ISO 9001:2008 for Small Businesses
Fifth edition

D0226317

Small businesses face many challenges today, including the increasing demand by larger companies for ISO compliance. Compliance is a challenging task for any organisation and can often be time consuming and costly, particularly for small businesses who are unlikely to have quality assurance experts on the payroll. However, it is still possible to achieve compliance without the need for expensive consultancy or training that takes you out of the office!

Ray Tricker has already guided hundreds of businesses through the challenge and this, the fifth edition of his life-saving ISO guide, has been rewritten and refined following five years' field use of working with the standard.

The one area that an organisation (particularly a small business) always wants to know is 'how much is it going to cost to implement and operate a QMS compliant with ISO 9001:2008 – and is it going to be worth the trouble?!' Due to popular demand, the fifth edition now includes a brand new chapter on the cost of implementing ISO 9001:2008.

This edition provides:

- relevant examples that put the concepts and requirements of the standard into a real-life context;
- down-to-earth explanations to help you determine what you need to work in compliance with and/or achieve certification to ISO 9001:2008;
- an example of a complete, generic, Quality Management System consisting of a Quality Manual plus a whole host of Quality Processes, Quality Procedures and Work Instructions; and
- access to a free, software copy of this generic QMS, to give you a starting point from which to develop your own documentation.

ISO 9001:2008 is the most widely followed quality management standard and the rewards can be great, opening up new business opportunities, as well as bringing real improvements to your processes and outputs.

Ray Tricker (MSc, IEng, FIET, FCMI, FCQI, FIRSE) is currently working as the Senior Management Consultant for Herne European Consultancy Ltd – a company specialising in offering organisations access to a range of highly skilled and specialist consultants to help these companies enhance their business performance.

ISO 9001:2008 for Small Businesses

Fifth edition

Ray Tricker

DiPietro Library
Franklin Pierce University
Rindge, NH 03461

First published 1997
by Butterworth-Heinnemann

Reprinted 1997, 1998, 1999, 2001
Second edition 2001

Reprinted 2001, 2002, 2003
Third edition 2005

Fourth edition 2010
by Routledge

Fifth edition published 2014
by Routledge
2 Park Square, Milton Park, Abingdon, Oxon OX14 4RN

and by Routledge
711 Third Avenue, New York, NY 10017

Routledge is an imprint of the Taylor & Francis Group, an informa business

© 1997, 2001, 2005, 2010, 2014 Ray Tricker

The right of Ray Tricker to be identified as author of this work has been asserted in accordance with sections 77 and 78 of the Copyright, Designs and Patents Act 1988.

All rights reserved. No part of this book may be reprinted or reproduced or utilised in any form or by any electronic, mechanical, or other means, now known or hereafter invented, including photocopying and recording, or in any information storage or retrieval system, without permission in writing from the publishers.

Trademark notice: Product or corporate names may be trademarks or registered trademarks, and are used only for identification and explanation without intent to infringe.

British Library Cataloguing in Publication Data
A catalogue record for this book is available from the British Library

Library of Congress Cataloging in Publication Data
    Tricker, Ray
    ISO 9001:2008 for small businesses / Ray Tricker. – Fifth edition.
    pages cm
    Includes bibliographical references and index.
    1. ISO 9000 Series Standards. 2. Small business–Quality control. I. Title.
    TS156.6.T753 2013
    658.02'2–dc23
    2013014681

ISBN: 978–0–415–70387–1 (hbk)
ISBN: 978–0–415–70390–1 (pbk)
ISBN: 978–1–315–89006–7 (ebk)

Typeset in Minion Pro and Optima
by Florence Production Ltd, Stoodleigh, Devon, UK

MIX
Paper from
responsible sources
FSC
www.fsc.org   FSC® C013056

Printed and bound in Great Britain by
TJ International Ltd, Padstow, Cornwall

Contents

Preface   xi

1   The importance of quality to small businesses   **1**

1.1   Why manage quality?   1
1.2   The importance of quality   2
1.3   Quality – the fundamentals   5
1.4   Quality Control   5
1.5   Quality Assurance   6
1.6   Specifications   7
      1.6.1   The significance of specifications   8
      1.6.2   Types of specification   8
      1.6.3   Supplier's responsibilities   10
      1.6.4   Purchaser's responsibilities   12
1.7   Quality Assurance during a product's life cycle   14
      1.7.1   Design stage   15
      1.7.2   Manufacturing stage   17
      1.7.3   Acceptance stage   18
      1.7.4   In-service stage   18
1.8   Benefits and costs of Quality Assurance   20
1.9   Costs of quality failure   21
      1.9.1   The supplier   22
      1.9.2   The purchaser   22
1.10 What are the costs involved in an organisation obtaining
      registration to this standard?   22

2   The background to ISO 9000   **25**

2.1   What is ISO 9000?   25
2.2   What national and international standards are available
      (and what is their interoperability)?   27
2.3   What about the growth of quality-specific standards?   31
2.4   But who are ISO?   34

2.5   What is the background to ISO 9000 and its current status?   35
       2.5.1 ISO 9000:1987   36
       2.5.2 ISO 9000:1994   36
       2.5.3 ISO 9001:2000   37
       2.5.4 ISO 9001:2008   39
       2.5.5 ISO 9001:2015   41
2.6   What are the Current ISO 9000 Standards?   42
       2.6.1 ISO 9000:2005 Quality Management Systems –
              Fundamentals and Vocabulary   42
       2.6.2 ISO 9004:2009 Quality Management Systems –
              Guidelines for Performance Improvement   43
       2.6.3 ISO 9001:2008 Quality Management Systems –
              Requirements   44
2.7   Quality management principles   45
2.8   ISO 9001:2008's compatibility with other management
       systems   48
       2.8.1 The OHSAS 18000 Series   49
       2.8.2 ISO 14000   50
       2.8.3 What is the difference between ISO 9000 and
              ISO 14000?   51
2.9   What other standards are based on ISO 9001:2008?   51
       2.9.1   Aerospace   52
       2.9.2   Automotive industry   52
       2.9.3   Computer software   52
       2.9.4   Crop production   53
       2.9.5   Data   54
       2.9.6   Education   54
       2.9.7   Energy   54
       2.9.8   Explosive atmospheres   54
       2.9.9   Food safety   54
       2.9.10 Good manufacturing practice   55
       2.9.11 Health care   55
       2.9.12 Information security   55
       2.9.13 Local government   55
       2.9.14 Measurement manufacturing systems   55
       2.9.15 Medical devices   56
       2.9.16 Multilayer piping systems   56
       2.9.17 Packaging – transport packages for dangerous goods   56
       2.9.18 Petroleum, petrochemical and natural gas industries   56
       2.9.19 Plastics piping systems   56
       2.9.20 Quality plans   57
       2.9.21 Ships and marine technology   57
       2.9.22 Space systems   57
       2.9.23 Supply chain management   57
       2.9.24 Systems engineering   57

Contents

    2.9.25 Telecommunications industry   57
    2.9.26 Testing and calibration laboratories   58
    2.9.27 Welding materials and fluxes   58
2.10 What is ISO 9001:2008's basic process?   58
2.11 What is the structure of ISO 9001:2008?   60
    0   Introduction   60
    1   Scope   60
    2   Normative references   60
    3   Terms and definitions   61
    4   Quality management system   62
    5   Management responsibility   63
    6   Resource management   64
    7   Product realisation   65
    8   Measurement, analysis and improvement   67
2.12 What about auditing ISO 9001:2008?   68
    2.12.1 Purpose of an audit   69
    2.12.2 Types of audit   69
    2.12.3 Audit categories   69
    2.12.4 ISO 19011:2002   71
2.13 Certification   71
    2.13.1 As a small business do I need to be certified and/or
            registered to ISO 9001:2008?   71
    2.13.2 Who can certify an organisation?   72
    2.13.3 What is required for certification?   72
    2.13.4 What is the difference between being certified and
            being registered?   72
    2.13.5 What is the difference between being certified and
            being compliant?   72
    2.13.6 What is the difference between being certified and
            being accredited?   73
2.14 Who will be responsible for quality within an organisation?   73
2.15 What is the future evolution of ISO 9000?   74

3   The process approach   75

3.1 Background   75
    3.1.1 Example of a simple process flow chart   78
    3.1.2 ISO 9001:2008's mandatory processes   79
3.2 But what is the process approach?   79
3.3 Planning an organisation's business processes   83
    3.3.1 Core Business Process   85
    3.3.2 Supporting processes   86
    3.3.3 Primary supporting processes   87
    3.3.4 Secondary supporting processes   88
3.4 Inter-relationship of process documentation   88

4   Quality Management System   **91**

4.1   Quality Management System – requirements   91
       4.1.1   Basic requirements of a Quality Management
               System   91
4.2   Quality Management System – principles   93
4.3   Quality Management System – approach   96
       4.3.1   What is a quality system?   97
       4.3.2   What is the difference between a quality manual
               and a quality system?   97
4.4   Quality Management System – structure   97
       4.4.1   QMS documentation   97
4.5   Quality Manual   99
4.6   Processes   100
4.7   Quality Procedures   102
       4.7.1   What documented procedures are required by
               ISO 9001:2008?   102
4.8   Work Instructions   103
       4.8.1   What is the difference between a Work Instruction
               and a record?   103
4.9   Quality Plan   104
       4.9.1   Management responsibility   106
       4.9.2   Contract review   107
       4.9.3   Design control   107
       4.9.4   Document and data control   107
       4.9.5   Purchasing   108
       4.9.6   Customer supplied product   108
       4.9.7   Product identification and traceability   108
       4.9.8   Process control   108
       4.9.9   Inspection and testing   109
       4.9.10 Inspection, measuring and test equipment   109
       4.9.11 Non-conforming service/product   109
       4.9.12 Other considerations   110
4.10   Quality Records   110

5   The Structure of ISO 9001:2008   **113**

5.1   Section 1 – Scope   113
       5.1.1   Section 1.1 – General   113
       5.1.2   Section 1.2 – Application   114
5.2   Section 2 – Normative reference   114
5.3   Section 3 – Terms and definitions   115
5.4   Section 4 – Quality Management System   116
       5.4.1   Section 4.1 – General requirements   117
       5.4.2   Section 4.2 – Documentation requirements   118

5.5   Section 5 – Management responsibility   123
       5.5.1   Section 5.1 – Management commitment   124
       5.5.2   Section 5.2 – Customer focus   126
       5.5.3   Section 5.3 – Quality policy   127
       5.5.4   Section 5.4 – Planning   129
       5.5.5   Section 5.5 – Responsibility, authority and
                communication   132
       5.5.6   Section 5.6 – Management review   134
5.6   Section 6 – Resource management   138
       5.6.1   Section 6.1 – Provision of resources   139
       5.6.2   Section 6.2 – Human resources   140
       5.6.3   Section 6.3 – Infrastructure   143
       5.6.4   Section 6.4 – Work environment   143
5.7   Section 7 – Product realisation   144
       5.7.1   Section 7.1 – Planning and realisation   145
       5.7.2   Section 7.2 – Customer-related processes   147
       5.7.3   Section 7.3 – Design and development   150
       5.7.4   Section 7.4 – Purchasing   163
       5.7.5   Section 7.5 – Production and service provision   168
       5.7.6   Section 7.6 – Control of measuring and monitoring
                equipment   174
5.8   Section 8 – Measurement, analysis and improvement   177
       5.8.1   Section 8.1 – General   178
       5.8.2   Section 8.2 – Monitoring and measurement   178
       5.8.3   Section 8.3 – Control of non-conforming product   185
       5.8.4   Section 8.4 – Analysis of data   187
       5.8.5   Section 8.5 – Improvement   189

6   **Example Quality Management System**   **201**

7   **Self-assessment**   **469**

7.1   How ISO 9000 can be used to check small businesses'
       Quality Management Systems   470
7.2   Internal audit   470
       7.2.1   Audit plan   472
       7.2.2   Internal audit programme   473
7.3   External audit   481
       7.3.1   Supplier evaluation   482
7.4   The surveillance or quality audit visit   485
       7.4.1   Multiple evaluations and audits   486
       7.4.2   Secondary audit   486
       7.4.3   Third-party evaluation   486
       7.4.4   Conformity assessment   486
7.5   Self-assessment checklists   487

7.5.1   Documentation required by an organisation to meet ISO 9001:2008 requirements   487
7.5.2   ISO 9001:2008 requirements of management   487
7.5.3   Example checklists of typical auditors' questions for ISO 9001:2008 compliance   487
7.5.4   Example internal stage audit checklists   488

7.6   Documentation requirements   488
7.6.1   The requirement   489
7.6.2   Control of documents   491
7.6.3   Software programs for document control   491

Annex A   Documentation required by an organisation to meet ISO 9001:2008 requirements   494
Annex B   ISO 9001:2008 requirements of management   505
Annex C   Example checklists of typical auditors' questions for ISO 9001:2008 compliance   524
Annex D   Example internal stage audit checklists   542

8   What are the costs involved in an organisation obtaining Registration to this standard?   **547**

8.1   Can I just work 'in compliance' with ISO 9001?   548
8.2   So why should I bother about getting ISO 90001 certification?   549
8.3   But what is the difference to being a certified, accredited and/or a registered ISO 9001:2008 organisation?   549
8.4   But is it worth the cost and trouble to become ISO 9001:2008 certified?   549
8.5   What are the benefits of ISO International Standards?   550
8.6   How do I become an ISO 9001 registered organisation?   551
8.7   What other national certification bodies are there?   553
8.8   What will be the budgetary costs for doing all this?   555
8.9   How long will it take to become certified?   555
8.10   How is the certification completed?   555
8.11   What happens during the actual ISO 9001 audit?!   556
8.12   What happens after certification and beyond?   556
8.13   How can I maintain my certification?   556
8.14   What are the advantages of maintaining my ISO 9001:2008 certification?   556

Abbreviations and acronyms   561
Books by the same author   565
References   573
Index   579

Preface

Many books have already been written on the topic of Quality Management and ISO 9000, but most of these appear to automatically assume that the reader belongs to a large company which already has an established management system in place and a full-time Quality Manager and probably a Quality Team to keep an eye on things. Small to medium-sized businesses, however, cannot afford these sort of 'luxuries' but nevertheless still need to set up similar systems (but on a far smaller scale) and show that they too can work in compliance with ISO 9001:2008 and produce consistent quality deliverables.

This fifth edition of 'ISO 9001:2008 for Small Businesses', with its series of examples and self-audit procedures, tries to show how a smaller company can benefit by meeting the requirements of ISO 9001:2008 and in so doing, gain entry into more lucrative markets. Indeed, the main aim of my writing this book in the first place was to help readers, at very little expense, to set up an ISO 9000, fully compliant, Quality Management System for themselves.

But this latest edition of my book (updated to take into account 5 years' field use and experience of the 2008 version of the standard) is **not** meant to be 'just another reference book', it **also** includes a fully worked, generic Quality Management System that can be quickly customised to suit any company – without having to rely on a specialist or a consultant to complete the task for them.

 To be of any real use, however, the customisation of the generic QMS **must** be completed on a page-by-page basis, to suit your own purposes. Chapter 6 is **not** meant as a 'one stop, quick fix product'!!

As you will doubtless recall, prior to the reissue of the ISO 9000 series in 2001, the majority of organisations simply wrote their Quality Manuals to indicate how they met the 20 requirements of the 1994 standard – clause-by-clause. Although this made it easier for the authors of the manual to show the auditors that all of the requirements of the standard had been met, quite often (especially for very small businesses), the manual was of little use to the organisation itself in actually running their business.

The current ISO 9001:2008 standard now requires the Quality Manual to 'include the scope of the system, any justifications for exclusions, refer to established procedures and describe the interaction between processes'. A Quality Manual that simply echoes the requirements of ISO 9001:2008 will, therefore, **not** be compliant, as certain sections of the standard's content may not be applicable to a particular organisation. It is essential, however, that an organisation's Quality Manual serves a useful purpose and clearly just paraphrasing ISO 9001:2008's requirements or using an 'off the shelf' Quality Manual to show compliance is not the answer **unless** it has been suitably customised to suit that particular organisation.

The prime aim of my book, therefore, is to help small businesses (who probably will have insufficient time to thoroughly read, understand, extract and implement all of the requirements of the ISO 9001:2008 standard and its supporting guidance documents) by providing them (in Chapter 6) with a fully worked example. For simplicity my generic QMS is based on one particular type of company (i.e. NAFAAD – a 'paper producing' consultancy) and you should use Chapter 6 as a template to describe the way that your organisation does business by leaving out those bits that are not particularly relevant and/or amplifying/writing new policies, processes and procedures to cover the organisation-specific areas that I have not covered in my book.

WHAT IS THE BACKGROUND TO ISO 9001:2008?

With the increased demand for quality in everything that we do or make nowadays has come the need to have some formalised set of rules to work to. Fifty years ago, however, there were no formalised standards for recognising a manufacturer's (or supplier's) quality. Quality procedures and guarantees were therefore required and the Military – as so often happens in these cases – came to the rescue.

NASA (in their capacity as controlling body for the US Space Program and with their requirement for the highest level of equipment reliability) was the first to produce a set of procedures, specifications and requirements. These became Military Specifications (Mil Specs) and manufacturers and suppliers, regardless of their size, were required to conform to these requirements if they wanted to provide equipment for the lucrative military market.

The North Atlantic Treaty Organisation (NATO), under the American influence, then produced a series of quality assurance procedures which were known as the NATO Allied Quality Assurance Publications (AQAPs). These were republished by the British Ministry of Defence (MOD-UK) as the Defence Standard (DEF STAN) 05 series of procedures.

Civilian firms and contractors quickly realised the necessity of ensuring that manufacturers and suppliers should abide by an agreed set of quality standards and the British Standards Institution (BSI) formally adapted the DEF STAN 05 series into a virtually identical set of documents known as the BS 5750 series. This standard was then copied by other nations and a common series of recommendations known as the ISO 9000:1994 series of 'Standards for Quality Assurance' were produced.

Under existing international agreement, all international standards have to be re-inspected five years after publication. In accordance with this agreement, the 1994 versions of ISO 9000 series were revised with more emphasis being placed on the need for customer satisfaction and the use of a more modular, process approach to quality management. The main change caused by this new review process, however, was the amalgamation of the previous (similar) requirements contained in the ISO 9001:1994, ISO 9002:1994 and ISO 9003:1994 standards into a single ISO 9001:2000 standard – which was then updated in 2008 and became the current ISO 9001:2008 – which (by international agreement) is due to be updated for 2015.

> Although not officially referred to as a 'requirements standard', ISO 9001:2008 does, nevertheless, still contain 141 'shalls' and 2 'musts' as opposed to 4 'shoulds' and 1 'could'!

ISO 9001:2008 specifies the national, regional and international accepted procedures and criteria that are required to ensure that products and services meet customers' requirements. It identifies the basic disciplines of a Quality Management System and can be used by manufacturers, suppliers, service industries and end users – large or small – with equal effect.

These processes, procedures, disciplines and criteria can be applied to ANY firm, no matter its size – whether they employ just a few people or many thousands. It can also be used by companies to set up their own Quality Management System and can form the basis for assessing an organisation's Quality Management System (i.e. to ensure that a supplier or service industry has the ability to provide satisfactory goods and/or services).

It therefore shouldn't come as too big a surprise to learn that since the publication of the new process orientated ISO 9001:2008, there has been a growing demand for an assurance of quality **before** a contract is let. This is not an entirely new concept, of course, because quality has always played an important role in securing new markets as well as retaining those markets that already exist, but without doubt, in these days of competitive world markets, quality assurance has become far more relevant.

To meet this requirement, manufacturers and suppliers have had to recognise the importance of quality and the fact that it can **only** be achieved through efficient company organisation and a determination by Top Management to meet the increased quality requirements of their potential customers.

This concept is not just related to large manufacturing companies and suppliers; it also has a huge impact on smaller organisations – even those employing just one or two people – because no matter how large or small the company, there has to be an increasing reliance on quality and the requirements and recommendations of ISO 9001 in order to meet customers' specifications. In fact, for anyone wanting to sell their product in today's multi-national European or American market, the ISO 9000 standards are essential publications. Together they provide a comprehensive set of rules and regulations, specifications and recommendations that enable an organisation, manufacturer or supplier, large or small, to set up a workable Quality Management System with in-built processes and procedures that enable them to operate within their constraints.

BUT WHAT IS A 'SMALL BUSINESS'?!

A small business is a business that is independently owned and operated, with (obviously!) a small number of employees and relatively low volume of sales. Small businesses can be involved in all aspects of design as well as the manufacture, supply, installation and maintenance of products, services and information technology. They are normally privately owned corporations, partnerships or sole proprietorships.

The legal definition of 'small' varies between countries, but within the European Union, the official definition of a Micro, Small and Medium-sized Enterprise (SME) – as provided by Directive 2003/361/EC – is:

Enterprise category	Headcount	Turnover	or	Balance sheet total
Medium-sized	< 250	≤ €50 million		≤ €43 million
Small	< 50	≤ €10 million		≤ €10 million
Micro	< 10	≤ € 2 million		≤ € 2 million

By comparison, the definition of mid-sized business in the USA is one employing fewer than 500, whilst in Australia, a small business is defined as 1–19 employees and a medium business as 20–200 employees. The American definition of a micro-business is the same (i.e. under 10 employees).

In the USA, the term SMB (Small and Medium-sized Businesses) is normally used whilst in Africa it is SMME (Small, Medium and Micro-Enterprises). Elsewhere in Africa, MSME is used, for Micro, Small and Medium Enterprises and, of course, the size thresholds vary from country to country.

Micro, small and medium-sized enterprises are socially and economically important, since they represent 98% of all enterprises in the EU, provide around 80 million jobs and contribute to entrepreneurship and innovation. Globally, SMEs account for 99% of business numbers and 40–50% of GDP. According to World Bank statistics, just over 40% of SMEs, worldwide, are involved in the manufacturing industry.

ADVANTAGES OF SMALL BUSINESSES

- Small businesses can be started at a very low cost and on a part-time basis and are well suited to Internet marketing because they can easily serve specialised niches – something that would have been more difficult prior to the Internet Marketing revolution which began in the late 1990s.
- Not being tied to any bureaucratic inertia, it is much easier for a small business to respond to the marketplace quickly. In addition, small businesses are usually able to work on a fairly informal basis with their customers and clients, which results in greater accountability and responsiveness.

PROBLEMS FACED BY SMALL BUSINESSES

- Small businesses often face a variety of problems related to their size – for example a frequent cause of bankruptcy is undercapitalization, which is often a result of poor planning rather than economic conditions.
- Whilst independence is an advantage of owning a small business, entrepreneurs usually have to work very long hours and understand that ultimately their customers are their bosses.
- Other problems include insurance costs (such as liability and health), rising energy costs and taxes, and small business owners tending to be overwhelmed by excessive governmental red tape.

WHAT ARE THE COSTS INVOLVED IN AN ORGANISATION OBTAINING REGISTRATION TO THIS STANDARD?

- The one thing that an organisation (particularly a small business) always wants to know is '*how much is it going to cost to implement and operate a QMS compliant with ISO 9001:2008 – and is it going to be worth the trouble?!*'
- Obviously each business is different and the cost of ISO 9001 Registration will vary depending on the size and complexity of your organisation and on whether you already have some elements of a Quality Management System in place.
- Consequently no book could answer this question with any accuracy, however, at the specific request of a number of my readers I have included (see Chapter 8) some tables with examples which I hope will be beneficial to you.

WHAT ARE THE CHANGES IN THIS EDITION OF 'ISO 9001:2008 FOR SMALL BUSINESSES' FROM PREVIOUS VERSIONS OF THE BOOK?

The main advantage of this book over other ISO 9000 books has **always** been the availability of a **free copy** of the generic Quality Management System featured in Chapter 6 as this can be customised to suit **any** sort of business, industry and/or service. Although the actual requirements of ISO 9001 have not changed since publication of Edition 4, it was felt that with the benefit of five years' field experience of the standard, now was an appropriate time to completely update Chapter 6 so that it could include examples of **all the mandatory ISO 9001:2008** formal Quality Procedures, namely:

- Document Control
- Quality Records
- Quality Audits
- Control of Non Conforming Products
- Corrective Action
- Preventative Action

Other changes in Chapter 6 include:

- reference to and an explanation of the Deming PDCA circle;
- a new section about meeting customers' requirements;
- further explanation about the interrelationship of the various levels of quality documentation;
- further explanation concerning the meaning of having a Core Business Process;
- a new Sub Process for Customer Satisfaction;
- turning some of the 'explanations' into proper formal Quality Procedures (e.g. 'Approval Procedure');

. . . and:

- updated information about the current status of ISO 9000 standards;
- emphasis on the growth of quality standards in the USA;
- complete revision (and expansion) on the sub section concerning other standards that are based on ISO 9001:2008;
- changes to existing Procedures to reflect current ISO 9001:2008 thinking as well as inclusion of additional text to reflect ongoing experience;
- revision of Customer Feedback to include Customer Satisfaction;
- production of new Work Instructions for e-mail control;
- the addition of some minor manuscript amendments, additions and a couple of new illustrations to emphasise the growing importance of ISO 9001:2008 outside Europe and the Americas.

 Note: For the benefit of Master's Degree students (and other interested parties) a reduced record of ISO 9000's development is still available in the text.

The main parts of the book are as follows:

- *The importance of Quality to Small Businesses;*
- *The background to ISO 9000;*
- *The process approach;*
- *Quality Management System;*
- *The Structure of ISO 9001:2008;*
- *Example Quality Management System;*
- *Self-assessment;*
- *What are the costs involved in an Organisation obtaining Registration to this standard?*

AUTHOR'S NOTE

For convenience (and in order to reduce the number of equivalent and/or similar terms) the following, unless otherwise stated, are considered interchangeable terms within this book:

product – hardware, software, service or processed material;
organisation – manufacturer and/or supplier.

Within the text, you will find the following symbols which are designed to help you get the most out of this book:

 An important requirement or point

 A good idea or suggestion

 Note: these are used to provide further amplification or information.

Italic text, indicates a direct quotation from an ISO 9000 standard, Guidance Note, ISO, National Standard etc.

Shaded boxes are used in Chapter 6 to show either the full text of the ISO 9001:2008 *legal requirements* or a paraphrased version of these requirements.

OBTAINING THE CUSTOMISABLE QUALITY MANAGEMENT SYSTEM

'*ISO 9001:2008 for Small Businesses*', fifth edition, is accompanied by a full customisable copy of the QMS files presented in the book and to save you having to copy or retype the Quality Manual, Quality Procedures and/or Work Instructions and so on, 'unlocked', fully accessible, non .PDF soft copies of all of these files are available – **at no additional charge** – direct from the author.

To obtain copies of these files, simply send an e-mail to ray@herne.org.uk containing details of your name, address and where you purchased the book, and I will send you the link to download a full copy.

 This QMS is provided free of charge and whilst the original files obviously remain copyright of the author, you are welcome to tailor them to suit the needs of your own organisation's QMS.

 Please note, however, that the author cannot enter into any further correspondence or offer any additional support for these freely provided files. Users requiring additional support or information should see below.

DISCLAIMER

Material provided by this service is provided 'as is' without warranty of any kind, either expressed or implied. Every effort has been made to ensure accuracy and conformance to standards accepted at the time of publication. The user assumes the entire risk as to the accuracy and use of this material. This material may be copied and distributed subject to the following conditions:

(1) '*Ray Tricker, ISO 9001:2008 for Small Businesses, Published by Routledge*' must be credited as the source of the QMS template;
(2) The QMS document may not be distributed for profit. All trademarks acknowledged.

Other ISO 9001:2008 related books by the same author

Title	*ISO 9001:2000 Audit Procedures* (Second Edition)
Details	A complete set of audit check sheets and explanations to assist quality managers and auditors in completing internal, external and third-party audits of ISO 9001:2000 Quality Management Systems
ISBN	978–0–7506–6615–2
Imprint	Routledge

Title	*ISO 9001:2000 in Brief* (Second Edition)
Details	Revised and expanded, this new edition of an easy-to-understand guide provides practical information on how to set up a cost-effective ISO 9001:2000 compliant Quality Management System
ISBN	978–7506–4814–1
Imprint	Butterworth Heinemann

Title	*MDD Compliance using Quality Management Techniques*
Details	This book is a good reference for understanding the Medical Device Directive's (MDD) requirements and would aid companies of all sizes in adding these requirements to an existing QMS
ISBN	978–0–7506–4441–9
Imprint	Butterworth Heinemann

Title	*ISO 9001:2000 The Quality Management Process* (Third Edition)
Details	Revised and expanded, this new edition will prove invaluable to all quality managers, internal auditors and anyone involved in the management and understanding of ISO 9001:2000. It also acts as a handy reference for professional auditors to the requirements for auditing ISO 9001:2000 System
ISBN	978–9077212776
Imprint	Van Haren Publishing

Note: A complete list of Ray Tricker's other titles on Integrated Quality Management currently in print is contained at the end of this book, together with details of other books that Ray has written in the past.

FURTHER ASSISTANCE

For further details about these and other ISO 9001 consulting services, please email ray@herne.org.uk or visit www.thebestqms.com

About the author

Ray Tricker (MSc, IEng, FIET, FCMI, FCQI, FIRSE) is a senior Consultant with over 50 years' continuous service in Quality, Safety and Environmental Management, Project Management, Communication Electronics, Railway Command, Control and Signalling systems and the development of molecular nanotechnology.

He served with the Royal Corps of Signals (for a total of 37 years) during which time he held various managerial posts culminating in being appointed as the Chief Engineer of NATO's Communication Security Agency (ACE COMSEC).

Most of Ray's work since leaving the services has centred around the European Railways. He has held a number of posts with the Union International des Chemins de fer (UIC) [e.g. Quality Manager of the European Train Control System (ETCS)] and with the European Union (EU) Commission [e.g. T500 Review Team Leader, European Rail Traffic Management System (ERTMS) Users Group Project Coordinator, HEROE Project Coordinator] and currently (as well as writing books on such diverse subjects as ISO 9001:2008 and Building, Wiring and Water Regulations for Taylor & Francis and Elsevier) he is busy assisting Small Businesses from around the world (usually on a no cost basis) to produce their own auditable Quality and/or Integrated Management Systems to meet the requirements of ISO 9001:2008, ISO 14001 and OHSAS 18001. He is also a UKAS Assessor (for the assessment of certification bodies for the harmonisation of the Trans-European, High Speed Railway Network) and recently he was the Quality, Safety and Environmental Manager for the Project Management Consultant overseeing the multi-billion Dollar Trinidad Rapid Rail System.

Currently he is working as the Senior Management Consultant for Herne European Consultancy Ltd – a company specialising in offering organisations access to a range of highly skilled and specialist consultants to help these companies enhance their business performance.

One day he may retire!!

To Lalita with Love – As Always

Chapter 1

The importance of quality to small businesses

Author's Note

The aim of this short chapter is to introduce the reader to the requirements and benefits of quality, quality control and quality assurance.

The significance and the types of specification are explained, supplier's and purchaser's responsibilities are defined and a thorough review of quality during a product's life cycle enables the reader to appreciate the costs and associated benefits of quality.

For this particular Edition (and as a result of requests from previous readers of my book) I have also included a small section concerning the possible costs involved in an Organisation obtaining Registration to ISO 9001:2008.

Note: for a more in-depth explanation of potential costs, how to prepare for your first Certification Audit and how to assist in its execution, please see Chapter 8.

Although I have written Chapter 1 primarily from the point of view of a manufactured product (bearing in mind that 41% of all small businesses are actually manufacturers), it is equally applicable to the design of a product or piece of software, the production of a document or, indeed, any other form of deliverable.

I consider that this part of the book is essential reading, regardless of the type of business you are involved in.

Note: Throughout the text of this book, wherever the term 'product' occurs, it can also mean 'service', and vice versa.

1.1 WHY MANAGE QUALITY?

The Chartered Quality Institute (CQI) have carried out extensive research (see Note below) on this point and have advised that the effective management of quality not only creates value for an organisation and its stakeholders but also manages its exposure to risk and can make the difference between success and failure.

A properly implemented and effective business management system identifies and manages organisational risks to ensure that:

- the organisation consistently delivers the products and services that customers want, when they want them and to the quality they expect;
- customer satisfaction and loyalty is improved;
- organisational goals and objectives are achieved;
- organisational risk is identified and effectively managed;
- products, services and the processes that deliver them to customers are continually improved through innovation;
- waste throughout the organisation is identified and eliminated;
- partnerships and the supply chain deliver value to the parties involved.

 Note: The CQI's Case Studies of the:

- Manufacturing sector;
- Defence engineering sector;
- Engineering and construction sector;
- Legal services sector;
- Business services sector;
- Transport and telecommunications sector;
- Voluntary sector; and the
- Public sector

are available at http://www.thecqi.org/Knowledge-Hub/Research-and-reports/The-economic-contribution-of-quality.

1.2 THE IMPORTANCE OF QUALITY

First of all, what is meant by the word – **Quality**?!

Basically, the quality of a product or service refers to the degree to which the product or service meets, and continues to meet, customer expectations.

In business, there are many meanings of *quality* such as:

- '*A product or service free of deficiencies*' (Deming);
- '*Conformance to requirements*' (Cosby);
- '*Fitness for use*' (Juran);
- '*Meeting or exceeding customer expectations*' (Juran);
- '*The characteristics of a product or service that bear on its ability to satisfy stated or implied needs*' (American Society for Quality);
- '*The degree of excellence of something*' (Oxford Dictionary);
- '*The number of defects per million opportunities*' (Six Sigma);
- '*The result of care*' (Page);
- '*The standard of something as measured against other things of a similar kind*' (Oxford Dictionary);

- '*Uniformity around a target value*' (Kano);
- '*The loss a product imposes on society after it is shipped*' (Taguchi);
- '*Value to some person*' (Weinburg); and even
- '*Quality in a product or service is not what the supplier puts in – it is what the customer gets out and is willing to pay for*' (Drucker).

But today's internationally accepted definition of quality (i.e. as defined in ISO 9000) is that:

'Quality is the degree to which a set of inherent characteristics fulfils requirements.'

However, quality has no specific meaning unless related to a specific function and/or object. Quality is a perceptual, conditional and somewhat subjective attribute.

Quality (particularly with reference to ISO 9001:2008) is a reference to a set of predetermined, well-organised actions that can be used by **any** organisation whether it is a large or small business and regardless of whether it is a manufacturer, producer, supplier or end user. It is a method of ensuring that the producers or final users get a standard quality product or service that satisfies their individual and collective needs (Fig. 1.1).

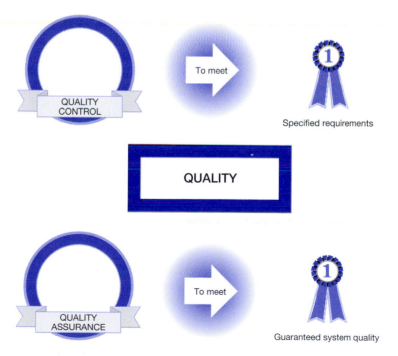

FIGURE 1.1 Quality

Quality consists of two separate yet connected activities, Quality Control (QC) and Quality Assurance (QA) as shown below.

Quality Control	Quality Assurance
• A procedure (or set of procedures) to make sure that a product or service adheres to required quality standards.	• Confirms the degree of excellence of a product or service, measured against its defined purpose.
• A regulating process through which actual quality performance can be measured and compared to quality standards.	• Ensures that a set of activities are carried out to agreed standards.
• A control (such as inspection or testing, introduced into an industrial or business process) to ensure quality.	• Ensures that all those planned or systematic actions that are necessary to provide adequate confidence that a product or service is of the type and quality needed have been fully implemented.
• A control meant to guarantee, by periodic inspections, that a certain amount of quality is being maintained during the production, completion and use of the product or service.	• Is a formal process of implementing quality assessment and quality improvement in programmes.
• A management procedure(s) for evaluating and guaranteeing quality against reference standards.	• Is a process for evaluating overall project performance on a regular basis to ensure that it will satisfy relevant quality standards.
• A process for developing and applying systems to ensure products or services are designed and produced to meet and even exceed customer requirements and expectations.	• Is a programme by which continual improvement and customer satisfaction can be monitored.
• A process to ensure that all of the execution procedures and actions undertaken in order to fulfil the demands for quality products or services have been included and have been tailored to suit the final users' needs.	• Is a systematic process for verifying that a product or service being developed is meeting specified requirements.
Quality Control also ensures:	• Is a systematic programme of controls and inspections that can be applied by any organisation or body.
• The maintenance of standards of quality of goods and/or services.	• Provides a method for monitoring and improving performance.
	• Provides confidence that quality requirements will be fulfilled to ISO 9001:2008.
• The operational techniques and activities that are used to fulfil the requirements for quality.	• Provides systematic production processes that ensure confidence in a product or service's suitability for use.
• The process of making sure that products or services are made to consistently high standards.	

1.3 QUALITY – THE FUNDAMENTALS

- **Business process management** – delivering results through business processes to increase efficiency.
- **Continual improvement** – making performance improvement a perpetual objective.
- **Customer focus** – delivering customer value while anticipating future needs and potential markets.
- **Fact-based decision making** – ensuring good decision making by using accurate data and facts.
- **Leadership and business results** – providing vision and direction, gaining commitment and achieving collective results.
- **People and organisational culture** – delivering maximum value through development and involvement of individuals working in a productive organisational culture.
- **Suppliers and partners** – maintaining mutually beneficial relationships to enable value creation.
- **Systems thinking** – managing interrelated processes with an integrated approach.

1.4 QUALITY CONTROL

The definition of Quality Control (QC) is:

'That part of quality management focussed on fulfilling quality requirements.'

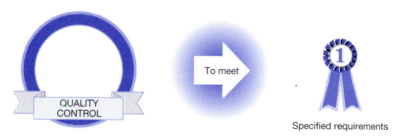

FIGURE 1.2 Quality Control

In other words, the operational techniques and activities that are used to fulfil the requirements for quality. It is the amount of supervision that a deliverable (product or service) is subjected to so as to be sure that the workmanship associated with that deliverable meets the quality level required by the design. Or – to put it another way – it is the control exercised by the organisation (small, medium or large) to certify that **all** aspects of its activities during the design, production, installation **and** in-service stages are to the desired standards.

Quality Control is exercised at all levels, and, as all personnel are responsible for the particular task they are doing, they are **all** quality controllers to some degree or other.

In large organisations, managers, because of their positions and responsibilities, will have more control over their own particular process and therefore have more control over the final quality. It is true, therefore, to say that in these sorts of organisation, while **all** personnel are quality controllers and that managers are the Principal Quality Controllers, within their own particular part of that organisation.

1.5 QUALITY ASSURANCE

The recognised definition of Quality Assurance (QA) is:

'That part of quality management focussed on providing confidence that quality requirements are fulfilled.'

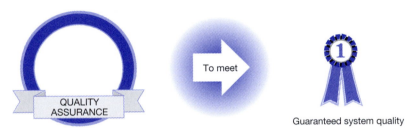

FIGURE 1.3 Quality Assurance

In other words, all those planned and systematic actions necessary to provide adequate confidence that a product or service will satisfy given requirements for quality.

Quality	is fit for intended use
Assurance	is a declaration given to inspire confidence in an organisation's capability
Quality Assurance	in a product (or service) is a declaration given to inspire confidence that a particular organisation is capable of consistently satisfying need as well as being a managerial process designed to increase confidence

Quality Assurance ensures that a product has achieved the highest standards and that its production, modification or repair (for example, in the case of a manufactured item) has been completed in an efficient and timely manner.

The purpose of Quality Assurance is, therefore, to:

- provide assurance to a customer that the standard of workmanship within a contractor's premises is of the highest level and that all products leaving that particular organisation are above a certain fixed minimum level of specification;
- ensure that production standards are uniform throughout the organisation and remain constant despite changes in personnel.

In a nutshell, Quality Assurance is concerned with:

- an agreed level of quality;
- a commitment within an organisation to the fundamental principle of consistently supplying the right quality product;
- a commitment from a customer to the fundamental principle of only accepting the right quality product;
- a commitment within **all** levels (contractor and/or customer) to the basic principles of Quality Assurance and Quality Control.

The main benefits of Quality Assurance are:

- an increased capability of supplying a product which consistently conforms to an agreed specification;
- a reduction in supply and production costs;
- a greater involvement and motivation within an organisation's workforce;
- an improved customer relationship through fewer complaints, thus providing increased sales potential.

1.6 SPECIFICATIONS

Without proper specifications it is impossible to expect an organisation to produce a product or service (i.e. deliverable) that completely satisfies the purchaser's requirements. Equally, if the organisation does not work within laid-down specifications it will be unable to produce something that comes up to the purchaser's required standard.

If an organisation does not meet required specifications, then the document, part, equipment or system will not work as expected or the components will be the wrong dimensions and not fit properly etc. Worst of all, the deliverable will not be exactly what the purchaser wanted.

Correct specifications are, therefore, very much the responsibility of the purchaser **as well as** the manufacturer/supplier.

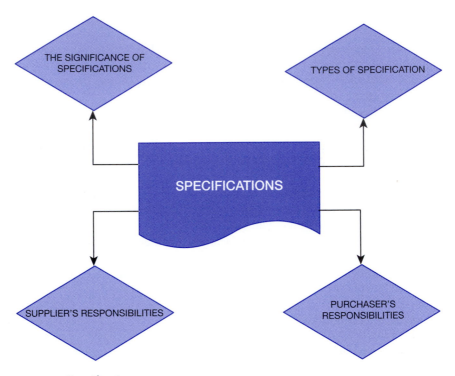

FIGURE 1.4 Specifications

1.6.1 The significance of specifications

Specifications always form the basis of a contract and as such they need to be a comprehensive and precise description of exactly what the purchaser requires. The document must, therefore, avoid ambiguous words, mixed systems of units (e.g. metric and imperial) and, in particular, avoid over specification such as listing extremely close tolerances (i.e. with respect to dimensions, colour, surface finishes and/or performance – particularly when it is software related) which are liable to increase the cost of the deliverable unnecessarily.

Specifications can be very simple and just covered by a few words, or they can be extremely rigid and run into many volumes. It all depends on the size of the assignment and the level of accuracy that the purchaser requires.

1.6.2 Types of specification

There are three main ways in which the purchaser's requirements can be specified:

- general specifications;
- overall performance specifications; and
- standard specifications.

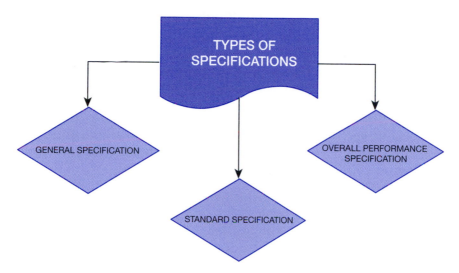

FIGURE 1.5 Types of specification

Although slightly different in content, each of these specifications closely examines the procedures used by the supplier (be they a software designer, manufacturer, installer, maintainer or a trader).

1.6.2.1 General specification

A general specification requires the purchaser to produce a detailed written description of the deliverable. If it is an article that is going to be constructed, then its function, construction, the materials to be used and the level of performance that is required need to be clearly established and agreed. The general specification is usually written by a member of the design team and then passed to an experienced engineer (independent of that particular design team) for final verification (and in some cases, validation and approval).

This also applies to other products (e.g. Information Technology (IT) services and deliverables) where the general specification **must** to be clearly stated.

To avoid any problems later on, specifications must always guard against using such words as 'suitable', 'appropriate' or 'conventional'. In a similar manner, inclusion of 'possible alternatives' and 'by agreement' clauses should also be avoided.

If in-house specifications are produced in quantity, it is essential that any amended specification is published and immediately issued to all concerned. To make life simpler and avoid future problems, it is equally important that these amendments are numbered, dated and the recipients are made to destroy all previous copies and issues.

 See the Section on Document Control later on in this book for further details.

1.6.2.2 Overall performance specification

An overall performance specification tells the organisation responsible for supplying the product or service, in comprehensive terms, exactly what the purchaser is looking for. The obvious disadvantage of this method is that it leaves the design of the deliverable completely up to the supplier. This can often lead to arguments later on, especially when the purchaser realises that the product is either too big, too small, the wrong shape, not up to (or exceeding) his or her engineering requirements, not (especially in IT) capable of producing what he or she requires and, as frequently happens, is **far** more expensive than the purchaser really intended.

1.6.2.3 Standard specification

A standard specification is a list that describes, in detail, the type of service that is to be provided, the kind of software that the purchaser requires or the items or materials that are to be used in the manufacture and/or production of a deliverable.

In the case of a manufactured item, without any real experience of manufacturing, it would obviously take a purchaser a long time to compile such a list of what he or she requires or even be able to express – in technical terms – exactly what he or she wants. To overcome these problems, National Standards Organisations (NSOs) publish lists of all the materials and sub assemblies commonly used by manufacturers as well as information concerning off the shelf software programmes etc.

In the United Kingdom (UK) the British Standards Institution (BSI) has produced these lists in the BS 9000 series (**NOT** to be confused with the ISO 9000 quality series!). In Europe they are made available by the CENELEC Electronic Components Committee (CECC) and internationally by the Quality Assessment System for Electronic Components (IECQ).

1.6.3 Supplier's responsibilities

The suppliers' prime responsibility must always be to ensure that anything **and everything** leaving their organisation conforms to the specific requirements of the purchaser – particularly with regard to quality.

The simplest way to be a 'responsible supplier' is for suppliers to ensure that their particular office, production facility or manufacturing outlet fully complies with the requirements of the quality standards adopted by the country in which they are working and the country to whom they intend supplying the component, equipment, system or product.

To do this they must, of course, first be aware of the standards applicable to that country, know how to obtain copies of that country's standards, how to adapt them to their own particular environment and how to get them accepted by the relevant authorities (for example Notified Bodies).

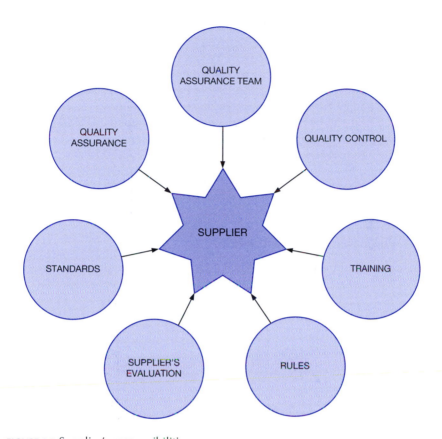

FIGURE 1.6 Supplier's responsibilities

Although an organisation can set out to abide by accepted standards, unless it achieves its aim it will fail in its attempt to become a recognised supplier of quality goods. The main points that it should note are:

- that all managerial staff, from the most junior to the most senior, firmly believe in the importance of Quality Control and Quality Assurance and understand how to implement them;
- that managerial staff **must** create an atmosphere in which Quality Assurance rules are obeyed and not simply avoided just because they are inconvenient, time consuming, laborious or just too boring to bother with;
- that there has to be an accepted training scheme to ensure that all members of the organisation are regularly brought up to date with the ongoing and the latest requirements of Quality Assurance;
- that there must (especially in large businesses) be a Quality Assurance team available to oversee and make sure that Quality Control and Quality Assurance are carried out at all times and **at all levels**, within their premises.

In a very small business this will quite often be one of the Managing Directors' duties.

In addition, suppliers will have to provide proof that they are providing a quality product. This is actually a '*measurement of their Quality Control*' and usually takes the form of a supplier's evaluation, surveillance and/or audit.

National and international Quality Management Systems (QMSs) will also require suppliers to establish and maintain a fully documented procedure for the inspection of their system for Quality Control. Procedures must be developed and identified for classifying lots, cataloguing characteristics, selecting samples and rules for acceptance and/or rejection criteria, together with procedures for segregating and screening rejected lots.

1.6.4 Purchaser's responsibilities

Quite a number of problems associated with a product's quality are usually the fault of the purchaser! Obviously the purchaser can only expect to get what he or

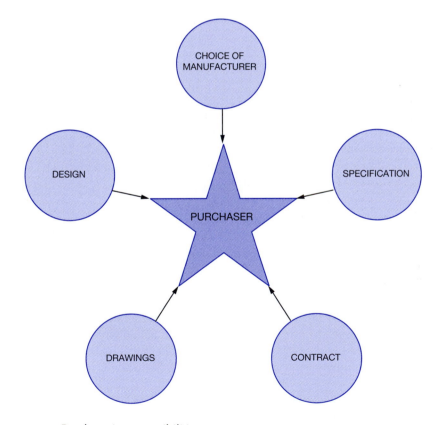

FIGURE 1.7 Purchaser's responsibilities

she ordered. It is, therefore, extremely important that the actual order is not only correct, but also provides the supplier with all the relevant (and accurate) information required for completing the task.

There is little point in trying to blame the supplier when an article or service doesn't come up to expectation because of an unsatisfactory design that has been provided by the purchaser. If an IT company has been asked to produce a new software product, then it needs to know the input and output requirements. If a designer has been asked to produce a Functional Requirements Specification (FRS) for a railway system, then he or she needs to be aware of the Infrastructure, Rolling Stock, Signalling and Power requirements envisaged.

In certain cases (particularly when the requirements for an article that is going to be manufactured **cannot** easily be described in words), it could be very helpful if the purchaser was to provide a drawing as a form of graphic order. In such cases, this drawing should contain all the relevant details such as type of material to be used, the material's grade or condition, the specifications that are to be followed and, where possible, the graphic order/drawing should be to scale. If this approach proves impractical, then the order would have to include all the relevant dimensional data, sizes, tolerances etc., or refer to one of the accepted standards.

Having said all that, it must be appreciated that the actual specification being used is also very important for it sets the level of quality required and, therefore, directly affects the price of the article. Clearly, if specifications are too demanding then the final cost of the article will be too high. If specifications are too vague or obscure, then the supplier will have difficulty in producing or providing the object and/or service – or may even be unable to get it to work correctly!

The purchaser's choice of supplier is equally important. It is an unfortunate fact of life that purchasers (particularly Governments!!) usually consider that the price of the article is the prime and (in some cases) even the only consideration. Buying cheaply is obviously **not** the answer because if a purchaser accepts the lowest offer, then all too often he or she will find that delivery times are lengthened (because the supplier can make more profit on other orders), the article or service produced does not satisfy his or her requirements, or worst of all, the quality of the article is so poor that he or she has to replace the device or system well before its anticipated life cycle has been completed.

If a supplier has received official recognition that the quality of his or her work is up to a particular standard, then the purchaser has a reasonable guarantee that the article being produced will be of a reasonable quality – always assuming that the initial order was correct – and the easiest way of recognising if a supplier is a quality supplier is to see if he or she is Registered to ISO 9001:2008!

 See later sections of this book on Subcontracting and Auditing.

1.7 QUALITY ASSURANCE DURING A PRODUCT'S LIFE CYCLE

Author's Note

Although I have written section 1.7 of this book primarily from the point of view of a manufactured product, the design, production, acceptance and in-service stages are equally applicable whether you are designing a product, producing a document or have influence on any other form of deliverable such as Information Technology (IT) products.

Please, therefore, study the bits that are applicable to your own type of business – and at the same time realise what the poor manufacturer has to put up with!

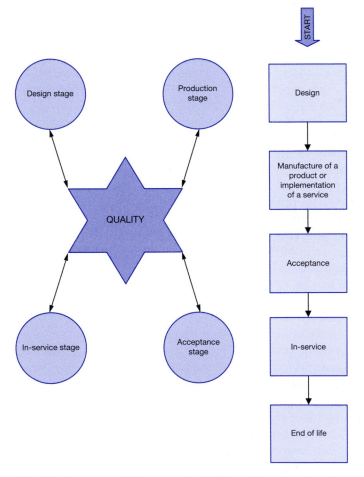

FIGURE 1.8 Quality Assurance during a product's life cycle

The life of a product is made up of five stages (see Fig. 1.8). Each of these stages has specific requirements that need to be correctly managed and which need to be regulated by Quality Controls.

As Quality Assurance affects the product throughout its life cycle, it is important that Quality Assurance procedures are introduced for design, manufacturing (if applicable to the product) and acceptance stages, as well as in service utilisation.

1.7.1 Design stage

'Quality must be designed into a product before manufacture or assembly.'

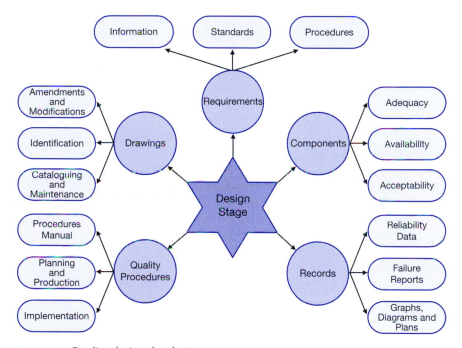

FIGURE 1.9 Quality during the design stage

Throughout the design stage of a product or service, the quality of that design must be regularly checked. Quality procedures have to be planned, written and implemented so as to predict and evaluate the fundamental and intrinsic reliability of the proposed design.

It doesn't matter whether the responsibility for the design of a product rests purely with the supplier, the purchaser or is a joint function. It is essential that the designer is fully aware of the exact requirements of the project and has a sound background knowledge of the relevant standards, information and procedures that will have to be adopted during the design stages.

This is extremely important, because the actions of the design office will not only influence the maintenance of quality during manufacture or supply of the product, but will also play a major part in setting the quality level of the eventual product. If there is no Quality Control in the drawing office, there is little chance of there ever being any on the shop floor. When the engineers are trying to manufacture or design something (or a technician is attempting to assemble a system or module) to a set of drawings that have countless mistakes on them, what chance is there of them ever being able to produce an acceptable item?! The same applies to all types of product or service – even the production of a simple document or report requires a design stage to show what it is supposed to cover and in what detail etc.

Design problems, although not specifically stipulated in ISO 9001:2008, should nevertheless be addressed. The design office (or team) should produce some sort of '*Procedures Manual*' which lists and describes the routine procedures that are required to turn a concept into a set of functional drawings.

These procedures will cover such activities as the numbering of drawings, authorisation to issue amendments and modifications, how to control changes to drawings, the method of withdrawing obsolete drawings and the identification, cataloguing and maintenance of drawings.

In addition to these procedures, the design office will also have to provide a complete listing of all the relevant components, availability, acceptability and adequacy and be aware of all the advances in both materials and equipment that are currently available on today's market which are relevant to the product.

It is imperative that the design team maintains a close relationship with the remainder of the organisation throughout these initial stages so as to be aware of the exact requirements, the problems, the choice of components etc., assist in the analysis of failures, swiftly produce solutions and forestall costly work stoppages. One of the main problems to overcome is the ease with which the design office can make an arbitrary selection, but then find that the size and tolerance is completely inappropriate (for example) to the manufacturing or assembly process.

In order that the statistical significance of a particular failure can be assessed and correct retroactive action taken, it is essential that the design team has access to all the records, failure reports and other data as soon as they are available within the design office or shop floor.

The storage, maintenance and analysis of reliability data will require the design team to follow the progress of the product throughout its productive life cycle, its many maintenance cycles and to take due note of customers' comments.

The compilation and retention of design office reliability data is essential to the reliability of the product and the manufacturing facility.

Nowadays, of course, most design offices – particularly in larger organisations – are computerised and use processors to store their records on internal or external hard drives so that these records can be continually updated and amended. This information (data) can then be used with standard software such as Computer

Aided Design (CAD) programs and computer aided design facilities to produce lists, graphs and drawings. The possibilities are almost endless but there are associated problems such as security against virus attack and computer crashes.

1.7.2 Manufacturing stage

'Manufacturing operations must be carried out under controlled conditions.'

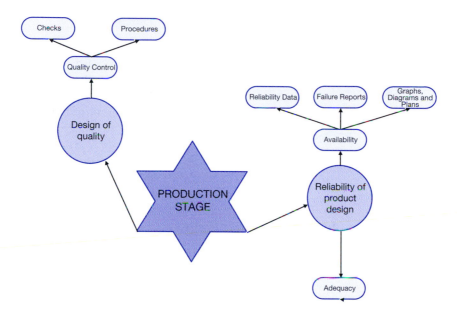

FIGURE 1.10 Quality during the production stage

During all production and manufacturing processes (and throughout early in-service life), the product must be subjected to a variety of Quality Control procedures and checks in order to evaluate the degree of quality.

One of the first things that must be done is to predict the reliability of the product's design. This involves obtaining sufficient statistical data so as to be able to estimate the actual reliability of the design before a product is manufactured.

All the appropriate engineering data has to be carefully examined, particularly the reliability ratings of recommended parts, components, software etc. The designer then extrapolates and interpolates this data and uses probability methods to examine the reliability of a proposed design.

Design deficiencies such as assembly errors, operator learning, motivational or fatigue factors, latent defects and improper part selection are frequently uncovered during this process.

1.7.3 Acceptance stage

'The quality of a product must be proved before being accepted.'

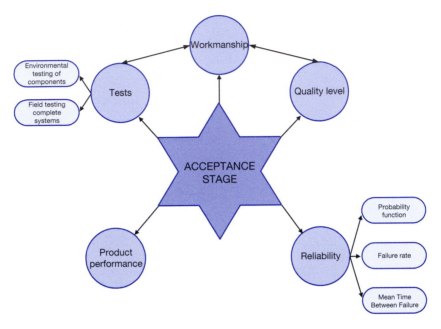

FIGURE 1.11 Quality during the acceptance stage

As stated in ISO 9001:2008: '*The outputs of design and development shall be provided in a form that enables verification against the design and development input and shall be approved prior to release.*'

During the acceptance stage, the product is subjected to a series of tests designed to confirm that the workmanship of the product fully meets the levels of quality required, or stipulated by the user, and that the product performs the required function correctly. Tests will range from environmental tests of individual components to field testing complete systems.

Three mathematical expressions are commonly used to measure reliability and each of these expressions can be applied to a part, component assembly or an entire system. They are: Probability Function (PF), Failure Rate (FR) and Mean Time Between Failures (MTBF).

1.7.4 In-service stage

'Evaluation of product performance during typical operating conditions and feedback of information gained through field use improves product.'

During the in-service stage the equipment user is, of course, principally concerned with system, product and equipment reliability.

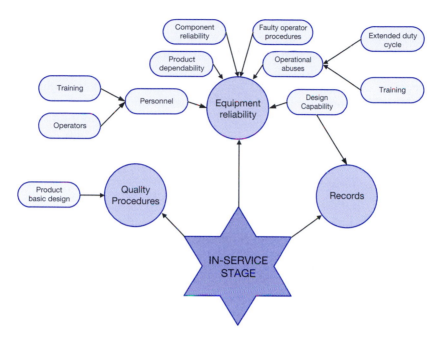

FIGURE 1.12 Quality during the in-service stage

Although reliability is based on the product's generic design (and can be easily proved by statistics), its practical reliability is often far less design dependent. This difference can be due to poor or faulty operating procedures, operating the system beyond its design capability or operational abuses (e.g. personal, extended duty cycles, neglected maintenance, training etc.). Each of these hazards can damage individual components, sub assemblies and soft and/or firmware and each will, in turn, reduce the product's dependability.

It is interesting to note that according to studies completed by the British Chartered Management Institute (CMI) in 2008 (**and** reconfirmed by another survey in 2012), the maintenance technician (or engineer) **still** remains the primary cause of reliability degradations during the in-service stage. The problems associated with poorly trained, poorly supported or poorly motivated maintenance personnel with respect to reliability and dependability cannot be over emphasised and requires careful assessment and quantification.

The most important factor that affects the overall reliability of a modern manufactured product, nevertheless, is the increased number of individual components that are required in that product. Since most system failures are actually caused by the failure of a single component, the reliability of each individual component must be considerably better than the overall system reliability.

Information obtained from in-service use and field failures are enormously useful (always assuming that they are entirely accurate, of course!) in evaluating a product's performance during typical operating conditions. But the main reason for accumulating failure reports from the field is to try to improve the product. This can be achieved by carefully analysing the reports, finding out what caused the failure and taking steps to prevent it from recurring in the future.

Because of this requirement, quality standards for the maintenance, repair and inspection of in-service products have had to be laid down in engineering standards, handbooks and local operating manuals (written for specific items and equipment). These publications are used by maintenance engineers and should always include the most recent amendments. It is **essential** that Quality Assurance personnel also use the same procedures for their inspections!

 See section later on in this book concerning Document Control Procedures.

1.8 BENEFITS AND COSTS OF QUALITY ASSURANCE

'An effective QMS should be designed to satisfy the purchaser's conditions, requirements and expectations whilst serving to protect the manufacturer's best interests.'

In practice, some Quality Assurance programmes can be very expensive to install and operate, particularly if inadequate Quality Control methods were used previously. If the purchaser requires consistent quality he or she must pay for it, regardless of the specification or order which the manufacturer has accepted. However, against this expenditure must always be offset the savings in scrapped material, rework and general problems arising from lack of quality.

From the producers' and/or suppliers' point of view, there is a business requirement to obtain and maintain the desired quality at an optimum cost. The following represent some of the additional expenses that will probably be incurred in a large company:

- salaries for the Quality Manager and Quality Assurance Team;
- training for the Quality Assurance Team;
- visits by the Quality Assurance staff to other companies, subcontractors and the eventual consumer, for evaluation and audit of their facilities and products;
- test equipment that is of a recognised type, standard and quality; and which is regularly maintained and calibrated by an accredited calibration centre;
- better storage facilities.

Note: obviously this would not be such a problem with a very small business; nevertheless, account should still be taken of these potential costs – especially if it is the ultimate aim of the small business to eventually gain ISO 9001:2008 Registration.

'But why bother with "Quality Assurance"?! It is all very expensive to set up and extremely expensive to run – is it really worth it?!'

The short answer is, 'YES' – it is!!

In order to be part of the enormous European and world market, designers, producers, manufacturers, suppliers **and** sole traders must not merely be aware of the requirements and need for Quality Assurance, they **must** also be able to prove that they are capable of constantly producing a quality product that is as good as, if not better than, any others available.

Hopefully they will take pride in producing an item of equipment or the design of a system or a piece of software that operates correctly and which will fully satisfy the purchaser – as opposed to something that goes wrong as soon as it is 'switched on'. There will not be many reorders for that particular model!

Insisting on an assurance of quality has got to save money in the long run. It ensures that the deliverable's design features are more dependable and efficient, and built-in quality at every stage will obviously reduce wastage and increase customer satisfaction.

1.9 COSTS OF QUALITY FAILURE

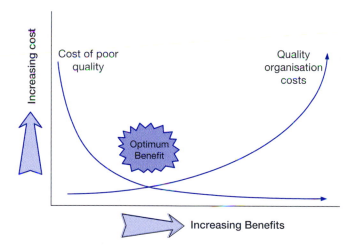

FIGURE 1.13 Quality Management System costs

With an effective QMS in place, the supplier will achieve increased profitability and market share and the purchaser can expect reduced costs, improved product fitness for role, increased satisfaction and, above all, growth in confidence.

1.9.1 The supplier

Lack of Quality Control and Quality Assurance can cause the supplier to:

- replace scrapped products or have to redo unsatisfactory services;
- re-inspect and reprocess products returned as unsatisfactory by the purchaser;
- lose money by having to send staff to the purchasers' premises to sort out their complaints of unsatisfactory labour;
- lose money through a major quality failure halting production;
- lose money through field repairs, replacements and other work having to be carried out under warranty;
- lose money by having to carry out investigations into claims of unsatisfactory work;
- lose money by having to investigate alternative methods of producing a deliverable without quality failures;
- lose his or her image and reputation;
- lose market potential;
- have to acknowledge complaints, claims, liabilities and be subject to waste of human and financial resources;

But most of all . . .

- lose customers!

1.9.2 The purchaser

By not insisting that the supplier abides by a set of recognised quality standards, the purchaser can be involved in:

- delays in being able to use the product and the possibility of the purchaser losing orders because of it;
- possible increases in his or her organisation, operation, maintenance downtime and repair costs;
- dissatisfaction with goods and services;
- health and safety aspects (now a mandatory requirement of ISO 9001:2008);
- lack of confidence in the manufacturer.

1.10 WHAT ARE THE COSTS INVOLVED IN AN ORGANISATION OBTAINING REGISTRATION TO THIS STANDARD?

The one area that an organisation (particularly a small business) will want to know, is how much is it going to cost to implement and operate a QMS compliant with ISO 9001:2008 – and is it going to be worth all the trouble and cost?!!

Obviously each business is different and the cost of ISO 9001 registration will vary depending on the size and complexity of your organisation and on whether you already have some elements of a quality management system in place.

Consequently no book could answer this question with any accuracy; however the following table with examples may, I hope, be beneficial to you.

The first question to be answered, however, is do you actually need to become an ISO 9001 registered company or would simply 'working in compliance with ISO 9001:2008' be sufficient?!

Quite often the answer to this question is 'yes' because in order to tender for a particular project, service or deliverable quite often there is a tender requirement that your company is ISO 9001:2008 registered.

So the next question that is immediately asked by the Managing Director to the Quality Manager is 'how much will it cost' and 'who can we get to do it'?

There is no general rule to the amount that it will cost a particular organisation to become ISO 9001:2008 registered as it will depend very much on the size of the company, its type of product, its client range and a whole host of other questions but at the time of writing this book (September 2013) the budgetary cost for an organisation seeking Registration in the UK would be in the region of that shown below:

Enterprise Category	Headcount	1st Stage 3rd Party Audit	2nd Stage 3rd Party Audit	Yearly assessments
Medium sized	< 250	£600	£2400	£1200
Small	< 50	£600	£1200	£600–1200
Micro	< 10	£300	£600	£600

 If your organisation, on the other hand, does **not** actually require the ISO 9001:2008 certificate on the wall of the office and simply needs to prove to its customers that it is capable and really does work in compliance with the requirements of ISO 9001:2008, then all that is required is to fully read and understand Chapter 6 of this book. This chapter contains a generic QMS that can be customised to suit any form of business no matter whether it produces equipment, widgets, software or simply professional advice etc. – But although this is a fully compliant generic example of a QMS, it **must** be fully customised to suit your own organisation's work methods etc.

The generic example contained in Chapter 6 is **not** meant as a simple, quick, pretty meaningless cut and paste exercise!!

To save you having to copy or retype the Quality Manual, Quality Procedures and/or Work Instructions, 'unlocked', fully accessible, non .PDF, soft copies of all of the files presented in the book, are available – at no additional charge – direct from the author.

To obtain copies of these files, simply send an e-mail to ray@herne.org.uk containing details of your name, address, where you purchased the book from etc., and I will send you the link to download a full copy.

Good Luck!!

Author's Note

Having appreciated the requirements and benefits of quality, quality control and quality assurance, in Chapter 2 the necessity and inter-operability of quality standards is discussed, the historical background of ISO 9000 is presented and the basic requirements of ISO 9001:2008 are explained.

The background to ISO 9000

Author's Note

In Chapter 2, the necessity and interoperability of quality standards is discussed, the historical background of ISO 9000 is presented, the basic requirements of ISO 9001 are explained and certification and registration to ISO 9001:2008 is clarified.

2.1 WHAT IS ISO 9000?

Wherever you go nowadays, it seems that you are always hearing the word 'quality', especially in relation to the requirements of 'ISO 9000', but even though these have become everyday words, they are often misused, misquoted and misunderstood. But why is this? Well, normally you will find that when most people talk about the quality of an object, they are talking about its excellence, perfection and/or value. In reality, of course, they should be talking about how much it meets its designed purpose and comes up to the manufacturer's or supplier's original specifications. Referring to the quality of a single article is, of course, fairly simple. Problems occur, however, when one has to talk about complex systems. Then it can become very difficult indeed to assess a level of quality.

So what exactly is **meant** by the word quality? As explained in Chapter 1, there are many definitions, but the most commonly accepted (as provided by ISO 9000) is 'The degree to which a set of inherent characteristics fulfils requirements'. Another definition (as provided by ISO 9126 for Software product evaluation) is 'The totality of features and characteristics of a product or service that bears its ability to satisfy stated or implied needs'. Both of these definitions are equally applicable whether you are a designer, manufacturer, supplier, maintainer or end user.

But customers are not just interested in the level of quality 'intended' by the manufacturer or supplier, they are far more interested in the maintenance of quality level and want an assurance that the product (i.e. hardware, software, service or processed material) that they are buying truly meets the quality standard that they were initially offered and/or recommended.

**THE TOTALITY OF FEATURES AND CHARACTERISTICS OF A
PRODUCT OR SERVICE THAT BEARS ITS ABILITY TO
SATISFY STATED AND IMPLIED NEEDS**

FIGURE 2.1 A definition of quality

This customer requirement has, quite naturally, had a sort of knock-on effect which has meant that manufacturers and suppliers (especially in large companies) have now had to pay far more attention to the quality of their product than was previously necessary.

Organisations have had to set up proper Quality Management Systems (QMS) in order to control and monitor all stages of the production process **and** they have had to provide proof to a potential customer that their product has the guaranteed – and in some cases certified – quality required **by** that customer. In other words, manufacturers or suppliers have had to work within a Quality Management System in order to provide some degree of quality assurance for their product.

Unfortunately, with the current trend towards microminiaturisation, nano and information technology, most modern day products and supplies have become extremely complex assemblies of components compared to those which were available a few years ago. This has meant that many more people are now involved in the design, production and/or supply of a relatively simple object and this has increased the likelihood of a '*production fault*' occurring.

In much the same way, the responsibility for the quality of a product or service has also been spread over an increasing number of people which has meant that the manufacturer's and/or supplier's guarantee of quality has, unfortunately, become less precise.

With the growing expansion of the European Union (EU), there is now a potential marketplace of some 700–800 million people generating a combined world domestic product of between 40 and 50%. In North America the potential is very similar and selling products and services to these markets has, therefore, become an extremely competitive business which (in order to gain a foothold in

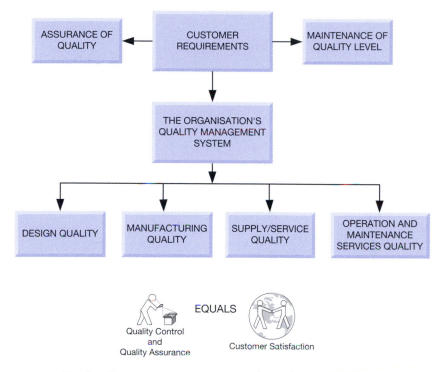

FIGURE 2.2 Meeting the customer's requirements for quality

these markets) has meant an increased reliance on internationally recognised quality procedures and recommendations. This is, of course, an area where ISO 9001:2008 has proved its worth.

2.2 WHAT NATIONAL AND INTERNATIONAL STANDARDS ARE AVAILABLE (AND WHAT IS THEIR INTEROPERABILITY)?

Standards, of course, are as international as the markets they serve and currently the main producers of national standards in Europe are:

- United Kingdom – British Standards Institution (BSI);
- Germany – Deutsch Institut fur Normung e.v. (DIN);
- France – Association Français de Normalisation (AFNOR).

Outside Europe the most widely used standards come from:

- America – American National Standards Institute (ANSI);
- Canada – Canadian Standards Association (CSA).

FIGURE 2.3 Main producers of national standards in Europe

There are, of course, others (for example Japan and Saudi Arabia) but Europe and North America are the main two.

Although these countries publish what are probably the most important series of standards, virtually every country with an industrial base has its own organisation producing its own set of standards. This can obviously lead to a lot of confusion, especially with regard to international trade and tenders.

For example, if America were to invite tenders for a project quoting American (ANSI) national standards as the minimum criteria, other countries might find it difficult to submit a proposal, either because they didn't have a copy (or a translation) of the relevant standard, or because they wouldn't find it cost effective to retool their entire works in order to conform to the requirements of that particular national standard.

FIGURE 2.4 Main producers of national standards outside Europe

The situation in Europe has been made even more difficult by the EU – in an attempt to stop national standards forming trade barriers to community trade – producing even more regulations!

From a Defence Force point of view, there is little change. The United Kingdom Ministry of Defence (MOD-UK) use Defence Standards (DEF STANS), the American Division of Defense (DOD) use Military Standards (Mil-Stds), the North Atlantic Treaty Organisation (NATO) use NATO Allied Quality Assurance Publications (AQAPs) and most other nations have their own particular variations.

From a more civilian point of view the International Telecommunications Union (ITU) Committees (i.e. The International Telegraph and Telephony Consultative Committee (CCITT) and the International Radio Consultative Committee (CCIR)) also publish recommendations.

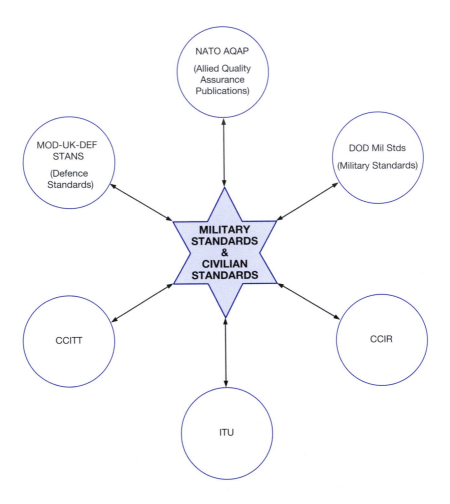

FIGURE 2.5 Military and civilian standards

For this reason there has been a steady growth in international standardisation, and ISO (International Organization for Standardization) and the IEC (International Electrotechnical Commission) are now the standards bodies that most countries are affiliated to – via, that is, their own particular National Standards Organisation (NSO).

Note: If you find this list of acronyms confusing – think what it is like for the poor author trying to get to grips with it – in fact, I could do with a DOA (Dictionary of Abbreviations) to remember them all! For your convenience, however, a complete list of all the abbreviations used is available at the end of this book.

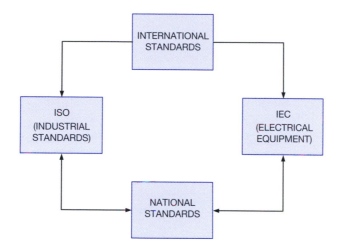

FIGURE 2.6 International standards

Like ITU documents, these ISO and IEC standards (ISO is mainly concerned with industrial standards whilst IEC refers to electrical equipment) were initially published as 'recommendations', but they are now accepted as international standards in their own right.

The standards themselves are drawn up by International Technical Committees which have been approved by ISO or IEC member countries and there are now many hundreds of different ISO and IEC standards available.

But national bodies and national standards cannot dictate customer choice. A product that may legally be marketed need not be of universal appeal. Indeed, where different national standards persist they will do so as a reflection of different market preferences. For industry to survive in this 'liberalised' market, therefore, it must have a sound technological base supported by a comprehensive set of internationally approved standards.

Quality has thus become the key word in today's competitive markets and there are now more than 80 countries with similar organisations – most of which are members of ISO and IEC. Figure 2.7 shows the inter-relationship of these standards and committees.

2.3 WHAT ABOUT THE GROWTH OF QUALITY-SPECIFIC STANDARDS?

The growing demand for assurance of quality **before** a contract is awarded has reinforced the already accepted adage that quality products and services play an important role in securing new markets as well as retaining those markets that already exist. Without doubt, in these days of competitive world markets, quality assurance has never been more relevant. No longer can suppliers rely on their reputation alone.

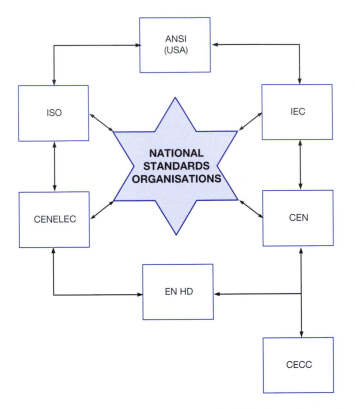

FIGURE 2.7 Inter-relationship of the standards bodies and committees

This drive towards quality-led production now means that today's major purchasers are not just **expecting** a quality product but are also **demanding** proof that a company is capable of producing quality products and/or providing quality services. The provision of this proof is normally in the form of an independent third-party certification and this is possibly the single most important requirement for a manufacturer, company or supplier.

Up until the early 1970s, however, there were no viable third-party certification schemes available. But with an increased demand for quality assurance during all stages of the production process, came the requirement for manufacturers to work to a recognised set of standards.

Within the United Kingdom the BSI had already published a number of guides to quality assurance (for example BS 4891:1972 – 'A guide to Quality Assurance') and quickly set about providing an acceptable document that would cover the requirements for a two-party manufacturing or supply contract.

This became the BS 5750 series of standards which were first published in the United Kingdom during 1979. These standards supplied guidelines for internal quality management as well as external quality assurance and they were quickly accepted by manufacturers, suppliers and purchasers as being a reasonable

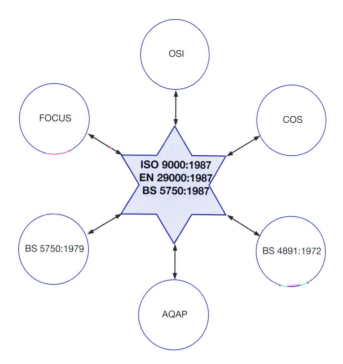

FIGURE 2.8 The background to ISO 9001:1987

minimum level of quality assurance that they could be expected to work to. The BS 5750:1979 series thus became the *'cornerstone for national quality'*.

But in the meantime America had been working on their ANSI 90 series and other European countries were also busily developing their own sets of standards. Quite naturally, however, as the BSI had already produced and published an acceptable standard, most of these national standards were broadly based on BS 5750.

In 1981, the UK Department of Trade and Industry (DTI) formed a committee called FOCUS to examine areas where standardisation could benefit the competitiveness of British manufacturers and users of high technology – for instance Local Area Network (LAN) standardisation. Owing to the wider international interest concerning quality assurance, ISO then set up a Study Group during 1983 to produce an international set of standards that all countries could use.

This initiative, the Open Systems Interconnection (OSI), ensured that products from different manufacturers and different countries could exchange data and interwork in certain defined areas. In the United States, the Corporation of Open Systems (COS) was formed in 1986 to pursue similar objectives.

2.4 BUT WHO ARE ISO?

ISO (the International Organization for Standardization) was first established as a United Nations Agency in 1947 and is a network of national standards bodies. These national standards bodies make up the ISO membership and they represent the ISO in their country.

There are three member categories. Each enjoys a different level of access and influence over the ISO system which helps ISO to be inclusive while also recognising the different needs and capacity of each national standards body.

Note: Countries with limited resources or without a fully developed national standards system can still observe and keep up to date with international standardisation in ISO.

From the consumer's point of view, however, the importance of international (i.e. ISO) standards is that all major agencies are committed to recognising their

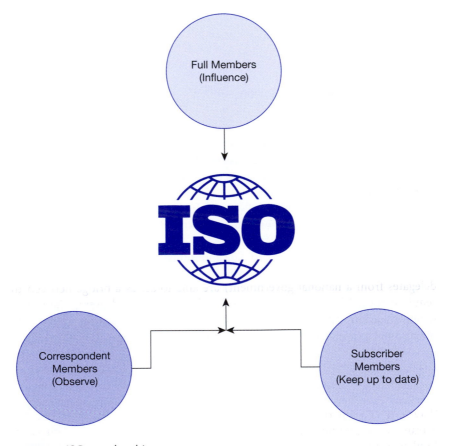

FIGURE 2.9 ISO membership

TABLE 2.1 ISO membership

Type of membership	Responsibility	Total membership*
Full members (or member bodies)	**Influence** ISO standards development and strategy by participating and voting in ISO technical and policy meetings. Full members sell and adopt ISO International Standards nationally	114
Correspondent members	**Observe** the development of ISO standards and strategy by attending ISO technical and policy meetings as observers. Correspondent members can sell and adopt ISO International Standards nationally.	45
Subscriber members	**Keep up to date** on ISO's work but cannot participate in it. They do not sell or adopt ISO International Standards nationally	4

* Accurate at the time of publication.

requirements. Equipment, modules and components as well as systems and software can be designed and produced so that they will be acceptable to all member countries and in this way interoperability is assured.

As the term 'ISO' actually stands for the 'International Organization for Standardization' one would normally assume that the acronym should be 'IOS'! Apparently there are two reasons why ISO was chosen instead of IOS. The first is that 'iso' in Greek means 'equal' (and this mirrors ISO's aim to develop standards that will enable organisations to be on an equal footing and, therefore, conveys the idea of equality). The second (and probably the main reason) is that 'ISO' (International Standard Organisation) is spelt the same (and, therefore, has the same acronym) in most languages spoken by the members of the original organisation.

ISO is a non-governmental organisation and its members (as opposed to being delegates from a national government) are able to act as a bridge between the requirements of business and the needs of consumers and users. Many of its member bodies are part of the governmental structure of their own countries, while other members come from the private sector.

2.5 WHAT IS THE BACKGROUND TO ISO 9000 AND ITS CURRENT STATUS?

'ISO 9000' is a generic name given to a family of standards developed to provide a framework around which a quality management system can effectively be implemented.

2.5.1 ISO 9000:1987

Similar to quality standards from other countries, ISO's first attempt at producing an international standard for quality management (i.e. the ISO 9000:1987 set of standards) were very heavily based on BS 5750 Parts 1, 2 and 3. They followed the same sectional layout except that an additional section (ISO 9000:1987 Part 0 Section 0.1) was introduced to provide further guidance about the principal concepts and applications contained in the ISO 9000 series.

When ISO 9000 was first published in 1987 it was immediately ratified by the UK (under the direction of the Quality Management and Statistics Standards Committee) and republished by the BSI (without deviation), as the new BS 5750:1987 standard for QMSs.

Similarly, on 10 December 1987 the Technical Board of the European Committee for Standardisation (Commission European de Normalisation Electrotechnique – CEN) approved and accepted the text of ISO 9000:1987 as **the** European Standard – without modification – and republished it as EN 29000:1987.

At that time official versions of EN 29000:1987 existed in English, French and German. CEN members were allowed, however, to translate any of these versions into their own language and they then had the same status as the original official versions.

 Up-to-date lists and bibliographical references concerning these and other European standards may be obtained on application to the CEN Central Secretariat (Rue Brederode 2, Boite 5, B–1000, Brussels, Belgium) or from any CEN member.

BS 5750:1987 was, therefore, identical to ISO 9000:1987 and EN 29000:1987 except that BS 5750 had three additional guidance sections.

Consequently, BS 5750 was not just the British Standard for Quality Management Systems, it was also the European **and** the international standard!

2.5.2 ISO 9000:1994

As ISO 9000:1987 became more popular, ISO realised that calling the same document by a variety of different names could cause a certain amount of confusion, and so in March 1994 the ISO 9000:1994 series of Quality Management documents were published.

Although the most notable change between the 1987 and the 1994 versions of the ISO 9000 standard was the streamlining of the numbering system, there were also around 250 other changes, the main ones being that:

- it became an explicit requirement that all members of an organisation (down to supervisory level at least) had job profiles (descriptions) to define their authority and responsibility;

- design reviews were now compulsory throughout the Work Package lifetime;
- documentation control was extended to ensure that all data was kept up to date.

Most of the 250 changes were intended to clarify the standard, making it easier to read. They did not significantly alter the way in which most companies were running their businesses; they simply sought to improve it.

2.5.3 ISO 9001:2000

When ISO 9000 was first released in 1987, it was recognised as being mainly aimed at manufacturers, and largely incomplete and it required the auditors to fill in lots of the gaps. The first revision of ISO 9000 in 1994 got rid of many of these problems. However, an organisation could still conform to the standard **but** at the same time produce sub standard products that were of a consistent poor quality! There was clearly a major loophole that enabled organisations to comply with the requirements of ISO 9000:1994 – without having to **improve** the quality of their product or service!

Some managers also found it extremely difficult to see the real benefit of having to commit more and more manpower and finance in maintaining their ISO 9000 certification and whilst most organisations accepted that the initial certification process was worthwhile and could result in some very real benefits, these were mainly one-offs and it was felt that once ISO 9000 had been fully adopted within an organisation, these savings could not be repeated. The ISO 9000 certificate had been hanging on the wall in the reception office for many years but third-party surveillance visits didn't tell the management much more than they already knew from their own internal audits! Quite a few organisations also felt that they had gone well beyond ISO 9000 and apart from associating their organisation with a quality standard, there was little or no actual benefit to be gained from having to continually pay out for re-certification and surveillance fees.

On the other hand, however, BSI frequently came across organisations who initially sought ISO 9000 registration (because it was a requirement to continue business with a client), but having seen the benefits they, in turn, had pushed it on down their own supply chain, thus **increasing** the requirement for ISO 9000 certification.

So as the 1990s progressed, more and more organisations started reaping benefits from the existing ISO 9000:1994 requirements but as the standard became more popular the inadequacies of ISO 9000:1994 became more apparent. For example:

- some organisations were not manufacturers and did not need to carry out all the 20 elements making up ISO 9000:1994 in order to be a quality organisation;
- the standard was too biased towards manufacturing industries thus making it difficult for service industries to use;

- there was growing confusion about having three quality standards available for certification (i.e. ISO 9001:1994 (*Model for quality assurance in design, development, production, installation, and servicing*), ISO 9002:1994 (*Model for quality assurance in production, installation, and servicing*) and ISO 9003:1994 (*Model for quality assurance in final inspection and test*)) and there was a need for the requirements for all three standards to be combined into one overall standard (i.e. ISO 9001:2000);
- the requirements were repeated in other management systems, resulting in duplication of effort (e.g. ISO 14001 Environmental Management and OHSAS 18001 for Occupational Health and Safety);
- many organisations wanted to progress beyond the confines of ISO 9000 towards Total Quality Management (TQM);
- the documents were viewed by many as **not** being very user-friendly;
- the language used was **not** clear and could be interpreted in many different ways;
- the standard was very inflexible and could **not** be tailored to specific industries, etc;
- the standard did **not** cater for continual improvement;
- the standard did **not** fully address customer satisfaction.

The reasons went on and on and there was clearly a need for revision with the overall aim of making a new ISO 9001:2000 that was:

- more compatible with the other management systems;
- more closely associated to business processes;
- more easy to understand;
- capable of being used by all organisations, no matter their size;
- capable of being used by all types of industry and profession (i.e. manufacturers **and** service providers);
- a means of continually improving quality; and above all
- future proof.

A decision was made, therefore, to provide a revised standard which would:

- be split, so that one standard (i.e. ISO 9001:2000) would address requirements, whilst another standard (ISO 9004:2009) would address the gradual improvement of an organisation's overall quality performance;
- be simple to use, easy to understand and only use clear language and terminology (a definite plus for most readers of current international standards!);
- have a common structure based on a '*process model*';
- be capable of being '*tailored*' to fit all product and service sectors and all sizes of organisation (and not just the manufacturing industry);
- be more orientated toward continual improvement and customer satisfaction;

- be capable of demonstrating continuous improvement and prevention of non-conformity;
- provide a natural stepping stone towards performance improvement;
- have an increased compatibility with other management system standards;
- provide a basis for addressing the primary needs and interests of organisations in specific sectors such as aerospace, automotive, medical devices, telecommunication and others.

ISO emphasised, however, that this revision of the ISO 9000 standards would **not** require the rewriting of the organisation's current QMS documentation! They pointed out that the only real change had been from a 'system based' to a more 'process orientated' management approach, which could be easily addressed by organisations on an as-required basis.

2.5.4 ISO 9001:2008

According to the rules of ISO, the ISO 9001 standard is required to undergo review and revision every 6–8 years.

The ISO 9001 standard was first revised in 1994 and then underwent a major revision in 2000. In November 2008, ISO published the current revision, which is called ISO 9001:2008.

2.5.4.1 What is new in ISO 9001:2008?

Thankfully the changes made in ISO 9001:2008 were relatively minor and of little concern to most companies. The new standard does **not** contain any **new** requirements nor does it contain changes to any of the requirements of ISO 9001:2000, and more importantly, it does not change the intent of ISO 9001:2000.

For all intents and purposes, therefore, the structure and outline of ISO 9001:2008 is identical to that of ISO 9001:2000 and only introduces clarifications to the existing requirements of ISO 9001:2000 based on eight years of experience of implementing the standard worldwide with over one million certificates issued in over 175 countries. It also introduces some changes to the wording intended to improve consistency with the other Safety (OHSAS 18001) and Environmental (ISO 14001) Management Systems.

According to ISO, the benefits of the changes to the wording in ISO 9001:2008 are as follows:

- easier to use
- clearer language
- easier to translate into other languages
- better compatibility with the environmental and safety management standards.

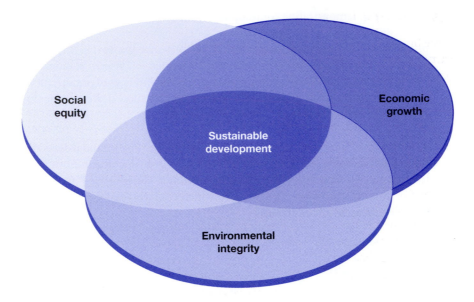

FIGURE 2.10 Three aspects of sustainable development

2.5.4.2 When is the next revision due?

Building on 25 years of success of the ISO 9000, ISO technical committee ISO/TC 176, Quality management and quality assurance, subcommittee SC 2, Quality systems (ISO/TC 176/SC 2) is currently laying the groundwork for the next generation of quality management standards with the overall aim of ensuring that ISO 9000 continues to provide a solid foundation for quality management over the next 25 years.

As ISO state in their initial announcement *'This pivotal role of quality management systems as a basis for the economic growth component of the sustainability agenda has often been overlooked, with attention in recent years being focused on the more topical elements of environmental integrity and social equity'* (see Figure 2.10).

It should not be forgotten, though, that ISO 9001 is, and will probably continue to be, the entry point for most organisations seeking to implement any type of formal management system. Although not a requirement, third-party certification to ISO 9001 will still remain a key driver.

It is important, however, to ensure that quality management is seen as much more than just certification to ISO 9001 and that it really helps organisations to achieve long-term success. This means that quality needs to be promoted in the widest sense of the word and encouragement given to organisations to look beyond compliance to ISO 9001 by providing linkages to ISO 9004 and other ISO management system standards.

2.5.5 ISO 9001:2015

Since the publication of the minor amendment to ISO 9001 in 2008, ISO has been carrying out extensive research and preparation for the next major revision (currently forecast for 2015). This involves activities such as:

- developing a long-term strategic plan for ISO/TC 176/SC 2 and its products;
- conducting several open workshops during SC 2 Plenary Meetings including interactions with users of the ISO 9001 and ISO 9004 standards;
- participating in the work of the ISO/TMB Joint Technical Coordination Group, aimed at increasing the alignment of ISO's management system standards by developing a common high-level structure, common definitions and some common text;
- studying the latest trends in quality management that might be considered for incorporation into future revisions of ISO 9001 and ISO 9004;
- analysing data received from a web-based survey that was conducted in 10 languages (and which gained a total of 11,722 responses from 122 countries) of users and potential users of ISO 9001 and ISO 9004.

The results of these activities indicate that whilst there is still significant satisfaction with the current version of the standard, most people consider that in order to keep ISO 9001 relevant and reflect changes in its environment (whilst ensuring that it still continues to deliver *confidence in the organization's ability to consistently provide product that meets customer and applicable statutory and regulatory requirements*') a revision of ISO 9001:2008 is appropriate and that this revised standard should (among other things):

- provide a stable core set of requirements for the next 10 years or more;
- remain generic, and relevant to all sizes and types of organisation operating in any sector;
- maintain the current focus on effective process management to produce desired outcomes;
- take account of changes in quality management systems practices and technology since the last major revision in 2000;
- reflect changes in the increasingly complex, demanding and dynamic environments in which organisations operate;
- enhance compatibility and alignment with other ISO management system standards;
- facilitate effective organisational implementation and effective conformity assessment by first, second and third parties;
- use simplified language and writing styles to aid understanding and consistent interpretations of its requirements.

2.5.5.1 ISO 9001:2015 timeline

The proposed timeline for the development of ISO 9001:2015 is shown in Figure 2.11.

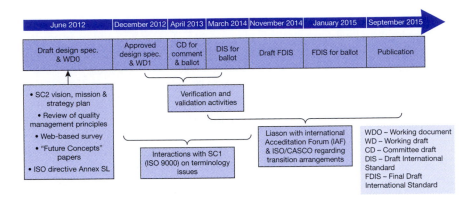

FIGURE 2.11 Proposed high-level timing for development of ISO 9001:2015

It is intended that the development of ISO 9001:2015 will be wide ranging and involve specific sectors whose own requirements standards are based on ISO 9001, organisations that have systems certified to ISO 9001:2008, certification bodies, accreditation bodies as well as regulators.

All of this is good news for current ISO 9001 users. They can update their existing systems without the dramatic upheaval some would have experienced in the last major revision that happened 15 years before when ISO 9001:2000 was published. It also allows technical experts to take the time needed to fully address the changes required without damaging the effectiveness of the existing standard.

2.6 WHAT ARE THE CURRENT ISO 9000 STANDARDS?

There are three main standards that make up the ISO 9000 family (as shown in Figure 2.12 and described below).

2.6.1 ISO 9000:2005 Quality Management Systems – Fundamentals and Vocabulary

ISO 9000:2005 is (i.e. at the time of writing this book) the latest version of a standard that defines the vocabulary and describes the fundamental principles of Quality Management Systems (QMS). It also provides details of the basic QMS terminology such as:

- the product – the 'thing' that your company provides to the customer;
- the organisation – your company;

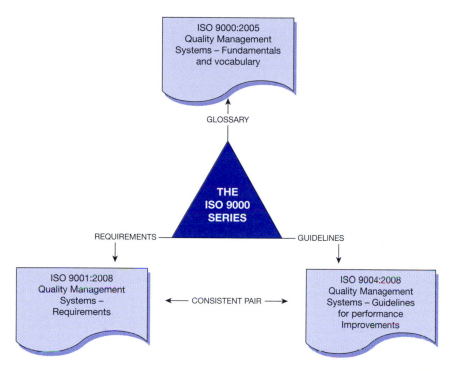

FIGURE 2.12 The ISO 9000 series of standards

- the customer – the people you supply the product to;
- the supplier – the people who supply you with something that contributes to your product;
- top management – the company directors and executive management;

and

 emphasises that 'shall' means '**you must**' and that you will always be audited to ensure you comply with the 'shalls'!

2.6.2 ISO 9004:2009 Quality Management Systems – Guidelines for Performance Improvement

ISO 9004:2009 provides useful guidance for the development of a QMS, including the processes for continual improvement that will contribute to the satisfaction of an organisation's customers and other interested parties.

This guidance is generic and, therefore, applicable to all organisations, regardless of their type, size and the product provided. It also supplies a link to other, wider, quality standards such as Six-Sigma and Business Excellence and is aimed at improving an organisation's overall quality performance. In effect, it provides a stepping-stone to Total Quality Management (TQM).

 ISO 9004:2009 is **not** intended for certification, regulatory or contractual use.

2.6.3 ISO 9001:2008 Quality Management Systems – Requirements

ISO 9001 is the definitive requirements standard which specifies the requirements for a Quality Management System (QMS) which can be used when an organisation's capability to provide products that meet customer and applicable regulatory requirements needs to be demonstrated.

Unlike the 1994 version of the standard, which concentrated on 20 auditable elements (and virtually ended up as a '*tick in the box*' conformity standard) ISO 9001:2008 focuses on four major generic business processes covering the management of resources, the quality of the product, the maintenance of quality records and the requirements for continual improvement:

Section 5 – Management Responsibility
Section 6 – Resource Management
Section 7 – Product Realization
Section 8 – Measurement Analysis and Improvement

These processes are backed up by Section 4 (Quality Management System) which covers the requirements for the control of documents and records as well as the need to establish a Quality Manual to describe the interaction between the processes of the QMS.

ISO 9001:2008, by being much less prescriptive than the 1994 version, has significantly reduced the amount of documentation an organisation has to produce to show compliance. This allows organisations to develop their own style of documentation to show the effectiveness of their planning, operation and control of processes and the implementation and continual improvement of their QMS.

Note: For certification purposes, an organisation will have to possess a documented management system that takes the inputs and transforms them into targeted outputs. Something that (in an effective manner):

- says what it is going to do;
- does what it has said it is going to do;
- keeps records of everything that it does – especially when things go wrong.

ISO 9001:2008 provides detailed assistance in producing an auditable management system, no matter whether the user is a manufacturer or supplier, or if it is a producer or service-provider.

2.7 QUALITY MANAGEMENT PRINCIPLES

The eight quality management principles defined in ISO 9000:2008 can be used by senior management as a basis for improving their organisation's performance. They have been derived from the collective experience and knowledge of the international experts making up the technical committee responsible for developing and maintaining ISO 9000 (i.e. ISO-TC 176).

FIGURE 2.13 The eight principles of quality management

Note: ISO 9000:2008 also provides examples of the benefits that can be derived from the use of these eight principles and some of the actions that managers could typically take in applying them to improve their organisations' performance.

Principle 1 Customer focus

Organisations depend on their customers and therefore should understand current and future customer needs, should meet customer requirements and strive to exceed customer expectations.

Key benefits:

- Better use of the organisation's resources.
- Enhanced customer satisfaction.

- Flexible and fast response to market opportunities.
- Improved customer loyalty.
- Increased revenue and market share.
- Repeat business.

Principle 2 Leadership

Leaders establish unity of purpose and direction of the organisation. They should create and maintain the internal environment in which people can become fully involved in achieving the organisation's objectives.

Key benefits:

- Better communication levels throughout the organisation.
- Better understanding of the reasons for achieving the organisation's goals and objectives.
- Evaluation of activities.
- Minimising the possibilities for error.

Principle 3 Involvement of people

People at all levels are the essence of an organisation and their full involvement enables their abilities to be used for the organisation's benefit.

Key benefits:

- Helping people to be motivated, committed and involved.
- Inspiring people to continually improve on their organisation's objectives.
- Making people accountable for their own performance.
- Stimulating people to always aim for continual improvement.

Principle 4 Process approach

A desired result is achieved more efficiently when activities and related resources are managed as a process.

Key benefits:

- Lower costs and shorter cycle times.
- Effective use of resources.
- Improved, consistent and predictable results.
- Focused and prioritised opportunities for improvement.

Principle 5 System approach to management

Identifying, understanding and managing interrelated processes as a system contributes to the organisation's effectiveness and efficiency in achieving its objectives.

Key benefits:

- Being able to focus effort on the key processes.
- Being better able to achieve desired results.
- Integration and alignment of business processes.
- Promoting confidence (to interested parties) about the organisation's effectiveness, efficiency and capability.

Principle 6 Continual improvement

Continual improvement of the organisation's overall performance should be a
permanent objective of the organisation.

Key benefits:

- Coordination of all improvement possibilities and activities.
- Improving the organisational capability.
- Providing the flexibility to react to opportunities quickly.

Principle 7 Factual approach to decision making

Effective decisions are based on the analysis of data and information.

Key benefits:

- Ability to review, challenge and change opinions and decisions.

Principle 8 Mutually beneficial supplier relationships

An organisation and its suppliers are interdependent and a mutually beneficial
relationship enhances the ability of both to create value.

Key benefits:

- Ability to react quickly to a changing market and/or customer needs and expectations.
- Costs optimised.
- Possibilities for creating value for both parties.
- Resources used to their best advantage.

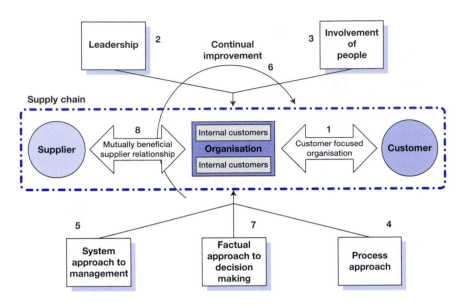

FIGURE 2.14 The process model

ISO has recently undertaken a full review of these eight quality management principles. From this, it is pleasing (but not surprising) to report that they have stood the test of time, and that only a few minor adjustments are needed to update them for the next generation of Quality Management Standards.

2.8 ISO 9001:2008'S COMPATIBILITY WITH OTHER MANAGEMENT SYSTEMS

Similar to its 2000 predecessor, ISO 9001:2008 is intended to be compatible with other internationally recognised management system standards – particularly those relating to Environmental Management and Occupational Health and Safety (OHS).

Although ISO 9001:2008 does not include any requirements that are actually specific to any of these other management systems, it does, nevertheless, allow an organisation to align and integrate its own ISO 9001:2008 QMS with other (related) management system requirements. In many cases, it may even be possible for an organisation to adapt an existing Environmental, Health and/or Safety Management System so that it can establish a QMS that complies with the requirements of ISO 9001:2008. For example, a company designing, producing and installing a hand-held medical device such as a TENS (Transcutaneous electrical nerve stimulation) electrotherapy machine (similar to that shown in Figure 2.15), would require Registration to ISO 13485 for Medical Devices as well as ISO 9001.

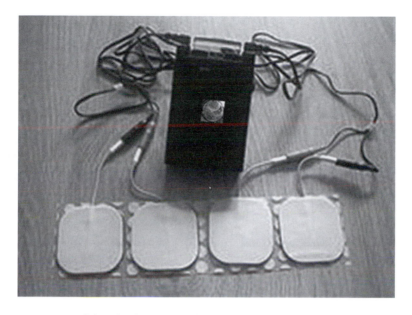

FIGURE 2.15 Typical four lead TENS machine

2.8.1 The OHSAS 18000 Series

OHSAS (short for the Occupational Health & Safety Assessment Series) 18000 is the internationally recognised assessment specification for OHS Management Systems. It has been specifically designed to be compatible with ISO 9001 and ISO 14001 and its aim is to help organisations meet their health and safety obligations in an efficient manner.

OHSAS 18000 is made up of two standards (ISOs 18001 and 18002) and includes the requirements of BS8800:1996 (Guide to Occupational Health and Safety Management Systems) as well as other internationally recognised OHS publications.

OHSAS 18001

OHSAS 18001 is the assessment specification for Occupational Health and Safety Management Systems. It can be used by any organisation wishing to implement a formal procedure for reducing the risks associated with health and safety in the working environment for employees, customers and the general public by addressing the following key areas:

- planning for, risk assessment, risk control and hazard identification and analysis;
- the OHSAS management programme;
- structure and responsibility;
- training, awareness and competence;

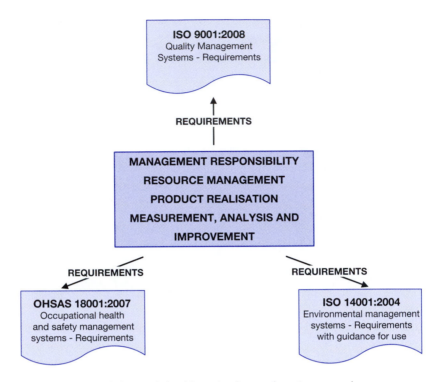

FIGURE 2.16 Compatibility with health and safety and environmental management systems

- consultation and communication;
- operational control;
- emergency preparedness and response;
- performance measuring, monitoring and improvement.

Note: To compliment OHSAS 18001, BSI published OHSAS 18002, which explains the requirements of the specification and shows you how to work toward implementation and registration.

2.8.2 ISO 14000

The ISO 14000 Environmental Management series help organisations to minimise the negative effect that their operations have on the environment (such as causing unfavourable changes to air, water or land).

Similar to ISO 9001, ISO 14000 makes use of processes to describe how a product or service is produced, and in doing so, systematically reduce the impact of the environmental aspects which an organisation can control.

This standard is applicable to any organisation that wishes to:

- implement, maintain and improve an environmental management system;
- ensure compliance with environmental laws and regulations;
- assure itself of its conformance with its own stated environmental principles and activities;
- demonstrate conformance;
- seek certification of its environmental management system by an external third-party organisation;
- make a self-determination and self-declaration of environmental conformity.

The ISO 14000 family addresses various aspects of environmental management and its structure is very similar to the ISO 9001 series; ISO 14001 provides the requirements for an Environmental Management System (EMS) whilst ISO 14004 provides general EMS guidelines.

2.8.3 What is the difference between ISO 9000 and ISO 14000?

ISO 9001:2000 has been closely aligned with ISO 14001:1996 so as to *'enhance the compatibility of these two standards for the benefit of the user community'*.

Whilst both of these standards are effectively *'generic management system standards'*, the ISO 9000 family is primarily concerned with 'quality management' and:

- what the organisation does to fulfil the customer's quality requirements;
- how it meets the applicable regulatory requirements;
- how it enhances customer satisfaction; and
- how it achieves continual improvement of its performance, product and/or service.

On the other hand, the ISO 14000 is aimed at continually reducing pollution (through the more efficient and responsible use of raw materials) and the minimisation of energy usage and waste. It is concerned with how an organisation:

- minimises harmful effects on the environment caused by its activities; and
- achieves continual improvement of its environmental performance.

2.9 WHAT OTHER STANDARDS ARE BASED ON ISO 9001:2008?

During the last decade, registration to the ISO 9000 series of quality standards has become a growing trend worldwide and particularly within Europe and the United States where it has had an impact on a large part of the business community. Larger companies have seen the immediate benefits of becoming registered, particularly for those expanding into the global marketplace.

Smaller American companies, although they have not been as quick to jump on the bandwagon (mainly due to the perceived cost of registration) are now seeing the benefit of working in compliance with ISO 9000 and because of the reduced fees associated with registering a small company (indeed of those companies registered since 2000, about 50% were able to recover their ISO 9000 implementation costs in three years or less – according to a recent McGraw-Hill study) America is now one of the world leaders in ISO 9001:2008 SME registered companies.

ISO and ANSI work closely together in producing interpretative standards for both sides of the Atlantic, and the 1994 and 2000 versions of ISO 9000 have been frequently used as the generic template for other industry management system standards. Currently, although there are still a number of these other industry standards available, they are all gradually being rewritten around the requirements and recommendations of ISO 9001:2008 and Table 2.2 shows a selection of some of the more important ones.

2.9.1 Aerospace

AS/EN/JIS Q 9100: 2009 (*Quality Management Systems – Aerospace – Requirements*) is an international aerospace standard for quality assurance in design, development, production, installation and servicing of aircraft and aircraft systems.

2.9.2 Automotive industry

ISO/TS 16949:2009 (*Quality management systems – Particular requirements for the application of ISO 9001:2008 for automotive production and relevant service part organizations*), in conjunction with ISO 9001:2008, defines the quality management system requirements for the design and development, production and, when relevant, installation and service of automotive-related products.

2.9.3 Computer software

ISO/IEC 90003:2004 (*Software engineering – Guidelines for the application of ISO 9001:2000 to computer software*) provides guidance for organisations using ISO 9001 to purchase, supply, develop, operate and maintain computer software and related support services.

Note: TickIT procedures relate directly to the requirements set out in ISO 9001:2008 and similar to this standard, certification is conducted by an independent third-party certification body using specialist auditors trained by the International Register of Certificated Auditors (IRCA) with the support of the British Computer Society.

TABLE 2.2 Other standards based on ISO 9001:2008

Aerospace	AS 9100:2009
Automotive industry	ISO 16949:2009
Computer software	ISO 90003:2004
Crop production	ISO 22006:2009
Data	ISO/TS 8000–150:2011
Education	IWA 2:2007
Energy	ISO 50001:2011
Explosive atmospheres	ISI/IEC 80079–34:2011
Food safety	ISO 22000:2005
Good manufacturing practice	ISO 1538:2011
Health care	IWA 1:2005
Information security	ISO/IEC 27001:2005
Local government	IWA 4:2009
Measurement manufacturing systems	ISO 10012:2003
Medical devices	ISO 13485:2003
Multilayer piping systems	ISO/TS 21003–7:2008
Packaging	ISO 16106:2006
Petroleum, petrochemical and natural gas industries	ISO/TS 29001:2010
Plastics piping systems	ISO/TS 15887–7:2009
Quality plans	ISO 10005:2005
Ships and marine technology	ISO 30000:2009
Space systems	ISO 16192:2010
Supply chain management	ISO 28000:2007
Systems engineering	ISO TR 90005:2008
Telecommunications industry	TL 9000
Testing and calibration laboratories	ISO/IEC 17025:2005
Welding materials and fluxes	ISO 13444:2010

2.9.4 Crop production

ISO 22006:2009 (*Quality management systems – Guidelines for the application of ISO 9001:2008 to crop production*) gives guidelines to assist crop producers in the adoption of ISO 9001:2008 for crop production processes. The term 'crop' includes seasonal crops (such as grains, pulses, oilseeds, spices, fruit and vegetables), row-planted crops that are cultivated, perennial crops that are managed over a period of time, and wild crops that are not formally planted or managed. Horticultural crops provide an even broader range of types from annual and perennial fruits, vegetables and ornamental flowering plants to perennial shrubs and trees, and root crops. These diverse crops require a broad range of planting, cultivating, pest control and harvesting methods and practices. Decisions regarding planting, growing and harvesting activities can be similar, although specific steps can be quite different when considering the range of crops.

2.9.5 Data

ISO/TS 8000–150:2011 (*Data quality – Part 150: Master data: Quality management framework*) specifies fundamental principles of master data quality management, and requirements for implementation, data exchange and provenance. ISO/TS 8000–150:2011 also contains an informative framework that identifies processes for data quality management. This framework can be used in conjunction with, or independently of, quality management systems standards, for example, ISO 9001.

2.9.6 Education

IWA 2:2007 (*Quality management systems – Guidelines for the application of ISO 9001:2000*) provides guidance for a quality management system in educational organisations.

2.9.7 Energy

ISO 50001:2011 (*Energy management systems – Requirements with guidance for use*) specifies requirements for establishing, implementing, maintaining and improving an energy management system, the purpose of which is to enable an organisation to follow a systematic approach in achieving continual improvement of energy performance, including energy efficiency, energy use and consumption.

2.9.8 Explosive atmospheres

ISO/IEC 80079–34:2011 (*Part 34: Application of quality systems for equipment manufacture*) specifies particular requirements and information for establishing and maintaining a quality system to manufacture Ex equipment including protective systems in accordance with the Ex certificate.

2.9.9 Food safety

ISO 22000:2005 (*Food safety management systems – Requirements for any organization in the food chain*) specifies requirements for a food safety management system where an organisation in the food chain needs to demonstrate its ability to control food safety hazards in order to ensure that food is safe at the time of human consumption.

2.9.10 Good manufacturing practice

ISO 1538:2011 (*Primary packaging materials for medicinal products – Particular requirements for the application of ISO 9001:2008, with reference to Good Manufacturing Practice (GMP)*) specifies requirements for a quality management system where an organisation needs to demonstrate its ability to provide primary packaging materials for medicinal products which consistently meet customer requirements, including regulatory requirements and International Standards applicable to primary packaging materials.

2.9.11 Health care

IWA 1:2005 (*Quality management systems – Guidelines for process improvements in health service organizations*) provides guidance for any health service organisation involved in the management, delivery or administration of health service products or services, including training and/or research, in the life continuum process for human beings, regardless of type, size and the product or service provided.

2.9.12 Information security

ISO/IEC 27001:2005 (*Information technology – Security techniques – Information security management systems – Requirements*) specifies the requirements for establishing, implementing, operating, monitoring, reviewing, maintaining and improving a documented Information Security Management System, taking into consideration the organisation's overall business risks. It includes requirements for the implementation of security controls customised to the needs of individual organisations or parts thereof.

2.9.13 Local government

IWA 4:2009 (*Quality management systems – Guidelines for the application of ISO 9001:2008 in local government*) provides local governments with guidelines for the voluntary application of ISO 9001 on an integral basis.

2.9.14 Measurement manufacturing systems

ISO 10012:2003 (*Measurement management systems – Requirements for measurement processes and measuring equipment*) specifies generic requirements and provides guidance for the management of measurement processes and metrological confirmation of measuring equipment used to support and demonstrate compliance with metrological requirements. It specifies quality management requirements of a measurement management system that can be used by an organisation performing measurements as part of the overall management system, and to ensure metrological requirements are met.

2.9.15 Medical devices

ISO 13485:2003 (*Medical devices – Quality management systems – Requirements for regulatory purposes*) specifies the requirements for a QMS where an organisation needs to demonstrate its ability to provide medical devices and related services that consistently meet customer requirements and regulatory requirements applicable to medical devices and related services.

 As patient safety is involved, **ALL** of the requirements of ISO 13485:2003 are mandatory!

2.9.16 Multilayer piping systems

ISO/TS 21003–7:2008 (*Multilayer piping systems for hot and cold water installations inside buildings – Part 7: Guidance for the assessment of conformity*) is applicable, in conjunction with the other parts of ISO 21007, to multilayer piping systems intended to be used for hot and cold water installations inside buildings for the conveyance of water – whether or not the water is intended for human consumption (domestic systems) or for heating systems – under specified design pressures and temperatures appropriate to the class of application. It gives guidance for the assessment of conformity, to be included in the manufacturer's quality plan as part of the quality system.

2.9.17 Packaging – transport packages for dangerous goods

ISO 16106:2006 (*Packaging – Transport packages for dangerous goods – Dangerous goods packagings, intermediate bulk containers (IBCs) and large packagings – Guidelines for the application of ISO 9001*) gives guidance on quality management provisions applicable to the manufacture, measuring and monitoring of design type approved dangerous goods packagings, intermediate bulk containers (IBCs) and large packagings.

2.9.18 Petroleum, petrochemical and natural gas industries

PD ISO/TS 29001:2010 (*Petroleum, petrochemical and natural gas industries – Sector specific quality management systems – Requirements for product and service supply organisations*) defines the quality management system for product and service supply organisations for the petroleum, petrochemical and natural gas industries.

2.9.19 Plastics piping systems

ISO/TS 15887–7:2009 (*Plastics piping systems for hot and cold water installations – Chlorinated poly(vinyl chloride) (PVC-C) – Part 7: Guidance for the assessment of conformity*) gives guidance for the assessment of conformity included in the manufacturer's quality plan as part of its quality system.

2.9.20 Quality plans

ISO 10005:2005 *(Quality management systems – Guidelines for quality plans)* provides guidelines for the development, review, acceptance, application and revision of quality plans (it is applicable whether or not the organisation has a management system in conformity with ISO 9001).

2.9.21 Ships and marine technology

ISO 30000:2009 *(Ship recycling management systems – Specifications for management systems for safe and environmentally sound ship recycling facilities)* specifies requirements for a management system to enable a ship recycling facility to develop and implement procedures, policies and objectives in order to be able to undertake safe and environmentally sound ship recycling operations in accordance with national and international standards.

2.9.22 Space systems

ISO 16192:2010 *(Space systems – Experience gained in space projects (Lessons learned) – Principles and guidelines)* outlines lessons learned principles and guidelines that are applicable in all space project activities (management, technical, quality, cost and schedule).

2.9.23 Supply chain management

ISO 28000:2007 *(Specification for security management systems for the supply chain)* specifies the requirements for a security management system, including those aspects critical to security assurance of the supply chain.

2.9.24 Systems engineering

ISO TR 90005:2008 *(Systems engineering – Guidelines for the application of ISO 9001 to system life cycle processes)* provides guidance for organisations in the application of ISO 9001:2000 to the acquisition, supply, development, operation and maintenance of systems and related support services.

2.9.25 Telecommunications industry

TL 9000 *(Quality management standard for the telecommunication sector)* is a set of quality system requirements for the telecommunications industry which were originally developed by the QuEST Forum (Quality Excellence for Suppliers of Telecommunications Leadership) and was first published in November 1999. It has now been updated to conform to ISO 9001:2008.

2.9.26 Testing and calibration laboratories

ISO/IEC 17025:2005 (*General requirements for the competence of testing and calibration laboratories*) specifies the general requirements for the competence to carry out tests and/or calibrations, including sampling. It covers testing and calibration performed using standard methods, non-standard methods, and laboratory-developed methods. It is applicable to all organisations performing tests and/or calibrations, regardless of the number of personnel or the extent of the scope of testing and/or calibration activities.

2.9.27 Welding materials and fluxes

ISO 13444:2010 (*Welding consumables – Procurement of filler materials and flux*) specifies tools for communication between a purchaser and a supplier of welding consumables within quality systems, such as those based upon ISO 9001.

2.10 WHAT IS ISO 9001:2008'S BASIC PROCESS?

With the publication of ISO 9001:2008, there is now, therefore, a single quality management '**requirements**' standard that is applicable to **all** organisations, products and services. It is the **only** standard that can be used for the certification of a QMS and its generic requirements can be used by **any** organisation (whether they are Huge Conglomerates, Medium Sized Enterprises, Small Businesses or just '*One Man Bands*' and no matter whether you are a designer, manufacturer, supplier or maintainer) to:

- address customer satisfaction;
- meet customer and applicable regulatory requirements;
- enable internal and external parties (including certification bodies) to assess the organisation's ability to meet these customer and regulatory requirements.

For certification purposes, an organisation will have to possess a documented management system which takes the inputs and transforms them into targeted outputs. Something that effectively:

- says what it is going to do;
- does what it has said it is going to do;
- keeps records of everything that it does (especially when things go wrong!)

The basic process to achieve these targeted outputs will encompass:

- the client's requirements;
- the inputs from management and staff;
- documented controls for any activities that are needed to produce the finished article;

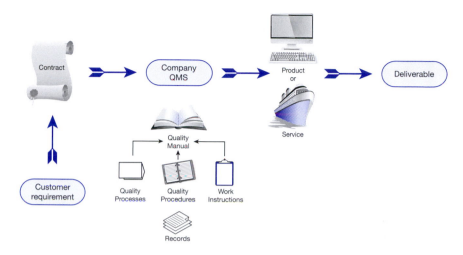

FIGURE 2.17 The basic process

- and, of course, delivering a product or service, which satisfies the customer's original requirements.

The adoption of a QMS has to be a strategic decision for any organisation and the design and implementation of its QMS will be influenced by its varying needs, objectives, products provided, processes employed and the size and structure of that organisation. As ISO are quick to point out, however, it is not the intention of ISO 9001:2008 to insist on a uniform structure to a QMS or uniformity of documentation. The QMS requirements specified in this standard should always be viewed as complementary to the product's technical requirements.

ISO 9001:2008 is a generic management standard that adopts the process management approach widely used in business today and more clearly addresses the QMS requirements for an organisation in order to demonstrate its capability of meeting customer requirements. It is now also more compatible (indeed linked with) the ISO 14001 standard for environmental management and includes the relevant managerial requirements found in national/international health and safety management standards.

As previously mentioned, the ISO 9001:2008 standard is the **only** standard within the current ISO 9000 series to which an organisation can be certified. It includes all the key points from the previous quality standards, but integrates them into four major generic business processes, namely:

- management responsibility (policy, objectives, planning, system, review);
- resource management (human resources, information, facilities);
- product realisation (customer, design, purchasing, production, calibration);
- measurement, analysis and improvement (audit, process/product control, improvement).

2.11 WHAT IS THE STRUCTURE OF ISO 9001:2008?

ISO 9001:2008 commences with an introductory section containing the following headings:

0 Introduction

General	0.1
Process approach	0.2
Relationship with ISO9004	0.3
Compatibility with other management systems	0.4

This is then followed by the eight sections that make up ISO 9001:2008 and which are summarised below.

1 Scope

This short section explains what the standard covers and emphasises that:

> **'All requirements of this International Standard are generic and are intended to be applicable to all organizations, regardless of type, size and product provided.'**

It goes on to explain that ISO 9001:2008 specifies the requirements for a QMS where an organisation:

- needs to demonstrate its ability to consistently provide a product that meets customer and applicable statutory and regulatory requirements; and
- aims to enhance customer satisfaction through the effective application of the system, including processes for continual improvement of the system and the assurance of conformity to customer and applicable statutory and regulatory requirements.

The term 'product' only applies to:

- a product intended for, or required by, a customer;
- any intended output resulting from the product realisation processes.

2 Normative references

Another small section that directs the reader to other standards that form a **mandatory** input to ISO 9001:2000. In this instance the only reference is 'ISO 9000:2005, *Quality Management Systems – Fundamentals and vocabulary*'.

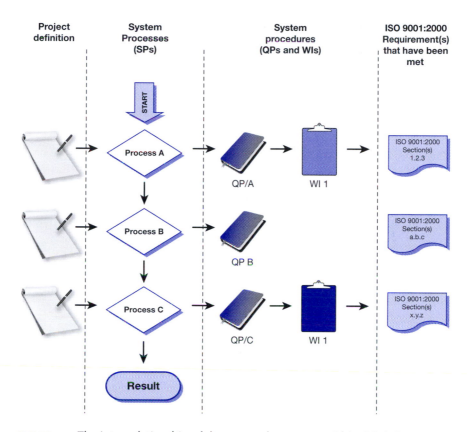

FIGURE 2.18 The inter-relationship of documented processes within QPs/WIs

3 Terms and definitions

This third section explains how the standard is based on the supply chain (see Figure 2.19).

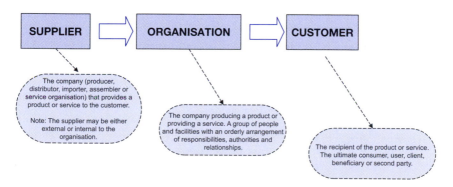

FIGURE 2.19 The supply chain

4 Quality management system

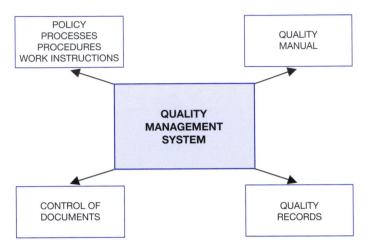

FIGURE 2.20 Quality Management System

This basically states that an organisation **shall** have a documented QMS that defines the processes necessary to ensure that the product conforms to customer requirements and that this QMS must be implemented, maintained and, most importantly, continually improved by the organisation.

This section also clearly states the types of documentation required to comply with the standard, as follows:

- **Quality manual** – establishing and maintaining an organisational '*Rule Book*';
- **Control of documents** – establishing and maintaining a documented procedure for the control of QMS documents;
- **Quality records** – controlling and maintaining quality records;
- **System level processes** – used to detail the activities needed to implement the QMS;
- **Procedures** that clearly describe the sequence of processes necessary to ensure the conformity of a product or service;
- **Instructions** that describe the physical operating practices and controls within each process.

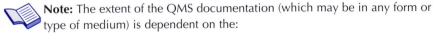 **Note:** The extent of the QMS documentation (which may be in any form or type of medium) is dependent on the:

- size and type of the organisation;
- complexity and interaction of the processes;
- competency of personnel.

General requirements	4.1
Documentation requirements	4.2
• General	4.2.1
• Quality manual	4.2.2
• Control of documents	4.2.3
• Control of records	4.2.4

5 Management responsibility

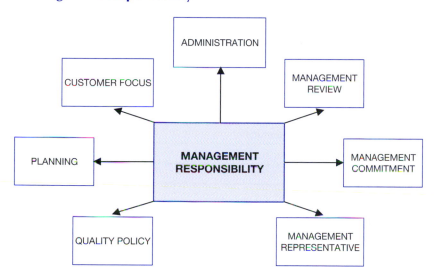

FIGURE 2.21 Management responsibility

This section consists of the majority of the old ISO 9001:1994 management responsibility and quality requirements all rolled together. It is broken down into the following sub sections that cover the requirements for:

- **Management commitment** – top (i.e. senior) management committing, fully, to the development and improvement of the QMS. (Without their commitment the system will fall at the first hurdle);
- **Customer focus** – determining, fully understanding and documenting customer requirements; ensuring compliance with identified statutory legislation (e.g. EC Directives, other national and international standards etc.);
- **Quality policy** – ensuring that it is appropriate for the purpose, understood by everyone and reviewed for continued suitability;
- **Planning** – clearly stating management's quality objectives and policy on quality in an established, fully documented QMS;

- **Administration** – identifying and planning the activities and resources required to achieve quality objectives;
- **Management representative** – appointing someone (or some people) to be responsible for the implementation and improvement of the organisation's QMS;
- **Management review** – carrying out regular reviews of the QMS to ensure it continues to function correctly (and to identify areas for improvement).

Management commitment	5.1
Customer focus	5.2
Quality policy	5.3
Planning	5.4
• Quality objectives	5.4.1
• Quality management system planning	5.4.2
Responsibility, authority and communication	5.5
• Responsibility and authority	5.5.1
• Management representative	5.5.2
• Internal communication	5.5.3
Management review	5.6
• General	5.6.1
• Review input	5.6.2
• Review output	5.6.3

6 Resource management

This section covers resources with regard to training, induction, responsibilities, working environment, equipment requirements, maintenance etc. It is broken down into the following sub sections:

- **Provision of resources** – identifying the resources required to implement and improve the processes that make up the QMS;
- **Human resources** – assigning personnel with regard to competency, education, training, skill and/or experience;
- **Infrastructure** – identifying, providing and maintaining the workspace, facilities, equipment (hardware and software) and supporting services to achieve conformity of product;
- **Work environment** – identifying and managing the work environment (e.g. health and safety, ambient conditions etc.).

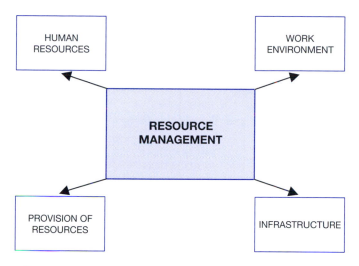

FIGURE 2.22 Resource management

Provision of resources	6.1
Human resources	6.2
• General	6.2.1
• Competence, training and awareness	6.2.2
Infrastructure	6.3
Work environment	6.4

7 Product realisation

Section 7 absorbs most of the 20 elements of the old ISO 9000:1994 standard, including process control, purchasing, handling and storage and measuring devices. This section is broken down into a number of sub sections that cover the requirements for:

- **Planning of realisation processes** – clearly defining and documenting the processes used to ensure reliable and consistent products (e.g. verification and validation activities, criteria for acceptability and quality records etc.);
- **Customer-related processes** – identifying customer, product, legal and design requirements;
- **Design and development planning** – controlling the design process (e.g. design inputs, outputs, review, verification, validation and change control);
- **Purchasing** – having documented processes for the selection and control of suppliers and the control of purchases that affect the quality of the finished product or service;

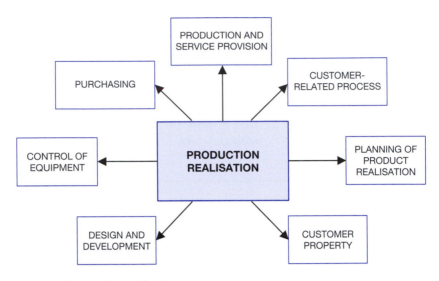

FIGURE 2.23 Production realisation

- **Production and service provision** – having documented instructions that control the manufacture of a product or delivery of a service;
- **Customer property** – identifying, verifying, protecting and maintaining customer property provided for use or incorporation with the product;
- **Control of monitoring and measuring devices** – their control, calibration and protection.

Planning of product realisation	7.1
Customer-related processes	7.2
• Determination of requirements related to the product	7.2.1
• Review of requirements related to the product	7.2.2
• Customer communication	7.2.3
Design and development	7.3
• Design and development planning	7.3.1
• Design and development inputs	7.3.2
• Design and development outputs	7.3.3
• Design and development review	7.3.4
• Design and development verification	7.3.5
• Design and development validation	7.3.6
• Control of design and development changes	7.3.7
Product and service provision	7.4
• Purchasing process	7.4.1

• Purchasing information	7.4.2
• Verification of purchased product	7.4.3
Production and service provision	7.5
• Control of production and service provision	7.5.1
• Validation of processes for production and service	7.5.2
• Identification and traceability	7.5.3
• Customer property	7.5.4
• Preservation of product	7.5.5
Control of monitoring and measuring equipment	7.6

8 Measurement, analysis and improvement

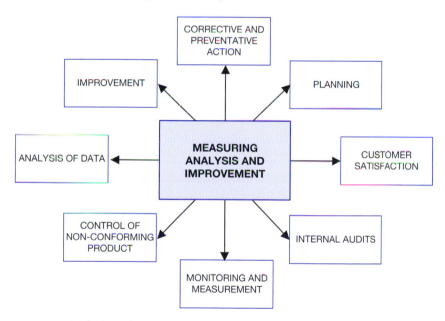

FIGURE 2.24 Analysis and improvement

This section absorbs the former inspection and measurement control sections of ISO 9001:1994 and includes requirements for:

- **Planning** – defining the requirements for measurement analysis and improvement (including statistical analysis);
- **Customer satisfaction** – monitoring customer satisfaction (and dissatisfaction) as a measurement and improvement of the QMS;
- **Internal audits** – conducting periodic internal audits to confirm continued conformity with ISO 9001:2000;

- **Monitoring and measurement of processes and product** – defining processes to monitor the performance of the QMS and the products and services delivered by the organisation;
- **Non-conformity** – controlling non-conformity and its rectification;
- **Data analysis** – collecting and analysing statistical data obtained from the organisation's measuring and monitoring activities to find areas of improvement;
- **Improvement** – planning for continual improvement of the QMS;
- **Corrective and preventive action** – having available procedures to address corrective and preventive action.

General	8.1
Monitoring and measurement	8.2
• Customer satisfaction	8.2.1
• Internal audit	8.2.2
• Monitoring and measurement of processes	8.2.3
• Monitoring and measurement of product	8.2.4
Control of non-conforming product	8.3
Analysis of data	8.4
Improvement	8.5
• Continual improvement	8.5.1
• Corrective action	8.5.2
• Preventive action	8.5.3

2.12 WHAT ABOUT AUDITING ISO 9001:2008?

One of the requirements of ISO 9001:2008 (Section 8.2.2) is that:

'The organisation shall conduct internal audits at planned intervals to determine whether the quality management system:

   a. **conforms to the requirements of the ISO 9001:2008 standard and to the quality management system requirements established by the organisation; and,**

   b. **is effectively implemented and maintained.'**

2.12.1 Purpose of an audit

The primary purpose of an audit is to enable an organisation to evaluate its process management systems, determine deficiencies and generate cost effective and efficient solutions. An audit is performed to check practice against procedure and to thoroughly document any differences. It is used to measure an organisation's ability 'to do what it says it is going to do'.

2.12.2 Types of audit

There are several types of audit that can be completed under the general umbrella of 'audits measuring conformance with ISO 9001:2008', such as:

Quality system audits	An overall measurement of an organisation's capability to meet the requirements of ISO 9001:2008.
Management audits	Confirmation that an organisation's strategic plan reflects their business objectives and continues to meet their Clients' requirements.
Process audits	Checks that focus specifically on a single process to verify if an organisation is capable of delivering the outputs expected of them.
Procedural audits	Verification that documented practices are sufficient to ensure the implementation of approved policies and are capable of controlling the organisation's operations.
System audits	Checks to ensure that a business management system is sufficiently comprehensive to control all of the activities within that business. (Generally, this type of audit would look for gaps in the management system that may result in them not achieving their business objectives.)
Product/service audits	Verification that an organisation's plans and proposals for supplying a product or service will ensure that product or service fully meets specified requirements.

2.12.3 Audit categories

Whilst the common aim of all audits is to establish that an organisation's documented policies, processes and procedures, when implemented, are fit for their purpose and satisfy the needs of those who require them, the actual type of audit will depend on whether it is a First-, Second- or Third-Party Audit. These are the three main types of audit associated with ISO 9001:2008 and are used as follows:

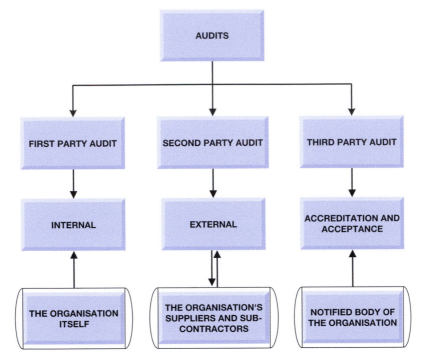

FIGURE 2.25 Types of audit

First party	First-Party Audits of an organisation, or parts of an organisation, are completed by personnel employed by that organisation. These audits are usually referred to as Internal Audits where (as the name suggests) members of an organisation look inwards at their own processes. This is the least effective form of auditing, as generally most auditors will find it difficult to criticise their own or their workmates' work.
Second party	Second-Party Audits are carried out by customers upon their suppliers or subcontractors and are completed by an organisation independent of the organisation being audited. These audits are usually referred to as External Audits or Vendor Audits.
Third party	Third-Party Audits are carried out by personnel who are neither employees of the customer nor the supplier. They are usually employees of certification bodies or Registrars such as BSI, TÜV and Yardley. External Audits are sometimes referred to as Certification Audits, Compliance Audits or Quality System Assessments.

2.12.4 ISO 19011:2002

ISO 19011:2002 (*Guidelines for quality and/or environmental management systems auditing*) provides guidance on the principles of auditing, managing audit programmes, conducting quality and environmental management system audits, as well as guidance on the competence of quality and environmental management system auditors.

It is applicable to all organisations needing to conduct internal or external audits of quality and/or environmental management systems or to manage an audit programme and it is intended that, by using this standard, organisations will be able to save time, effort and money by:

*   avoiding confusion about the objectives of the audit programme;
*   conducting a combined environmental/quality audit;
*   ensuring audit reports follow the best format and contain all the relevant information;
*   evaluating the competence of audit team members against the appropriate criteria.

2.13 CERTIFICATION

2.13.1 As a small business do I need to be certified and/or registered to ISO 9001:2008?

It is widely acknowledged that proper quality management improves business, which often has a positive effect on investment, market share, sales growth, sales margins, competitive advantage and avoidance of litigation. Being able to provide proof of conformity to ISO 9001:2008 has, therefore, almost become a prerequisite of business today.

To obtain ISO 9001:2008 certification and registration, your Quality Management System must meet all of the requirements of the Standard. To do this, you will have to undergo an audit (i.e. a detailed test and examination) to establish if the management system your organisation uses complies with (and meets) **all** of the requirements of ISO 9001. This audit cannot be done internally. It has to be completed by a properly accredited certifier or registrar.

If successful, you get a certificate (which will please your Managing Director as it can go in pride of place on his or her office wall!) and you can then advertise the fact (on marketing material, letterheads and so on) that you are a fully certified and registered quality organisation.

Note: A word of warning, however. You must ask yourself, '*Is certification itself important to the marketing plans of our company?*' If not, then do not rush to certification, because even without it, your company can still utilise the ISO 9000 model as a benchmark to assess the adequacy of your quality programmes.

2.13.2 Who can certify an organisation?

There are a number of companies (i.e. Notified Bodies and/or Registrars) available to carry out ISO 9001:2008 certification (e.g. TÜV, BSI, SGS, Yarsley etc.) and it really depends on where your organisation's main market is going to be as to which one you eventually choose. Organisations are, therefore, recommended to review quotes and get feedback from at least two or three organisations to assess their experience and suitability to fit with their specific organisational needs.

2.13.3 What is required for certification?

A fully documented, auditable QMS that is totally supported by senior management and one that is implemented throughout the organisation.

The QMS shall consist of:

- **Quality Manual** – describing how an organisation meets the requirements of ISO 9001:2008 (objectives, goals, roles, organisation and responsibilities etc.);
- **Processes** – describing the end-to-end activities involved in project management;
- **Quality Procedures** – describing the method by which the processes are managed;
- **Work Instructions** – describing how individual tasks and activities are carried out.

Note: Organisations who are **not** involved in certain aspects of quality management (e.g. they do not manufacture anything) are allowed to be certified to ISO 9001:2008 through '*permissible exclusions*' of the standard's requirement – i.e. by omitting those requirements that do not actually apply to their particular organisation.

2.13.4 What is the difference between being certified and being registered?

Actually there is no difference! In some countries companies/organisations will say that they are certified, in others they will say that they are registered – but it means the same thing.

2.13.5 What is the difference between being certified and being compliant?

When an organisation claims that it is ISO 9000 certified or registered, it means that a Notified Body (i.e. an independent registrar) has audited its QMS, certified that it meets the requirements of ISO 9001:2008, given the organisation a written assurance that ISO's quality management system standard has been met and registered it as having been certified.

On the other hand, when an organisation says that it is '*ISO 9000 compliant*', it usually means that it has met ISO's quality system requirements but has **not** been formally certified by an independent registrar. In effect, it is self-certified and whilst this is perfectly acceptable for many organisations, especially the smaller ones, an official certificate issued by an independent registrar does tend to carry more weight in the market place.

 Note: As ISO 9001:2008 is a process standard (and not a product standard), when a company says that it is certified or compliant, it is **not** saying that its products and/or services meet the ISO 9000 requirements!

2.13.6 What is the difference between being certified and being accredited?

Registrars audit and certify organisations that wish to become ISO 9000 registered. Accreditation Bodies, like UKAS (United Kingdom Accreditation Service), on the other hand, evaluate and accredit the Registrars. In effect accreditation bodies audit the auditors and certify that the Registrars are competent and authorised to issue ISO 9001:2008 certificates in specified business sectors.

See Chapter 8 for details of world-wide Accreditation Bodies that have the power to certify a Notified Body to assess whether a product meets certain preordained standards.

2.14 WHO WILL BE RESPONSIBLE FOR QUALITY WITHIN AN ORGANISATION?

ISO 9001:2008 requirement 5.5.2 (Management representative) states that:

> **'Top management shall appoint a member of management who, irrespective of other responsibilities, shall have responsibility and authority that includes:**
>
> - **ensuring that processes needed for the quality management system are established, implemented and maintained;**
> - **reporting to top management on the performance of the quality management system, and any need for improvement;**
> - **ensuring the promotion of awareness of customer requirements throughout the organisation;**
> - **liaison with external parties on matters relating the quality management system.'**

In a small business where there are only two or three people, the Quality Manager's function will more than likely be the owner or (if the business has one) the Managing Director.

A large organisation, however, will need to appoint a Quality Manager who has the full support of senior management. This person will need to be fully versed in the requirements of ISO 9001:2008 and be capable of acting as a catalyst and management coach. This post will initially have to be full-time whilst the organisation is setting up its QMS, but (dependent on the size of the company) could probably reduce to part-time following certification.

The Quality Manager's prime qualities (no matter the size of the organisation) should include

- approachability; and
- an ability to establish two-way communication with **all** levels of the company personnel.

The Quality Manager reports directly to the Managing Director and must be independent of all responsibilities that may adversely affect quality performance.

2.15 WHAT IS THE FUTURE EVOLUTION OF ISO 9000?

To ensure that the current ISO 9000 family can continue to benefit from new developments within the quality management field, ISO (TEC-176) continuously monitor the use of the ISO 9000 standards.

Similar to other ISO standards, ISO 9000 is reviewed every five years and so a new version is scheduled to be published during 2015 (i.e. five years after ISO 9001:2008 becomes the mandatory standard for quality management). As well as customer feedback, ISO have stated that the review will take into consideration all of the other system-specific industrial standards and specifications and be aimed at producing an even more generic standard than ISO 9001:2008 already is.

Author's Note

Chapter 2 has explained the background to the ISO 9000 standards, its requirements and recommendations. It has described how ISO 9001:2008 can be used to the best advantage and it has shown how much importance is being placed on companies (large and small) in having ISO 9001:2008 certification or possessing an effective QMS that ensures they work in conformance with that standard.

In Chapter 3, ISO 9001:2008's Quality Process Approach will be explained.

The process approach

Author's Note

This short chapter provides the background to and the inter-relationship of processes as recommended by ISO 9001:2008.

Also explained is the Plan-Do-Check-Act (PDCA) cycle and the links between process documentation.

3.1 BACKGROUND

The success of the ISO 9001:2008 Quality Management Systems (QMS) relies on the universally adopted process approach to monitoring the quality of a product or system. Summarised, *'a process is an integrated set of activities that uses resources to transform inputs into outputs and it is quite normal for processes to be interconnected because the output from one process frequently becomes the input for another process.'*

A QMS is, therefore, a collection of management processes which are made up of people, work, activities, tasks, records, documents, forms, resources, rules, regulations, reports, materials, supplies, tools and equipment etc. – in other words, all those things that are required to regulate, control and improve the quality of products and services. For organisations to function effectively they will have to identify and manage a number of interlinked processes and this identification and the associated management of the processes (and particularly the interactions between these processes) is referred to as the *'process approach'*.

Any activity that receives inputs and converts them to outputs can, therefore, be considered as a process and often the output from one process becomes the input for another process.

As the process approach is now central to ISO 9001:2008, ISO's Committees have identified 12 primary processes that will make up a Quality Management System (QMS).

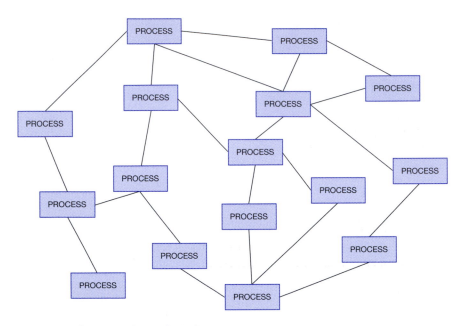

FIGURE 3.1 The inter-relationship of processes

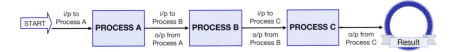

FIGURE 3.2 ISO 9001:2008's basic process approach

1. Quality Management Process
2. Resource Management Process
3. Training and Awareness Process
4. Product Purchasing Process
5. Design and Development Process
6. Production Management Process
7. Service Provision Process
8. Product Management Process
9. Customer Relationship Management Process
10. Internal Quality Management Audit Process
11. Monitoring and Measuring Process
12. Management Review Process.

Note: Obviously this does not include a list of all possible processes that could be used by you to establish your own QMS, nor does it exhaust the many ways in which your processes can be grouped into larger processes or subdivided into smaller ones. Your own particular organisation's list of processes will probably be different from the ones ISO have listed and that is perfectly OK, as long as your QMS meets your organisation's needs and complies with the requirements of ISO 9001:2008.

Throughout ISO 9001:2008, the requirement for continuous improvement is frequently (and heavily) emphasised. '*Continual improvement*' (i.e. in the context of ISO 9001:2008) requires an organisation to concentrate on continually increasing the effectiveness and efficiency of its business processes whilst carrying out the policies and objectives of that organisation.

The ISO 9001:2008 process model approach requires the organisation to:

- identify the processes;
- decide the order in which they are carried out;
- ensure that appropriate resources are provided; and
- establish appropriate methods to operate and control them.

Most organisations will diagram one process at a time using a single flowchart on a single page, as shown in Figure 3.3. This will allow you to identify the most important input–output relationships without having to resort to a more intricate drawing. By way of explanation, in the figure, the process shown at the centre is the main process and the four surrounding processes are there to provide inputs to this central process, and receive outputs from it on an as-required basis.

ISO 9001:2008 requires that each of your processes will need to be designed, fully documented, implemented, supported, monitored, controlled and subject to continual improvement.

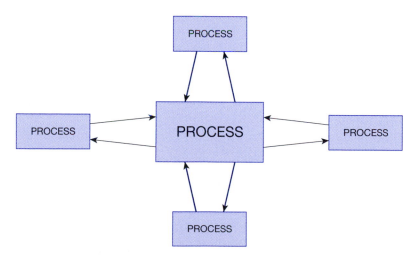

FIGURE 3.3 Initial process diagram

When designing an internal organisational process, the most efficient way of completing a process map is to either walk through the process or get someone from that particular department or section to walk you through the process describing the various steps and how they interact.

3.1.1 Example of a simple process flow chart

When producing or supplying a service for other organisations (e.g. customers), one of the following steps would normally be required:

For a small manufacturing business	For a small business providing a service (e.g. selling a product)	For a small business designing software or providing IT products
• Receive enquiry • Identify specifications and standards • Cost and identify necessary material suppliers • Provide quotation • Receive order • Complete design • Provide sample • Receive sample approval • Purchase materials • Goods receipt • Goods-in stores – manufacture • Test • Goods-out stores • Despatch • Provide training • Customer after care • Despatch	• Receive enquiry • Provide quotation • Receive order • Purchase materials • Goods receipt • Goods-in stores • Test • Goods-out stores • Despatch • Provide training • Customer after care	• Receive enquiry • Identify specifications and standards • Complete initial breadboard design • Provide quotation • Receive order • Complete design • Provide sample • Receive sample approval • Produce software package • Write manual and user instructions • Purchase materials • Goods receipt • Goods-in stores • Assemble package • Test • Goods-out stores • Install (but not always) • Provide training • Customer care

Note: 'Customer Care' would ensure customer satisfaction and provide a template for continual improvement (both of which are mandatory aims of the ISO 9001:2008 standard).

3.1.2 ISO 9001:2008's mandatory processes

Within ISO 9001:2008, you will find a number of mandatory requirements for developing a number of specific processes (see Table 3.1).

TABLE 3.1 ISO 9001:2008 QMS Development Plan

Requirement	ISO 9001:2008 section
Design a management review process	4.1
Document your management review process	4.2
Implement your management review process	4.1
Support your management review process	4.1
Monitor your management review process	8.2.3
Control your management review process	4.1
Improve your management review process	4.1

3.2 BUT WHAT IS THE PROCESS APPROACH?

In accordance with Section 4.2.2 of ISO 9001, an organisation is required to develop a Quality Manual that:

- describes how your quality system processes interact;
- defines the scope of your quality management system;
- explains any reductions in the scope of your system;
- justifies all exclusions (reductions in scope);
- documents your procedures or refers to them.

The Quality Manual is **not** in itself a quality system, it is just a document that contains outline details of how all your processes inter-react and how they are documented and recorded.

With a well structured, planned process, continual improvement will respond to the growing needs and expectations of customers and ensure a dynamic evolution of the Quality Management System.

Continual improvement is assured by utilisation of the PDCA model which was developed by the US mathematician Dr Walter Shewart (1891–1967), reinforced and used by the American statistician, professor, author, lecturer and consultant William Deming (1900–1993) and eventually adopted by ISO (see Figure 3.5) as the Plan-Do-Check-Act (PDCA) cycle.

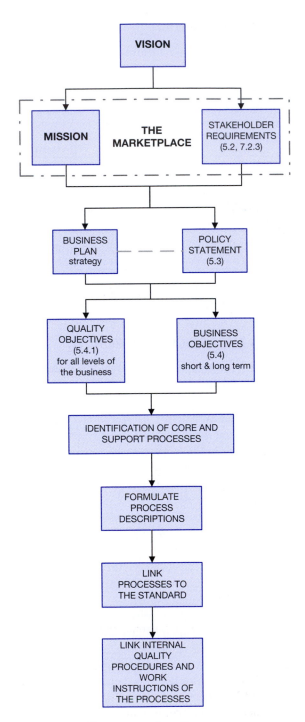

FIGURE 3.4 The integration of business and quality

This is a very simple four-step management method used in business for the control and continuous improvement of processes and products. The steps are:

1. **Plan** – determine what needs to be done, when, how, and by whom;
2. **Do** – carry out the plan, on a small scale first;
3. **Check** – analyse the results of carrying out the plan;
4. **Act** – take appropriate steps to close the gap between planned and actual results.

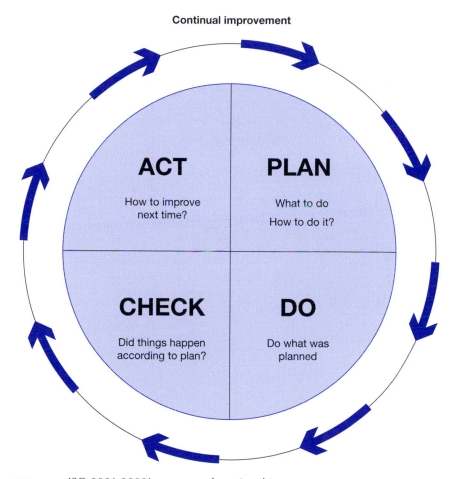

Continual improvement

ACT — How to improve next time?

PLAN — What to do / How to do it?

CHECK — Did things happen according to plan?

DO — Do what was planned

FIGURE 3.5 ISO 9001:2008's concept of continual improvement

The following process model (see Figure 3.6) seeks to show how the four major sections of ISO 9001:2008 (i.e. Management Responsibility, Resource Management, Product Realisation and Measurement, Analysis and Improvement) inter-relate and how the improvement processes continuously revolve around all other aspects of quality management.

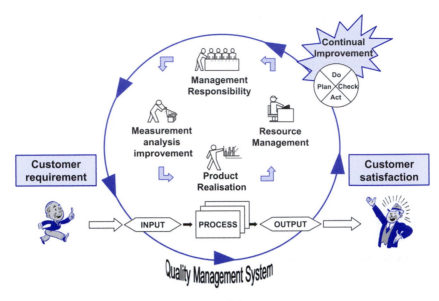

FIGURE 3.6 The ISO 9001:2008 process model

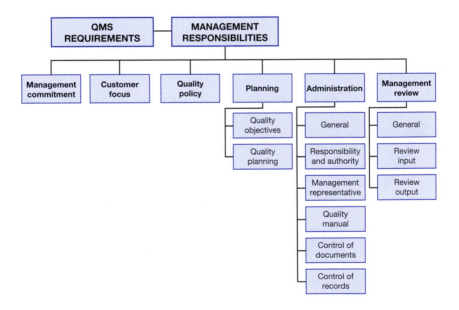

FIGURE 3.7 Quality Management System requirements and management responsibilities

For clarity, the QMS requirements and management responsibilities can be combined, as shown in Figure 3.7.

> **Note:** If your **current** Quality Management System is successfully implemented, satisfies the needs and objectives of your organisation, reflects the way your organisation works and addresses all of the requirements detailed in the ISO 9001:2008 standard, then no changes are required. However, if your current documented system does **not** address all of these requirements, additional documentation may be necessary.

3.3 PLANNING AN ORGANISATION'S BUSINESS PROCESSES

All businesses are made up of a series of processes which, when placed together, make the business operate. In a similar manner, ISO 9001:2008 is based around four generic business processes, these being Management Responsibility, Resource Management, Product and/or Service Realisation, and Measurement, Analysis and Improvement. All processes within businesses will contain an element of these four business processes.

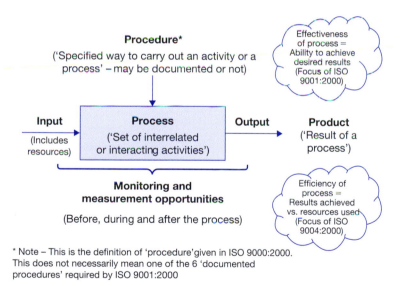

* Note – This is the definition of 'procedure' given in ISO 9000:2000.
This does not necessarily mean one of the 6 'documented procedures' required by ISO 9001:2000

FIGURE 3.8 Schematic representation of a process

Processes are the keys to providing a clear understanding of what an organisation does and the quality controls it has in place to control its business activities. ISO 9001:2008 recommends the use of '*processes*' to define how resources and activities are combined, controlled and converted into deliverables.

These business processes could (depending on the organisation) include one (or all) of the following:

- customer communications process;
- continual improvement process;
- customer needs assessment process;
- document control process;
- general systemic process
- internal audit process;
- internal communications process;
- management review process
- market research process;
- measurement process;
- monitoring process;
- non-conformance management process;
- planning process;
- product design process;
- product protection process;
- production process;
- purchasing process;
- record keeping process;
- regulatory research process;
- resource management process
- service provision process;
- training process;

and of course, the

- Quality Management Process

There are three types of processes associated with an organisation's QMS (see Table 3.2).

TABLE 3.2 Core Business and Supporting Processes

Core business process	Describing the end-to-end activities involved in an organisation manufacturing or supplying a deliverable.
Primary supporting processes	The basic set of activities which, when combined into a logical sequence, takes you from receipt of an order (or marketing opportunity) through to the realisation of the finished product or service.
Secondary supporting processes	Those activities that are vital to attaining the desired levels of quality but which are seen as supporting the primary supporting processes.

3.3.1 Core Business Process

A company's organisational processes making up their QMS normally comprise a Core Business Process supplemented by a number of Supporting Processes which describe the infrastructure required to produce the contact deliverable, service or market opportunity on time, on budget and to the satisfaction of the customer or end user (see Figure 3.9).

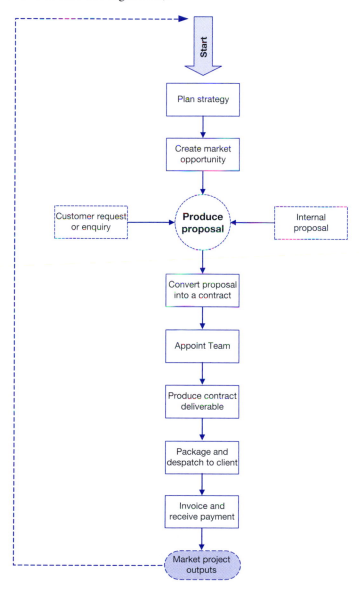

FIGURE 3.9 Core business process

The Core Business Process describes the end-to-end activities involved in producing a contract deliverable, service or marketing opportunity. It commences with the definition of corporate policy and ends when the product or system is designed, created and marketed. Marketing and product information is then used to plan future strategies.

 Note: A process owner with full responsibility and authority for managing the process and achieving process objectives should always be nominated.

3.3.2 Supporting processes

The Core Business Process may then (depending on the size of the business) be supplemented by a number of supporting processes that describe the infrastructure required to produce a deliverable on time.

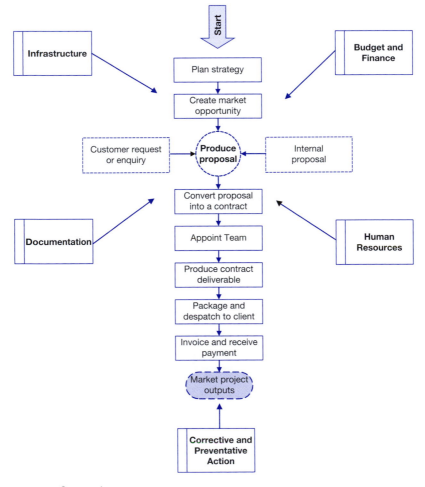

FIGURE 3.10 Supporting processes

3.3.3 Primary supporting processes

All businesses revolve around taking inputs and putting them through a series of activities that turn them into useful outputs, be they a product or service. These activities are the supporting processes.

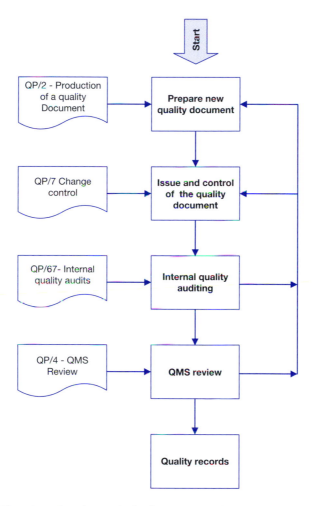

FIGURE 3.11 Flowchart showing typical primary supporting processes

Of course, the only way to ensure repeat orders is to control the quality of not only the deliverable, but also the organisation itself. Consequently, it is essential that you define your quality policy and objectives for each supporting process.

For each process within the flowchart there needs to be an organisational documentation detailing:

- **objective** – what the process aims to achieve;
- **scope** – what the process covers;
- **responsible owner** – who is ultimately responsible for implementing the process;
- **policy** – what the organisation intends doing to ensure quality is controlled;
- **key performance indicators** – those items of objective evidence that can be used as a way of monitoring performance of the process;
- reference to **supporting system documentation** (QPs and WIs).

3.3.4 Secondary supporting processes

In addition to primary supporting processes there may also be a number of **secondary supporting processes** that run in parallel with (and support the) primary supporting processes. These secondary supporting processes are equally important as they control all other activities that may influence the quality of the product.

Secondary supporting processes may include such things as:

- identification and provision of suitable staff;
- management and support of staff;
- identification and provision of information;
- identification and provision of materials;
- identification and provision of equipment and facilities;
- management of the QMS;
- continual improvement.

The purpose of secondary supporting processes is to document those activities that are essential for supporting and achieving the primary supporting processes. An example of a secondary supporting process is shown in Figure 3.12.

These secondary supporting processes will have an identical structure to the primary supporting processes, and will also have their own associated supporting documentation (e.g. Quality Procedures (QPs) and Work Instructions (WIs)).

3.4 INTER-RELATIONSHIP OF PROCESS DOCUMENTATION

All processes are documented so as to provide a complete picture of how to perform the activity to a consistent level of quality. The level of detail varies depending on whether it is a:

- **Process** – an outline of its objective, scope and key performance indicators;
- **Quality Procedure (QP)** – an enlargement of the process explaining how it is controlled;
- **Work Instruction (WI)** – the 'fine print' required to perform a specific activity.

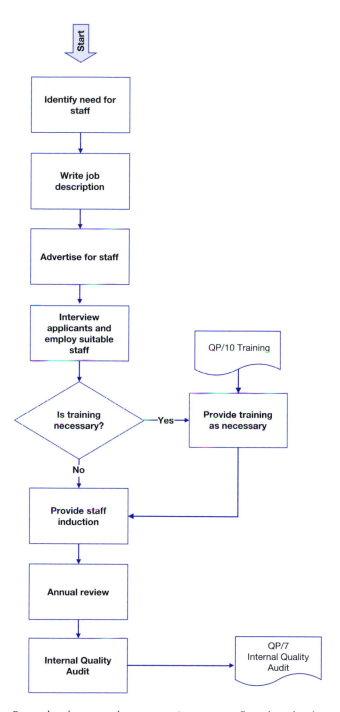

FIGURE 3.12 Example of a secondary supporting process flowchart for the identification, provision, management and support of staff

Notes:
1. All of these documents are explained in more detail elsewhere in this book.
2. By using a matrix such as that shown in Figure 4.1, it is possible to identify the parts of ISO 9001:2008 which are met by each process.

 Author's Note

Chapter 3 has shown the inter-relationships between business processes.

In Chapter 4, the structure of a business Quality Management System is described.

Quality Management System

Author's Note

In this chapter, the basic requirements of a Quality Management System are discussed and the reader is shown how an organisation's Quality Management System becomes the documented proof of a firm's commitment to quality management.

The reader is shown how a Quality Management System can be structured to an organisation's particular type of business and how a Quality Management System will cover such functions as customer liaison, design, purchase, subcontracting, manufacturing, training and installation.

4.1 QUALITY MANAGEMENT SYSTEM – REQUIREMENTS

'A Quality Management System is a management system to direct and control an organisation with regard to quality.'

A Quality Management System (QMS) is an organisational structure of responsibilities, activities, resources and events that together provide procedures and methods of implementation to ensure the capability of an organisation to meet quality requirements.

Having seen in Chapter 2 the advantages and benefits of quality control and quality assurance, what about the QMS that needs to be set up so as to adapt and instigate these procedures?

4.1.1 Basic requirements of a Quality Management System

To be successful, a small business must:

- be able to offer products and services that satisfy a customer's expectations;
- agree with the relevant standards and specifications of a contract;

- be available to provide products and services at competitive prices; **and**
- supply deliverables at a cost that will still bring a profit to that organisation.

They must, above all, provide a quality product that will promote further procurement and recommendations.

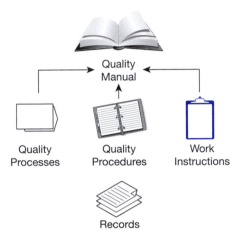

FIGURE 4.1 Quality Management System

So how can your organisation become a quality organisation? Well, I can assure you that it is not just a case of simply claiming that you are a reliable organisation and then telling everyone that you will be able to supply a reliable product or service! Nowadays, especially in the European and American markets, purchasers are demanding proof of these claims. Proof that you are the organisation that **they** should be dealing with.

How can anyone supply this proof? Well, the obvious answer is to use the internationally recognised ISO 9000 series of standards. These standards provide the requirements and guidelines for organisations wishing to establish their own QMS and in doing so control the quality of their organisation – from within their organisation.

You may also find that some contracts stipulate that the product '*must*' comply with the requirements of (such and such) a standard. For example, for a British component manufacturer it might be BS EN 60191–4:2000 '*Mechanical standardisation of semiconductor devices*', or for a test house in the USA, it could be ASTM E1212–04:2008 '*Standard Practice for Quality Management Systems for Non-destructive Testing Agencies*'.

But perhaps we are moving on too fast. Before an organisation is even **qualified** to tender for a contract to produce something, it must first **prove** its capability by showing that it can operate a Quality Management System.

To satisfy these requirements an organisation's QMS has to encompass all the different levels of quality control that are required during the various stages of

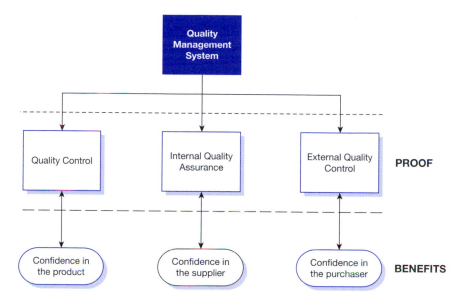

FIGURE 4.2 Quality Management System – organisational structure

design, manufacture and acceptance of a product and be capable of guaranteeing quality acceptance.

These requirements are covered by national, European and international standards. But although these standards may vary slightly from country to country, basically they are very similar and cover the following topics:

- organisational structure;
- measurement of quality assurance;
- the contract;
- design control;
- purchasing and procurement;
- production control;
- product testing;
- handling, storage, packaging and delivery;
- after sales service.

4.2 QUALITY MANAGEMENT SYSTEM – PRINCIPLES

The first thing that ISO 9001:2008 requires is for an organisation to set up and fully document its position with regard to quality assurance. These documents comprise the organisation's QMS and describe its capability to supply goods and services that will comply with laid-down quality standards. They contain a general description of the organisation's attitude to quality assurance and specific details about the quality assurance and quality control from within that organisation.

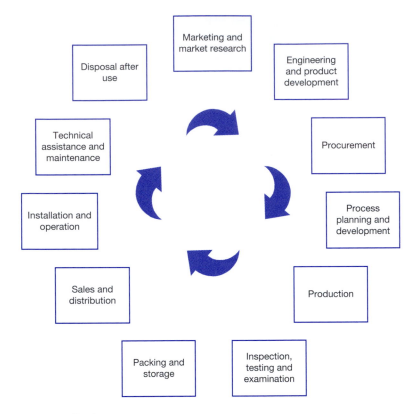

FIGURE 4.3 Quality loop

To be successful, an organisation must be able to prove that it is capable of producing the component, product or service to the customer's complete satisfaction so that it conforms exactly to the purchaser's specific requirements and that it is always of the desired quality.

An organisation's QMS is, therefore, the organisational structure of responsibilities, procedures, processes and resources for carrying out quality management and as such must be planned and developed in order to be capable of maintaining a consistent level of quality control.

The QMS must be structured to the organisation's own particular type of business and should consider all functions such as customer liaison, designing, purchasing, subcontracting, manufacturing, training, installation, updating of quality control techniques and the accumulation of quality records. In most organisations this sort of information will normally be found in the organisation's Quality Manual.

The type of QMS chosen will, of course, vary from organisation to organisation depending upon its size and capability. There are no set rules as to exactly how these documents should be written. However, they should – as a minimum – be

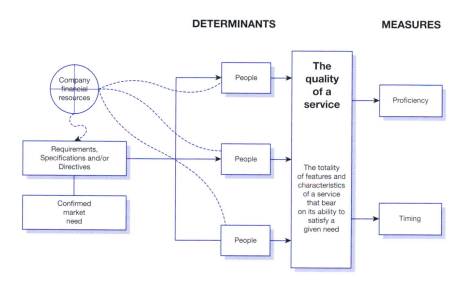

FIGURE 4.4 Some of the determinants and measurements of the quality of a service

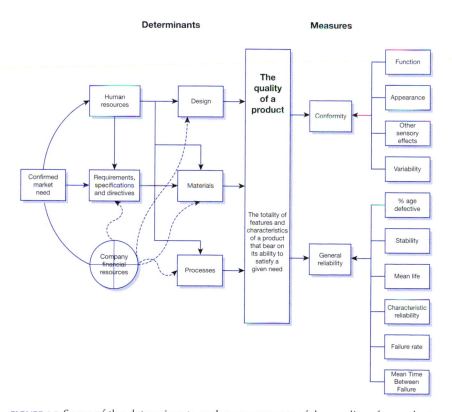

FIGURE 4.5 Some of the determinants and measurements of the quality of a product

capable of showing the potential customer exactly how the manufacturer or supplier is equipped to achieve and maintain the highest level of quality throughout the various stages of design, production, installation and servicing.

As an example, some of the determinants and measures of the quality of a service are shown in Figure 4.4 whilst those affecting the quality of a product are shown in Figure 4.5.

Note: Figures 4.4 and 4.5 are extracts from BS 4778:1979 and have been reproduced with the kind permission of BSI. Although the 1979 edition has been superseded these figures are included here since they illustrate the concept.

4.3 QUALITY MANAGEMENT SYSTEM – APPROACH

Customers require products that continually meet their needs and expectations and in order to be profitable, an organisation must be able to offer products that continually achieve customer satisfaction and satisfy its customers' requirements. As well as providing a framework for providing customer satisfaction, a QMS also provides confidence (to the organisation **and** to its customers) that the organisation is capable of providing products that consistently fulfil requirements. This is achieved by:

- determining the needs and expectations of the customer;
- establishing the quality policy and quality objectives of the organisation;
- determining the processes and responsibilities necessary to attain the quality objectives;
- establishing measures for the effectiveness of each process towards attaining the quality objectives;
- applying the measures to determine the current effectiveness of each process;
- determining means of preventing non-conformities and eliminating their causes;
- looking for opportunities to improve the effectiveness and efficiency of processes;
- determining and prioritising those improvements which can provide optimum results;
- planning the strategies, processes and resources to deliver the identified improvements;
- implementing the plan;
- monitoring the effects of the improvements;
- assessing the results against the expected outcomes;
- reviewing the improvement activities to determine appropriate follow-up actions.

Any organisation that adopts the above approach will create confidence in the capability of its processes and the reliability of its products. It will also provide a basis for continual improvement and can lead to increased customer satisfaction.

4.3.1 What is a quality system?

In terms of the ISO standard, 'Quality System' and 'Quality Management System' mean one and the same thing. A 'quality system', however, is neither a manual (i.e. a document) nor a computer program (which is an information system as opposed to being a real quality system); it is a system that contains all the things that are used to regulate, control and improve the quality of your products and/or services. It is a network of inter-related processes with each process being made up of people, work, activities, tasks, records, documents, forms, resources, rules, regulations, reports, materials, supplies, tools, equipment etc. that are required to transform inputs into outputs.

4.3.2 What is the difference between a quality manual and a quality system?

Basically, a quality manual is all about paperwork and is just a document whereas a quality system is about a network of processes. Your quality manual is **not** supposed to be your system; it merely documents your quality system.

4.4 QUALITY MANAGEMENT SYSTEM – STRUCTURE

An organisation's QMS defines the policy, organisation and responsibilities for the management of quality within that organisation.

It ensures that all of your organisation's activities comply with an agreed set of rules, regulations and guidelines and that the end product (i.e. the deliverable) conforms to the customer's (i.e. the user's) contractual requirements.

4.4.1 QMS documentation

'A QMS can only be effective if it is fully documented, understood and followed by all.'

Within the ISO 9001:2008 quality model, there are four levels of documentation (see Figure 4.6). When trying to work out which processes should be documented, the organisation may wish to consider factors such as:

- effect on quality;
- risk of customer dissatisfaction;
- statutory and/or regulatory requirements;
- economic risk;
- competence of personnel;
- complexity of processes.

FIGURE 4.6 ISO 9001:2008 Quality Management System structure

TABLE 4.1 QMS Documentation

Level 1	Quality Manual	The main policy document that establishes the QMS and how it meets the requirements of ISO 9001:2008.
Level 2	Processes	The Core Business Process plus Supporting Processes that describe the activities required to implement the QMS and to meet the policy requirements made in the Quality Manual.
Level 3	Quality procedures	A description of the method by which quality system activities are managed.
Level 4	Work instructions	A description of how a specific task is carried out.

Where it is found necessary to document processes, a number of different methods (such as graphical representations, written instructions, checklists, flow charts, visual media or electronic methods) can be used.

4.5 QUALITY MANUAL

The Quality Manual is at the very heart of an organisation's Quality Management System and describes the inter-relationships between:

- **A Process** – an outline of its objective, scope and key performance indicators;
- **Quality Procedures** – an enlargement of the process explaining how it is controlled;
- **Work Instructions** – the 'fine print' required to perform a specific activity.

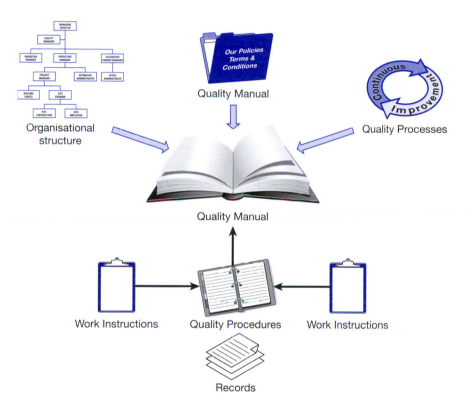

FIGURE 4.7 Quality Manual

It is the main policy document that establishes the QMS and how it meets the requirements of ISO 9001:2008 – particularly the six mandatory requirements for:

- Document Control
- Control of Records
- Internal Auditing
- Control of Non Conforming Product
- Corrective Action
- Preventative Action

. . . and it provides general information on the system (i.e. objectives, goals, roles, organisation and responsibilities).

The Quality Manual (see example in Chapter 6) is the formal record of that organisation's QMS. It:

- is a rule book by which an organisation functions;
- is a source of information from which the client may derive confidence;
- provides consistent information, both internally and externally, about the organisation's QMS;
- is a means of defining the responsibilities and inter-related activities of every member of the organisation;
- is a vehicle for auditing, reviewing and evaluating the organisation's QMS.

The Quality Manual will identify the organisation's business-critical processes and their associated Quality Procedures (QPs) and Work Instructions (WIs). The Quality Manual will also provide examples of the various forms and documentation used by the organisation – such as production control forms, inspection sheets and documents used to purchase components, systems and software etc. from subcontractors.

 For a complete description and guidance on how to develop a Quality Manual, the reader is referred to ISO/TR 10013:2001 'Guidelines for quality management system documentation'.

4.6 PROCESSES

Processes describe the activities required to implement the QMS and to meet the policy requirements set out in the Quality Manual.

Typically, the organisational processes making up a company's QMS will normally comprise a Core Business Process supplemented by a number of supporting processes which describe the infrastructure required to produce the contract deliverable (or market opportunity) on time and within budget. (See Table 4.2.)

Note: A process owner with full responsibility and authority for managing the process and achieving process objectives should be nominated. In many small businesses, one person might be responsible for a number of processes or even all of them. This is particularly so in the case of an extremely small business or a 'one-man-band' sort of organisation.

For each process there will be an organisation document detailing:

- **Objective** – what the process aims to achieve;
- **Scope** – what the process covers;

- **Responsible owner** – who is ultimately responsible for implementing the process;
- **Policy** – what the organisation intends doing to ensure quality is controlled;
- **Key performance indicators** – those items of objective evidence that can be used as a way of monitoring performance of the process;
- **Cross reference** to supporting system documentation (QPs and WIs).

TABLE 4.2 Core Business and Supporting Processes

Core Business Process	Which describes the end-to-end activities involved in producing a contract deliverable or marketing opportunity. It commences with the definition of corporate policy and ends when the product is manufactured and marketed.
	The Core Business Process is then supplemented by a number of supporting processes that describe the infrastructure required to manufacture (or supply) the product on time.

 Note: All businesses revolve around taking inputs and putting them through a series of activities that turn them into useful outputs, be that a product or service. These activities are the supporting processes.

Primary supporting processes	The basic set of activities which when combined into a logical processes sequence takes you from receipt of an order (or marketing opportunity) through to the realisation of the finished product or service.
Secondary supporting processes	The purpose of secondary supporting processes is to document those activities that are essential for supporting and achieving the primary supporting processes.
	Secondary supporting processes will have an identical structure to the primary supporting processes and will also have their own associated supporting documentation [e.g. Quality Procedures (QPs) and Work Instructions (WIs)].
	Secondary supporting processes may include such things as:

- Identification and provision of suitable staff;
- Management and support of staff;
- Identification and provision of information;
- Identification and provision of materials;
- Identification and provision of equipment and facilities;
- Management of the QMS;
- Continual improvement.

All processes should be documented to give a complete picture of how to perform the activity to a consistent level of quality. The level of detail varies from:

- **Process** – an outline of its objective, scope and key performance indicators;
- **Quality Procedures** – an enlargement of the process explaining how it is controlled;
- **Work Instructions** – the 'fine print' required to perform a specific activity.

4.7 QUALITY PROCEDURES

QPs are formal documents that describe the method by which the Core Business and its Supporting Processes are managed. They describe how the policy objectives of the Quality Manual can be met in practice and how these processes are controlled. They contain the basic documentation used for planning and controlling all activities that impact on quality.

There are two types of procedure, namely:

- system-level procedures that are used to detail the activities needed to implement the QMS;
- procedures that describe the sequence of processes necessary to ensure the conformity of a product or service.

4.7.1 What documented procedures are required by ISO 9001:2008?

In section 4.2.2 of ISO 9001:2008, the standard requires the organisation to:

'Establish and maintain a quality manual that includes the documented procedures established for the quality management system.'

There is **no** restriction about how many of these documented procedures an organisation should have to cover; ISO 9001:2008 does, however, contain six **mandatory requirements** for formal documented procedures to be produced for the:

1. Control of documents (4.2.3);
2. Control of quality records (4.2.4);
3. Internal audits (8.2.2);
4. Control of non-conforming products (8.3);
5. Corrective actions (8.5.2);
6. Preventative actions (8.5.3).

Note: Where the term 'documented procedure' appears within this International Standard, this means that *the procedure has to be established, documented, implemented and maintained.*

By implication documented procedures should also be included for:

1.   Customer communications (7.2.3)

(which states that: '*The organisation shall determine and implement effective arrangements for communication with customers*').

2.   Purchasing process (7.4.1)

(which states that: '*Criteria for selection, evaluation and re-evaluation shall be established*').

 Procedures can take any suitable form. They can be a narrative, a flow chart, a process map or indeed any other suitable structure. As long as the procedure is effective, it really doesn't matter what it looks like.

4.8 WORK INSTRUCTIONS

WIs describe in detail how individual tasks and activities are to be carried out. For example, what is to be done, by whom and when it has to be completed.
   Work Instructions describe:

*   the physical operating practices and controls within each process;
*   how individual tasks and activities are to be carried out.

They will normally also provide examples of the various forms and documentation used by the organisation. For instance:

*   production control forms;
*   inspection sheets;
*   documents used to purchase components from subcontractors.

Note: Work Instructions, similar to the remainder of the QMS documentation, can take any appropriate form. However, one of the best ways to document a Work Instruction is probably to use a flow chart associated with a form which can then become a record once it is filled in.

4.8.1 What is the difference between a Work Instruction and a record?

Work Instructions describe how tasks should be done and are used before the task is performed. Records document how tasks **were** completed and are used after the task has been performed. Work Instructions come before the fact, while records come after the fact.

4.9 QUALITY PLAN

When complex assemblies or multi-part contracts are required, separate instructions may have to be included in the Quality Manual in order to cover individual parts of the contract. These types of instruction are called Quality Plans.

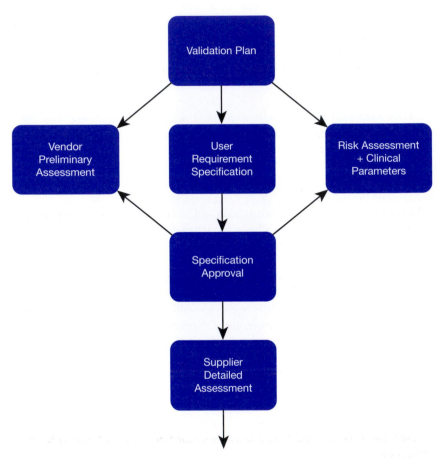

FIGURE 4.8 Quality Plan

The accepted definition (as provided in ISO 9000:2005 *'Quality management systems – fundamentals and vocabulary'*) of a Quality Plan is that it is *'a document specifying which procedures and associated resources shall be applied, by whom and when to a specific project, product, process or contract'.*

A Quality Plan – in setting out the specific quality practices, resources and sequence of activities – therefore, ensures that specific requirements for quality are appropriately planned and addressed. Ideally the Plan should state its purpose, how and to what it applies, its quality objectives (in measurable terms), any specific exclusions and, of course, its period of validity.

Quality Plans normally describe how the QMS is applied to a specific deliverable. They may also be used to demonstrate how the quality requirements of a particular contract will be met, and to monitor and assess adherence to those requirements. While a Quality Plan normally refers to the appropriate parts of the Quality Manual, it can be used in conjunction with a QMS or in some circumstances, as a standalone document.

Quality Plans provide a collated summary of the requirements for a specific activity. They include less information than the organisation's QMS but, with all the detail brought together in one document, the requirement for performance should be more readily understandable and the risk of non-conformance and misinterpretation of intentions should be reduced.

Quality assurance for the supply of complex products can be very difficult to stipulate in a contract especially if (in the case of a manufactured product) the most important inspections have to be left until the assembly is almost complete – by which time many of the sub assemblies and components will have become almost inaccessible! In these cases it is essential for the organisation's Quality Manager to develop and produce a Quality Plan that details all the important information that has to be provided to the shop floor management.

The Quality Plan will cover all of the quality practices and resources that are going to be used, the sequence of events relevant to that product, the specific allocation of responsibilities, methods, QPs and WIs, together with the details of the testing, inspection, examination and audit programme stages.

The Quality Plan should, nevertheless, be flexible and written in such a way that it is possible to modify its content to reflect changing circumstances.

At all work places, QPs and WIs must be readily available. These will include the specifications that must be obeyed, particulars of the drawings, documentation, the sampling method, the tests which have to be made, the test specifications and procedures, the acceptance/ rejection criteria – and so on.

The main requirement of a Quality Plan, however, is to provide the customer (and the organisation) with clear, concise instructions and guidance as well as the appropriate inspection methods and procedures; the results of inspections (including rejections) and details of any concessions issued for rework or repair. All these must be clearly recorded and available for a purchaser's future (possible) examination.

A well thought out Quality Plan will divide the product or service being supplied into stages, show what type of inspection has to be completed at the beginning, during, or at the end of each stage and indicate how these details should be recorded on the final document. The Quality Plan should be planned and developed in conjunction with all the business stages (be they design, development, manu-facturing; subcontract and/or installation and after-sales work) and ensure that all functions have been fully catered for.

One of the main objectives of quality planning is to identify any special or unusual requirements, processes and techniques – including those requirements that are unusual by reason of newness, unfamiliarity, lack of experience and/or absence of precedents. As ISO 9004:2005 points out, if the contract specifies that

Quality Plans are required, then these Quality Plans should fully cover the following areas and ensure that:

- design, contract, development, manufacturing and installation activities are well documented and adequate;
- all controls, processes, inspection equipment, fixtures, tooling, manpower resources and skills that an organisation must have to achieve the required quality, have been identified, recorded and the necessary action taken to obtain any additional components, documentation etc. that is required;
- quality control, inspection and testing techniques (including the development of new instrumentation) have been updated;
- any new measurement technique (or any measurement involving a measurement capability that exceeds the known state of the art) that is required to inspect the product, has been identified and action taken to develop that capability;
- standards of acceptability for all features and requirements (including those which contain a subjective element) have been clearly recorded;
- compatibility of design, manufacturing process, installation, inspection procedures and applicable documentation has been assured well before production begins;
- as each special requirement is identified, the means for testing and being able to prove successfully that the product or service is capable of successfully complying with the requirements has to be considered.

The integration of special or unusual requirements into the QMS must be carefully investigated, planned and documented.

A Quality Plan is effectively a sub set of the actual Quality Manual. The layout of the Quality Plan is very similar to that of the Quality Manual and refers (other than system-specific QPs and WIs) normally to the QPs and WIs contained in that Quality Manual.

The following briefly describes how each of the ISO 9000 elements is covered in a Quality Plan.

4.9.1 Management responsibility

The Quality Plan should show who is responsible for:

- ensuring activities are planned, implemented, controlled and monitored;
- communicating requirements and resolving problems;
- reviewing audit results;
- authorising exemption requests;
- implementing corrective action requests.

Where the necessary documentation already exists under the present QMS, the Quality Plan need only refer to a specific situation or specification.

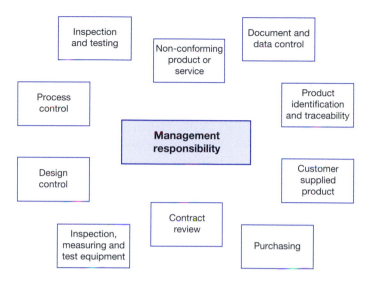

FIGURE 4.9 Management responsibility

4.9.2 Contract review

Contract review should cover:

- when, how and by whom the review is made;
- how the results are to be documented;
- how conflicting instructions or ambiguities are resolved.

4.9.3 Design control

Design control should indicate:

- when, how and by whom the design process, validation and verification of the design output is carried out, controlled and documented;
- any customer involvement;
- applicable codes of practice, standards, specifications and regulatory requirements.

4.9.4 Document and data control

Document and data control should refer to:

- what is provided and how it is controlled;
- how related documents will be identified;
- how and by whom access to the documents can be obtained;
- how and by whom the original documents are reviewed and approved.

4.9.5 Purchasing

Under the heading of purchasing the following should be indicated:

- the important products that need to be purchased;
- the source and requirements relating to them;
- the method, evaluation, selection and control of subcontractors;
- the need for a subcontractor's Quality Plan in order to satisfy the regulatory requirements applicable to purchase products/services.

4.9.6 Customer supplied product

Customer supplied products should refer to:

- how they are identified and controlled;
- how they are verified as meeting specified requirements;
- how non-conformance is dealt with.

4.9.7 Product identification and traceability

If traceability is a requirement then the Plan should:

- define its scope and extent (including how services/products are identified);
- indicate how contractual and regulatory authority traceability requirements are identified and incorporated into working documents;
- indicate how records are to be generated, controlled and distributed.

4.9.8 Process control

Process control may include:

- procedures/instructions;
- process steps;
- methods to monitor and control processes;
- service/product characteristics.

The Plan could also include details of:

- reference criteria for workmanship;
- special and qualified processes;
- tools, techniques and methods to be used.

4.9.9 Inspection and testing

Inspection and testing should indicate:

- any inspection and test plan;
- how the subcontractors' product (if used) shall be verified;
- the location of inspection and test points;
- procedures and acceptance criteria;
- witness verification points (customers as well as regulatory);
- where, when and how the customer requires third parties to perform:
  - o type tests;
  - o witness testing;
  - o service/product verification;
  - o material, service/product, process or personnel certification.

4.9.10 Inspection, measuring and test equipment

Inspection, measuring and test equipment should:

- refer to the identity of the equipment;
- refer to the method of calibration;
- indicate and record calibration status and usage of the equipment;
- indicate specific requirements for the identification of inspection and test status.

4.9.11 Non-conforming service/product

Under the heading of non-conforming service/product, an indication should be given of:

- how such a service/product is identified and segregated;
- the degree or type of rework allowed;
- the circumstances under which the supplier can request concessions.

Details should also be provided with respect to:

- corrective and preventive action;
- handling, storage, packaging, preservation and delivery.

4.9.12 Other considerations

Quality Plans should:

- indicate key quality records (i.e. what they are, how long they should be kept, where and by whom);
- suggest how legal or regulatory requirements are to be satisfied;
- specify the form in which records should be kept (e.g. paper, microfilm, disc, hard drive etc.);
- define liability, storage, retrievability, disposition and confidentiality requirements;
- include the nature and extent of quality audits to be undertaken;
- indicate how the audit results are to be used to correct and prevent recurrence of deficiencies;
- show how the training of staff in new or revised operating methods is to be completed.

Where servicing is a specified requirement, suppliers should state their intentions to assure conformance to applicable servicing requirements, such as:

- regulatory and legislative requirements;
- industry codes and practices;
- service level agreements;
- training of customer personnel;
- availability of initial and ongoing support during the agreed time-period;
- statistical techniques, where relevant.

Note: For further information I would recommend looking at ISO 10005:2005 which provides the reader with guidance on how to produce Quality Plans as well as including helpful suggestions on how to maintain an organisation's quality activities.

4.10 QUALITY RECORDS

Quality records provide objective evidence of activities performed or results achieved.

Records of QMS inspections and tests concerning the design, testing, survey, audit and review of a product or service are the evidence that a supplier is capable of and is indeed meeting the quality requirements of the customer.

Records such as QMS audit reports, calibration of test and measuring equipment, inspections, tests, approvals, concessions etc., ensure that an organisation is capable of proving the effectiveness of its QMS.

Records, therefore, are an important part of quality management and the QMS will have to identify exactly what type of record is to be made, at what stage of the production process it should be made and who should make it. To be of any real

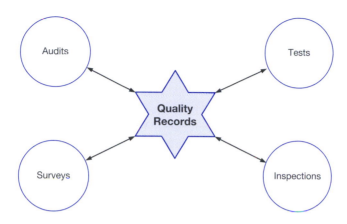

FIGURE 4.10 Quality records

value it is essential that these records are covered by clear, concise instructions and procedures. Above all, the storage of records should be systematic and capable of being easily and quickly accessed.

Having agreed and decided on the necessity for records, the next step is to:

- establish methods for making changes, modifications, revisions and additions to these records;
- establish methods for accounting for the documents;
- show their retention time;
- lay down methods for the disposal of those that are superseded or become out of date;
- show how they should be stored.

These procedures will normally have already been written up as QPs and been included in the organisation's QMS. WIs should also be available to show how important it is to keep records of defects, diagnosis of their causes and details of the corrective action that was carried out together with the success or failure of this corrective action.

If this information is stored in a computer, then it is essential that the integrity of that system **must** also be satisfactorily assured.

The retention of records is an aspect that is far too often overlooked by organisations. Records are very important, not only from an historical point of view, but also as a means of settling disputes about bad workmanship, identifying faults and settling production problems whether this be internally, by the supplier, or externally, by the organisation.

 Use of 'Cloud' storage is another option.

Author's Note

In Chapter 4 of this book we have addressed the basic requirements for a Quality Management System and shown how ISO 9000 can be structured to suit a particular business or profession.

In Chapter 5, the requirements and recommendations of ISO 9001:2008 are described in detail and guidance notes provided to suggest ways of meeting and implementing these requirements and regulations in practice.

The structure of ISO 9001:2008

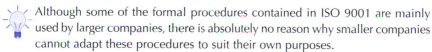

Author's Note

Having reviewed the basic requirements for a Quality Management System and seen how ISO 9000 can be structured to suit a particular business or profession, Chapter 5 now takes us a step nearer to fully understanding what is required for an organisation to become ISO 9001:2008 compliant.

In this chapter, the structure of ISO 9001:2008 is explained, details are provided of the various clauses, and elements contained in the ISO 9001:2008 sections and sub sections are reviewed.

Although some of the formal procedures contained in ISO 9001 are mainly used by larger companies, there is absolutely no reason why smaller companies cannot adapt these procedures to suit their own purposes.

For example, ISO 9001:2008 Section 7.3 states that 'an organization shall plan and control the design and development of a product'. Perhaps your company does not have a design office and this activity is achieved by an individual. Although most of the requirements of Section 7.3 are probably inappropriate, the procedures required are still the same – so why not make use of them!

A detailed description of the main sections making up ISO 9001:2008 now follows.

5.1 SECTION 1 – SCOPE

5.1.1 Section 1.1 – General

Section 1.1 General requirements	The organisation shall demonstrate its ability to: • consistently provide a product that meets customer and regulatory requirements; • enhance customer satisfaction through the application of their QMS.

This short section contains an explanation of the contents of the standard and states the basic requirements for achieving customer satisfaction through the effective application of a Quality Management System (QMS).

 Note: In this international standard the word '*product*' applies to the product intended for (or required by) a customer, or any intended output resulting from the product relationship process. Thus, a 'product' can be one of many things such as a design, a plan, a manufactured item, a system or even a service of some description.

5.1.2 Section 1.2 – Application

Section 1.2 Permissible exclusions	If there are clauses that an organisation does not need to meet in order to fulfil the requirements of this standard, these clauses may be excluded. They may be due to: • the nature of the product; • customer requirements; • applicable regulatory requirements.

Section 1.2 emphasises that all the requirements of this International Standard are generic and are, therefore, applicable to **all** organisations regardless of type, size and product provided.

If any of the requirements contained in Section 7 cannot be applied owing to the nature of the organisation, then provided that the exclusion(s) do not affect the organisation's ability, or responsibility to provide a product that fulfils customer and/or applicable regulatory requirements, then it can be considered an exclusion.

For example, if the organisation manufactures a product that does not have any design and development input, then Clause 7.3.2 is not really relevant.

In all cases, exclusions are permitted **provided** that the reason(s) why they are not entirely applicable to that particular organisation are fully documented in the organisation's Quality Manual.

The **only** clauses that may be excluded from ISO 9001:2008 are those within Section 7.

5.2 SECTION 2 – NORMATIVE REFERENCE

Section 2 Normative reference	This section lists standards that form a mandatory input to ISO 9001:2008.

This short section requires an organisation to take into consideration ISO 9000:2005: '*Quality Management Systems – Fundamentals and vocabulary*', when applying ISO 9001:2008.

5.3 SECTION 3 – TERMS AND DEFINITIONS

Section 3 Terms and definitions	In addition to those terms defined within ISO 9000:2005, an organisation shall make a note of the specific terms used to describe the supply chain.

This section covers the specific use of terminology to describe the supply chain.

The word '*product*' is defined so as to cover all manufacturing and service outputs and so, whenever the term '*product*' occurs, it can also mean '*service*' (and, of course, vice versa).

In this particular ISO standard, the definition of a product is '*the result of a process*'. A product may be defined as:

- hardware;
- software;
- services;
- processed materials.

Note: Most products are, of course, combinations of one of these four generic product categories and whether the combined product is then called hardware, processed material, software or service depends on the dominant element. For example, if the product were an '*automobile*', it would consist of hardware (e.g. tyres), processed materials (e.g. fuel, cooling liquid), software (e.g. engine control software, driver's manual), and service (e.g. operating explanations provided by the salesman).

The definition of a supply chain is shown in Figure 5.1.

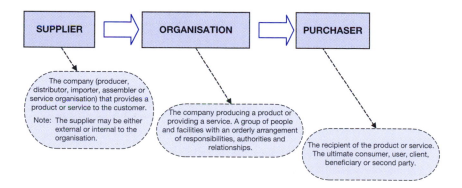

FIGURE 5.1 The supply chain

5.4 SECTION 4 – QUALITY MANAGEMENT SYSTEM

Section 4 of ISO 9001:2008 covers the requirements for all organisations to establish, document, implement, maintain and continually improve a QMS in accordance with the requirements of this standard.

It is broken down into the following sub clauses:

* **Quality Manual** – establishing and maintaining an organisational '*Rule Book*';
* **Control of documents** – establishing and maintaining a documented procedure for the control of QMS documents;
* **Quality records** – controlling and maintaining quality records.

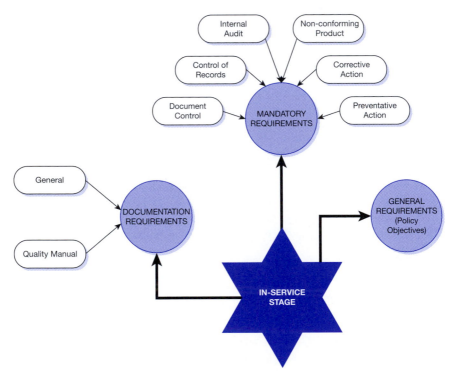

FIGURE 5.2 Quality Management System

Note: The extent of the QMS documentation (which may be in any form or type of medium) is dependent on the:

* size and type of the organisation;
* complexity and interaction of the processes;
* competency of personnel.

5.4.1 Section 4.1 – General requirements

Section 4.1 General requirements	The organisation shall establish, document, implement, maintain and continually improve a QMS, that ensures and covers: • identification of processes; • their operation and control; • the availability of resources and information; • measurement, monitoring, analysis and support; • achievement of planned results; • continual improvement; • management (in accordance with the requirements of ISO 9001:2008).
Proof	A definition of the processes necessary to ensure that a product conforms to customer requirements which is capable of being implemented, maintained and improved.

The management of any organisation will rely on a number of different management disciplines, the most important of which is quality management. As this is the core of all organisational structures, the activities and processes that affect performance improvement will need to be described and defined by management. They will also need to ensure that they are clearly understood by the whole workforce, monitored (i.e. to evaluate improvement on a continuing basis) and managed. Self-assessment can be a very useful tool to evaluate improvement and ISO 9004:2005 helps organisations by providing an annex containing '*Guidelines for self-assessment*'.

Note: For the assistance of small businesses (in particular) I have also included a section (see Chapter 7 of this book) on '*self-assessment*' which includes check sheets against the requirements of ISO 9001:2008 and examples of stage audit checklists.

An organisation's self-assessment should be completed on a regular basis as it will provide an overall view of the performance of the organisation and the degree of maturity of its QMS. It can also help to identify areas that need improving and determine priorities.

Where an organisation chooses to outsource any process that affects product conformity to requirements, the organisation shall ensure control over such processes.

5.4.2 Section 4.2 – Documentation requirements

Section 4.2.1 – General

Section 4.2 General documentation requirements	The QMS documentation shall include: • a Quality Manual; • specific statements regarding quality policy and quality objectives • documented procedures that clearly describe the sequence of processes necessary to ensure the conformity of the product; • documented instructions to ensure the effective operation and control of the processes; • quality records.

Note: Where the term *'documented procedure'* appears within ISO 9001:2008, this means that the procedure is established, documented, implemented and maintained. A single document may address the requirements for one or more procedures and a requirement for a documented procedure may be covered by more than one document.

As ISO 9001:2008 is a generic requirements standard it doesn't state exactly what an organisation's quality documentation should look like. It merely provides details of the mandatory requirements and then leaves it up to the organisation to determine the appropriate documentation to suit its own size and type of business.

Note: This is a good point to be remembered by small businesses who, whilst wanting to *'work in compliance with the requirements of ISO 9001:2008'* do **not** necessarily see the **need** for their system to be certified against that standard.

The standard goes on to state that the QMS documentation and records can be in any form or in any medium provided that they meet:

• the needs of that particular organisation;
• customer and contractual requirements;
• the relevant international, national, regional and industry sector standards;
• the relevant statutory and regulatory requirements.

Section 4.2.2 – Quality Manual

Section 4.2.2 Quality Manual	The organisation shall: • establish and maintain a Quality Manual; • include details of any ISO 9001:2008 exclusions; • include details of associated documented procedures; • indicate the sequence and interaction of processes.
Proof	A document which describes an organisation's quality policies, procedures and practices that makes up its Quality Management System.
Likely documentation	A controlled document (i.e. Quality Manual) containing everything related to quality control and quality assurance within an organisation.

One of the requirements of ISO 9001:2008 (see Section 4.2.1) is to define the documentation required to support an organisation's QMS. The primary purpose of this quality documentation is to express the quality policy and describe the QMS. This documentation serves as the basis for implementing and maintaining the system and should be capable of controlling the effective operation of the QMS.

Details of the quality documentation are usually found in an organisation's Quality Manual, which will provide information about all of the quality policies, processes and their associated Quality Procedures (QPs) and Work Instructions (WIs). Depending on the size of the organisation, the Quality Manual will also, probably, include standard formats for data collection, data reporting and quality records. It will also have to show (and justify) if certain requirements from ISO 9001:2008 have been omitted.

There are no set rules about what should or should not be included in a Quality Manual. It all rather depends on the structure and business of the organisation concerned.

 As a Quality Consultant, I always recommend that organisations address **each** requirement contained in ISO 9001:2008 separately, and in turn, to ensure that none of the essential (i.e. mandatory) requirements are left out.

As previously described, organisations are allowed to leave out the non-relevant sections of ISO 9001:2008 **provided**, that is, that the relevant detail and reasons are included in the organisation's Quality Manual. In Chapter 6 I have provided a complete example of a generic Quality Manual together with a number of example QPs and WIs which can be used as a template for your own Quality Manual.

Note: For your assistance, a soft copy of this *'generic Quality Manual'* is available: please see p. xvii for details of how to obtain these files. If you then wish to customise this publication to suit your own purposes, the easiest method is to instruct your computer (using the 'find and replace all' facility) to replace *'NAFAAD Consultancy Ltd'* with your own company's name.

It is important that **each** section of the Quality Manual is read and carefully modified so that it reflects your own organisation's business.

If you require further Help Line assistance or feel the need for a copy of the complete QMS described in this Book **plus** additional Quality Procedures and Work Instructions **plus** copies of audit checklists etc. then please feel free to contact me at *'ray@herne.org.uk'*.

Section 4.2.3 – Control of documents

'A documented procedure SHALL be established to define the control of documents.'

(This is a ISO 9001:2008 mandatory requirement.)

Section 4.2.3 Control of documents	The organisation shall instigate a documented procedure for the quality control of documents. This procedure shall include processes for: • controlled distribution of documents; • approval of documents prior to issue; • review, updating and re-approval of documents; • identifying the current revision status of documents; • ensuring that only relevant versions of applicable documents are available at points of use; • ensuring that documents remain legible, readily identifiable and retrievable; • identifying, distributing and controlling documents from an external source; • controlling obsolete documents.
Proof	A documented procedure.
Likely documentation	• Document control procedures; • Work Instructions.

ISO 9001:2008 requires an organisation to establish and maintain procedures for the control of all its documents and data (i.e. hard copy as well as electronic media) especially those relating to quality assurance and quality control.

Indeed, where the term '*documented procedure*' appears within ISO 9001:2008, this requires the procedure to be *established, documented, implemented and maintained.*

All documentation used by the organisation in support of its QMS and/or the execution of a contract (e.g. specifications, customer orders, plans, drawings, manuals, operating procedures, national and international standards and codes of practice etc.) must be controlled to ensure that:

- they are issued to the appropriate personnel;
- they are revised and reissued as necessary;
- all obsolete versions are removed from the point of use.

Value of documentation

Documentation enables communication of intent and consistency of action. It is therefore a necessary element within a QMS and its use contributes to:

- the achievement of product quality and quality improvement;
- the provision of appropriate training;
- ensured repeatability and traceability;
- the provision of objective evidence;
- the evaluation of the effectiveness of the system.

The production of documentation should not be an end in itself but should be a value-adding activity.

Quality Manual

Normally the Quality Manual and its associated processes, procedures, plans and instructions are maintained by the Quality Manager (or in the case of an extremely small business, probably the Owner) who ensures that the appropriate items, at the correct revision levels, are issued (or at least made available) to all who need them within the organisation.

Support documentation

National and international standards, codes of practice and so on should (particularly in large organisations) normally be maintained by the General Manager and/or the Engineers who would then be responsible for ensuring that appropriate documents are available within the organisation and that they are issued and maintained at the correct revision levels. External suppliers of documentation should be contacted on a regular basis to ascertain that the documents held by the organisation remain current.

Document distribution

The distribution of standard documents should be controlled and recorded on distribution lists, which also show the current issue status. A master list of all documents should be maintained which clearly shows the current status of each document. This list needs to be available at all locations where operations effective to the functioning of the QMS are performed and this distribution list needs to be reviewed and updated as changes occur and all invalid and/or obsolete documents/data must be immediately removed.

Document changes

All changes (e.g. modified wording, new procedures to be adopted etc.) that need to be made to a previously issued document or data should, ideally, be approved by the same person who performed the original review and approval. Where appropriate, the nature of the change should be indicated on the document and master copies of the revised documents retained as records of the changes.

Contract documents

Each contract should have a separate file which contains all the relevant information applicable to that contract.

Section 4.2.4 – Control of records

'The organization shall establish a documented procedure to define the controls needed for the identification, storage, protection, retrieval, retention and disposition of records.'

(This is an ISO 9001:2008 mandatory requirement.)

Section 4.2.4 Control of records	The organisation shall establish a documented procedure for the: • control; • maintenance; • identification; • storage; • retrieval; • protection; • retention time; • disposition; of all quality records.
Proof	A documented procedure.
Likely documentation	Record keeping procedures.

The question is often asked, 'why bother to keep records?'

Nothing is worse than ordering a product or service, finding a firm to meet the delivery time, but then not being able to use it because the relevant documentation (for example a specific working instruction), has still to arrive. It is, therefore, vitally important for the supplier to ensure that the documentation for the assembly, installation, commissioning, use and/or operation of a deliverable are provided to the purchaser **well** before delivery and that these are both comprehensive and clear.

The progress of a product throughout its life cycle, its many maintenance cycles, during storage and operational use etc. will doubtless produce a considerable number of records. Product improvement relies heavily on the availability of records such as the results of previous audit reports, customer feedback and failure reports gathered in the design office and from the shop floor. From a contract point of view, the maintenance of a complete historical record of all the alterations made to a contract, concessions allowed, variations permitted by the purchaser and specifications changed need to be recorded. Indeed it is usually a contract requirement for organisations to have available, at all times, sufficient records to be able to demonstrate that their products continue to comply with the relevant contract requirements and specifications. Quality records that can be analysed to provide inputs for corrective and preventive action, process improvements etc. are also very important to the quality of the product.

The above are only a few examples which show why records should be maintained and ISO 9001:2008 makes it a mandatory requirement that all records that are required for the QMS **shall** be controlled.

Today, of course, many organisations rely on computers and electronic storage devices to store records. Whilst this is a convenient method of storing and retrieving files and information, it is important to remember the need for backup and restore processes for electronic data. Also, in some organisations the use of electronic signatures is becoming commonplace and some form of record and control may well be required.

5.5 SECTION 5 – MANAGEMENT RESPONSIBILITY

This section contains the majority of the old ISO 9001:1994 management responsibility and quality requirements all rolled together. It is broken down into sub clauses that cover the requirements for:

- **Management commitment** – Top (i.e. senior) Management committing, fully, to the development and improvement of the QMS. (Without their commitment the system will fall at the first hurdle);
- **Customer focus** – determining, fully understanding and documenting customer requirements; ensuring compliance with identified statutory legislation (such as EC Directives, regional, national and international standards etc.);
- **Quality policy** – ensuring that a product or service is appropriate for the purpose, understood by everyone and reviewed for continued suitability;
- **Planning** – clearly stating management's quality objectives and policy on quality in an established, fully documented QMS;
- **Responsibility, authority and communication** – identifying and planning the activities and resources required to achieve quality objectives. Appointing

someone (or some people) to be responsible for the implementation and improvement of the organisation's QMS;

- **Management review** – carrying out regular reviews of the QMS to ensure it continues to function correctly (and to identify areas for improvement).

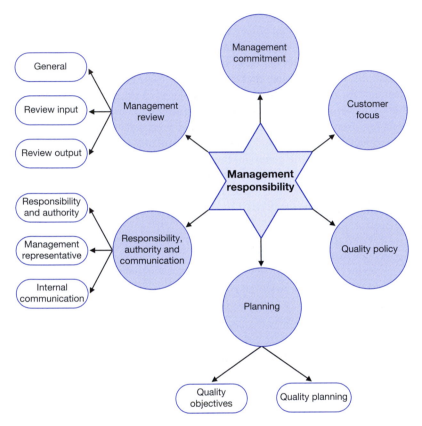

FIGURE 5.3 Management responsibility

5.5.1 Section 5.1 – Management commitment

Section 5.1 Management commitment	Management shall demonstrate their commitment to developing and improving their QMS by: • conducting regular management reviews; • establishing organisational objectives and quality policies; • ensuring the availability of necessary resources; • ensuring everyone is aware of the importance of meeting customer, regulatory and legal requirements.

Proof	A description of management responsibility and quality requirements. A written demonstration of an organisation's commitment to sustainable quality management.
Likely documentation	A Quality Manual containing: 1 A high-level policy statement concerning organisational objectives and quality policies. 2 A list of government regulatory, legal and customer-specific requirements. 3 Procedures describing: • resource management; • contract review procedures; • management reviews; • financial business plan(s).

Top Management should always try to create an environment where people are fully involved and in which their QMS can operate effectively. They should use the principles of quality management as a basis for:

- establishing the organisation's quality policies and quality objectives;
- ensuring that customer requirements are recognised;
- ensuring that processes are available (and implemented) that enable customer requirements to be fulfilled and quality objectives to be achieved;
- ensuring that an effective QMS is established, implemented and maintained to achieve these objectives;
- ensuring the availability of necessary resources;
- comparing the achieved results against the quality objectives that were set by Top Management;
- evaluating the ongoing effectiveness of their organisation's quality policies and quality objectives;
- deciding on actions for improvement;
- defining responsibilities and authorities – e.g. the person or persons responsible for managing, performing and verifying that the end product meets the organisation's quality requirements;
- nominating a management representative (or representatives – depending on the size of the organisation) for quality matters.

Note: For small businesses, management commitment is extremely important as the success and failure of many systems typically lies with Top Management's commitment or lack of enthusiasm. It is important for small businesses to remember this when establishing and implementing their quality management system.

5.5.2 Section 5.2 – Customer focus

Section 5.2 Customer focus	Customer needs and expectations shall be: • determined; • converted into requirements; • fulfilled.
Proof	Auditable proof that all of the customer's requirements are (and have been) fully met.
Likely documentation	Procedures describing: • resource management; • contract review procedures; • management reviews; • financial business plan(s).

To satisfy customer requirements, organisations must fully understand the customer's current (and future) needs and expectations. In an ideal world, of course, management should always attempt to exceed their customers' needs and expectations and in so doing, stand to gain follow-on orders. To define customer and end-user needs and expectations, an organisation should:

- identify its customers (including potential customers);
- determine the customer's key product characteristics;
- identify and assess market competition;
- identify opportunities and weaknesses;
- define financial and future competitive advantages;
- ensure that it has sufficient knowledge of the statutory and regulatory requirements (and is capable of implementing them);
- identify the benefits to be achieved from exceeding compliance;
- identify the role of the organisation in the protection of community interests.

In addition to their customers' needs and expectations, organisations may also have a number of other 'interested parties' whose needs and expectations will have to be addressed. For quality management purposes, these interested parties may include:

- people within the organisation;
- owners, partners, investors and shareholders;
- suppliers;
- the general public.

The needs and expectations of these interested parties will be similar to the customers' **except** that they will be more directed to recognition, work satisfaction, competencies and development of knowledge.

Involving motivated people in the finalisation of a product can be a key to success!

5.5.3 Section 5.3 – Quality policy

Section 5.3 Quality policy	Top management shall ensure that the quality policy is: • controlled; • appropriate; • committed to meeting requirements; • communicated and understood throughout the organisation; • capable of continual improvement; • a framework for establishing and reviewing quality objectives; • regularly reviewed.
Proof	A description of how an organisation approaches quality and how they ensure that this approach is appropriate for both the customer and their own organisation.
Likely documentation	A high-level managerial statement on an organisation's quality policy containing clear responsibilities, training and resources required for each organisational activity.

Quality policies and quality objectives need to be established in order to provide a general focus for the organisation. Policies and objectives determine the intended results and assist the organisation in applying its resources to achieve these results.

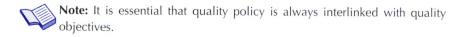 **Note:** It is essential that quality policy is always interlinked with quality objectives.

First step

The first step that an organisation must take is to define and document its quality management policy. That is, produce a mission statement that covers the organisation's objectives for quality and its commitment to quality. This quality policy must be relevant to the company's organisational goals and take into account the expectations and needs of the customer. The organisation then needs to ensure that its quality management policy is understood and implemented by all staff members and used to provide confidence that the application of management (as described in the Quality Manual) is efficient, comprehensive and effective in ensuring that the organisation delivers the right product:

- on time;
- to the agreed specifications;
- within budget.

The purpose and benefits of establishing a quality policy and quality objectives

The organisation's quality policy should always be to achieve '*sustained, profitable growth by providing products which consistently satisfy the needs and expectations of its customers*'. This level of quality can be achieved by adopting a system of procedures that reflect the competence of the organisation to existing customers, potential customers and independent auditing authorities and which is aimed at:

- maintaining an effective QMS that complies with ISO 9001:2008;
- achieving and maintaining a level of quality which enhances the organisation's reputation with customers;
- ensuring compliance with all the relevant statutory and safety requirements;
- endeavouring, at all times, to maximise customer satisfaction with the products provided by the organisation.

Quality policy structure

Summarised, the quality management policy **shall** include the requirement that:

- clear responsibilities for each activity and development task are identified;
- each organisational activity is defined and controlled by a Quality Process, Quality Procedure (QP) or Quality Plan;
- staff are trained to the requirements listed in the company's Quality Manual;
- compliance with company procedures detailed in the Quality Manual and associated Quality Plans are audited;
- remedial action is taken whenever appropriate;
- the QPs contained in the Quality Manual and associated Quality Plans themselves are regularly reviewed.

Quality Management System review

One of the responsibilities of Top Management is to carry out regular systematic evaluations of their organisation's QMS to confirm its continued suitability, adequacy, effectiveness and efficiency with regard to their organisation's quality policy and objectives. This review should include the need to adapt and respond to changing needs, customer expectations, the market it serves and include details of any remedial actions that are required.

5.5.4 Section 5.4 – Planning

Section 5.4 Planning	Quality planning shall be documented and shall include: • quality objectives; • resources.
Proof	Planned resources and infrastructure etc. to meet an organisation's overall business objectives.
Likely documentation	Quality Manual.

Having defined its overall business objectives, the organisation is then in a position to define its quality objectives and to plan the resources etc. that it will need to meet these objectives.

 Note: The key is to make these objectives SMART – Specific, Measurable, Agreed upon, Realistic and Time-based.

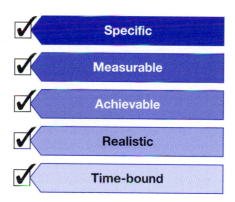

FIGURE 5.4 Planning Objectives

The acronym SMART has a number of slightly different variations, which can be used to provide a more comprehensive definition for goal setting:

S – specific, significant, stretching;
M – measurable, meaningful, motivational;
A – agreed upon, attainable, achievable, acceptable, action-orientated;
R – realistic, relevant, reasonable, rewarding, results-orientated;
T – time-based, timely, tangible, traceable.

Section 5.4.1 – Quality objectives

Section 5.4.1 Quality objectives	Top management shall ensure that quality objectives, including those needed to meet requirements for product, are established at relevant functions and levels within the organization. These quality objectives shall: • be established; • be measurable; • be consistent with quality policy; • include a commitment for continual improvement; • cover product requirements.
Proof	Quality objectives that Top Management expect to achieve within each function and level of the organisation.
Likely documentation	Policy statements defining the objectives of the company and those responsible for achieving these objectives.

 Note: Normally these will be found in the Quality Manual.

The overall quality objectives of the organisation need to be firmly established during the planning stage and then circulated to all personnel involved so that they can easily translate them into individual (and achievable) contributions. These objectives should be periodically reviewed and should:

- be relevant to the various levels and functions within the organisation;
- be consistent with the organisation's quality policy;
- be capable of being measured.

They should consider:

- current and future requirements;
- the markets served;
- the output from management's previous reviews;
- current product and process performance
- the required (and anticipated) levels of satisfaction of all interested parties.

Section 5.4.2 – Quality management system planning

Section 5.4.2 Quality management system planning	Quality planning shall be documented and shall: • meet the requirements contained in section 4.1; • provide QMS processes; • identify resources; • identify requirements for continual improvement; • identify requirements for change control.
Proof	The identification and planning of activities and resources required to meet an organisation's quality objectives. • Current and future requirements; • the markets served; • the output from management previous reviews; • current product and process performance.
Likely documentation	Processes and procedures used by senior management to define and plan the way that their organisation is run.

Having defined its quality objectives, the next step will be to plan how to meet these objectives (i.e. the processes, resources, responsibilities, methodologies, procedures etc. that will be needed). As ISO is quick to point out '*Quality planning is an integral part of the QMS*' and so organisations should take into careful consideration the:

- needs and expectations of the customers;
- required product performance;
- previous experiences and lessons learned;
- improvement opportunities;
- risk assessment;
- performance indicators;
- results of reviews and the need for change control;
- the need for documentation and records.

Customer satisfaction and quality can only be achieved by operating in accordance with the documented QMS. Specific customer requirements need to be identified and documented during the contract review process and these requirements need to be communicated and achieved in order to ensure customer satisfaction.

5.5.5 Section 5.5 – Responsibility, authority and communication

Section 5.5 Responsibility, authority and communication	Administration of the QMS shall be documented and shall cover: • responsibilities and authorities; • management representative's duties; • internal communication.
Proof	How the organisation documents and administers its QMS.
Likely documentation	A Quality Manual containing everything related to quality controls within the organisation.

Management need to define and implement their QMS so that it provides confidence that the organisation can satisfy the needs and expectations of interested parties and in such a way that is consistent with its size, culture and products.

The following sub sections describe how an organisation's QMS should be administered.

Section 5.5.1 – Responsibility and authority

Section 5.5.1 Responsibility and authority	The organisation shall define and communicate throughout the organisation: • functions and their interrelationships; • responsibilities and authorities.
Proof	The definition of the roles, responsibilities, lines of authority, reporting and communication relevant to quality.
Likely documentation	• job descriptions and responsibilities; • organisation charts showing lines of communication.

The QMS is effectively the organisation's rule book. As such it has to be accepted and implemented by everyone. There needs to be a feeling of involvement **and** commitment in achieving the organisation's quality objectives, from Top Management right down to the newest employee. Personnel need, however, to know exactly what they are responsible for and so management must clearly define functions, levels of responsibility and authority for all personnel, in order to implement and maintain their QMS effectively and efficiently.

It is essential that Top Management ensures that the responsibilities, authorities (and their relationship) for documenting, planning and implementing the QMS are defined and communicated throughout the organisation.

Top Management should continually review the organisation's resources to ensure that adequate staff, equipment and materials are available to meet customer requirements. All staff should be allocated authority to perform their allocated responsibilities and they should have a share in the responsibility for identifying non-compliance or possible improvements and recording these instances so that corrective action can be taken, both to rectify the immediate situation and to prevent recurrence.

Section 5.5.2 – Management representative

Section 5.5.2 Management representative	The organisation shall appoint a member who, irrespective of all other duties, is responsible for: • establishing, administering and maintaining the QMS processes; • advising top management on the performance of and improvements to the organisation's QMS; • promoting awareness of customer requirements; • liaising with external parties on all matters relating to the organisation's QMS.
Proof	The identification and appointment of a 'Quality Manager' with overall responsibility for the organisation's QMS.
Likely documentation	• job description and responsibilities; • organisation charts showing lines of communication.

Whilst Top Management can all agree that they are going to have a QMS, they need to nominate someone from within management (and at managerial level) with responsibility and authority to see its successful implementation. This person (usually referred to as the Quality Manager) is responsible for:

- ensuring that the organisation's QMS is (at all times) relevant, effective and appropriate – usually achieved by completing internal quality audits;
- ensuring that the organisation meets the customer's quality requirements;
- ensuring that all personnel are aware and capable of meeting and (when required) administering the organisation's quality processes;
- producing and maintaining the quality documentation (i.e. procedures and instructions) required for those processes;

- managing, performing and verifying that the end product meets the company's quality requirements;
- supplying regular reports to Top Management on the performance of the QMS and making recommendations for its improvement;
- liaising with external parties on all matters relating to the QMS.

Section 5.5.3 – Internal communication

Section 5.5.3 Internal communication	The details of the organisation's QMS processes shall be given to all those responsible for their effectiveness.
Proof	Confirmation that the requirements of an organisation's QMS are communicated throughout the company.
Likely documentation	• notice boards; • in-house journals/magazines; • audio-visual; • e-information. Also: • team briefings; • organisational meetings.

To ensure the continued effectiveness of the organisation's QMS, it is important that everyone involved in the implementation of the system is aware of the Quality Processes that have been agreed by management. It is the responsibility of the Quality Manager (as management's representative) to inform everyone about the requirements, objectives and accomplishments of and from the Quality Processes. There are no set rules about how this sort of information should be distributed; it really depends on how the organisation is set up. Choices can include (but not necessarily be restricted to) team briefings, organisational meetings, notice boards, in-house journals/magazines/memos, audio-visual and other forms of e-information systems.

5.5.6 Section 5.6 – Management review

Section 5.6 Management review	The QMS shall be regularly reviewed to ensure its continued suitability, effectiveness and adequacy. Opportunities for improvement shall be assessed and records of all reviews shall be maintained.
Proof	How Top Management reviews the QMS.

Likely documentation	Procedures concerning: • **process and product performance;** • **audits of process, product and service;** • **customer feedback;** • **corrective and preventive action;** • **supplier performance;** • **record keeping.**

Although, when first written, an organisation's QMS is assumed to cover all eventualities, doubtless there are parts of the system that will need further definition.

ISO 9001:2008 has recognised this possibility and has made it a **mandatory** requirement for Top Management to complete a review of their organisation's QMS (for continued suitability and effectiveness) on a bi-annual basis. Records of these reviews should be retained and details of all actions agreed, allocated and minuted.

The objective of these management reviews is to establish that the QMS:

- is achieving the expected results;
- meets the organisation's requirements;
- conforms to the requirements of ISO 9001:2008;
- continues to satisfy the customers' needs and expectations;
- is functioning in accordance with the established operating procedures;
- is capable of identifying irregularities, defects and/or weaknesses in the system (and to evaluate possible improvements).

During the review, management will also review:

- the effectiveness of previous corrective actions;
- the adequacy and suitability of the QMS for current and future operations of the organisation;
- any complaints received (identifying the cause and recommending corrective action if required);
- previous internal and external audits and identify any areas of recurring problems or potential improvements;
- reports of non-conforming items and trend information to identify possible improvements.

Evaluation and auditing

When evaluating a QMS, there are four basic questions that should be asked in relation to every process being evaluated:

- Is the process identified and appropriately described?
- Are responsibilities assigned?
- Are the procedures implemented and maintained?
- Is the process effective in providing the required results?

There are three basic types of audit to choose from:

- **First-party audits** – conducted by, or on behalf of, the organisation itself for **internal** purposes, which can form the basis for an organisation's self-declaration of conformity.
- **Second-party audits** – conducted by customers of the organisation or by other persons on behalf of the customer (i.e. an **external** audit).
- **Third-party audits** – conducted by **external** independent audit service organisations. Such organisations, usually accredited, provide certification or registration of conformity with requirements such as those of ISO 9001:2008.

Section 5.6.1 General

Section 5.6.1 General	Top Management shall review the organization's quality management system, at planned intervals, to evaluate the: • need for changes; • effectiveness of the organisation's quality policies; • effectiveness of the organisation's quality objectives.
Proof	How Top Management reviews the QMS to ensure its continued suitability, adequacy and effectiveness, in the context of an organisation's strategic planning cycle.
Likely documentation	• Management review; • QMS audit procedures.

Management need to establish a process for periodically reviewing the organisation's QMS to ensure that it continues to meet the requirements of ISO 9001:2008, agrees with the organisation's policies and objectives, and continues to provide customer satisfaction. Current performance, client feedback and opportunities for improvement all need to be evaluated and possible alterations have to be made to the relevant quality documentation analysed.

It is essential that records are retained of all these management reviews and that any change that might have an effect on existing work practices is subjected to a change control procedure.

Section 5.6.2 Review input

Section 5.6.2 Review input	The input to management reviews shall include results from: • earlier management reviews (e.g. follow-up actions); • previous internal, third-party and external audits; • customer feedback; • process performance; • product conformance; • preventive and corrective actions; • changes that could affect the QMS and recommendations for improvement.
Proof	How a Top Management review of the QMS is completed.
Likely documentation	Results of audits, customer feedback, analysis of product conformance with process and procedural rules, corrective and preventive action reports and supplier performance records.

For completeness, inputs to management reviews should include everything concerned with the performance, conformance and improvement of the product. The review body should evaluate new technologies, statutory conditions, regulatory changes and environmental conditions for their effect on their product. Inputs would include, but are not restricted to:

- results from previous internal, customer and third-party audits;
- analysis of customer feedback;
- analysis of process performance;
- analysis of product conformance;
- the current status of corrective and preventive actions;
- the results of self-assessment of the organisation;
- supplier performance.

Section 5.6.3 Review output

Section 5.6.3 Review output	Management reviews shall be aimed at: • improving the organisation's overall QMS and its processes; • improving the product; • enhancing customer satisfaction; • confirming the resources required.

Proof	How the results of management reviews of the QMS are documented.
Likely documentation	Minutes of the meetings where the overall running of the company is discussed.

The aim of completing management reviews is to provide a continuing record of the organisation's capability to produce quality products that meet the quality objectives, policies and requirements (contained in their QMS) and which continue to provide customer satisfaction.

Review output should be centred on:

- improved product and process performance;
- conformation of resource requirements and organisational structure;
- meeting market needs;
- risk management;
- change control;
- continued compliance with relevant statutory and regulatory requirements.

The actual management review process should also be evaluated to confirm its continued effectiveness and a complete record of all reviews must be retained for future use.

5.6 SECTION 6 – RESOURCE MANAGEMENT

This section covers resources with regard to training, induction, orientation, responsibilities, working environment, equipment requirements, maintenance etc.

It is broken down into sub sections that cover the requirements for:

- **Provision of resources** – identifying the resources required to implement and improve the processes that make up the QMS;
- **Human resources** – assigning personnel with regard to competency, education, training, skill and experience;
- **Infrastructure** – identifying, providing and maintaining the workspace, facilities, equipment (hardware and software) and supporting services to achieve conformity of product;
- **Work environment** – identifying and managing the work environment (e.g. health and safety, ambient conditions etc.).

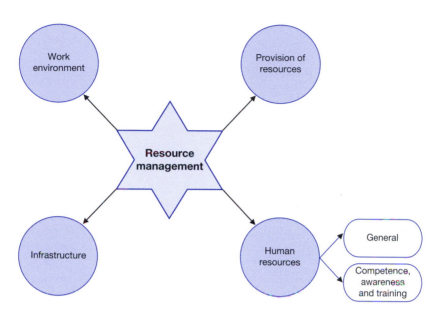

FIGURE 5.5 Resource management

5.6.1 Section 6.1 – Provision of resources

Section 6.1 Provision of resources	The organisation shall provide resources to: • implement, maintain and continually improve its QMS and its processes; • enhance customer satisfaction; • meet customer requirements.
Proof	How resource needs (i.e. humans, materials, equipment, and infrastructure) are identified with regard to training, induction, responsibilities, working environment, equipment needs, maintenance, etc.
Likely documentation	• Quality Plans; • Quality Procedures; • Work Instructions.

The organisation needs to identify and make available all the resources (e.g. information, infrastructure, people, work environment, finance, support etc.) required to implement and improve its QMS and its associated quality processes.

Resources can include (but not be limited to):

- natural resources;
- tangible resources (e.g. support facilities);
- intangible resources (e.g. intellectual property);
- future resources;
- organisational resources;
- information management systems;
- training and education;
- resources to encourage continual improvement.

Suppliers

A complete historical record should be maintained by an organisation to register variations to the contract, concessions made, variations allowed by the purchaser and specifications altered. In a sizeable business, the design office often carries out this activity.

In a similar manner, suppliers must provide the purchasers with an assurance that they are capable of continuing to supply logistic support for the product for as long as can reasonably be expected. This logistic support may include the provision of spares, updating of documentation, details of product improvement etc., depending upon the purchaser's requirements.

5.6.2 Section 6.2 – Human resources

Section 6.2 Human resources	The organisation shall establish procedures for: • the assignment of personnel; • training, awareness and competency.
Proof	How human resources to implement and improve the QMS are identified.
Likely documentation	• Quality Plans; • Quality Procedures; • Work Instructions.

The organisation needs to identify and make available human resources to implement and improve its QMS and comply with contract conditions. Consideration must be given to its competency for the job that it is selected to complete and the possible requirements for additional training.

Section 6.2.1 – General

Section 6.2.1 General	Assigned personnel shall be: • competent; • educated and trained; • skilled and experienced.
Proof	How an organisation assigns personnel.
Likely documentation	• job descriptions and responsibilities; • training records; • staff evaluations; • Quality Plans, QPs and WIs identifying human resources required to complete a task.

Human resources are the principal method of achieving product completion and customer satisfaction. The old adage '*a happy worker is a good worker*' still stands true in this age of information technology and with the increased training and education opportunities currently available, highly motivated, well-qualified personnel are at a premium. To employ and retain the right sort of person for the job, management must, when determining the resources required, adequately define their responsibilities and authorities, establish their individual and team objectives and encourage recognition and reward. They must also:

- consider career planning and On-The-Job Training (OJT);
- encourage innovation and effective teamwork;
- make use of information technology;
- measure people's satisfaction.

Section 6.2.2 – Competence, awareness and training

Section 6.2.2 Competence, awareness and training	The organisation shall: • identify the requirements for training personnel; • provide appropriate training; • evaluate the effectiveness of the training provided; • maintain records of all training.
Proof	Documents showing how an organisation assigns personnel to specific tasks.
Likely documentation	System level procedures for: • training; • staff evaluations; • review of work assignments and staff assessments; • records.

The organisation is responsible for ensuring that all personnel are trained and experienced to the extent necessary to undertake their assigned activities and responsibilities effectively. Thus, whenever training needs have been identified, Top Management should endeavour to make the relevant training available and full records must be maintained of all training undertaken by employees.

Most organisations will recruit employees who are already well qualified and quite capable of meeting the relevant technical, skill, experience and educational requirements of the organisation. There will still, however, be a need for some additional system or contract-specific training and all staff have a responsibility for identifying and recommending the training needs of others and for ensuring that all employees allocated specific tasks are suitably qualified and experienced to execute those tasks.

It is very important for an organisation's staff to receive sufficient training to enable them to carry out their functions. Organisations should, therefore, determine the competence levels required, assess the competence of its people and develop plans to close any gaps. Then, based on an analysis of the present and expected needs of the organisation (compared with the existing competence of its people and the requirements of related legislation, regulation, standards and directives) determine the type and amount of training required.

Training plan

Training should cover the organisation's policies and objectives and, as well as having introductory programmes for new people, there should also be available periodic refresher programmes for people already trained. The training should emphasise the importance of meeting requirements and the needs of customers and other interested parties. It should also include an awareness of the consequences to the organisation and its people of failing to meet the requirements.

A typical training plan would include:

- training objectives;
- training programmes and methodologies;
- the training resources needed;
- identification of necessary support;
- evaluation of training in terms of enhanced competence of people;
- measurement of the effectiveness of training and the impact on the organisation.

5.6.3 Section 6.3 – Infrastructure

Section 6.3 Infrastructure	The organisation shall identify, provide and maintain the necessary: • **workspace and associated facilities;** • **equipment, hardware and software;** • **supporting services.**
Proof	How an organisation defines, provides and maintains the infrastructure requirements to ensure product conformity.
Likely documentation	• Policies, procedures and regulatory documents stating organisation and customer requirements; • budget and financial documents; • maintenance plans; • project plans identifying the human resources required to complete the task.

Depending on the size of the organisation and the products that it is offering, the infrastructure (e.g. workspace and facilities) required may include plant, hardware, software, tools and equipment, communication facilities, transport and supporting services.

The organisation should define, provide, develop, implement, evaluate and consider its requirements in terms of product performance, customer satisfaction and controlled improvement.

5.6.4 Section 6.4 – Work environment

Section 6.4 Work environment	The organisation shall identify and manage the work environment required to achieve conformity of product.
Proof	How an organisation defines and organises its work environment.
Likely documentation	• environmental procedures; • project plans; • budgetary processes; • legal processes and procedures.

An organisation's work environment is a combination of human factors (e.g. work methodologies, achievement and involvement opportunities, health and safety rules and guidance, ergonomics etc.) and physical factors (e.g. heat, hygiene, vibration, noise, humidity, pollution, light, cleanliness and air flow). All of these factors influence motivation, satisfaction and performance of people and as they have the potential for enhancing the performance of the organisation, they must be taken into consideration by the organisation when evaluating product conformance and achievement.

5.7 SECTION 7 – PRODUCT REALISATION

This section absorbs most of the 20 elements of the old ISO 9000:1994 standard, including process control, purchasing, handling and storage, and measuring devices.

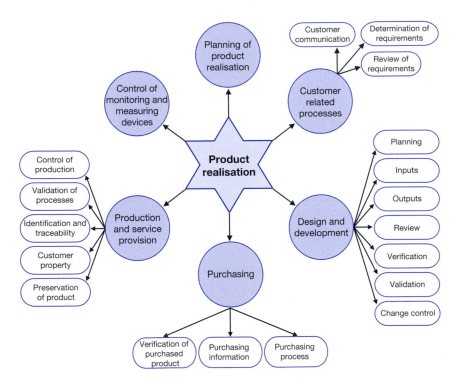

FIGURE 5.6 Product realisation

It is broken down into a number of sub sections that cover the requirements for:

- **Planning of realisation processes** – clearly defining and documenting the processes used to ensure reliable and consistent products (e.g. verification and validation activities, criteria for acceptability and quality records etc.);

- **Customer-related processes** – identifying customer, product, legal and design requirements;
- **Design and development** – controlling the design process (e.g. design inputs, outputs, review, verification, validation and change control);
- **Purchasing** – having documented processes for the selection and control of suppliers and the control of purchases that affect the quality of the finished product or service;
- **Production and service provision** – having documented instructions that control the manufacture of a product or delivery of a service as well as identifying, verifying, protecting and maintaining customer property provided for use or incorporation with the product;
- **Control of monitoring and measuring equipment** – their control, calibration and protection.

5.7.1 Section 7.1 – Planning and realisation

Section 7.1 Planning and realisation	The organisation shall plan and develop the processes needed for product realisation. These shall include: • product, contract quality objectives and requirements; • product processes and their associated documentation, resources and facilities; • verification, validation, monitoring, inspection and test requirements; • criteria for acceptability; • details of the records that are required.
Proof	The availability of documented plans for processes that are required to realise a product – and the sequences in which they occur.
Likely documentation	• process models (flow charts) showing the sequence of activities that an organisation adopts in order to produce a product; • quality plan • documented QPs and WIs to ensure that staff work in accordance with stipulated requirements; • records that prove the results of process control.

Note: A document specifying the processes of the quality management system (including the product realisation processes) and the resources to be applied to a specific product, project or contract can also be referred to as a 'Quality Management Plan'.

A process can be represented as a flow of activities consisting of three separate elements, as shown in Figure 5.7.

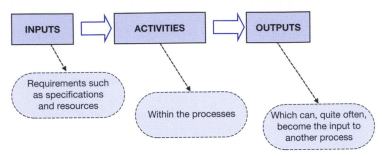

FIGURE 5.7 Planning realisation processes

Realisation processes result in the products of an organisation. Support processes include all the other management processes that are necessary to the organisation, but do not directly add any value. To ensure product realisation, therefore, consideration should be given to desired outputs, process steps, activities, workflow, control measures, training needs, equipment, methodologies, information, materials and other resources. In fact, anything that might have an effect on the output.

Identification of processes

The organisation needs to identify the processes required to realise products that satisfy the requirements of customers and a plan has to be defined to manage these processes, especially their input and output stages. The documentation that describes how the QMS processes are applied for a specific product, project or contract is usually contained in a separate Quality Plan.

In ISO 9001:2008 the organisation is recommended to identify and plan all of the production, installation and servicing processes that directly affect quality. Procedures should be available to ensure that these processes are completed under controlled conditions especially with respect to special processes such as those for defining work to be carried out where no previous procedure exists.

Process planning

Special equipment or environmental conditions; compliance with relevant standards (national, European and international); criteria for workmanship (e.g. written standards, representative samples or illustrations) need to be planned. Procedures must be available to ensure that there is an appropriate system for the maintenance of equipment to ensure a continuing process capability. Records of all these procedures and processes must be maintained, controlled and fully documented.

Indeed, all productive work should be planned and undertaken in accordance with the organisation's procedures and any specific documents that have been detailed for that particular contract (e.g. contract specifications).

5.7.2 Section 7.2 – Customer-related processes

Section 7.2 Customer-related processes	The organisation shall establish procedures for the: • identification of customer requirements; • review of product requirements; • customer communication.
Proof	The identification, review and interaction with customers and customer requirements.
Likely documentation	• Quality Manual; • Quality Plans.

Before entering into a contract situation, an organisation needs to find out exactly what the customer wants in terms of product specification, availability, delivery, support etc. It also needs to confirm that it has sufficient resources to complete the contract and is capable of satisfying the customer's requirements, in full.

Section 7.2.1 – Determination of requirements related to the product

Section 7.2.1 Determination of requirements related to the product	The organisation shall determine: • product requirements specified by the customer; • product requirements not specified by the customer; • regulatory and legal product requirements.
Proof	How an organisation determines and implements customer, product and regulatory requirements.
Likely documentation	• formal contracts; • contract review specifications and procedures; • regulatory and legal product requirements.

On receipt of an order and/or contract, the organisation should thoroughly review it to ensure:

- customer requirements are fully understood and documented;
- the organisation has the ability to meet the customer's requirements;
- any differences between a quotation and the order are identified and resolved.

The customer's requirements can include many elements (e.g. product, options, delivery method, terms of contract, method of payment etc.) and the organisation's ability to meet these requirements will rely on:

- people and their skills, experience and motivation;
- production tools and equipment;
- raw materials;
- stock availability;
- information, drawings and instructions.

Once the organisation has successfully proved to the customer that its QMS is acceptable (see preceding paragraphs), the next step is to commence contract negotiations.

Section 7.2.2 – Review of requirements related to the product

Section 7.2.2 Review of requirements related to the product	Prior to submission of a tender or acceptance of a contract, the organisation shall ensure that: • product requirements have been defined; • contract requirements have been fully established; • all requirements differing from those previously expressed are resolved; • the organisation has the ability to meet defined requirements.
Proof	How an organisation reviews product and customer requirements to check that they can actually do the job.
Likely documentation	• contract review procedures; • project plans showing lines of communication with the customer.

Most organisations will offer their standard products in a catalogue for the customer to make a selection from. These products will be identified against a design specification and normally be accompanied by a picture and/or technical description. Most organisations will also usually be willing to provide system-specific products to suit individual customer requirements. These specialist service requirements will differ from one customer to another (and from one contract to another) and will, therefore, possibly need to be covered by an individual tender, quotation and/or contract.

 Note: In some situations, such as internet sales, a formal review is impractical for each order. Instead the review can cover relevant product information such as catalogues or advertising material.

The contract document

The contract will specify which part of ISO 9001:2008 is to be used, what portions can be deleted and what additional conditions have to be inserted. The contract will also specify the use of quality plans, quality programmes, quality audit plans and other relevant technical specifications.

Once the customer has accepted a proposal, or an order is placed, it should be recorded and reviewed in order to establish that the requirements of the order are adequately defined and documented. Any differences from the proposal should be resolved and the organisation should have established that it is fully capable of meeting and satisfying the customer's requirements. Most of the larger organisations will rely on some form of computerised order processing system to ensure rapid fulfilment of customer orders. Whilst this is a preferred method, it is not an essential ISO 9001:2008 requirement.

Contract signature

Before signature, both parties must thoroughly review the contract and be absolutely sure that:

- the QMS requirements are fully understood;
- all the requirements, clauses and provisions are complete, unambiguous, mutually acceptable (considering the economics and risks in their respective situations);
- the requirements are adequately documented and defined;
- the organisation is able to meet all the contractual requirements.

Where product requirements are changed, the organisation **shall** ensure that the relevant documentation is amended and that the relevant personnel are made aware of the changed requirements. Where the customer provides no documented statement of requirement, the customer requirements must be confirmed before acceptance.

Any requirement differing from those in the original enquiry or tender should be resolved at this stage and it must be confirmed that all the contractual requirements can be met.

Servicing

Most service practices will vary widely between suppliers, distributors and users. If servicing is to be provided, or is required as part of the contract, then the supplier must establish procedures for controlling and authenticating the quality of the service performed and ensure that it meets the required standards.

Section 7.2.3 – Customer communication

Section 7.2.3 Customer communication	The organisation shall have procedures available to: • provide customers with product information; • handle customer enquiries, contracts or order handling including amendments; • cover customer feedback and/or customer complaints.
Proof	How an organisation communicates (i.e. liaises) with its customers, keeps them informed (of product progress etc.) and handles their enquiries and complaints.
Likely documentation	Project plans showing lines of communication with the customer.

The need to maintain open lines of communication with the customer cannot be over-emphasised and procedures should be put in place to ensure that the customers are kept fully up-to-date with the progress of their product/contract and that all customer comments and complaints are dealt with in a speedy and effective manner.

5.7.3 Section 7.3 – Design and development

Section 7.3 Design and development	The organisation shall develop procedures for design and development: • planning; • inputs; • outputs; • review; • verification; • validation; • change control.
Proof	The availability of a process to control design and development stages within an organisation.
Likely documentation	• processes and procedures for design and development; • design plans and development plans.

Design usually means the production of something new, although it can, in many circumstances, be a variation of an existing product or service. It could, therefore, be a new product or it could be a system made up of a variety of products. Either way, a process or design plan needs to be developed that confirms:

- what the customer needs;
- what the boundaries are (e.g. customer requirements);
- how the organisation is going to achieve it;
- how long it will take;
- who will undertake the task;
- who will check and verify the product.

 Note: Design and development is not always applicable to all small businesses, particularly if the organisation just manufactures a product for someone else. In this case, whilst it doesn't actually 'own' the design, it will probably have to develop a process to manufacture the product. In a small business, therefore, design control can be a very challenging process. Methods and controls for ensuring the success of a process need to be flexible and the process should be capable of being tailored to the size of any project.

Section 7.3.1 – Design and development planning

Section 7.3.1 Design and development planning	The organisation shall plan and control the design and development of the product through all processes. This planning shall include: • stage reviews; • verification and validation activities; • identification of responsibilities and authorities; • management of the interfaces between different groups that may be involved; • provision of effective communication; • clarity of responsibilities; • product and planning review procedures.
Proof	How an organisation goes about planning and controlling the design and development of a product.
Likely documentation	• design and development plans; • processes and procedures for design and development; • risk assessment; • job descriptions and responsibilities.

 Note: Design and development review, verification and validation have distinct purposes. They can be conducted and recorded separately or in any combination, as suitable for the product and the organisation.

The best production methods cannot compensate for an inadequate or mediocre design! Quality cannot be an '*add on*'; it has to be designed into a product before it is created and the only way of achieving that is through careful planning and controlled documentation throughout the design stage.

Whether the responsibility for the design of a product rests purely with the supplier, the purchaser or is a joint function, it is essential that the designer is fully aware of the exact requirements of the project and has a sound background knowledge of all the proper standards, information and procedures that will be required.

Functions of the design office

The functions of the design office are extremely important for they will not only influence the maintenance of quality throughout the manufacturing process, but also play a major part in setting the quality level of the final product. If there is no quality control in the drawing office, what chance is there of ever having quality on the shop floor? When the engineers are trying to manufacture something to a set of drawings that have countless mistakes on them, how on earth can they be expected to produce an acceptable item!

 Note: The same applies to the production of a service.

Thus, in close co-operation with the marketing, sales and production sections, the design office prepares business and performance specifications, sets target dates, provides technical specifications, reviews drawings, produces overall schemes to the estimating section, discusses these schemes with the production or manufacturing section and develops the design in conjunction with other supplier functions.

Design criteria

Design criteria will have to be clarified, documented and recorded in the design plan and used for reference throughout the design process. The level of detail on the design plan will vary depending upon the type and size of system, but at all times it should contain sufficient detail to control the design process in accordance with the customer's requirements. Where items require interpretation (e.g. positioning, practicality, maintainability etc.) they will need to be reviewed prior to design finalisation.

Section 7.3.2 – Design and development inputs

Section 7.3.2 Design and development inputs	Product requirement inputs shall be defined, documented and include: • functional and performance requirements; • regulatory and legal requirements; • information derived from previous similar designs; • other requirements essential for design and development.
Proof	How an organisation identifies the requirements to be met by a product.
Likely documentation	Project Plans detailing: • policies; • standards; • specifications and tolerances; • skill requirements; • regulatory and legal requirements; • information derived from previous (similar) designs or developments; • environmental requirements; • health and safety aspects.

Following initial contract approval, details of all the relevant standards, specifications and specific customer requirements that are going to be used during production will have to be identified and steps taken to ensure that they are available. Procedures will have to be established and maintained in order to make certain that the functions of the design office are in agreement with the specified requirements. Any incomplete, ambiguous or conflicting requirements must be resolved at this stage and revisions of the specification reviewed and agreed by both parties.

The design input items are documented on the design plan and reviewed by the designer prior to commencing design process. Where ambiguity exists, the designer will need to clarify this with the customer and document the results.

Design input may consist of:

- national/international codes of practice;
- customer supplied documents, drawings, specifications and samples;
- statutory regulations;
- previous and/or similar designs.

Process inputs for product design and/or development can be divided into three categories:

1. **internal** – policies, standards, specifications, skill and dependability requirements, documentation and data on existing products and outputs from other processes;
2. **external** – customer or marketplace needs and expectations, contractual requirements, interested party specifications, relevant statutory and regulatory requirements, international or national standards and industry codes of practice;
3. **other** – operation, installation and application, storage, handling, maintenance and delivery, physical parameters and environment and disposal requirements.

Staff

All staff should be capable of undertaking their tasks correctly. Guidance concerning tasks may be available from training, experience, detailed instructions, comparison with examples; or a mixture of these. Detailed instructions are only normally required where their absence could adversely affect the quality and acceptability of the product. Other items that need controlling (especially those that ensure that acceptable products are produced) include:

*   tools;
*   production equipment;
*   production environment.

Special processes

ISO 9001:2008 requires an approved control system for '*special processes*' that cannot easily be inspected on completion of the product (e.g. welding). The simplest means to ensure that they are correct each time is by experimenting, and then documenting the successful process (personnel, equipment, materials, sequence and environment). The process can then be repeated each time the product is required. Production of a reject then becomes an improbability but not, unfortunately, an impossibility!

Process control and instructions

As part of a contract, the supplier may be required to identify (and plan) any production and/or installation process that directly affects quality and (in particular) any special process that may only become apparent after production and/or when the product is used. These plans and instructions should be included in any representative samples that are provided.

Marketing implications

It would be totally unproductive for an organisation to make something (e.g. a product or a system), find that it is not required by anyone and consequently be unable to sell it! For this reason most organisations have a separate marketing section (or person) that is responsible for determining the need for a product or service and for estimating the market demand.

Customer requirements

Customer requirements will specify and detail the way the work is to be performed, the standard of workmanship and the degree of quality assurance needed. The marketing section must be capable of translating the user requirements into technical language that will be sufficient to enable the design staff to convert the requirements into practical designs and specifications that enable production, testing, maintenance and servicing to be technically and economically possible.

The customer's technical requirements should include:

- performance and environmental characteristics – specific use, reliability etc.;
- sensory characteristics – style, colour, taste, smell;
- installation configuration or fit;
- standards, specifications and specific user requirements;
- packaging;
- quality assurance.

Market readiness

In order for the management to always be aware of their organisation's market readiness, the marketing section needs to define and review market readiness, field support and production capability.

Components, parts and materials

For manufacturers, although the design office needs to be free to be creative, it is also imperative that they maintain a close relationship with the manufacturing section so that they can be aware of **their** exact requirements, **their** problems and **their** component preferences etc. It can be so easy for the design office to work in splendid isolation, make arbitrary decisions, select components that **they** think are suitable, but then find that the size and tolerance is completely inappropriate for the manufacture of that device.

The design office must have available complete listings of all the appropriate components, parts and materials, their reliability, availability, maintainability, safety, acceptability and adequacy. They must be aware of recent developments, new technologies and advances in both materials and equipment that are available on the market and applicable to that particular product.

Specifications and tolerances

Tolerances should never be unduly restrictive for this could create problems with respect to machine capabilities or require operator skills (and time) far beyond those, which are really essential. Tolerance specifications should also be flexible enough to allow for interchangeability of material where necessary.

Health and safety

As health and safety has now become a mandatory requirement of ISO 9001:2008, designers should be even more aware of the implications of the statutory national, European and international legal requirements for health and safety as they could well place constraints on their designs.

These regulations will not just be concerned with the condition and safety of the material but will also provide measures for overcoming the possibility of danger to persons and property when the material is being used, stored, transported or tested. All aspects of a product or service should be identified with the aim of enhancing product safety and minimising product liability. This can be achieved by:

- identifying the relevant safety standards that make a product or service more effective;
- carrying out design evaluation tests and prototype testing for safety;
- analysing instructions, warnings, labels and maintenance manuals etc. to minimise misinterpretation;
- developing a means of traceability to allow a product to be recalled if safety problems are discovered.

Computers

Nowadays, of course, most design offices have computers to record and store their information on, and they also have available disc retrieval systems that enable regular updating and amendment of data. This updated information is then available for use with standard software programs and Computer Aided Design (CAD) packages to produce accurate information either by list, graph or drawing.

Section 7.3.3 – Design and development outputs

Section 7.3.3 Design and development outputs	The organisation shall ensure that: • design output meets design input requirements; • sufficient information is available for production and service operations; • product acceptance criteria have been met; • the characteristics of the product that are essential to its safe and proper use have been defined.
Proof	How an organisation ensures that the design output meets the design input requirements.
Likely documentation	• drawings; • schematics; • schedules; • system specifications; • system descriptions, etc.

All documentation associated with the design output (e.g. drawings, schematics, schedules, system specifications, system descriptions etc.) needs to:

- be produced in accordance with agreed customer requirements;
- be reviewed (by another designer who has not been associated with the initial design) to ensure that it meets the design input;
- identify all of the characteristics which are critical to the effective operation of the designed system;
- be reviewed and approved by the customer prior to use.

Design office responsibilities

Another responsibility of the design office is to maintain a link with the production department so that they can assist in the analysis of failures, swiftly produce solutions and forestall costly work stoppages. This is often referred to as 'design output' and is covered by the activities of the 'internal audit' system that is required to ensure that the design output meets the specified requirements of the design input through design control methods such as:

- undertaking qualification tests and demonstrations;
- comparing the new design with a similar proven design;
- ensuring that it conforms to appropriate regulatory (for example safety) requirements, whether or not these have been stated in the input documentation;
- identifying those characteristics of the design that are crucial and establishing that these characteristics meet the design input criteria.

Examples of the output from design and/or development activities include:

- product specifications;
- training requirements;
- methodologies;
- purchase requirements;
- acceptance criteria.

Inspection and test status

Once products have been inspected, there needs to be a method for easily identifying them as being either acceptable or unacceptable. This can be achieved in many ways, including:

- marking;
- stamping;
- labelling;
- segregating;
- associated documents;
- test reports;
- physical location.

Note: Information for production and service provision can include details for the preservation of product.

Section 7.3.4 – Design and development review

Section 7.3.4 Design and development review	The organisation shall complete systematic reviews to: • evaluate the ability of the product to fulfil requirements; • identify problems; • propose follow-up actions.
Proof	How an organisation ensures that it is capable of meeting product requirements.
Likely documentation	• design process review procedures; • procedures detailing how changes are made to designs and how they are approved, recorded and distributed; • management reviews and audit procedures; • records.

Design process control

The process of translating the design input into design and developed output is primarily controlled by the design review, which ensures that:

• adherence to contractual and statutory requirements has been fully met;
• all alternative design concepts and items have been considered;
• all potential design problems have been identified and evaluated;
• all calculations have been correctly performed and re-checked;
• the suitability of the designed item/system with respect to environmental and operating conditions has been considered;
• the compatibility with existing (or proposed) items or systems is assured;
• the designed item or system is maintainable;
• all necessary working documents (e.g. calculations, notes, sketches etc.) accompany the design output documentation.

The majority of design activities can be verified during the design process review and a record maintained of all the items that have been considered together with their results. Whenever possible the use of computers is recommended for verifying designs and currently there are many proprietary brands being marketed.

Final verification of the design is usually completed during final inspection and test and the designer is responsible for specifying and supplying any inspections or tests that are required during system installation to practically verify the design.

Design process review

When designing and/or developing products or processes, as well as ensuring that the needs of all interested parties are satisfied, the organisation will have to take into consideration life cycle costs, environmental requirements, Reliability, Availability, Maintainability and Safety (RAMS) requirements and ergonomic considerations.

A risk assessment (using risk assessment tools such as Failure Mode and Effects Analysis (FMEA), Fault Tree Analysis (FTA), reliability assessment, simulation techniques etc.) will be required to assess the potential for, and the effect of, possible failures in products and/or processes and the results used to define and implement preventive actions to mitigate identified risks.

Periodic reviews

Periodic reviews should be completed throughout the design process (for example, preliminary, intermediate and final) with the aim of:

- confirming design and/or development objectives are being met;
- evaluating potential hazards and/or modes of failure found in product use;
- evaluating life-cycle product performance data;
- evaluating the impact of the product on the environment;
- ensuring all other viable paths have been considered;
- confirming that all statutory requirements have been considered and are complied with;
- ensuring that there is adequate supporting documentation available to define the design and how the product or service is to be used and maintained.

The tests should include:

- the evaluation of the performance, durability, safety, reliability and maintainability of the product under expected storage and operational conditions;
- inspection procedures to verify that all design features are as they were originally intended and that all authorised design changes have been carried out and that these have been properly recorded;
- validation of computer systems and associated software.

 Note: Participants in such reviews should include representatives of functions concerned with the design and/or development stage(s) being reviewed and the results of the reviews and subsequent follow-up actions need to be recorded.

Section 7.3.5 – Design and development verification

Section 7.3.5 Design and development verification	The organisation shall verify that: • design output meets the design and development inputs; • the results of the verification have been recorded.
Proof	How an organisation ensures that product specifications are fulfilled and that the finalised product meets the original input requirements.
Likely documentation	• design process review procedures; • procedures for periodic reviews; • records.

ISO 9001:2008 requires an organisation to verify that design outputs meet the design input specifications and that they meet the needs of the customer. In particular, verification of engineering designs (prior to construction, installation or application) software outputs (prior to installation or use) and direct customer services (prior to their widespread introduction) can prove very beneficial to an organisation! The aim should be to generate sufficient data through these verification activities to enable design and development methodologies and decisions to be reviewed.

Design verification and review is another form of periodic evaluation and uses one of the following methods:

- **alternative calculations** – to verify the precision of the original calculations and their analysis;
- **comparison** – with other similar designs;
- **third-party evaluation** – to verify that the original calculations and/or other design activities have been correctly carried out;
- **feedback** – from previous designs and experience;
- **information** – gained during manufacture, assembly, installation, commissioning, servicing and field use;
- **customer** – feedback (i.e. asking the customer);
- **testing** – by model or prototype.

Section 7.3.6 – Design and development validation

Section 7.3.6 Design and development validation	The organisation shall validate that the: • product is capable of meeting the requirements for its intended use; • results of the validation have been recorded.
Proof	How an organisation ensures that the design is actually capable of doing the intended job.
Likely documentation	• procedures for in-process inspection and testing; • final inspection and test procedures; • records.

As design work is normally performed in accordance with the customer's instructions, it is sometimes difficult for an organisation to validate the end product. In these situations, the organisation will normally only be required to validate that the design meets the customer's requirements. Installed systems (hardware and software) will then need to be inspected and tested to ensure compliance and customer satisfaction and acceptance and it is only **then** that the design can be finally validated.

In-process inspection and testing

Items that have been produced in accordance with an organisation's documented processes generally pass through a number of stages. Rather than leaving inspection and testing to when the last stage has been completed, it is more cost effective to check the items as they progress through the various stages of their production and/or installation. These are called '*in-process inspections*' and their objective is to identify rejects and inadequate processes as they happen and not at the end of a job lot.

The organisation must, therefore, establish effective stages of inspection, define the type of inspection to be performed and clarify the acceptance/rejection criteria. All the in-process inspections should be documented, and any faulty items must be identified and segregated.

Final inspection and testing

Once again, the principle of final inspection is similar to an in-process inspection, i.e. to identify acceptable products from faulty products, record the results and confirm the acceptance/rejection decision.

The tests will normally include the:

• evaluation of the performance, durability, safety, reliability and maintainability of the product under expected storage and operational conditions;

- inspection procedures to verify that all design features are as they were originally intended and that all authorised design changes have been carried out and that these have been properly recorded;
- validation of computer systems and associated software.

Note: Wherever applicable, validation should be completed prior to the delivery or implementation of the product. If this isn't possible or is impractical, then partial validation should be performed to the extent applicable.

Section 7.3.7 – Control of design and development changes

Section 7.3.7 Control of design and development changes	The organisation shall: • identify, document and control all design and development changes; • evaluate the effect of these changes; • verify, validate and approve these changes before implementation.
Proof	How changes to a design are identified, evaluated, recorded and approved.
Likely documentation	• change control procedures; • design process review procedures; • management reviews and audit procedures; • records.

Throughout the design and development phase, there are likely to be a number of changes, alterations, modifications and improvements made to the design of the product and its development processes. It is essential that:

- these are identified, documented and controlled;
- the effect of the changes on constituent parts and delivered products is evaluated;
- the changes are verified, validated and approved before implementation.

All changes to the design criteria (input and/or output) should be subject to strict documentation control and should be reviewed and verified by the designer and/or the customer, prior to incorporation within the design. All changes need to be subject to an agreed change control procedure to ensure that the changes have been fully evaluated, agreed (or concessions made) and that only the latest versions of design documents are available in work places. It is essential that the results of the review of changes and subsequent follow up actions are always documented.

It is essential that all of the design documentation, drawings and notes etc. are retained in a design project file so that it can be made immediately available and can be produced for reviews etc. The design output should be reviewed and approved by top management before being provided to the customer for approval and use.

5.7.4 Section 7.4 – Purchasing

Section 7.4 Purchasing	The organisation shall have documented procedures for: • purchasing control; • purchasing information; • verification of purchased product.
Proof	How an organisation controls the purchase of materials, products and services from suppliers and third parties.
Likely documentation	• documented procedures for the evaluation of suppliers; • documented procedures for the evaluation of a purchased product or service.

Note: Supplier selection and verification can be an absolute minefield for small businesses and the chosen process needs careful consideration – particularly with respect to reliability, availability and mutual respect.

When an organisation has to purchase products, materials and/or services from suppliers who have not been previously specified in a contract or by a customer, they are normally selected on their ability to meet the organisation's requirements given due consideration to the quality, statutory obligations, timescale and cost. A list of approved suppliers and subcontractors needs to be maintained by the organisation and this should contain the following information:

- previous performance in supplying to similar specifications and requirements;
- stocking of high-volume standard items conforming to relevant national and/or international standards (or supplied with a statement of conformity);
- compliance with an approved third-party product or quality registration scheme;
- recommendation by other similar purchasers or manufacturers of equipment;
- trial order and evaluation of performance.

Purchasing process

The organisation should have available a process to ensure appropriate selection, evaluation and control of all purchased products. All supplies and subcontracts should be subject to an authorised purchase order that provides full details of the type and extent of supply.

Section 7.4.1 – Purchasing process

Section 7.4.1 Purchasing process	The organisation shall have procedures to: • ensure purchased product conforms to purchase requirements; • evaluate, re-evaluate and select suppliers.
Proof	The controls that an organisation has in place to ensure purchased products and services are of an acceptable standard.
Likely documentation	• approved list of suppliers; • supplier evaluations; • purchasing procedures; • purchase orders.

Purchasing processes and procedures

The organisation is responsible for producing purchasing processes and procedures that include:

- identification of requirements;
- selection of suppliers;
- quotations and tenders;
- purchase price;
- order forms;
- verification of purchased products;
- non-conforming purchased products;
- contract administration and associated purchase documentation;
- supplier control and development;
- risk assessment.

Suppliers

Having identified its suppliers (usually selected from previous experience, past history, test results on similar projects or published experience from other users) an organisation should establish a system by which the supplier/subcontractor is clearly advised exactly what is required, and by when. This is often achieved by use of a purchase order system.

Note: The organisation shall evaluate and select suppliers based on their ability to supply product in accordance with the organisation's requirements. Criteria for selection, evaluation and re-evaluation shall be established and records of the results of evaluations and any necessary actions arising from the evaluation shall be maintained.

Subcontractors

If a supplier uses subcontractors, it is important that they can be relied on to produce a quality product, have the ability to meet subcontractual requirements, (including quality assurance) and do not reduce the quality of the final product. The supplier (who is normally referred to as the prime contractor) must ensure that all items purchased from a subcontractor are covered by a purchasing document. This document will contain details of the product ordered, type, class, style, grade and the title/number/issue of the relevant standard, specification, drawing, inspection instruction etc. that it must conform to. The prime contractor should ensure that subcontractors have their own QMS and that the purchased product or service is satisfactory.

Section 7.4.2 – Purchasing information

Section 7.4.2 Purchasing information	Purchasing documents shall describe: • the product to be purchased; • requirements for approval or qualification of product, service, procedure; • process, equipment and personnel; • QMS requirements.
Proof	The details that need to be provided by an organisation when placing an order with a supplier.
Likely documentation	• approved list of suppliers; • supplier evaluations; • purchasing procedures; • purchase orders; • stock control procedures.

A process should be established to ensure that purchasing documents contain sufficient details about:

- the product to be purchased;
- the necessary approval and qualification requirements (i.e. procedures, processes etc.) for product, equipment and personnel;
- the QMS requirements;
- agreement on quality assurance – whether the prime contractor can completely rely on the subcontractor's quality assurance scheme or whether some (or all)

of the product will have to be tested by the prime contractor or via a third party;

- agreement on verification methods by the purchaser at source or on delivery; whether this should be by sample or on a 100% basis; whether this inspection should be at the prime contractor's or the subcontractor's premises;
- settlement of quality disputes – who, how, when and where.

Section 7.4.3 – Verification of purchased product

Section 7.4.3 Verification of purchased product	The organisation shall establish procedures to verify that the purchased product meets specified purchase requirements.
Proof	The controls that an organisation has in place to ensure that products and services provided by suppliers meet their original requirements.
Likely	• approved list of suppliers; • supplier evaluations; • purchasing procedures; • purchase orders; • stock control procedures.

It is essential that all goods and services received from a third party are checked to confirm that they are those that were ordered, the delivery is on time and that they are of good quality. The amount of inspection will depend on how critical the supplied goods and service is to the end product and the amount of inspection should be compatible with the risk or inconvenience if the item is later found to be faulty.

A consumable item (e.g. low-cost items such as light bulbs, duplicating paper etc.) are normally only checked for correct identity, correct quantity and any signs of damage. It would be unwise to perform detailed inspections on these items which, if found to be faulty, could be replaced within a short time at little comparative expense. Conversely, detailed inspections should always be performed on major components, as, if they are faulty, the rectification could be expensive and time-consuming.

It should also be appreciated that the worst possible time to identify an item as a reject is when it is handed over to the final customer. If the product (or its components) can be checked at earlier stages, it is time well spent.

In-inspection

Receiving or in-inspection should be documented to confirm that it has taken place and that the goods or services are deemed fit for use in the next stage of the process.

This may often be by completing a goods received note, or marking the supplier's delivery note. The delivery should also be checked against the purchase order to ensure that it is complete. Should the inspection identify the delivery as reject, the items should be segregated, labelled or identified to avoid them being used in error.

Goods inwards

In industry there are very few suppliers who are not actually purchasers themselves. Large and small companies have to obtain consumables, components and sometimes complete assemblies from a subcontractor at some stage or other and therefore the quality of the supplier's final product, to a considerable degree, depends on the quality of the subcontractor's goods.

To be certain that the items purchased, or obtained, from a third party are up to the required standard, the prime contractor will have to set up some kind of quality inspection, unless that is, the supplier him- or herself operates a fully satisfactory and recognised QMS.

The term '*goods inwards*' describes the procedures designed to cover this type of inspection and it is a very important quality assurance function.

Inspection and testing

It is the prime contractor's responsibility to ensure that inspection and tests are always performed on all incoming goods and that no incoming material is used or processed until it has been inspected or otherwise verified to confirm that it is up to the specified requirements.

The prime contractor will have to show in his or her Quality Plan exactly how this is to be achieved and precisely what inspections and tests are to be carried out to confirm quality. It is then up to the purchaser to decide if this is enough or whether he or she would like to see additional or supplementary inspections carried out. The amount of inspection will, of course, vary according to the degree of control exercised by the subcontractor, his or her past performance and records – for example, is he or she assessed to ISO 9001:2008?

This inspection should complement and be in addition to the existing quality control procedures and must be clearly laid down. Records should detail who actually carried out the inspection that released the product, the assembly line and despatch services. The inspection must:

- consider that all incoming material where quality is unproved should remain suspect until proven as satisfactory;
- ensure that written control procedures are available to establish a product has:
  o not been inspected;
  o been inspected and approved or;
  o been inspected and rejected;
- ensure that any defective material that is received from a third party is subject to the same controls as defective material that may occur in the company's own production.

Inspection procedures

Ineffective or incomplete control usually leads to costly defects. The prime contractor must, therefore, ensure that all processes are carried out under strictly controlled conditions. These conditions should be covered by work instructions that define the process, suitable equipment and if a special working environment is required.

Workmanship criteria will have to be fully documented using either written standards, photographs, sketches or representative samples.

Control of quality

The choice of how quality is controlled and the type of inspection is normally left up to the prime contractor who may decide on a stage inspection, sampling inspection, final inspection or perhaps even a combination of all methods as being more appropriate. For manufacturers, the method chosen should cover every phase of manufacture, assembly and installation and the instructions should include the following details:

- identification of material;
- detailed operations to be performed;
- tools or test equipment required;
- requirements for operational checks, calibration and equipment availability;
- methods of inspection;
- environmental conditions to be maintained during operation or inspection;
- criteria for passing or failing the test;
- sampling techniques and related decision criteria if applicable.

Non-compliance

Inspection and testing is normally carried out on completion of installation and maintenance activities, with results being documented. If items fail to comply with agreed contract criteria, then they should either be repaired, replaced or identified for subsequent evaluation and decision. All repaired items need to be re-inspected to ensure their acceptability prior to being used.

5.7.5 Section 7.5 – Production and service provision

Section 7.5 Production and service provision	The organisation shall have procedures for the control of: • production and service operations; • validation of processes; • identification and traceability; • customer property; • preservation of product.

Proof	The availability of a process to cover all production and service operations.
Likely documentation	• processes; • Quality Procedures; • Work Instructions.

A documented process needs to be agreed and implemented by the organisation to cover all production and service operations.

Section 7.5.1 – Control of production and service provision

Section 7.5.1 Control of production and service provision	The organisation shall have the following available: • information concerning product characteristics; • appropriate work instructions; • suitable production equipment; • measuring and monitoring devices and facilities; • processes to cover the release, delivery and post-delivery activities.
Proof	The availability of all relevant information concerning control production and service operations.
Likely documentation	• procedures; • project plans; • resources.

The organisation should identify the requirements for product realisation and ensure that it has:

• the ability to comply with contractual requirements;
• the ability to train and have available competent people;
• a viable system for communication;
• a process for problem prevention.

Section 7.5.2 – Validation of processes for production and service provisions

Section 7.5.2 Validation of processes for production and service provisions	The organisation shall define validation arrangements for: • review and approval of processes; • approval of equipment; • qualification of personnel; • use of defined methodologies and procedures; • requirements for records; • re-validation.
Proof	How an organisation identifies processes which cannot be verified by subsequent monitoring/testing/inspection (including the validation of these processes to demonstrate their effectiveness).
Likely documentation	• processes; • Quality Procedures; • Work Instructions.

Where the resulting output cannot be verified by subsequent measurement or monitoring (and where deficiencies may become apparent **only** after the product is in use or the service has been delivered), the organisation needs to validate any production and/or service processes to demonstrate the ability of the processes to achieve their planned results.

The organisation should have procedures available to ensure that these processes are completed under controlled conditions especially with respect to special processes, and for defining work to be carried out where no previous procedure exists.

Note:
Design verification is a process whose purpose is to examine design outputs and to use objective evidence to confirm that outputs meet design input requirements. Your purpose here is to see whether your design outputs meet your organisation's design goals. On the other hand . . .

Design validation is a process whose purpose is to examine products and to use objective evidence to confirm that these products meet customer needs and expectations. Your purpose here is to see whether your product does what your customer or user wants it to do under real-world conditions.

Section 7.5.3 – Identification and traceability

Section 7.5.3 Identification and traceability	The organisation shall have procedures available for: • identification of product; • product status; • traceability.
Proof	How the status of a product is identified during all stages of its production/delivery.
Likely documentation	Documented: • processes; • Quality Procedures; • Work Instructions.

ISO 9001:2008 recommends organisations maintain documented procedures for identifying products (hardware, software, documents and/or data) throughout all stages of production, delivery, receipt and installation. This process should be documented and reviewed for its continued applicability on a regular basis.

If required, organisations can also establish a system for identifying individual products or batches.

All received goods should be inspected, their status defined and stored until required for use. Non-conforming items should be placed in a reject area or marked as 'reject for review'. The status of work in progress should be clearly indicated by markings or associated documentation recording the inspections undertaken and their acceptability.

 Note: In some industry sectors, configuration management is a means by which identification and traceability are maintained.

Section 7.5.4 – Customer property

Section 7.5.4 Customer property	The organisation shall: • retain records of all customer provided material; • protect and maintain all customer provided property.
Proof	How an organisation looks after property that has been provided by a customer.
Likely documentation	A documented procedure for the control of customer property.

Customer supplied products are goods which have been provided by the customer (or his/her agent), normally free of charge, for incorporation into the product. The existence of *'free issue'* products will only be relevant to certain organisations. However, it should be remembered that items returned to the organisation for repair or rectification are also within this category.

Goods received from customers need to be visually inspected at the receipt stage and any undeclared non-conformance immediately reported to the customer.

The organisation should ensure that all property belonging to the customer (including its intellectual or property rights) is protected and that care is taken to ensure that it is well maintained, used in accordance with the supplier's instructions and safeguarded at all times.

Should the items become lost, damaged or unserviceable while in the organisation's control, the problem should be recorded and the customer advised.

Purchaser supplied product

In some circumstances material, sub assemblies or components may have been supplied to the organisation by the purchaser as part of the contract. In these cases it is important that the organisation has a Goods Inwards inspection process to assure themselves that the item they are receiving is the correct one, has not been damaged in transit and is suitable for its purpose.

 'Customer property' can sometimes include *'intellectual property'*!

Section 7.5.5 – Preservation of product

Section 7.5.5 Preservation of internal product	The organisation shall have procedures available for identifying, handling, packaging, storing and protecting products during processing and delivery to their intended destination.
Proof	How an organisation looks after its own products.
Likely documentation	• product approval procedures; • procedures which ensure the safety and protection of products.

Part numbers and labels

A manufacturer's/supplier's part number or description label should identify any material or equipment that cannot be obviously identified. This identification can be on the packaging or on the item itself and should remain in place for as long as possible provided it does not hamper effective use of the item. If items have a serial number then this number should also be recorded.

Product protection

All materials and goods that are received, whether they are the property of the organisation or others, should, as far as practicable, be protected and their quality preserved until such time as they are transferred to a customer, disposed of to a third party or utilised. The overall objective should be to prevent deterioration and damage whilst in storage, or in the process of transportation, installation, commissioning and/or maintenance. Written instructions and procedures for the handling, identification and storage of documentation, materials, components, parts, sub assemblies and completed items will have to be established and made available. These instructions must contain details of quarantine areas or bonded stores and how they should be used, together with methods of cleaning, preserving and packaging.

Documented procedures

As previously mentioned, ISO 9001:2008 recommends that organisations maintain documented procedures for identifying products (e.g. hardware, software, documents and/or data) throughout all stages of production, delivery, receipt and installation. If required, organisations can also establish a system for identifying individual products or batches and consider the need for any special requirements (i.e. associated with software, electronic media, hazardous materials, specialist personnel and products or materials) arising from the nature of the product which are unique or irreplaceable.

In some cases (e.g. toxic contamination), in order to prevent damage and deterioration of the product (and harm to the product user!), it might even be necessary to refer to another document, regulation or standard to ensure that the items are correctly handled, stored and delivered.

Storage

All QMS standards emphasise the importance of having satisfactory storage facilities and stipulate that these must be available for **all** materials, consumables, components, sub assemblies or completed articles. In a similar manner, the standards specify that materials should always be properly stored, segregated, handled and protected during production so as to maintain their suitability.

The supplier will thus have to provide secure storage areas or stock rooms so that the materials can be isolated and protected (e.g. from harmful environments) pending use or shipment. Storage areas will have to be protected and kept tidy and the supplier must ensure that material only leaves the storage areas when it has been properly authorised.

Procedures for rotation of stock will need to be established and special consideration should always be given to items with limited shelf life and items that might require special protection during transit or storage. This is usually referred to as deterioration control. Where corrosive or toxic materials are stored in quantity, these items must be kept in a separate storage area.

Note: although the above explanation primarily concerns a manufactured item, storage facilities nevertheless still have to be considered for documents and/or software.

Delivery

The supplier must make arrangements to ensure that the quality of the product is protected following final inspection and test. Where contractually specified, this protection can even be extended to include delivery to the final destination. Some of the factors that should be considered by suppliers when delivering their product to the purchaser are:

- the nature of the material;
- the type(s) of transport to be used;
- environmental conditions during transit;
- time in transit;
- handling methods en route;
- storage en route and at the destination.

5.7.6 Section 7.6 – Control of measuring and monitoring equipment

Section 7.6 Control of measuring and monitoring devices	The organisation shall ensure that all measuring and monitoring equipment are: • calibrated and adjusted periodically or prior to use; • traceable to international or national standards; • safeguarded from adjustments that would invalidate the calibration; • protected from damage and deterioration during handling, maintenance and storage.
Proof	The controls that an organisation has in place to ensure that equipment (including software) used for proving conformance to specified requirements is properly maintained.
Likely documentation	• equipment records of maintenance and calibration; • Work Instructions.

Where applicable, the control of measuring and test equipment (whether owned by the supplier, on loan, hired or provided by the purchaser), should always include a check that the equipment is exactly what is required, has been initially calibrated before use, operates within the required tolerances, is regularly recalibrated and that facilities exist (either within the organisation or via a third party) to adjust, repair or recalibrate as necessary.

In particular, measuring and monitoring devices that are used to verify process outputs against specified requirements need to be maintained and calibrated against national and international standards. The results of all calibrations carried out must be retained and the validity of previous results re-assessed if they are subsequently found to be out of calibration.

All production and measuring equipment that is held needs to be well maintained, in good condition and capable of safe and effective operation within a specified tolerance of accuracy. Test and measuring equipment should be regularly inspected and/or calibrated to ensure that it is capable of accurate operation, by comparison with external sources traceable back to national standards. Any electrostatic protection equipment that is utilised when handling sensitive components should be regularly checked to ensure that it remains fully functional.

Control of inspection, measuring and test equipment

All production equipment including machinery jigs, fixtures, tools, templates, patterns and gauges should always be stored correctly and satisfactorily protected between use to ensure its bias and precision. It should be verified or recalibrated at appropriate intervals.

 Special attention should be paid to computers if they are used in controlling processes and particularly to the maintenance and accreditation of any related software.

Software

Software used for measuring and monitoring of specified requirements should be validated prior to use.

 Note: also see ISO 10012:2003 Measurement management systems. Requirements for measurement processes and measuring equipment.

Calibration

Without exception, all measuring instruments can be subject to damage, deterioration or just general wear and tear when they are in regular use in workshops and factories. The organisation's QMS should take account of this fact and ensure that **all** test equipment is regularly calibrated against a known working standard held by the manufacturer.

Of course, calibrating against a standard is pretty pointless if that particular standard cannot be relied upon and so the 'workshop standard' **must** also be calibrated, on a regular basis, at either a recognised calibration centre or at the UK Physical Laboratory (or similar) against one of the national standards.

The supplier's QMS will thus have to make allowances for:

- the calibration and adjustment of all inspection, measuring and test equipment that can affect product quality;
- the documentation and maintenance of calibration procedures and records;
- the regular inspection of all measuring or test equipment to ensure that it is capable of the accuracy and precision that is required;
- the environmental conditions being suitable for the calibrations, inspections, measurements and tests to be completed.

The accuracy of the instrument will depend very much on what items it is going to be used to test, the frequency of use of the test instrument, industry standards of acceptability etc., and the organisation will have to decide on the maximum tolerance of accuracy for each item of test equipment.

Calibration methods

There are various possibilities, such as:

- send all working equipment to an external calibration laboratory;
- send one of each item (i.e. a 'workshop standard') to a calibration laboratory, then sub calibrate each working item against the workshop standard;
- testing by attributes – i.e. take a known 'faulty' product, and a known 'good' product; and then test each one to ensure that the test equipment can identify the faulty and good product correctly.

Calibration frequency

The calibration frequency depends on how much the instrument is used, its ability to retain its accuracy and how critical the items being tested are. Infrequently used instruments are often only calibrated prior to their use whilst frequently used items would normally be checked and re-calibrated at regular intervals depending, again, on product criticality, cost, availability etc. Normally 12 months is considered as about the maximum calibration interval.

Calibration ideals

Each instrument should be uniquely identified, allowing it to be traced.

- The calibration results should be clearly indicated on the instrument.
- The calibration results should be retained for reference.
- The instrument should be labelled to show the next 'calibration due' date to easily avoid its use outside the period of confidence.
- Any means of adjusting the calibration should be sealed, allowing easy identification if it has been tampered with (e.g. a label across the joint of the casing).
- If the instrument is found to be outside its tolerance of accuracy, any items previously tested with the instrument must be regarded as suspect. In these

circumstances, it would be wise to review the test results obtained from the individual instrument. This could be achieved by compensating for the extent of inaccuracy to decide if the acceptability of the item would be reversed.

 Note: Records of the results of calibration and verification shall be maintained.

5.8 SECTION 8 – MEASUREMENT, ANALYSIS AND IMPROVEMENT

This part of the standard absorbs the former inspection and measurement control sections of ISO 9001:1994. It includes requirements for:

- **General** – defining the requirements for measurement analysis and improvement (including statistical analysis);
- **Monitoring and measurement** – monitoring customer satisfaction/ dissatisfaction as a measurement and improvement of the QMS. Conducting periodic internal audits to confirm continued conformity with ISO 9001:2008 and defining processes to monitor the performance of the QMS and the products and services delivered by the organisation;
- **Control of non-conforming product** – controlling non-conformity and its rectification;
- **Analysis of data** – collecting and analysing statistical data obtained from the organisation's measuring and monitoring activities to find areas of improvement;
- **Improvement** – planning for continual improvement of the QMS, including having available procedures to address corrective and preventive action.

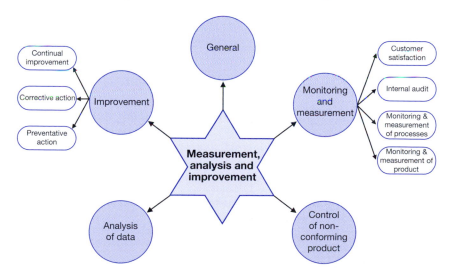

FIGURE 5.8 Measurement, analysis and improvement

5.8.1 Section 8.1 – General

Section 8.1 General	The organisation shall define the activities needed to measure and monitor: • product conformity; • product improvement.
Proof	Documented procedures to ensure product conformity and product improvement.
Likely documentation	Procedures for: • product conformity; • product improvement; • statistical process review.

Under ISO 9001:2008 the organisation is required to determine and implement procedures to ensure product and QMS conformity and improvement.

The use of statistical techniques can help to understand the variability of a product and in so doing, help organisations to solve problems and improve efficiency. Basically, statistical techniques:

- make better use of available data to assist in decision making;
- help to measure, describe, analyse, interpret and model variability;
- help to provide a better understanding of the nature, extent and causes of variability;
- help to solve and even prevent problems that may result from such variability;
- promote continual improvement.

Details of the application of statistical techniques are given in ISO TR 10017:2003 – *Guidance on Statistical Techniques for ISO 9001:2000*.

5.8.2 Section 8.2 – Monitoring and measurement

Section 8.2 Monitoring and measurement	The organisation shall have procedures available to: • ensure customer satisfaction; • control internal audits; • ensure effective monitoring and measurement of product and processes.
Proof	The analysis of customer satisfaction and the control of products and processes.
Likely documentation	Procedures for inspection and measurement.

For an organisation to measure customer satisfaction, evaluate its product and the efficiency of its processes, it needs to establish a method to monitor, measure, collect, analyse and record the relevant data using statistical or other appropriate techniques such as:

- customer satisfaction measurement;
- internal audits;
- financial measurements;
- self-assessment methodologies.

Collection of this data should not be purely for the accumulation of information. This process should always be aimed at progressive improvement of the organisation's QMS. The results of this analysis will then be one of the inputs to the management review process.

Section 8.2.1 – Customer satisfaction

Section 8.2.1 Customer satisfaction	The organisation shall monitor customer satisfaction and/or dissatisfaction.
Proof	The processes used to establish whether a customer is satisfied with a product.
Likely documentation	Procedures for: • customer feedback; • change control; • customer complaints.

The organisation should establish processes to gather, analyse and make effective use of all customer-related information as one of the measurements of performance of its QMS. This information can come from many sources such as:

- customer requirements and contract information;
- feedback from the delivery of a product;
- market needs;
- service delivery data;
- information relating to competition.

The organisation's process should address conformance to requirements, meeting the needs and expectations of customers, price and delivery of product and overall customer satisfaction. Examples of sources of information on customer satisfaction include:

- customer complaints;
- direct communication with customers;

- questionnaires and surveys;
- focus groups;
- reports from consumer organisations;
- reports in various media;
- sector studies.

Section 8.2.2 – Internal audit

'A documented procedure shall be established to define the responsibilities and requirements for planning and conducting audits, establishing records and reporting results. Records of the audits and their results shall be maintained.'

 This is mandatory ISO 9001:2008 requirement!

Section 8.2.2 Internal audit	The organisation shall plan and conduct periodic internal audits to determine whether the QMS: • continues to conform to the requirements of ISO 9001:2008; • has been effectively implemented and maintained. The organisation shall plan the audit programme taking into account: • the status and importance of the activities and areas to be audited; • the results of previous audits. The organisation shall have a documented procedure which includes: • the responsibilities and requirements for conducting audits; • the scope, frequency, methodologies used; • the method for recording results and reporting to management.
Proof	The in-house checks made to determine if the QMS is: • functioning properly; • continues to comply with the requirements of ISO 9001:2008.
Likely documentation	• audit procedures; • audit schedules; • audit plans, check sheets and records.

An organisation **shall** establish an internal audit process to assess the strengths and weaknesses of its QMS, to identify potential danger spots, eliminate wastage and verify that corrective action has been successfully achieved. The internal audit process should also be used to review the efficiency and effectiveness of other organisational activities and support processes including:

- existence of adequate documentation;
- effective implementation of processes;
- identification of non-conformance;
- documentation of results;
- competence of personnel;
- opportunities for improvement;
- capability of processes;
- use of statistical techniques;
- use of information technology;
- analysis of quality cost data;
- assigned responsibilities and authorities;
- performance results and expectations;
- adequacy and accuracy of performance measurement;
- improvement activities;
- relationships with interested parties, including internal customers.

To be effective, an '*internal audit*' must be completed by trained personnel and in the larger organisation, by members of the quality control staff – provided, that is, that they are not responsible for the quality of that particular product and they are **not** associated with the activity being audited. In addition to documenting non-conformances, internal audits should also indicate areas for improvement (with recommendations), as well as areas of outstanding performance.

There are three basic types of audit to choose from:

- **First-party audits** – conducted by, or on behalf of, the organisation itself for **internal** purposes and can form the basis for an organisation's self-declaration of conformity.
- **Second-party audits** – conducted by customers of the organisation or by other persons on behalf of the customer (these are classified as **external** audits).
- **Third-party audits** – conducted by **external** independent audit service organisations. Such organisations (normally accredited by a Notified Body) provide certification or registration of conformity with requirements such as those of ISO 9001:2008.

It is essential that management take timely corrective action on all deficiencies found during the audit. Follow-up actions should include the verification of the implementation of corrective action, and the reporting of verification results.

Financial approach

As part of their overall management system, organisations should establish a methodology for linking financial considerations with the QMS. This could include:

- prevention, appraisal and failure costs analysis;
- costs of conformance and non-conformance;
- life-cycle approach.

Self-assessment

Organisations should consider establishing and implementing a self-assessment process. The range and depth of the assessment should be planned in relation to the organisation's objectives and priorities.

Self-assessment can be a very useful tool to evaluate improvement and so (for the assistance of small businesses) I have also included a section in this book (see Chapter 7) on 'self assessment' which includes check sheets against the requirements of ISO 9001:2008 and examples of Stage Audit checklists.

Section 8.2.3 – Monitoring and measurement of processes

Section 8.2.3 Monitoring and measurement of processes	The organisation shall measure and monitor QMS processes to ensure they: • meet customer requirements; • satisfy their intended purpose.
Proof	The methods used to check if processes continue to meet their intended purpose.
Likely documentation	• audit schedules, plans, check sheets and records; • processes for product assessment, failure cost analysis, conformity, non-conformity, life cycle approach, self-assessment; • compliance with environmental and safety policies, laws, regulations and standards; • procedures for testing and monitoring processes.

The organisation should identify measurement methodologies, perform measurements to evaluate their process performance and use the results obtained to improve the product realisation process. Examples where process performance measurements can be used to improve processes include:

- timeliness;
- dependability;

- reaction time of processes and people to special internal and external requests;
- cycle time or throughput;
- effectiveness and efficiency of people;
- utilisation of technologies;
- cost reduction.

Section 8.2.4 – Monitoring and measurement of product

Section 8.2.4 Monitoring and measurement of product	The organisation shall: • monitor and measure the characteristics of a product; • document evidence of conformity with the acceptance criteria; • indicate the authority responsible for release of product; • not release the product until all the specified activities have been satisfactorily completed.
Proof	How an organisation ensures that product characteristics meet customer's specified requirements.
Likely documentation	• audit schedules; • audit plans, check sheets and records; • approval procedures for product acceptance; • processes for failure cost analysis, conformity, non-conformity, life cycle approach and self-assessment; • compliance with environmental and safety policies, laws, regulations and standards; • procedures for testing and monitoring processes; • performance and product measurement procedures; • supplier approval procedures.

The organisation should establish, specify and plan their measurement requirements (including acceptance criteria) for its products taking into consideration the:

- location of each measurement point in its process sequence;
- characteristics to be measured at each point;
- documentation and acceptance criteria to be used;
- any equipment and/or tools that are required;
- inspections and tests that need to be witnessed or performed by the customer, statutory and/or regulatory authorities;

- possible requirements for qualified third parties to perform type testing, in-process inspections, product verification and/or product validation;
- necessary qualification requirements of material, product, process, people or the QMS;
- requirements for final inspection;
- outputs of the measurement process of the product;
- conformance to customer, statutory and regulatory requirements.

Typical examples of product measurement records include:

- inspection and test reports;
- material release notices;
- certificates as required;
- electronic data.

To be of any use it is very important that the inspection and test status of a product is immediately clear. The QMS will have to show exactly how this will be achieved (using such methods as markings, stamps, tags, labels, routing cards, inspection records, test software, physical location or other suitable means) to indicate the conformance or non-conformance of the product, and whether it has been inspected and approved, or inspected and rejected.

Production control

To reduce the possibility of manufacturing or design errors causing production line and product delays, the quality status of the product, process, material or environment must be checked at various stages during the production sequence. The use of control charts, statistical sampling procedures and plans are some of the techniques that are used for production and process control.

Product testing

Product testing (i.e. final inspection and testing), are methods of testing whether the product is acceptable or not. These methods have to be developed by the supplier in conjunction with the purchaser and should be included in the supplier's QMS, Quality Manual and/or Quality Plan. These methods would normally contain:

- confirmation that all the relevant inspections and tests have been carried out during production, are fully documented and are recorded in accordance with the Quality Plan or agreed procedure;
- details of the acceptance and rejection criteria that are to be used;
- the measurement and acceptance criteria;
- the quantity to be inspected;
- the sampling plan;
- who is to complete the inspection processes;
- details of the equipment that requires statistical analysis.

Special processes

Occasionally (especially when manufacturing an item) the supplier will be required to perform an inspection on components or activities that cannot normally be verified or inspected at a later stage. The purpose of these inspections is to detect, at an early stage, non-conforming material. If these inspections are required, then the prime contractor will have to establish '*special manufacturing processes*' (such as welding, forging, plastic and wood fabrication, heat treatment and the application of protective treatments) and inspection and testing processes (such as temperature and humidity cycling, vibration, radiography, magnetic particle inspection, penetrant inspection, ultrasonic inspection, pressure testing, chemical and spectrographic analysis and salt spray tests).

5.8.3 Section 8.3 – Control of non-conforming product

'The organization shall ensure that product which does not conform to product requirements is identified and controlled to prevent its unintended use or delivery. A documented procedure shall be established to define the controls and related responsibilities and authorities for dealing with nonconforming product.'

 This is mandatory ISO 9001:2008 requirement!

Section 8.3 Control of non-conforming product	The organisation shall define documented procedures to ensure that: • products which do not conform to requirements are prevented from unintended use or delivery; • non-conforming products that have been corrected are re-verified to demonstrate conformity; • non-conforming products detected after delivery or use are either corrected or removed from service.
Proof	The methods used to prevent the use or delivery of non-conforming products as well as their storage and disposal.
Likely documentation	• documented procedure to identify and control the use and delivery of non-conforming products; • approval procedures; • quarantine procedures; • change control procedure; • corrective and preventive action.

Material control and traceability

To ensure that a non-conforming or hazardous product is not delivered by mistake to a customer, the organisation must establish and maintain procedures for identifying the product (from drawings, specifications or other documents), during all stages of production, delivery and installation. This also ensures that all parts of the product are capable of being traced and recalled if necessary.

Control of non-conformity

To cover the possibility of confusing an acceptable quality product with a defective, non-conforming or unacceptable product (and accidentally using this material or despatching it to the purchaser!), all non-conforming articles **must** be clearly identified and kept completely separate from **all** other acceptable (conforming) products. Non-conforming products can then be:

- documented and steps taken to see that they do not occur again;
- reworked so that they meet the specified requirement;
- accepted with or without repair by concession;
- regraded for possible use elsewhere;
- rejected or scrapped.

Since most production processes inevitably yield some kind of defective material, the organisation must investigate methods for preventing this from happening again and arrange for its immediate disposal. The most obvious method of disposing of a non-conforming material is to scrap it. First making sure, of course, that it cannot be confused with any other material or accidentally used again!

Whatever the choice, details about the non-conformance must be fed back into the system so that action (where economically feasible) can be taken to establish and correct the cause of the non-conformance and hopefully prevent its recurrence.

Supplier responsibility

BS 6143–2:1990 '*Guide to the Economics of Quality – Prevention, appraisal and failure model*' provides detailed information concerning the procedures that should be adopted. In précis form they stipulate that the supplier must:

- investigate the cause of any non-conforming product and have a corrective course of action available to prevent its recurrence;
- analyse all processes, work operations, concessions, quality records, service reports and customer complaints to eliminate the causes of non-conforming products;
- initiate preventive actions;
- change any designs, specifications or work methods that may be unsatisfactory; ensure that the responsibilities for corrective action are clearly assigned to personnel and that these responsibilities are carried out correctly;
- apply controls to ensure that corrective actions are taken and that the existing (as well as the modified) work, methods and designs are effective and suitable;

- implement and record changes in procedures that result from this corrective action.

BS 6143–2:1990 emphasises that this control of quality is not only limited just to the design, manufacture, production and/or installation facilities under the supplier's direct control. It also extends to those services, parts, materials or products that are provided by subcontractors. In some circumstances, if a subcontractor's work is found to be unsatisfactory this could mean dispensing with that particular subcontractor and having to find another one. This can, however, cause additional problems such as finding another one capable of supplying the same service and the materials before the lack of those materials (or service) causes product delays.

Permanent changes

If there are any permanent changes resulting from this corrective action, then they should be recorded in Work Instructions, manufacturing processes, product specifications and in the organisation's QMS. In some cases it might even be necessary to revise the procedures used to detect and eliminate potential problems.

5.8.4 Section 8.4 – Analysis of data

Section 8.4 Analysis of data	The organisation shall collect data for the analysis of: • customer satisfaction; • conformance to product requirements; • characteristics and trends (and opportunities) for preventive action.
Proof	The methods used to review data that will determine the effectiveness of the QMS.
Likely documentation	Data or statistics produced as a result of audits, customer satisfaction surveys, complaints, non-conformances, supplier evaluations, etc.

Customers may often require confirmation that the organisation is capable of continuing to produce a quality article or process. One of the methods frequently used to provide this sort of confirmation is statistical analysis. Nowadays there are many methods of statistically analysing whether the product is:

- what the market requires;
- the correct design;
- derived from a reliable specification and one that can be relied upon to stand the test of time (i.e. durability);
- subject to the correct process control and capabilities;
- covered by relevant quality standards, specifications and plans.

Statistical analysis

Statistical analysis can also include data analysis, performance testing and defect analysis. Other forms of analysis are design process review and design verification. Statistical analysis is, of course, a subject on its own and vast amounts of information about statistical methods, reliability and maintainability data are readily available. An exceedingly good overview of statistical analysis is provided in *Statistical Process Control* by John Oakland and other sources of information such as *Quality and Standards in Electronics.*

With the use of statistical methodologies, the organisation should analyse data in order to assess, control and improve the performance of processes and products and to identify areas for improvement. Analysis of data can help determine the cause of many problems and the results of this analysis can be used to determine:

- trends;
- operational performance;
- customer satisfaction and dissatisfaction;
- satisfaction level of other interested parties;
- effectiveness and efficiency of the organisation;
- economics of quality and financial and market-related performance;
- benchmarking of performance.

Records

In order that the statistical significance of a failure can be properly assessed and that the correct retrospective action may be taken, it is essential that the design section has access to all the records and other pertinent data gathered in the design office and on the shop floor.

The storage, maintenance and analysis of reliability data will require the design section to follow the progress of the product throughout its productive life cycle, through its many maintenance cycles and take due note of any customer comments. The compilation and retention of design office reliability data is not only very important, but essential to the reliability of the product and the manufacturing facility.

Storage of records

Storage facilities should be available to ensure that all stored records are identifiable and retrievable and that the storage areas are free from damp and other agents which could cause premature deterioration. If records are maintained on computers, then these should be subject to 'back-up' at regular intervals, with the 'back-up' information being stored in a protected location to ensure security from loss or damage of active data. All records are normally retained for a minimum of two years after contract completion – but this can be longer in the case of some contracts.

5.8.5 Section 8.5 – Improvement

Section 8.5 Improvement	The organisation shall have procedures available for: • planning for continual improvement; • corrective action; • preventive action.
Proof	How an organisation controls corrective and preventive actions and how it ensures the continual improvement of its product.
Likely documentation	Documented procedures for: • corrective action; • preventive action; • product/process improvement; • customer complaints/feedback; • non-conformity reports; • management reviews; • staff suggestions scheme.

The organisation **shall** plan and manage the processes, policies and objectives that are required for the continual improvement of its QMS as well as its products using audit results, analysis of data, corrective and preventive action and management reviews.

Non-conformity

Once non-conforming items have been recognised, they should be identified by location, associated documents or specific markings in order to prevent their inadvertent use. All non-conforming items and customer complaints should be subject to review and rectification by nominated personnel. The type and extent of non-conformity needs to be documented in order to establish trends and identify possible areas for improvement.

Corrective action

The corrective action required to prevent recurrence should be evaluated, documented and its effective implementation monitored. All rectification should subsequently be re-inspected to ensure complete customer satisfaction.

Preventive action

All employees should be encouraged to suggest improvements in methods, materials, suppliers and subcontractors and organisations should have an established procedure for review of all activities in order to identify and evaluate all possible improvements in methods/materials and its procedures.

Section 8.5.1 Continual improvement

Section 8.5.1 Continual improvement	The organisation shall plan, manage and ensure the continual improvement of their QMS.
Proof	How an organisation goes about continually improving its QMS.
Likely documentation	• procedures, minutes of meetings (where improvement to the organisation's business is discussed); • management reviews.

The organisation should continually seek to improve its processes and procedures (rather than just waiting for a problem to come along) and have available documented procedures to identify, manage and improve them. Such actions would include the following:

- defining, measuring and analysing the existing situation;
- establishing the objectives for improvement;
- searching for possible solutions;
- evaluating these solutions;
- implementing the selected solution;
- measuring, verifying, and analysing results of the implementation;
- formalising changes.

Section 8.5.2 Corrective action

'All organisations are required to have a documented quality procedure for corrective action.'

 This is mandatory ISO 9001:2008 requirement!

Section 8.5.2 Corrective action	The organisation shall have documented procedures for: • identifying non-conformities (including customer complaints); • determining the causes of non-conformity; • evaluating the need for action to ensure non-conformities do not recur; • implementing corrective action; • recording results; • reviewing corrective action taken.

Proof	What an organisation does to identify and put right non-conformities.
Likely documentation	• process for eliminating causes of non-conformity; • documented complaints; • complaints procedure; • staff suggestions scheme.

The organisation should plan and establish a process for corrective action, the results of which **shall** be included in the management review process. The input information for this activity can derive from a number of sources such as:

- customer complaints;
- non-conformance reports;
- outputs from management review;
- internal audit reports;
- outputs from data analysis;
- relevant QMS records;
- outputs from satisfaction measurements;
- process measurements;
- results of self-assessment.

The corrective action process should include:

- a definition of the causes of non-conformances and defects;
- elimination of causes of non-conformances and defects;
- appropriate actions to avoid recurrence of problems (i.e. preventative action);
- a record of the activity and results.

The necessity for corrective action should be evaluated in terms of the potential impact on operating costs, costs of non-conformance, performance, dependability, safety and customer satisfaction.

Concessions and approvals

No matter how much an organisation may pay attention to the control of quality and no matter how hard it tries to avoid problems with both manpower and the product, all too often things go wrong. There could, for instance, be a problem in the production shop, an accident could happen, piece-part material could be damaged or a mistake could be made by an engineer when reading a drawing or setting up an electrical or electronic machine. Or the print shop could print the deliverable incorrectly or leave out sections.

In all of these cases there has to be a recognised method of accepting the problem instead of just trying to hide the blunder through either unofficial 'modifications' or, even worse, trying to cover it up! As the saying goes 'honesty is always the best policy' and in any case, '*Murphy's Law*' says that more than likely the hidden '*repairs*' will be found out and the manufacturer will consequently lose his or her customer's trust and any chance of follow on orders.

Concession scheme

The machinery for overcoming these problems is called the '*concession scheme*'. This will normally consist of a form that has to be completed by the manufacturer/supplier **and** the customer. Details of each document, component, sub assembly, defect or mistake that is identified has to be recorded together with the action that was taken to rectify, scrap, modify or accept the problem.

The Quality Plan will indicate the acceptance or rejection criteria that will be adopted. It will describe compulsory methods that must be taken to mark imperfect or faulty material and indicate how they should be separated from any other material before it is scrapped, reworked or repaired.

If the problem is the result of a faulty design or specification that originated from the purchaser any problems must of course be referred back to him or her. If the fault is found to be the fault of the purchaser (e.g. unsatisfactory design) the manufacturer/supplier may, of course, be able to insist on having an exgratia payment to overcome the problem. If the problem originated from the manufacturer/supplier, then the purchaser is perfectly within his or her rights to insist on a reduction in the agreed price.

In cases where a subcontractor requests a concession, then the prime contractor has to carry out a full investigation and agree to the subcontractor's proposal before asking the purchaser to consider the request.

A concession system is a very important part of the supplier/purchaser relationship. It also promotes better discipline within the factory, shows up re-occurring problem areas and ensures that the supplier's standard of workmanship is maintained.

Defects and defect reports

One of the requirements of the QMS is that signatures **shall** be required from inspectors at each stage of the production to show that the product is of the required standard and assured quality.

When an item fails to meet these criteria, then the inspector must submit a defect report, showing exactly what is defective, how it affects the product and, where possible, what steps can be taken to overcome these failures in future productions.

Bonded store

Owing to the possibility of having unacceptable goods inside his or her premises, the manufacturer must also set up some kind of '*bonded store*' where all incoming material is placed pending inspection.

Even when goods have left the bonded store it is still necessary to have some form of marking (e.g. labels or tags) to distinguish between those awaiting inspection, those inspected and accepted, and those rejected and awaiting return.

> **Author's Hint**
>
> In a very small business, 'a bonded store' could be just a cupboard or somewhere where goods cannot be inadvertently used.

Section 8.5.3 – Preventive action

'All organisations are required to have a documented quality procedure for preventative action.'

This is mandatory ISO 9001:2008 requirement!

Section 8.5.3 Preventive action	The organisation shall have documented procedures for: • identifying potential non-conformities; • implementing preventive action; • recording and reviewing all preventive action taken.
Proof	The proactive methods an organisation employs to prevent non-conformities from happening in the first place.
Likely documentation	• process for the prevention of non-conformity; • complaints procedure; • staff suggestions scheme.

The organisation should use preventive methodologies such as risk analysis, trend analysis, statistical process control, fault tree analysis, failure modes and effects and critical analysis to identify the causes of potential non-conformances. Examples of sources are:

- customer needs and expectations;
- market analysis;
- management review output;
- outputs from data analysis;
- satisfaction measurements;
- process measurements;
- systems that consolidate many sources of customer information;
- relevant QMS records;
- results of self-assessment;
- processes that provide early warning of approaching out-of-control operating conditions.

Preventive actions should be considered for inclusion in the management review process.

 Note: Corrective actions are steps that are taken to remove the causes of existing non-conformities, while preventive actions are steps that are taken to remove the causes of potential non-conformities. Corrective actions address actual problems, ones that have already occurred, while preventive actions address potential problems, ones that haven't yet occurred. In general, the corrective action process is a problem solving process, while the preventive action process is a risk analysis process.

Author's Note

Chapter 5 has provided a complete overview and explanation of the various sections and sub sections making up ISO 9001:2008.

Having got to this point, you should now be completely aware of what is required for your organisation to achieve compliance with the recommendations and requirements of ISO 9001:2008 – and so now you need to put it into practice!

To help you on your way, therefore, in Chapter 6 I have provided you with a complete, generic example of a Quality Manual that can be customised to suit your own organisation, together with examples of the six mandatory Quality Procedures (that you **must** have in order to gain ISO 9001:2008 certification). Also included are some model Quality Procedures and Work Instructions for you to look at.

These examples can be adapted by **any** organisation to suit its own purposes and own processes – **provided** that they are customised so that they exactly describe your company's business model.

 Chapter 6 is **NOT**, however, intended to provide a quick fix. It is **NOT** intended to be just another off-the-shelf product!

You will need to carefully review the example, possibly modify the structure and wording – it certainly is **NOT** meant as a quick *cut and paste* exercise!!

Example Quality Management System

As mentioned in the Preface of this book, prior to the re-issue of the ISO 9000 series in 2008, the majority of organisations wrote their Quality Manuals to show how they met the 20 individual requirements of the 1994 standard. Although this made it easier for the manual's authors to show the auditors that all of the requirements of the standard had been covered, quite often (especially in a very small business), the manual was of little use to the organisation itself in actually running its own business.

The process-orientated ISO 9001:2008 standard now requires the Quality Manual to:

> **'Include the scope of the system; include any justifications for exclusions; refer to established procedures and describe the interaction between processes.'**

A Quality Manual that simply echoes the requirements of ISO 9001:2008 will, therefore, not be compliant, as certain sections of the standard's content may not be applicable to that particular organisation.

The Quality Manual should serve a useful purpose and so simply paraphrasing ISO 9001:2008's requirements is not the best approach and certainly won't impress an external auditor!! Thus, an organisation should no longer use an *'off the shelf'* generic Quality Manual to show compliance **unless** it has been **thoroughly customised** to suit that particular organisation.

The whole reason for my book is to try to help small businesses (who probably have insufficient time to thoroughly read, understand, extract and implement all of the recommendations and requirements of ISO 9001:2008 – and who quite likely cannot afford to employ a consultant to do the job for them) by providing them with a fully worked example. Although this generic QMS is based on one particular type of company (NAFAAD Consultancy who are a *'paper producing'* consultancy) it can be used as a basic template to describe the way that your particular organisation does business by leaving out those bits that are not particularly relevant to your company and/or amplifying/writing new policies, processes and procedures to cover your organisation-specific areas that I have not covered in my book.

Although a lot of consultants say that there is now no need to address each requirement, clause by clause, I tend to disagree because if you are having to identify the requirements that are not applicable to your organisation (i.e. the 'exclusions') and **then** say why they are permitted exclusions, surely there is less chance of missing a possible sub requirement by actually listing all of them and showing whether they are applicable or not?! If you are having to describe the interaction between processes (which probably result from different requirements or sub requirements scattered within ISO 9001:2008), then why not list them all, so as to ensure that you don't miss any? I sought ISO's advice on this matter and they said that '*Although ISO 9001:2008 does not state that there needs to be any reference to the requirements of the standard, if an organisation chooses to list all of the requirements, then that is its choice – and it will certainly assist external and third party auditors.*'

As I understand it, the Quality Manual should be an overview of the organisation's Quality Management System (QMS) and show how the organisation runs its business. The Manual is primarily intended for the Managing Director (to document his or her policy for running that organisation), the Quality Manager (to give him or her a set of rules with which to ensure that the organisation meets the policy requirements of the MD) and auditors (to quickly identify which of the standard's requirements are applicable to that organisation and how they have been met). Depending on the individual organisation, therefore, the Quality Manual could be just a few A4 sheets of paper simply listing the exclusions, procedures and interaction of processes. Or, similar to my generic example, it could be more of a reference document aimed at assisting internal and external auditors in understanding the organisation's policies and how it completes its business – as well as providing a checklist for the Quality Manager.

The same thing can be said about the Quality Procedures (QP) contained in Part 2. These again are meant as examples of the sort of QPs that will be needed by an organisation to show how it implements its policies and processes.

For your convenience, in addition to a few general purpose QPs that most organisations will need, I have also included generic examples of the **six** most important and **mandatory** documentary procedures that you **must** produce in order to claim compliance with ISO 9001:2008. These are:

1. **Control of documents** (ISO 9001:2008 section 4.2.3);
2. **Control of records** (ISO 9001:2008 section 4.2.4);
3. **Internal audit** (ISO 9001:2008 section 8.2.2);
4. **Control of non-conforming product** (ISO 9001:2008 section 8.3);
5. **Corrective action** (ISO 9001:2008 section 8.5.2);
6. **Preventative action** (ISO 9001:2008 section 8.5.3).

Note: Where the term 'documented procedure' appears within this International Standard, this means that *the procedure has to be established, documented, implemented and maintained.*

Author's Note

By implication, documented procedures should also be included for:

Customer Communications (7.2.3)
(which states that: 'The organisation shall determine and implement effective arrangements for communication with customers');

Purchasing process (7.4.1)
(which states that: 'Criteria for selection, evaluation and re-evaluation shall be established').

Note: Procedures can take any suitable form. They can be a narrative, a flow chart, a process map, or indeed any other suitable structure. As long as the procedure is effective, it really doesn't matter what it looks like.

There are so many different types of organisation that make use of ISO 9001:2008 (e.g. designers, manufacturers, producers, installers and maintainers of products and services; small shops and other service industries) that it was an impossible task to include examples for all of these organisations in this chapter. I have (as previously mentioned), therefore, chosen to base these procedures around the theoretical NAFAAD Consultancy with the intention that purchasers/users of my book can take this generic Quality Management System (and its associated Processes, Procedures and Work Instructions) and then modify, adjust and customise them so that they represent a true picture of what they actually do in 'real life'.

For example, the Document Control procedure shown in QP/1, whilst covering the requirements for quite a large organisation (e.g. 45 people) would probably be way over the top for a **very** small organisation. However, as 'Document Control' is one of ISO 9001:2008's mandatory procedures, you **do** need to have some method of controlling your organisation's documentation and one that you (or a potential customer or an auditor) can use to identify where your documents are located or where they are saved on the server etc. You may also want to show who is responsible for these documents, their revision status and their date of issue. In some circumstances (especially when dealing with foreign countries) you might even need to know who was responsible for translating a specific document.

One of the main advantages of ISO 9001:2008 is that it encourages organisations to develop systems that can be **specifically** tailored to their own needs – even if you are just a '*one man band*'. The QMS is an integral part of the business processes but you should not lose sight of the fact that it **still** has to meet the requirements of ISO 9001:2008.

'*ISO 9001:2008 for Small Businesses*' (Fifth Edition) is meant to save you time from having to constantly refer to the standard to see that you have covered everything. My generic example covers **all** of the standard's requirements and, similar to the actual standard itself, the intention is that organisations pick and choose what bits they need for themselves and then customise them so that they replicate – **exactly** – how their business is run.

 But, it is **not** meant to be used as an *'off the shelf'* product!!

 Note: To save you having to copy or retype the Quality Manual, Quality Procedures and/or Work Instructions, *'unlocked'*, fully accessible, non .PDF, soft copies of all of the files presented in the book are available – at no additional charge – direct from the author.

To obtain copies of these files, simply send an e-mail to ray@herne.org.uk containing details of your name, address and where you purchased the book from, and I will send you the link to download a full copy.

DISCLAIMER

Material provided by this service is provided *'as is'* without warranty of any kind, either expressed or implied. Every effort has been made to ensure accuracy and conformance to standards accepted at the time of publication. The user assumes the entire risk as to the accuracy and the use of this material.

This material may be copied and distributed subject to the following conditions:

(1) *'Ray Tricker, ISO 9000:2008 for Small Businesses, Published by Routledge'* must be credited as the source of the QMS template;
(2) The QMS document may **not** be distributed for profit. All trademarks acknowledged.

 This QMS is provided free of charge by the author. Whilst the original files remain copyright of the author, you are welcome to tailor them to suit the needs of your own organisation's business.

OBTAINING ADDITIONAL MATERIAL, INFORMATION AND SUPPORT

A CD (or e-mailed) soft copy of the generic Quality Management System featured in *ISO 9001:2008 for Small Businesses*, fifth edition, is available **plus** a soft copy of *Auditing Quality Management Systems* (containing all the major audit checksheets and forms required to conduct either an internal, external or third party review/assessment) is also available from the author for a small additional charge. All of these files can be quickly customised to suit your organisation's business and an ISO 9001:2008 Help Line is also available to purchasers of this product.

Users requiring additional support or more information about this and other ISO 9000 consulting services, please visit www.thebestqms.com or www.herne. org.uk or simply e-mail me at ray@herne.org.uk and I will do my best to help you.

Author's Hint

This following example of a Quality Manual has been based on the assumption that NAFAAD is an SME, employing between 45 and 50 people, which has a full-time Quality Manager plus a small part-time Quality Team.

If your organisation does **not** have a Quality Team, then you should leave out the irrelevant passages.

If you are a Micro Business (i.e. less than 10 employees) then you probably will not have a full-time Quality Manager and in that case it would normally be the Owner or Managing Director who performs the audits and checks.

When using this example, please do **not** be tempted to just 'find and replace' NAFAAD with your own business name in the hope that it will satisfy an auditor – because it won't! You **must** go through this example Quality Manual (and its supporting processes, procedures and Work Instructions) **sentence by sentence** to ensure that it replicates exactly what your own organisation does and the type of business that you provide!

NAFAAD Consultancy Ltd

Quality Management System

Part 1 – Quality Manual

This Quality Manual has been issued on the authority of the Managing Director of NAFAAD Consultancy Ltd for the use of all staff, subcontractors, clients and/or regulatory bodies to whom NAFAAD Consultancy Ltd may be required to provide such information to.

Approved	
	Date: 1 October 2013
Ray Rekcirt Managing Director NAFAAD Consultancy Ltd	

© 2013 by NAFAAD Consultancy Ltd, all rights reserved.

Copyright subsists in all NAFAAD Consultancy Ltd deliverables including magnetic, optical and/or any other soft copy of these deliverables. This document may not be reproduced, in full or in part, without written permission.

	Document Ref: **N-51–044RLR13**
	Version: 03.01
	Date: 1 October 2013
	Quality Management System
	Part One – Quality Manual
	Version 01.00

DOCUMENT CONTROL SHEET

Title	This version	Date
NAFAAD Consultancy Ltd		
Part 1	File Number	No of Pages
Quality Manual	N-51–044RLR13	102

ABSTRACT

The NAFAAD Consultancy Ltd Quality Management System is divided into four parts. This Quality Manual is Part 1 and describes the policies adopted by NAFAAD Consultancy Ltd. It defines:

- the overall Quality Management System adopted by NAFAAD Consultancy Ltd;
- the organisation that has been developed to implement that Quality Management System;
- the associated documentation (e.g. Quality Processes, Quality Procedures and Work Instructions) that have been designed to enable NAFAAD Consultancy Ltd to carry out the Quality Management System.

The Quality Processes designed to meet these policies are contained in Part 2 and the details of the Quality Procedures and Work Instructions are in Parts 3 and 4.

Name	Function	Level
	Quality Manager	Prepare
	Managing Director	Agree
	Managing Director	Approve

Document Ref: **N-51–044RLR13**
Version: 03.01
Date: 1 October 2013
Quality Management System
Part One – Quality Manual
Version 01.00

ATTACHMENTS

Attachments	Description
Annex A	NAFAAD Consultancy Ltd's organisation and responsibilities
Annex B	ISO 9001:2008 cross-check
Annex C	List of Quality Procedures
Annex D	Abbreviations and acronyms
Annex E	References

QMS REVISION HISTORY

No.	Chapter	Amendment details	Date
01.00	All	First published version in accordance with ISO 9001:1994	28.06.93
01.01	3	Inclusion of new chapter for customer satisfaction	05.04.94
01.02	4.2.3	Procedure for the control of documents changed	23.12.95
01.03	All	Minor editorial revisions of all sections and annexes	30.07.96
02.00	All	Second published version to conform to ISO 9001:2000	31.12.00
02.01	5	Management responsibility procedure updated to cover new (i.e. Fuels) Division	01.01.02
02.02	All	Minor editorial changes following three years' experience of ISO 9001:2000	01.01.05
03.00	All	Major revision following publication of ISO 9001:2008	01.11.09
03.01	All	Minor editorial changes following five years experience of ISO 9001:2008	01.10.13

	Document Ref: **N-51–044RLR13**
	Version: 03.01
	Date: 1 October 2013
	Quality Management System
	Part One – Quality Manual
	Version 01.00

CONTENTS

1. Quality assurance at NAFAAD 9
    1.1 Company profile 10
    1.2 Costs 11
    1.3 NAFAAD Consultancy Ltd – organisational chart 12
    1.4 Quality policy and objectives. 12
         1.4.1 Policy 12
         1.4.2 Objectives 13
    1.5 Implementation 13
         1.5.1 Overall responsibility. 13
         1.5.2 Responsibility for quality system. 13
         1.5.3 Responsibility for contract quality 14
         1.5.4 Responsibility for product quality. 14
         1.5.5 Responsibility for subcontractor(s) quality 14
    1.6 Registrations and approvals held 14

2   NAFAAD's Management System 14
    2.1 Requirements. 14
    2.2 Organisational goals 15
    2.3 Purpose 17

3   Quality policy 18
    3.1 Introduction. 18
    3.2 Quality Management System requirements 18
    3.3 Company requirements 19
    3.4 Company quality policy 20
    3.5 Adherence to standards 21
    3.6 Purpose of a Quality Management System 21
    3.7 Quality in performance 23
    3.8 Organisational goals 23
    3.9 Structure for quality management 24
         3.9.1 QMS document control 26
    3.10 The Quality Manual 27
    3.11 Quality processes. 28
    3.12 Quality Procedures 30
    3.13 Work Instructions. 31
    3.14 Records 32
    3.15 Project quality plans 32

Document Ref: **N-51–044RLR13**
Version: 03.01
Date: 1 October 2013
Quality Management System
Part One – Quality Manual
Version 01.00

4　Quality Management System (ISO 9001:2008 – 4) 32
　4.1　General requirements (ISO 9001:2008 – 4.1) 33
　4.2　Documentation requirements (ISO 9001:2008 – 4.2) 35
　　　4.2.1　General (ISO 9001:2008 – 4.2.1) 35
　　　4.2.2　Quality Manual (ISO 9001:2008 – 4.2.2) 36
　　　4.2.3　Control of documents (ISO 9001:2008 – 4.2.3) 37
　　　4.2.4　Control of quality records (ISO 9001:2008 – 4.2.4) 38

5　Management responsibility (ISO 9001:2008 – 5) 40
　5.1　Management commitment (ISO 9001:2008 – 5.1) 41
　5.2　Customer focus (ISO 9001:2008 – 5.2) 41
　5.3　Quality policy (ISO 9001:2008 – 5.3) 42
　5.4　Planning (ISO 9001:2008 – 5.4) 42
　　　5.4.1　Quality objectives (ISO 9001:2008 – 5.4.1) 43
　　　5.4.2　Quality Management System planning
　　　　　　(ISO 9001:2008 – 5.4.2) 43
　5.5　Responsibility, authority and communication
　　　　(ISO 9001:2008 – 5.5) 44
　　　5.5.1　Responsibility and authority (ISO 9001:2008 – 5.5.1) 44
　　　5.5.2　Management representative (ISO 9001:2008 – 5.5.2) 45
　　　5.5.3　Internal communication (ISO 9001:2008 – 5.5.3) 46
　5.6　Management review (ISO 9001:2008 – 5.6) 46
　　　5.6.1　General (ISO 9001:2008 – 5.6.1) 47
　　　5.6.2　Review input (ISO 9001:2008 – 5.6.2) 47
　　　5.6.3　Review output (ISO 9001:2008 – 5.6.3) 48

6　Resource management (ISO 9001:2008 – 6) 49
　6.1　Provision of resources (ISO 9001:2008 – 6.1) 50
　6.2　Human resources (ISO 9001:2008 – 6.2) 50
　　　6.2.1　General (ISO 9001:2008 – 6.2.1) 50
　　　6.2.2　Competence, training and awareness (ISO 9001:2008 –
　　　　　　6.2.2) 51
　6.3　Infrastructure (ISO 9001:2008 – 6.3) 52
　6.4　Work environment (ISO 9001:2008 – 6.4) 53

7　Product realisation (ISO 9001:2008 – 7) 54
　7.1　Planning of realisation processes (ISO 9000:2000 – 7.1) 54
　7.2　Customer-related processes (ISO 9000:2000 – 7.2) 56
　　　7.2.1　Determination of requirements related to the product
　　　　　　(ISO 9001:2008 – 7.2.1) 56

Document Ref: **N-51–044RLR13**
Version: 03.01
Date: 1 October 2013
Quality Management System
Part One – Quality Manual
Version 01.00

7.2.2 Review of requirements related to the product
(ISO 9000:2000 – 7.2.2) 57
7.2.3 Customer communication (ISO 9000:2000 – 7.2.3) 58
7.3 Design and development (ISO 9000:2000 – 7.3) 59
7.3.1 Design and development planning
(ISO 9001:2008 – 7.3.1) 59
7.3.2 Design and development inputs (ISO 9001:2008 – 7.3.2) 60
7.3.3 Design and development outputs (ISO 9001:2008 – 7.3.3) . . . 61
7.3.4 Design and development review (ISO 9001:2008 – 7.3.4) 62
7.3.5 Design and development verification (ISO 9001:2008 –
7.3.5) 63
7.3.6 Design and development validation
(ISO 9001:2008 – 7.3.6) 64
7.3.7 Control of design and development changes
(ISO 9001:2008 – 7.3.7) 65
7.4 Purchasing (ISO 9001:2008 – 7.4) 66
7.4.1 Purchasing process (ISO 9001:2008 – 7.4.1) 66
7.4.2 Purchasing information (ISO 9001:2008 – 7.4.2) 68
7.4.3 Verification of purchased product
(ISO 9001:2008 – 7.4.3) 69
7.5 Production and service provision (ISO 9001:2008 – 7.5) 70
7.5.1 Control of production and service provision
(ISO 9001:2008 – 7.5.1) 70
7.5.2 Validation of processes for production and service
provision (ISO 9001:2008 – 7.5.2) 72
7.5.3 Identification and traceability (ISO 9001:2008 – 7.5.3) 73
7.5.4 Customer property (ISO 9001:2008 – 7.5.4) 73
7.5.5 Preservation of product (ISO 9001:2008 – 7.5.5) 74
7.6 Control of monitoring and measuring equipment
(ISO 9001:2008 – 7.6) 76
8 Measurement, analysis and improvement (ISO 9001:2008 – 8) 77
8.1 General (ISO 9001:2008 – 8.1) 77
8.2 Monitoring and measurement (ISO 9001:2008 – 8.2) 78
8.2.1 Customer satisfaction (ISO 9001:2008 – 8.2.1) 78
8.2.2 Internal audit (ISO 9001:2008 – 8.2.2) 79
8.2.3 Monitoring and measurement of processes
(ISO 9001:2008 – 8.2.3) 80
8.2.4 Monitoring and measurement of product
(ISO 9001:2008 – 8.2.4) 81

Document Ref: **N-51–044RLR13**
Version: 03.01
Date: 1 October 2013
Quality Management System
Part One – Quality Manual
Version 01.00

8.3   Control of non-conforming product (ISO 9001:2008 – 8.3) 82
8.4   Analysis of data (ISO 9001:2008 – 8.4) 84
8.5   Improvement (ISO 9001:2008 – 8.5) 85
       8.5.1 Continual improvement (ISO 9001:2008 – 8.5.1) 85
       8.5.2 Corrective action (ISO 9001:2008 – 8.5.2) 86
       8.5.3 Preventive action (ISO 9001:2008 – 8.5.3) 87

Annex A   88
Annex B   92
Annex C   100
Annex D   101
Annex E   102

LIST OF ILLUSTRATIONS

Figure 6.1.1:   NAFAAD Consultancy Ltd – organisational chart 12
Figure 6.1.2:   Quality loop 16
Figure 6.1.3:   Some of the determinants and measurements of the
                 quality of a service 18
Figure 6.1.4:   Some of the determinants and measurements of the
                 quality of a product 19
Figure 6.1.5:   The PDCA cycle 22
Figure 6.1.6:   Quality Management System 24
Figure 6.1.7:   The eight principles of ISO 9001:2008 expressed
                 diagrammatically 26
Figure 6.1.8:   NAFAAD's Quality Manual 27
Figure 6.1.9:   NAFAAD's Core Business Process 29
Figure 6.1.10:   Inter-relationship of documented processes with
                 QPs and WIs 30
Figure 6.1.11:   Quality Management System 34
Figure 6.1.12:   Management responsibility 40
Figure 6.1.13:   Resources management 49
Figure 6.1.14:   Product realisation 54
Figure 6.1.15:   NAFAAD's organisational chart 88

LIST OF TABLES

Table 6.1.1:   QMS documentation 25

Document Ref: **N-51–044RLR13**
Version: 03.01
Date: 1 October 2013
Quality Management System
Part One – Quality Manual
Version 01.00

NAFAAD CONSULTANCY LTD – POLICY STATEMENT

Within NAFAAD Consultancy Ltd (hereinafter referred to as NAFAAD who are a subsidiary of the North American Field Advanced Audit Division) we are committed to provide products and services, which fully meet the customers' specified contractual requirements.

NAFAAD recognises that in order to provide and maintain a consistently high quality in the work it undertakes, an effective Quality Management System is necessary so as to ensure that proper communication, work control and accountable records are generated for all work undertaken. We are totally committed to setting and achieving quality standards that are capable of meeting (in **all** respects) the specified requirements and reasonable expectations of our customers.

It is the policy, therefore, of NAFAAD to control and conduct its business of producing and implementing integrated management services by means of a formalised system of modern quality management. This quality management shall be in accordance with the quality system requirements as specified in ISO 9001:2008.

The Quality Manual (i.e. this document) defines NAFAAD's Quality Management System which has been established and adopted as the means for achieving these declared objectives and which is detailed in the sections below.

All members of NAFAAD staff are charged with promoting these aims and are required to familiarise themselves with the contents of this Quality Manual and to observe and implement the systems and procedures defined in the performance of their work. Everyone connected with NAFAAD shall be supported according to their individual needs for personal development.

The Quality Manager based at the NAFAAD main office is my appointed management representative responsible for monitoring and ensuring the correct and effective implementation of NAFAAD's Quality Management System as a whole.

Ray Rekcirt
Managing Director
NAFAAD Consultancy Ltd

	Document Ref: **N-51–044RLR13** Version: 03.01 Date: 1 October 2013 Quality Management System Part One – Quality Manual Version 01.00

 Author's Hint

This Policy Statement **must** be changed so that it accurately reflects **your** own business!

MISSION STATEMENT

'To deliver effective, evidence-based management systems in accordance to the recommendations of ISO 9001:2008 and other industry equivalent standards.'

1 QUALITY ASSURANCE AT NAFAAD

This Quality Manual has been issued on the authority of the Managing Director of NAFAAD for the use of all staff, subcontractors, clients or regulatory bodies to whom NAFAAD may be required to provide such information.

This Quality Manual defines:

- the overall quality policy adopted by NAFAAD;
- the organisation that has been developed to implement this quality policy;
- the documentation (i.e. Quality Processes, Quality Procedures and Work Instructions) that has been designed to enable NAFAAD to carry out that policy.

Other than the permissible exclusions shown in the relevant parts of the text, NAFAAD's Quality Manual fully conforms to the requirements of ISO 9001:2008 (Ref 1). It takes into consideration the requirements of NAFAAD's Memorandum and Articles of Association (Ref 3), together with all other applicable national, European and international standards and procedures such as EN 50126–1 (Reliability, Availability, Maintainability and Safety (RAMS)), BS EN ISO 14001 (Environmental management systems) and BS OHSAS 18001 (Occupational health and safety management systems) that are associated with our organisation's involvement with the European railway industry.

	Document Ref: **N-51–044RLR13**
	Version: 03.01
	Date: 1 October 2013
	Quality Management System
	Part One – Quality Manual
	Version 01.00

Author's Hint

If you are not a Ltd Company then you probably won't have *Memorandum and Articles of Association* and so you can leave it out, or you could say *'objectives set out in Section 1 of the Quality Manual'* or something similar.

If there are any discrepancies between the NAFAAD Quality Manual and these other directives/standards, the requirements of the NAFAAD Quality Manual shall prevail.

Author's Hint

Insert the directives, standards and procedures etc. that are relevant to your particular organisation in here.

Changes in the organisation of NAFAAD or the environment in which it operates, may necessitate modifications, amendments, insertions and/or deletions to the overall quality management adopted by NAFAAD and its associated documentation (e.g. Quality Processes, Quality Procedures and Work Instructions). The contents of this Quality Manual may, therefore, be altered on an as-required basis. All changes shall be subject to QP/1 for 'Document Control'. Changes shall be deemed operational following approval by the authorised person(s) and published as updated sections of the Quality Manual.

Certain technical terms and usage in this Quality Manual, although only reflecting the masculine gender, are, in fact, the parlance of the field and should be interpreted to apply equally to both sexes.

1.1 Company profile

NAFAAD Consultancy Ltd (NAFAAD) is a Private Limited Company specialising in the production of integrated Quality, Safety and Environmental Management Systems for Small and Medium sized Enterprises (SME) as well as Large

	Document Ref: **N-51–044RLR13**
	Version: 03.01
	Date: 1 October 2013
	Quality Management System
	Part One – Quality Manual
	Version 01.00

Multinational Organisations (LMO). All deliverables are designed and supplied to the highest standards and conform to the relevant international and European standards.

NAFAAD's aim is to produce everything that you want in support of your company's Management System. NAFAAD provides advice and guidance on **all** quality matters. We can produce either a complete QMS or separate Quality Manuals, Quality Processes, Quality Procedures, Work Instructions or technical books to suit individual customer requirements. NAFAAD also provides qualified advice on health & safety and environmental requirements (particularly those for the railway industry) and are experts in fuel conservation, railway signalling systems and nano-technology.

NAFAAD controls and conducts its business of producing and implementing integrated management systems by means of a formalised system of modern quality management which is in accordance with the quality system requirements and recommendations specified in ISO 9001:2008.

At NAFAAD, we believe that it is important to develop a good working relationship with our customers at every level, ensuring that they always receive a quality product and service. Nothing is considered too small. Indeed NAFAAD have become renowned for assisting the smaller company (who rarely possess a quality infrastructure) in establishing their own Quality Management System in accordance with ISO 9001:2008 and working towards becoming an ISO 9001:2008 certified company.

Author's Hint

The Company Profile will need to be changed so that it accurately reflects your **own** business.

1.2 Costs

Each deliverable's budget is carefully prepared taking into account the type of product and the market to which it is aimed. Emphasis is placed on producing a quality product at a realistic cost thereby giving the customer value for money.

	Document Ref: **N-51–044RLR13**
	Version: 03.01
	Date: 1 October 2013
	Quality Management System
	Part One – Quality Manual
	Version 01.00

1.3 NAFAAD Consultancy Ltd – organisational chart

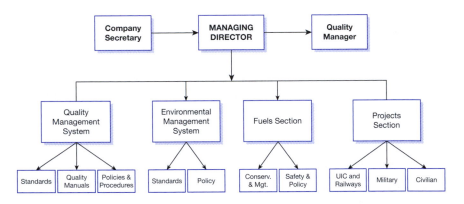

FIGURE 6.1.1 NAFAAD Consultancy Ltd – organisational chart

Author's Hint

This will obviously need amending to reflect your **own** organisation's structure.

1.4 Quality policy and objectives

1.4.1 Policy

NAFAAD shall define and manage the processes necessary to ensure that all project deliverables conform to customer requirements. As a means of continually improving project performance, NAFAAD shall establish a QMS covering the requirements of ISO 9001:2008. This QMS shall be implemented, maintained, continually improved and have the full support of Top Management.

NAFAAD shall prepare a series of supporting documents that describe the processes required to implement the QMS. These shall include:

- The Core Business Process and its Supporting Processes;
- The Quality Procedures required for ISO 9001:2008 compliance;

Document Ref: **N-51–044RLR13**
Version: 03.01
Date: 1 October 2013
Quality Management System
Part One – Quality Manual
Version 01.00

- Additional Quality Procedures that describe the methods adopted to manage the Core Business Process and Supporting Processes;
- Work Instructions that describe the operating methods, practice and control of the Core Business Process and Supporting Processes.

1.4.2 Objectives

The main objective of the NAFAAD QMS is to ensure that company activities, whether they are organisational (e.g. management and infrastructure) or technical (e.g. specification work, testing and simulation) comply with the Quality Manual and its associated Quality Plans.

1.5 Implementation

Quality management at NAFAAD is based on the Quality Management System described in ISO 9001:2008. The purpose of the NAFAAD QMS is to define the policy, organisation and responsibilities for the management of quality within NAFAAD.

The most important aspects of NAFAAD's QMS are to be found in the NAFAAD Quality Manual (i.e. this document) which describes, in detail, how the main elements of ISO 9001:2008 are catered for. The Quality Manual is then supported by individual Quality Plans (for each section or major contract/document) which in turn are supported by Quality Processes, Quality Procedures and Work Instructions.

All NAFAAD personnel shall have access to a copy of this Quality Manual (see Section 3.10 page 227) and as part of personnel induction training, the objectives of the manual shall be explained to them by the NAFAAD Quality Manager.

1.5.1 Overall responsibility

The responsibility of ensuring that NAFAAD has a quality policy and for ensuring that an organisation with the necessary resources is in place to implement the policy lies with the Managing Director.

1.5.2 Responsibility for quality system

The Managing Director has appointed the Quality Manager to have overall day-to-day responsibility for implementing and maintaining the NAFAAD quality system. The Quality Manager has the responsibility and the authority to ensure that adequate processes, procedures, plans and instructions are drawn up so as to provide a common approach to quality assurance throughout NAFAAD and to

	Document Ref: **N-51–044RLR13** Version: 03.01 Date: 1 October 2013 Quality Management System Part One – Quality Manual Version 01.00

ensure that the quality system is continuously monitored and improved by means of internal audits and management reviews.

1.5.3 Responsibility for contract quality

The responsibility for the development of contract quality rests with NAFAAD's Managing Director via the Company Managers.

1.5.4 Responsibility for product quality

The responsibility for ensuring that the product conforms to the defined quality requirements in this manual lies with **all** NAFAAD personnel.

1.5.5 Responsibility for subcontractor(s) quality

Specialised areas of operation and technical expertise may be required to meet the needs of NAFAAD. In many cases these shall have to be provided externally via a subcontractor. These subcontractors will need to provide evidence that their own organisation's QMS is in accordance with the requirements of the principles of ISO 9001:2008.

1.6 Registrations and approvals held

NAFAAD is a Registered Organisation certified by an Accredited Certification Body and verified as having quality documentation and effective practices in operation which are in accordance with the requirements of the international Quality System ISO 9001:2008.

 Author's Hint

You will need to include your own organisation's registrations and approvals in here.

2 NAFAAD'S MANAGEMENT SYSTEM

2.1 Requirements

NAFAAD's QMS is the organised structure of responsibilities, activities, resources and events that together provide procedures and methods of implementation to ensure the capability of NAFAAD meets the quality requirements of our customers.

	Document Ref: **N-51–044RLR13**
	Version: 03.01
	Date: 1 October 2013
	Quality Management System
	Part One – Quality Manual
	Version 01.00

NAFAAD has to develop, establish and implement a Quality Management System in order to ensure that the overall objectives and policies stated in NAFAAD's Memorandum of Articles and Association are met.

Author's Hint

If you are **not** a Ltd company then you might not have any Memorandum and Articles of Association, you could say 'objectives set out in Section 1 of the Quality Manual' or something similar.

To achieve these requirements, NAFAAD involves all phases of a quality loop (see Figure 6.1.2) that is derived from the requirements of ISO 9001:2008 and covers the initial identification of the requirement to the final satisfaction of the customer's needs and expectations.

Within NAFAAD an effective QMS ensures that all activities are fully understood, controlled and documented and that everyone knows exactly what they are supposed to be doing and how they should be doing it.

There are four main requirement sections making up the ISO 9001:2008 standard ranging from how to control a design process to how to audit an activity – but the most important element is the first one which demands that **everyone** shall be involved in quality in order for it to succeed and that it **must** be management led and that there **must** be a commitment to quality – **at the highest level**.

Within NAFAAD we have this commitment. It stems from NAFAAD's decisions in this respect and manifests itself throughout NAFAAD's management, at all levels.

2.2 Organisational goals

The primary goal of NAFAAD shall, at all times, be the quality of the end product and service.

To succeed, NAFAAD must be able to offer products and services that:

- meet the need, use and purpose as defined in NAFAAD's Memorandum and Articles of Association;
- satisfy the customer's requirements and expectations;
- comply with applicable international, European and national quality standards and specifications.

Document Ref: **N-51–044RLR13**
Version: 03.01
Date: 1 October 2013
Quality Management System
Part One – Quality Manual
Version 01.00

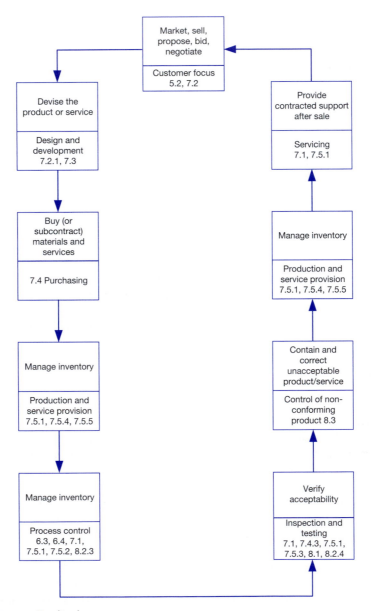

FIGURE 6.1.2 Quality loop

Document Ref: **N-51–044RLR13**
Version: 03.01
Date: 1 October 2013
Quality Management System
Part One – Quality Manual
Version 01.00

In order to meet these objectives, NAFAAD shall organise itself in such a way that the technical, administrative and human factors affecting the quality of NAFAAD products and services are always under control.

It is **imperative** that this control is orientated to the reduction, elimination and – of paramount importance – the prevention of quality deficiencies. The NAFAAD QMS, therefore, has to be developed and implemented for the purpose of accomplishing the objectives set out in NAFAAD's Memorandum and Articles of Association.

Author's Hint

If you are **not** a Ltd company then you might not have any Memorandum and Articles of Association, you could say 'objectives set out in Section 1 of the Quality Manual' or something similar.

Above all (and to achieve maximum effectiveness) it is essential that the NAFAAD QMS is designed so that it is appropriate to the type of contract and services being offered by NAFAAD.

Demonstration of the continued success of the QMS shall be achieved via regular audits and reviews.

2.3 Purpose

The purpose of a QMS is to ensure that the end product (i.e. the deliverable) conforms to the customer's (i.e. user's), contractual requirements.

NAFAAD's QMS, therefore, involves all NAFAAD's functions, wherever and however instigated (e.g. at Director level, Section Manager level etc.) that directly, or indirectly, affect NAFAAD deliverables and contracts.

In essence, NAFAAD's QMS essentially consists of the documented rules, procedures and instructions prepared in accordance with ISO 9001:2008. These are stated in the Quality Manual (QM) as well as the associated Core Business Process (CP), Supporting Processes (SPs), Quality Procedures (QPs) and Work Instructions (WIs).

The NAFAAD audit team (consisting of the Managing Director, Quality Manager and Company Secretary) plus Section Manager(s) may decide if additional documents are required for individual sections. In these cases, the requirement for an additional document shall be clearly stated and rules developed.

| Document Ref: **N-51–044RLR13** |
| Version: 03.01 |
| Date: 1 October 2013 |
| Quality Management System |
| Part One – Quality Manual |
| Version 01.00 |

3 QUALITY POLICY

3.1 Introduction

This section of the manual defines NAFAAD's quality policy and outlines the main responsibilities for its implementation.

3.2 Quality Management System requirements

'*A Quality Management System (QMS) is the organised structure of responsibilities, activities, resources and events that together provide procedures and methods of implementation to ensure the capability of an organisation meets the quality requirement of the client*' (ISO 10011:2002).

Quality is an objective concept. It is something that the whole workforce can understand and measure and for which they accept responsibility.

As an indicator, some of the determinants and measures of NAFAAD's quality of a service are shown in Figure 6.1.3, whilst those appertaining to the quality of a product are shown in Figure 6.1.4.

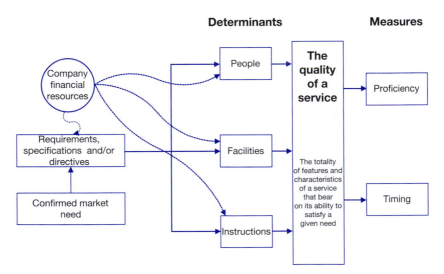

FIGURE 6.1.3 Some of the determinants and measurements of the quality of a service

	Document Ref: **N-51–044RLR13**
	Version: 03.01
	Date: 1 October 2013
	Quality Management System
	Part One – Quality Manual
	Version 01.00

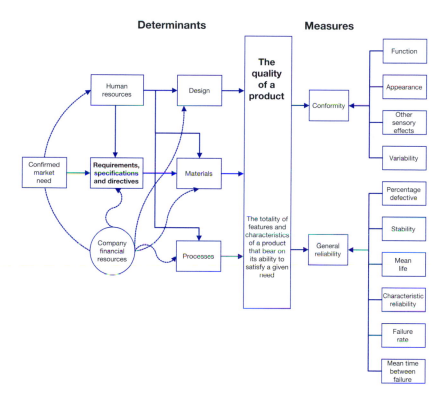

FIGURE 6.1.4 Some of the determinants and measurements of the quality of a product

3.3 Company requirements

As described in the company policy statement, within NAFAAD we are totally committed to setting and achieving quality standards that will enable the company to provide its customers with a high quality product and service.

To meet this commitment, NAFAAD shall develop and maintain a QMS that meets the requirements and the recommendations of ISO 9001:2008.

Total Quality Management (TQM) shall be applied to every aspect of our activity and quality shall be the responsibility of everyone, in every activity, throughout NAFAAD.

Document Ref: **N-51–044RLR13**
Version: 03.01
Date: 1 October 2013
Quality Management System
Part One – Quality Manual
Version 01.00

To achieve these objectives, everyone's involvement and commitment is vital in adhering to the system adopted and in fully appreciating their quality responsibilities. Everyone connected with NAFAAD shall be supported according to their individual needs for personal development, training and facilities.

3.4 Company quality policy

Quality management within NAFAAD is based on the quality system described in Section 4 of ISO 9001:2008 and the purpose of this quality system is to define the policy, organisation and responsibilities for the management of quality within NAFAAD.

Quality management, therefore, forms an integral part of our overall company management and the role of quality management within our company is an essential requirement. It provides confidence that application of company management (as described within this Quality Manual) is efficient, comprehensive and effective in ensuring that every stage of the product (or service) development is delivered:

- on time;
- to the agreed product specifications;
- within budget.

The main objective of NAFAAD's QMS is to ensure that all activities, whether they are managerial (e.g. organisation) or technical (e.g. specification work) comply with the Quality Manual and it is incumbent on **all** staff to have a day-to-day responsibility for ensuring conformance to the requirements and rules as stated in this Quality Manual.

Author's Hint

You may well need to change the above sentence to reflect your own type of business.

In cases of non-compliance (e.g. if part of the specified work is not carried out in accordance with the product and/or service requirements) a problem solving process shall be executed by the first responsible manager. This process shall

Document Ref: **N-51–044RLR13**
Version: 03.01
Date: 1 October 2013
Quality Management System
Part One – Quality Manual
Version 01.00

include the location of root causes, remedial action, review of NAFAAD's QMS and, if necessary, its adjustment and modification.

The Quality Manager plays an important part in this process. His role will be to suggest alternative solutions and help the First Line Manager to take the necessary remedial action. If no effective corrective action is taken, the Quality Manager has the duty to inform the Managing Director.

Summarised, NAFAAD's QMS shall ensure:

- clear responsibilities for all activities and tasks;
- confirmation that all activities are defined and controlled by a Quality Procedure or Work Instruction;
- staff are trained to the requirements listed in the Quality Manual and contract Quality Plans;
- compliance with NAFAAD's Quality Procedures detailed in the Quality Manual and Contract Quality Plans are audited;
- remedial action is taken whenever appropriate;
- the Quality Processes, Quality Procedures, Work Instructions (contained in the Quality Manual) and contract Quality Plans themselves are regularly reviewed.

3.5 Adherence to standards

NAFAAD's Quality Manual is based on the requirements of ISO 9001:2008 and takes into consideration the requirements of all other applicable national, European and international standards, procedures and directives. If there are any discrepancies between NAFAAD's Quality Manual and these other directives/standards, the requirements of NAFAAD's Quality Manual shall prevail.

3.6 Purpose of a Quality Management System

The purpose of having a QMS is to ensure that the end product or service conforms to the customer's (i.e. user's) contractual requirements. NAFAAD's Quality Management System, therefore, involves all NAFAAD functions, wherever and however instigated that directly, or indirectly, affect deliverables and contracts.

To ensure that we fully meet (and in many instances exceed) the requirements of ISO 9001:2008, NAFAAD have adopted the principles of the Deming four-step management PDCA method used throughout business for the control and continuous improvement of all our processes and products.

Document Ref: **N-51–044RLR13**
Version: 03.01
Date: 1 October 2013
Quality Management System
Part One – Quality Manual
Version 01.00

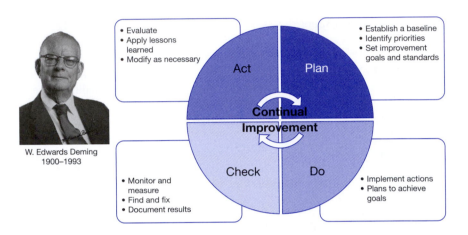

Act
- Evaluate
- Apply lessons learned
- Modify as necessary

Plan
- Establish a baseline
- Identify priorities
- Set improvement goals and standards

Check
- Monitor and measure
- Find and fix
- Document results

Do
- Implement actions
- Plans to achieve goals

Continual Improvement

W. Edwards Deming
1900–1993

FIGURE 6.1.5 The PDCA cycle

We ensure that every contract that we undertake and every improvement within NAFAAD's own internal management system(s) follow the internationally agreed steps of the cycle, namely:

PLAN – We establish the objectives and processes necessary to deliver results in accordance with the expected output – be that a deliverable, target or goal.

DO – Having planned our objectives, we then implement them and follow the agreed processes and procedures in order to produce a quality product.

CHECK – Throughout the planning and finalisation of the product, we carefully analyse the ongoing results (measured and collected in 'DO' above) and compare these against the expected results (targets or goals from the 'PLAN') to see if there are any differences. We look for any deviations and improvements that might have been made during the implementation of the 'PLAN'.

ACT – The results of the 'CHECK' stage are then carefully analysed to see if any further steps can be taken to refine and improve the 'PLAN'.

We also use the results of this PDCA cycle to further improve future products, processes and deliverables.

Demonstration of the continued success of our Quality Management System is then achieved via regular audits and reviews (for details see QP/3 – Internal Audits).

Document Ref: **N-51–044RLR13**
Version: 03.01
Date: 1 October 2013
Quality Management System
Part One – Quality Manual
Version 01.00

3.7 Quality in performance

The system adopted by NAFAAD to achieve quality in performance with accountability is based on the following four main items or activities:

1. **Quality Manual** – the Quality Manual (as the primary control document) which defines the policy, processes, responsibilities, procedures etc. that are to be used;
2. **Quality Manager** – the appointment of a Quality Manager within a defined organisational structure, who is responsible for operating the system and ensuring that the Quality Manual and its associated documentation is fully and effectively implemented;
3. **Documented Processes and Procedures** – the use of documented processes and procedures to define all activities which could lead to variability of execution with consequent loss of quality attainment, performance or safety if not rigorously controlled;
4. **Quality Management System reviews** – regular reviews of the Quality Manual (and its supporting documentation) together with auditing its effective implementation to ensure that the most suitable and effective methods and procedures are still prescribed and used.

3.8 Organisational goals

The primary goal of NAFAAD shall, at all times, be to ensure that the quality of the product and/or service:

- satisfies the customer's requirements and expectations;
- meets the need, use and purpose as defined in the approved product and/or service specifications;
- complies with the requirements of ISO 9001:2008;
- complies with applicable international, European and national quality standards, specifications and directives.

In order to meet these objectives, NAFAAD has to be organised in such a way that the technical, administrative and human factors affecting the quality of NAFAAD products and services are always under control. It is imperative that this control is orientated to the reduction, elimination and – very importantly – the prevention of quality deficiencies.

	Document Ref: **N-51–044RLR13** Version: 03.01 Date: 1 October 2013 Quality Management System Part One – Quality Manual Version 01.00

The NAFAAD QMS, therefore, has to be developed and implemented for the purpose of accomplishing the objectives set out above.

To achieve maximum effectiveness, it is essential that this QMS is designed so that it is appropriate to the type of contract and services being offered by NAFAAD.

3.9 Structure for quality management

NAFAAD's QMS defines the policy, organisation and responsibilities for the management of quality within NAFAAD. It ensures that all activities comply with an agreed set of rules, regulations and guidelines and that the end product or service (i.e. the deliverable) conforms to the customer's (i.e. the user's) contractual requirements. A QMS can only be effective if it is fully documented, understood and followed by all.

Within the ISO 9001:2008 Quality Model, there are four levels of documentation, and these are structured as shown in Figure 6.1.6.

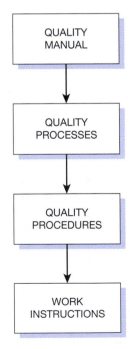

FIGURE 6.1.6 Quality Management System

	Document Ref: **N-51–044RLR13**
	Version: 03.01
	Date: 1 October 2013
	Quality Management System
	Part One – Quality Manual
	Version 01.00

TABLE 6.1.1 QMS documentation

Level 1 Quality Manual	The main policy document that establishes AAL's QMS and how it meets the requirements of ISO 9001:2008.
Level 2 Processes	The CP plus SPs that describe the activities required to implement the QMS and to meet the policy requirements made in the QM.
Level 3 Quality Procedures	A description of the method by which quality system activities are managed.
Level 4 Work Instructions	A description of how a specific task is carried out (supplemented by drawings, blueprints, forms, checklists, records and flowcharts).

The NAFAAD QMS relies on the eight quality management principles contained in ISO 9001:2008 to provide and enable a continual improvement of our business and our overall efficiency and to make us capable of responding to customer needs and expectations. These eight principles are shown in the following figure [Figure 6.1.7].

1. **Customer focused organisation** – NAFAAD depends on our customers and is committed to understanding, anticipating and responding to every customer requirement with product and service excellence.
2. **Leadership** – leaders establish unity of purpose and directions create the environment in which people can become fully involved in achieving NAFAAD's objectives.
3. **Involvement of people** – NAFAAD has created an environment which makes every employee a team member and encourages participation in achieving our goals.
4. **Process approach** – the desired result is achieved by relating resources and activities to managed processes.
5. **System approach to management** – identifying, understanding and managing a system of inter-related processes for a given objective contributes to the effectiveness and efficiency of NAFAAD.
6. **Continual improvement** – continual improvement is a permanent objective of NAFAAD.
7. **Factual approach to decision making** – effective decisions are based on the logical and intuitive analysis of data and information.

	Document Ref: **N-51–044RLR13**
	Version: 03.01
	Date: 1 October 2013
	Quality Management System
	Part One – Quality Manual
	Version 01.00

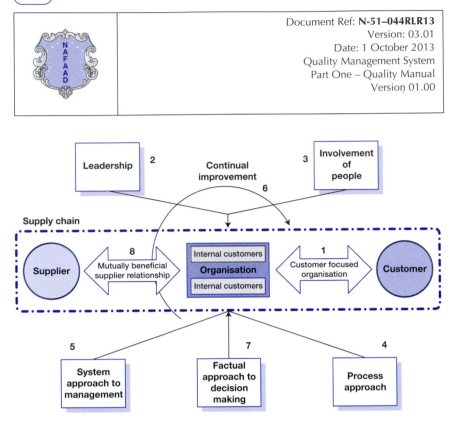

FIGURE 6.1.7 The eight principles of ISO 9001:2008 expressed diagrammatically

8. **Mutually beneficial supplier relationships** – mutually beneficial relationships between NAFAAD and its suppliers enhance the ability of both organisations to create value.

3.9.1 QMS document control

One copy of the QMS shall be held on the server and (for control purposes) the Quality Manager shall have sole access to this file. It is the Quality Manager's responsibility to modify, update, amend and approve these documents as required. In all cases, the procedures and instructions contained in this controlled copy shall be official company policy.

Uncontrolled copies of the Quality Manual (including Quality Procedures and Work Instructions) shall be available to all staff via a link on NAFAAD's Intranet Home Page. Uncontrolled copies (watermarked '*Uncontrolled Copy*' across each page) may be provided to outside organisations, or individuals, for publicity or information purposes.

	Document Ref: **N-51–044RLR13** Version: 03.01 Date: 1 October 2013 Quality Management System Part One – Quality Manual Version 01.00

 These copies will **not** be automatically updated!

Staff shall be informed by an e-mail from the Quality Manager when a controlled copy has been amended; it will include a request for all uncontrolled copies to be destroyed. All staff will reply by e-mail to the Quality Manager stating that they have complied with the request.

3.10 The Quality Manual

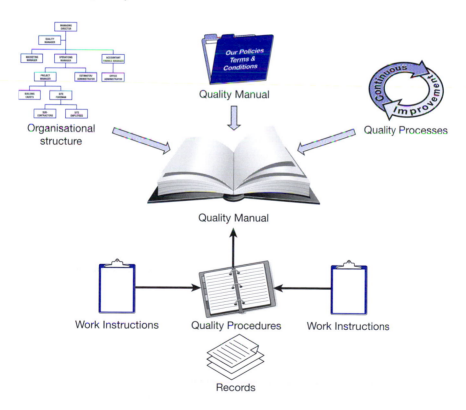

FIGURE 6.1.8 NAFAAD's Quality Manual

Document Ref: **N-51–044RLR13**
Version: 03.01
Date: 1 October 2013
Quality Management System
Part One – Quality Manual
Version 01.00

The Quality Manual is a statement of the managerial policy and the objectives for each element of ISO 9001:2008. For NAFAAD this is included in Section 4 and, having been established in response to the specified system requirements, it provides a statement of commitment to customers (or external approval and/or regulatory bodies) to which NAFAAD may be required to provide such information.

NAFAAD's Quality Manual describes a number of systematic controls and procedures for the staff in fulfilling their duties and responsibilities. It defines the lines of traceability, accountability and responsibility and whilst it exists primarily as an internal management control document, the Quality Manual also provides a definitive statement of the policy, objectives, operating systems, processes and procedures established by NAFAAD. The system recognises the established elements of modern formalised quality management as expressed in national and international standards and as appropriate to the nature of the work undertaken.

3.11 Quality Processes

NAFAAD's QMS is founded on the requirements of ISO 9001:2008, with a common structure based on a Core Business Process (CP) (describing the end-to-end activities involved in NAFAAD's project management and the production of contract deliverables) supplemented by a number of Supporting Processes (SPs) which describe the infrastructure required to complete NAFAAD's projects on time and within budget.

To ensure achievement of process objectives, a process owner with full responsibility and authority for managing the process and achieving process objectives shall be nominated.

From the initial identification of the task through to the final customer satisfaction all steps in NAFAAD's Core Business Process are supported by Quality Procedures (see Part 3 of this manual) that ensure that all activities are fully understood, controlled and documented and that everyone knows exactly what they are supposed to be doing and how they should be doing it.

Note: If a particular project requires additional quality controls for a specific product or service then project-specific QPs shall be written by the Quality Manager (in conjunction with the department or section concerned) as part of a separate project Quality Plan.

Document Ref: **N-51–044RLR13**
Version: 03.01
Date: 1 October 2013
Quality Management System
Part One – Quality Manual
Version 01.00

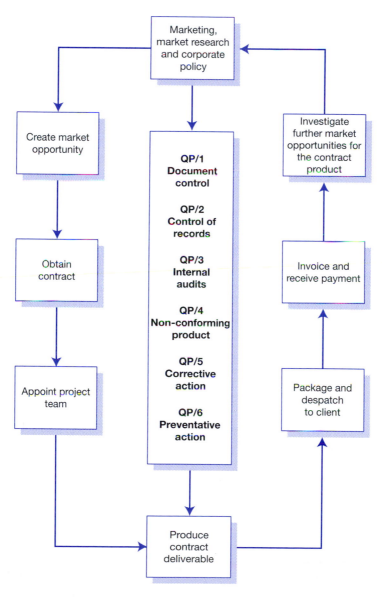

FIGURE 6.1.9 NAFAAD's Core Business Process

	Document Ref: **N-51–044RLR13**
	Version: 03.01
	Date: 1 October 2013
	Quality Management System
	Part One – Quality Manual
	Version 01.00

3.12 Quality Procedures

Quality Procedures (QPs) form the bulk of NAFAAD's QMS and describe how the policy objectives of the Quality Manual can be met in practice and how these processes are controlled. A list of the current NAFAAD Quality Procedures is shown in Annex C to this Quality Manual.

QPs shall cover all the applicable elements of ISO 9001 and shall detail procedures that concern NAFAAD's actual method of operation. They shall be used for planning and controlling all activities that impact on quality.

Each QP shall cover an easily identifiable and separate part of the quality system and shall be capable of being easily traced back to the policies dictated by senior management.

QPs should not normally include technical requirements or specialist procedures required for the manufacture of a product. This type of detail will generally be included in a Work Instruction.

The generation and control of QPs is defined in QP/7 – 'Production of a Quality Document' – and can be used as separate documents outside the Quality Manual in places of work. In addition to a descriptive title and a file number, each procedure shall be dated and is subject to regular review (during an internal audit) for possible amendments and/or updating. These documented procedures are made available as Uncontrolled Copies via a link on NAFAAD's Intranet Home Page.

A number of forms are used in the application of certain procedures, which mainly relate to the communication of data or instructions for keeping records.

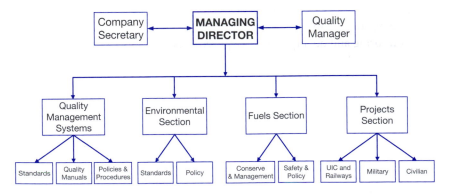

FIGURE 6.1.10 Inter-relationship of documented processes with QPs and WIs

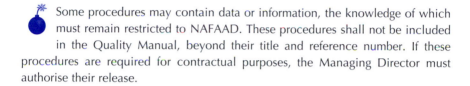

Document Ref: **N-51–044RLR13**
Version: 03.01
Date: 1 October 2013
Quality Management System
Part One – Quality Manual
Version 01.00

Copies of these forms are included in the relevant procedures and Work Instructions.

 Some procedures may contain data or information, the knowledge of which must remain restricted to NAFAAD. These procedures shall not be included in the Quality Manual, beyond their title and reference number. If these procedures are required for contractual purposes, the Managing Director must authorise their release.

3.13 Work Instructions

Work Instructions (WIs) describe, in detail, how NAFAAD implements its procedures, such as what is to be done, who should do it, when it should be done, what supplies, services and/or equipment are to be used and what criteria have to be satisfied. They describe how to perform specific operations and are produced for all of the relevant activities of NAFAAD so as to ensure that the whole company can work to the same format.

In order that NAFAAD Management can be sure that everything is being carried out under the strictest of controlled conditions, it is crucial that all WIs referring to a product, activity or service are clear, accurate and fully documented.

In summary a Work Instruction shall, as a minimum, define:

- the manner of production (and installation) where the absence of such controls would adversely affect quality;
- measurable criteria for workmanship to ensure the required level of quality is being adhered to;
- monitoring and quality control requirements;
- the approval processes by which compliance can be identified;
- who can carry out this procedure.

The generation and control of WIs is defined in QP/7 – 'Production of a Quality Document'. In addition to a descriptive title and a file number, each instruction is dated and shall be subject to regular review (during an internal audit) for possible amendment and/or updating. These documented instructions are made available as Uncontrolled Copies and can be used as separate documents outside the Quality Manual in places of work (see QP/1 'Document Control').

Current NAFAAD WIs are listed in Part 4 of the QMS.

	Document Ref: **N-51–044RLR13** Version: 03.01 Date: 1 October 2013 Quality Management System Part One – Quality Manual Version 01.00

 Note: If a particular project demands further detail then project-specific Work Instructions shall be created. These project-specific WIs shall appear in the Quality Plan applicable to that particular project.

3.14 Records

Records provide objective evidence of and demonstrate conformance to specified requirements contained in the QMS.

Normally records are retained for five years – except as required by local or national law.

See QP/2 *'Control of Records'* for more details.

3.15 Project quality plans

For larger and more complex projects and/or contracts, project-specific Quality Plans may have to be produced. These are effectively a sub set of the QM and describe additional procedures and controls that will have to be applied. The production of these Quality Plans shall be co-ordinated between the Quality Manager and Project/Contract Manager concerned.

4 QUALITY MANAGEMENT SYSTEM (ISO 9001:2008 – 4)

Subsequent sections of this QM are modelled on ISO 9001:2008 and describe the arrangements or systems that have been established to meet the specified requirements of this standard. As far as possible, the sections (i.e. 4–8) have been structured in a similar manner to those contained in ISO 9001:2008 (i.e. each section, sub section etc. directly corresponds in terms of number and content with the ISO equivalent number). This not only makes it easier for NAFAAD to ensure that our Quality Management System addresses all elements of ISO 9001:2008, but also makes it easier for an external auditor or client to quickly see that NAFAAD complies with (or has a very good reason for not complying with) all of the requirements of the standard. The correspondence between NAFAAD's Quality Manual and the requirements of ISO 9001:2008 is shown at Annex B.

	Document Ref: **N-51–044RLR13** Version: 03.01 Date: 1 October 2013 Quality Management System Part One – Quality Manual Version 01.00

Conformance with ISO 9001:2008

NAFAAD is, therefore, able to state, quite categorically, that other than the permissible exclusions shown in the relevant parts of the text and at Annex B, NAFAAD's QMS conforms to the requirements specified in ISO 9001:2008!

Quality Manual administration

The Quality Manager shall review the effectiveness and suitability of the Quality Manual at least twice a year. Where the system is found to be ineffective as a result of changed requirements and/or circumstances, amendments shall be made to the Quality Manual.

Confidentiality

This Quality Manual is the intellectual property of NAFAAD and may not be copied in whole or part, or transmitted to any third party without the express written permission of the Quality Manager.

 Author's Hint

Where the term *'documented procedure'* appears, this means that the procedure **MUST BE** established, documented, implemented and maintained. In accordance with ISO 9001:2008:

- a single document may address the requirements for one or more procedures; and
- a requirement for a documented procedure may be covered by more than one document.

4.1 General requirements (ISO 9001:2008 – 4.1)

NAFAAD recognises the need of adequate documentation for clarity and transparency of the system.

1. Policy and objectives

NAFAAD shall define and manage the processes necessary to ensure that all contract deliverables conform to customer requirements.

	Document Ref: **N-51–044RLR13**
	Version: 03.01
	Date: 1 October 2013
	Quality Management System
	Part One – Quality Manual
	Version 01.00

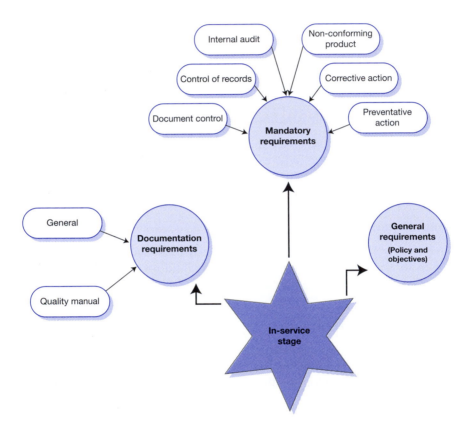

FIGURE 6.1.11 Quality Management System

As a means of continually improving performance, NAFAAD shall:

- ensure the availability of resources and information necessary to support the operation and monitoring of these processes;
- establish, document, implement and maintain a QMS and continually improve its effectiveness in accordance with the requirements and principles of ISO 9001:2008;
- prepare procedures that describe the processes required to implement the QMS.

Document Ref: **N-51–044RLR13**
Version: 03.01
Date: 1 October 2013
Quality Management System
Part One – Quality Manual
Version 01.00

 Author's Hint

All organisations should ensure that any outsourced processes that affect product conformity are thoroughly analysed, controlled and subject to continual improvement.

4.2 Documentation requirements (ISO 9001:2008 – 4.2)

NAFAAD shall establish and document the specified requirements for controlling the quality of a deliverable, in conformance with the appropriate regulatory requirements.

4.2.1 General (ISO 9001:2008 – 4.2.1)

1. Policy and objectives

NAFAAD's QMS documentation shall include:

- a Quality Manual;
- documented statements regarding quality policy and quality objectives;
- documented procedures, that clearly describe the sequence of processes necessary to ensure conformance with ISO 9001:2008;
- documented instructions to ensure the effective planning, operation and control of processes and quality records.

2. Responsibilities

The Quality Manager is responsible for overseeing the operation of NAFAAD's QMS; for ensuring that the Quality Manual is fully and effectively implemented and for co-ordinating the writing (as well as the availability) of the necessary processes, procedures and instructions.

3. Implementation

CP/1 – Core Business Process
SP/1 – Compliance and Approval
SP/2 – Subcontractors and Suppliers
SP/3 – Customer Satisfaction

| | Document Ref: **N-51–044RLR13**
Version: 03.01
Date: 1 October 2013
Quality Management System
Part One – Quality Manual
Version 01.00 |

 Author's Hint

The amount of documentation required for a QMS can vary from one organisation to another dependent on:

- the size of organisation and type of activity;
- the complexity of processes and their interactions; and
- the competence of personnel.

Note: The documentation can be in any form or type of medium and can consist of just a couple of pages or a large reference document such as NAFAAD's.

4.2.2 Quality Manual (ISO 9001:2008 – 4.2.2)

The Quality Manager shall establish and maintain the NAFAAD Quality Manual, which shall (inclusive of Annexes) be regularly reviewed and audited to ensure continuing acceptability, validity and effectiveness.

1. Policy and objectives

The Quality Manager shall ensure that NAFAAD's Quality Manual includes:

- the scope of the QMS;
- details of the documented procedures that need to be established as part of the QMS;
- the sequence and interaction between the processes of the quality management system;
- details of (and justification for) any ISO 9001:2008 exclusions.

2. Responsibilities

The Quality Manager is responsible for overseeing the operation of NAFAAD's QMS, for ensuring that the Quality Manual is fully and effectively implemented and for co-ordinating the writing (as well as the availability) of the necessary processes, procedures and instructions.

	Document Ref: **N-51–044RLR13** Version: 03.01 Date: 1 October 2013 Quality Management System Part One – Quality Manual Version 01.00

3. Implementation

CP/1 – Core Business Process
SP/1 – Compliance and Approval
SP/2 – Subcontractors and Suppliers
SP/3 – Customer Satisfaction
QP/7 – Production of a Quality Document
QP/9 – Approval Procedure
QP/10 – Quality Management System Review.

4.2.3 Control of documents (ISO 9001:2008 – 4.2.3)

> **Author's Hint**
>
> It is a **mandatory** requirement of ISO 9001:2008 for **all** organisations to
> have a documented procedure for the Control of documentation.

All documents required by, and used in support of NAFAAD's QMS shall be
controlled and maintained.

1. Policy and objectives

NAFAAD shall establish a documented procedure for the control of all
documents no matter their origin or topic. This procedure shall ensure that:

- documents are approved for adequacy prior to release;
- documents are reviewed, updated as necessary and re-approved;
- documents remain legible and readily identifiable and retrievable;
- documents of external origin can be identified, controlled and recorded;
- only relevant versions of documents are available at points of use;
- obsolete documents are removed from all points of issue and use, or otherwise
  controlled to prevent unintended use;
- any obsolete documents retained for legal or knowledge-preservation purposes
  are suitably identified;
- a master list identifying the current revision status of documents is established.

	Document Ref: **N-51–044RLR13** Version: 03.01 Date: 1 October 2013 Quality Management System Part One – Quality Manual Version 01.00

 Author's Hint

1. Only external documents that the organisation believes are necessary for the planning and operation of the QMS need to be identified and their distribution controlled.
2. Records are considered by ISO 9001:2008 as a special type of document that need to be controlled according to the requirements given in 4.2.4.

2. Responsibilities

The Quality Manager (in consultation with the Company Secretary) is responsible for the overall planning of document control procedures throughout NAFAAD.

3. Implementation

QP/1 – Document Control
QP/7 – Production of a Quality Document
QP/9 – Approval Procedure
QP/10 – Quality Management System Review
QP/14 – Change Control

4.2.4 Control of quality records (ISO 9001:2008 – 4.2.4)

 Author's Hint

It is a **mandatory** requirement of ISO 9001:2008 for **all** organisations to have a documented procedure for the Control of records.

NAFAAD shall maintain appropriate quality records that demonstrate conformance to the requirements and the effective operation of the QMS.

1. Policy and objectives

NAFAAD shall establish a documented procedure to define the controls required for the identification, storage, protection, retrieval, retention and disposition of records.

 Records shall remain legible, readily identifiable and retrievable.

Document Ref: **N-51–044RLR13**
Version: 03.01
Date: 1 October 2013
Quality Management System
Part One – Quality Manual
Version 01.00

2. Responsibilities

The Quality Manager (in consultation with the Company Secretary) is responsible for maintaining quality records demonstrating conformance to requirements and the effective operation of the QMS.

3. Implementation

QP/2 – Control of Records
QP/10 – Quality Management System Review

	Document Ref: **N-51–044RLR13** Version: 03.01 Date: 1 October 2013 Quality Management System Part One – Quality Manual Version 01.00

5 MANAGEMENT RESPONSIBILITY (ISO 9001:2008 – 5)

Top Management shall endeavour – at all times – to create an environment where people are fully involved and in which the organisation's QMS can operate effectively.

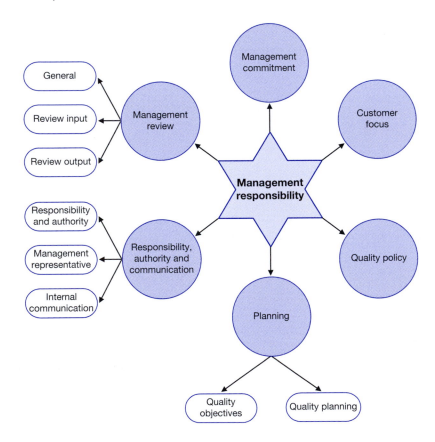

FIGURE 6.1.12 Management responsibility

Document Ref: **N-51–044RLR13**
Version: 03.01
Date: 1 October 2013
Quality Management System
Part One – Quality Manual
Version 01.00

5.1 Management commitment (ISO 9001:2008 – 5.1)

1. Policy and objectives

NAFAAD shall demonstrate its commitment to the development and implementation of the QMS and the continual improvement of its effectiveness by:

- establishing the quality policy and quality objectives;
- carrying out regular management reviews of the QMS and its associated documentation – aimed at ensuring the continual improvement of the system;
- ensuring the availability of necessary resources;
- ensuring that quality objectives are established;
- ensuring that all staff are aware of the importance of meeting customer, regulatory and legal requirements.

2. Responsibilities

The NAFAAD Executive Board is responsible for demonstrating their commitment to quality and for supporting management in achieving that commitment.

3. Implementation

The NAFAAD QM sections 5–8 together with its supporting annexes.

5.2 Customer focus (ISO 9001:2008 – 5.2)

Top Management shall ensure that customer requirements are determined and are met.

1. Policy and objectives

With the overall aim of achieving customer satisfaction, NAFAAD shall ensure that:

- customer needs and expectations are determined and converted into requirements;
- customer requirements are fully understood and met;
- customer satisfaction is enhanced.

2. Responsibilities

Top Management has overall responsibility for establishing, implementing and maintaining this activity.

	Document Ref: **N-51–044RLR13**
	Version: 03.01
	Date: 1 October 2013
	Quality Management System
	Part One – Quality Manual
	Version 01.00

3. Implementation

NAFAAD QMS Part 1 (i.e. this Quality Manual) and in particular:

SP/1 – Compliance and Approval
SP/2 – Subcontractors and Suppliers
SP/3 – Customer Satisfaction
QP/12 – Customer Feedback; and
QP/13 – Customer Awareness and Training.

5.3 Quality policy (ISO 9001:2008 – 5.3)

NAFAAD's quality policy shall provide a framework for establishing and reviewing quality objectives.

1. Policy and objectives

NAFAAD shall establish its quality policy and ensure that it:

- is appropriate for the needs of NAFAAD and its potential customers;
- includes a commitment to meeting requirements (and the continual improvement) of the NAFAAD QMS;
- provides a framework for establishing and reviewing quality objectives;
- is communicated, understood and implemented throughout NAFAAD;
- is regularly reviewed for continuing suitability.

2. Responsibilities

Top Management has overall responsibility for establishing, implementing and maintaining this activity.

3. Implementation

NAFAAD QM Section 1.4.
QP/7 – Production of a Quality Document
QP/10 – Quality Management System Review

5.4 Planning (ISO 9001:2008 – 5.4)

Top Management shall ensure that quality objectives are achieved and the Quality Plan is used consistently.

Document Ref: **N-51–044RLR13**
Version: 03.01
Date: 1 October 2013
Quality Management System
Part One – Quality Manual
Version 01.00

5.4.1 Quality objectives (ISO 9001:2008 – 5.4.1)

1. Policy and objectives

NAFAAD shall ensure that quality objectives:

- are established;
- are measurable;
- are consistent with quality policy;
- include a commitment for continual improvement;
- cover the requirements of the deliverable.

2. Responsibilities

Top Management has overall responsibility for establishing, implementing and maintaining this activity.

3. Implementation

NAFAAD QM Section 1.4

QP/7 – Production of a Quality Document
QP/10 – Quality Management System Review

5.4.2 Quality Management System planning (ISO 9001:2008 – 5.4.2)

1. Policy and objectives

NAFAAD shall identify and plan the activities and resources required to achieve quality objectives. This planning shall be consistent with the other requirements of the QMS and the results shall be documented.
    Planning shall cover the:

- processes required by the QMS;
- identification of resources;
- realisation processes;
- requirements for continual improvement;
- requirements for change control;
- verification activities, criteria for acceptability and the quality records that are needed.

	Document Ref: **N-51–044RLR13** Version: 03.01 Date: 1 October 2013 Quality Management System Part One – Quality Manual Version 01.00

 Author's Hint

ISO 9001:2008 is quite specific in stating that 'Planning' shall include and ensure that any organisational change is conducted in a controlled manner and that the QMS is maintained during such change(s).

---

2. Responsibilities

Top Management has overall responsibility for establishing, implementing and maintaining this activity.

3. Implementation

NAFAAD QM Sections 1.4, 2.1 and 2.2

SP/1 – Compliance and Approval
QP/7 – Production of a Quality Document
QP/8 – Design Control

5.5 Responsibility, authority and communication (ISO 9001:2008 – 5.5)

NAFAAD shall continually review the organisation's resources to ensure that adequate staff, equipment and materials are available to meet customer requirements.

5.5.1 Responsibility and authority (ISO 9001:2008 – 5.5.1)

1. Policy and objectives

NAFAAD shall:

- define the roles and their inter-relations, responsibilities and authorities in order to facilitate effective quality management and ensure that this inform-ation is communicated throughout NAFAAD;
- establish the inter-relations of personnel involved in managing, performing and/or assessing work that affects the quality of the deliverable (providing independence and authority as necessary);

Document Ref: **N-51–044RLR13**
Version: 03.01
Date: 1 October 2013
Quality Management System
Part One – Quality Manual
Version 01.00

2. Responsibilities

Top Management has overall responsibility for establishing, implementing and maintaining this activity.

3. Implementation

QM, Annex A – Duties and responsibilities

5.5.2 Management representative (ISO 9001:2008 – 5.5.2)

1. Policy and objectives

The Managing Director shall appoint a member of the management who, **irrespective of all other responsibilities**, has overall responsibility and authority to ensure that the NAFAAD's quality policies are implemented throughout NAFAAD.

The Quality Manager is responsible for:

- ensuring that all processes needed for the QMS are established, implemented and maintained;
- reporting to Top Management on the performance of the QMS and any need for improvement;
- ensuring the promotion of awareness of customer requirements throughout NAFAAD;
- liaising with external parties on matters relating to the NAFAAD QMS.

 Author's Hint

ISO 9001:2008 now makes it clear that the management representative **must** be a member of the organisation's own management and that *'outsiders'* (such as a subcontractor's Quality Manager) may no longer perform this important function.

2. Responsibilities

The Quality Manager reports directly to the Managing Director and is independent of all contractual and project responsibilities that may adversely affect quality performance. He is responsible for ensuring that the QM and its associated CPs, SPs, QPs and WIs (making up the NAFAAD QMS) are kept up-to-date,

	Document Ref: **N-51–044RLR13** Version: 03.01 Date: 1 October 2013 Quality Management System Part One – Quality Manual Version 01.00

administered and implemented correctly and efficiently according to the quality policy laid down by the Managing Director.

The Quality Manager has the overall responsibility for ensuring that the policies set out in this QMS are understood, implemented and maintained at all levels in the organisation and that the company works towards achieving its vision and key objectives.

The Quality Manager represents NAFAAD in all matters relevant to the QMS as established by customer, regulatory and ISO 9001:2008 requirements. He is responsible for ensuring that the system is effectively implemented and maintained, and reports on the performance of the QMS at management review meetings.

The Quality Manager is the prime point of liaison with certification bodies and customers' quality management representatives.

3. Implementation

Full details of the Quality Manager's duties and responsibilities are included at Annex A to the QM.

5.5.3 Internal communication (ISO 9001:2008 – 5.5.3)

1. Policy and objectives

NAFAAD shall ensure that suitable communication processes are established within the organisation and that these communication processes pay particular regard to the effectiveness of the QMS.

2. Responsibilities

The Quality Manager has overall responsibility for establishing, implementing and maintaining this activity.

3. Implementation

QP/13 – Customer Awareness and Training

5.6 Management review (ISO 9001:2008 – 5.6)

Top Management shall complete a review of the Quality Plan on a bi-annual basis in order to provide a long lasting record of NAFAAD's continued capability to produce deliverables that meet the quality objectives, policies and requirements that are contained in the QMS and that it continues to provide 'customer satisfaction'.

This review shall be chaired by the Quality Manager.

Document Ref: **N-51–044RLR13**
Version: 03.01
Date: 1 October 2013
Quality Management System
Part One – Quality Manual
Version 01.00

5.6.1 General (ISO 9001:2008 – 5.6.1)

1. Policy and objectives

NAFAAD shall establish a process for the periodic review of the QMS to ensure:

- its continuing suitability, adequacy and effectiveness;
- the effectiveness of its quality policies;
- the effectiveness of its quality objectives;
- NAFAAD's QMS's continued suitability and any need for changes;
- that the QMS continues to meet the requirements of ISO 9001:2008.

The review shall include an assessment of opportunities for improvement and the need for changes to the QMS.

 Records from management reviews shall be maintained (see 4.2.4).

2. Responsibilities

The Quality Manager (in consultation with the Company Secretary) is responsible for ensuring that quality records are maintained in a systematic and presentable form.

All staff are responsible for ensuring that they provide the necessary records as required from their involvement in implementing the quality systems.

3. Implementation

QP/2 – Control of Records
QP/10 – Quality Management System Review

5.6.2 Review input (ISO 9001:2008 – 5.6.2)

1. Policy and objectives

The QMS review input shall include (but not be limited to):

- results and follow-up actions from earlier management reviews;
- results of previous internal, customer and third-party audits;
- self-assessment results;
- analysis of customer feedback;
- analysis of process performance;

- analysis of product conformance;
- the current status of preventive and corrective action;
- supplier performance;
- changes that could affect the QMS;
- recommendations for improvement;
- new or revised regulatory requirements.

2. Responsibilities

All staff are responsible for ensuring that they provide the necessary records as required from their involvement in implementing the quality systems.

The Quality Manager (in consultation with the Company Secretary) is responsible for ensuring that quality records are maintained in a systematic and presentable form.

3. Implementation

QP/2 – Control of Records
QP/10 – Quality Management System Review

5.6.3 Review output (ISO 9001:2008 – 5.6.3)

1. Policy and objectives

The output of the QMS management review shall include:

- improved product and process performance;
- confirmation of resource requirements and organisational structure;
- market needs;
- risk management;
- change control;
- continued compliance with the relevant statutory and regulatory requirements (in particular ISO 9001:2008).

 Results of management reviews shall be recorded.

2. Responsibilities

All staff are responsible for ensuring that they provide the necessary records as required from their involvement in implementing the quality systems.

	Document Ref: **N-51–044RLR13** Version: 03.01 Date: 1 October 2013 Quality Management System Part One – Quality Manual Version 01.00

The Quality Manager (in consultation with the Company Secretary) is responsible for ensuring that quality records are maintained in a systematic and presentable form.

3. Implementation

QP/2 – Control of Records
QP/10 – Quality Management System Review

6 RESOURCE MANAGEMENT (ISO 9001:2008 – 6)

NAFAAD shall identify and make available all the resources required to meet customer requirements.

FIGURE 6.1.13 Resources management

	Document Ref: **N-51–044RLR13**
	Version: 03.01
	Date: 1 October 2013
	Quality Management System
	Part One – Quality Manual
	Version 01.00

6.1 Provision of resources (ISO 9001:2008 – 6.1)

1. Policy and objectives

NAFAAD shall identify, and make available, all the resources (e.g. information, infrastructure, people, work environment, finance, support etc.) required to:

- implement the QMS;
- maintain its effectiveness;
- meet regulatory and customer requirements;
- ensure that customer satisfaction is assured.

2. Responsibilities

The Managing Director (assisted by the Quality Manager, Company Secretary and Section Managers) has overall responsibility for establishing, implementing and maintaining this activity.

3. Implementation

QP/10 – Quality Management System Review
QP/11 – Purchasing
QP/13 – Customer Awareness and Training

6.2 Human resources (ISO 9001:2008 – 6.2)

NAFAAD shall identify and make available human resources to implement and improve its QMS and comply with contract conditions.

6.2.1 General (ISO 9001:2008 – 6.2.1)

1. Policy and objectives

NAFAAD shall **only** assign personnel who are competent (e.g. by appropriate education, training, skills and experience etc.). Their responsibilities and Job Descriptions are defined in NAFAAD's QM at Annex A.

2. Responsibilities

The Managing Director (assisted by the Quality Manager, Company Secretary and Section Managers) has overall responsibility for establishing, implementing and maintaining this activity.

	Document Ref: **N-51–044RLR13**
	Version: 03.01
	Date: 1 October 2013
	Quality Management System
	Part One – Quality Manual
	Version 01.00

3. Implementation

SP/1 – Compliance and Approval
SP/2 – Subcontractors and Suppliers
QP/11 – Purchasing
QP/13 – Customer Awareness and Training

6.2.2 Competence, training and awareness
(ISO 9001:2008 – 6.2.2)

1. Policy and objectives

NAFAAD shall establish and maintain system level procedures to:

- identify the requirements for training personnel;
- provide appropriate training;
- evaluate the effectiveness of the training provided;
- maintain records of all training;
- ensure that the necessary expertise and levels of skills etc. are available to handle the expected workload and range of activities.

Note: Certain national and/or regional regulations may require NAFAAD to establish additional documented procedures for identifying training needs to cover this possibility.

NAFAAD shall also establish and maintain procedures to make its employees, at each relevant function and level, aware of:

- the importance of conformance with the quality policy, and with the requirements of NAFAAD's QMS;
- the significant impact of its work activities on quality (actual or potential);
- the benefits of improved personal performance;
- its roles and responsibilities in achieving conformance with the quality policy and procedures and with the requirements of the QMS;
- the potential consequences of departure from specified procedures.

2. Responsibilities

Section Managers are responsible for ensuring that appropriate training is carried out and that all staff involved in their projects are aware of the requirements, rules

	Document Ref: **N-51–044RLR13**
	Version: 03.01
	Date: 1 October 2013
	Quality Management System
	Part One – Quality Manual
	Version 01.00

and procedures to which they are to conform and against which they will be audited.

The Quality Manager is responsible for providing internal QMS training.

3. Implementation

QP/13 – Customer Awareness and Training

6.3 Infrastructure (ISO 9001:2008 – 6.3)

1. Policy and objectives

NAFAAD shall determine, provide and maintain the infrastructure required to achieve product conformity requirements regarding (but not limited to) the following:

- workspace and associated facilities;
- hardware and software;
- tools and equipment;
- communication facilities;
- supporting services (such as transport, communication or information systems).

> **Author's Hint**
>
> ISO 9001:2008 now also expects an organisation to provide the infrastructure (including information systems) that is needed to ensure that product requirements are also being met!

2. Responsibilities

The Company Secretary (in consultation with the Quality Manager) has overall responsibility for establishing, implementing and maintaining this activity.

3. Implementation

QP/3 – Internal Audits
QP/8 – Design Control
QP/10 – Quality Management System Review

	Document Ref: **N-51–044RLR13** Version: 03.01 Date: 1 October 2013 Quality Management System Part One – Quality Manual Version 01.00

QP/11 – Purchasing
QP/15 – Meetings and Reports

6.4 Work environment (ISO 9001:2008 – 6.4)

NAFAAD's work environment is a combination of human factors (e.g. work methodologies, achievement and involvement opportunities, safety rules and guidance, ergonomics etc.) and physical factors (e.g. heat, hygiene, vibration, noise, humidity, pollution, light, cleanliness and air flow). All of these factors influence motivation, satisfaction and performance of people and as they have the potential for enhancing the performance of NAFAAD, they shall be taken into consideration when considering a deliverable's conformance and achievement.

1. Policy and objectives

NAFAAD shall define and manage those human and physical factors of the work environment required to achieve product conformity.
    This shall include:

* health and safety conditions;
* work methods;
* work ethics;
* ambient working conditions.

 Author's Hint

> ISO 9001:2008 has now clarified that 'work environment' includes conditions under which work is performed and that these 'conditions' can include environmental conditions such as noise, temperature, humidity, lighting and weather.

2. Responsibilities

Section Managers have overall responsibility for establishing, implementing and maintaining this activity.

3. Implementation

HSE relevant documents.

	Document Ref: **N-51–044RLR13** Version: 03.01 Date: 1 October 2013 Quality Management System Part One – Quality Manual Version 01.00

7 PRODUCT REALISATION (ISO 9001:2008 – 7)

NAFAAD shall ensure that customer requirements, including requirements for delivery and post-delivery activities, are fully understood, documented and implemented.

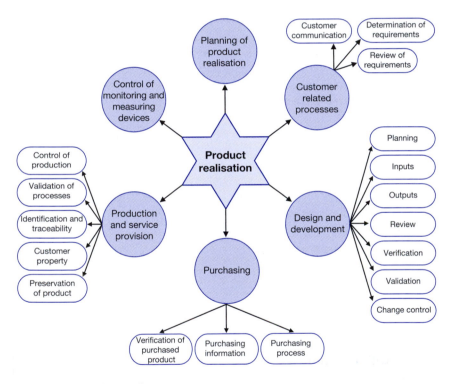

FIGURE 6.1.14 Product realisation

7.1 Planning of realisation processes (ISO 9000:2000 – 7.1)

1. Policy and objectives

Processes that are necessary to realise the required deliverable and their sequence and interaction shall be determined, planned and implemented taking into consideration the outputs from quality planning.

	Document Ref: **N-51–044RLR13**
	Version: 03.01
	Date: 1 October 2013
	Quality Management System
	Part One – Quality Manual
	Version 01.00

In planning product realisation, NAFAAD shall determine:

- the quality objectives and requirements for the product;
- the need to provide resources specific to the product;
- the amount of verification, validation, monitoring, measurement, inspection and test activities that will be required for product acceptance and to achieve product conformity with customer requirements;
- the type of records required to provide evidence that the realisation processes and resulting product meets requirements;
- the need to establish processes and documentation.

NAFAAD shall ensure these processes are operated under controlled conditions and produce outputs which meet customer requirements. NAFAAD shall determine how each process affects its ability to meet product requirements and shall:

- establish methods and practices relevant to these processes, to the extent necessary to achieve consistent operation;
- determine and implement arrangements for measurement, monitoring and follow-up actions, to ensure processes continue to operate to achieve planned results and outputs;
- ensure the availability of the information and data necessary to support the effective operation and monitoring of the processes;
- maintain (i.e. as quality records) the results of process control measures, to provide evidence of effective operation and monitoring of the processes.

 Author's Hint

A document specifying QMS processes (including the product realisation processes) and the resources to be applied to a specific product, project or contract is often referred to as a *'Quality Plan'*.

2. Responsibilities

Top Management has overall responsibility for establishing, implementing and maintaining this activity.

	Document Ref: **N-51–044RLR13** Version: 03.01 Date: 1 October 2013 Quality Management System Part One – Quality Manual Version 01.00

3. Implementation

CP/1 – Core Business Process
SP/1 – Compliance and Approval
SP/2 – Subcontractors and Suppliers
SP/3 – Customer Satisfaction
QP/8 – Design Control

7.2 Customer-related processes (ISO 9000:2000 – 7.2)

Understanding customer requirements is essential for the creation of a deliverable and for ensuring overall customer satisfaction (see SP/3 – Customer Satisfaction).

7.2.1 Determination of requirements related to the product (ISO 9001:2008 – 7.2.1)

1. Policy and objectives

NAFAAD shall establish a process for identifying customer requirements that determine the:

- completeness of the customer's product and/or service requirements;
- requirements not specified by the customer but necessary for fitness for purpose;
- statutory, regulatory and legal requirements;
- specific customer requirements for availability, delivery and support of product and/or service.

 Author's Hint

Post-delivery activities can include, for example, actions completed under warranty provisions, contractual obligations (such as maintenance services) and supplementary services (such as recycling and/or final disposal).

---

2. Responsibilities

The Managing Director (assisted by the Quality Manager, Company Secretary and Section Managers) has overall responsibility for establishing, implementing and maintaining this activity.

Document Ref: **N-51–044RLR13**
Version: 03.01
Date: 1 October 2013
Quality Management System
Part One – Quality Manual
Version 01.00

3. Implementation

CP/1 – Core Business Process
SP/1 – Compliance and Approval
SP/2 – Subcontractors and Suppliers
SP/3 – Customer Satisfaction
QP/1 – Document Control
QP/8 – Design Control

7.2.2 Review of requirements related to the product (ISO 9000:2000 – 7.2.2)

NAFAAD shall complete a thorough assessment of all requirements related to the deliverable.

1. Policy and objectives

Customer requirements, including any requested changes, shall be reviewed before a commitment to supply a product is provided to the customer (e.g. submission of a tender, acceptance of a contract or order) to ensure that:

- product and customer requirements are clearly defined;
- if the customer does not provide a written statement of requirement, the customer requirements are confirmed before acceptance;
- any contract or order requirements from those previously expressed (e.g. in a tender or quotation), are resolved;
- NAFAAD has the ability to meet the customer requirements for the product and/or service.

 The results of the review and any subsequent follow-up actions **shall** be recorded and the information disseminated to relevant personnel.

 Author's Hint

In some situations (such as internet sales) a formal review will obviously be impractical for each order. Instead the review can be completed by using relevant product information such as catalogues or advertising material.

Document Ref: **N-51–044RLR13**
Version: 03.01
Date: 1 October 2013
Quality Management System
Part One – Quality Manual
Version 01.00

2. Responsibilities

Section Managers have overall responsibility for establishing, implementing and maintaining this activity.

3. Implementation

CP/1 – Core Business Process
SP/1 – Compliance and Approval
QP/1 – Document Control
QP/8 – Design Control
QP/14 – Change Control

7.2.3 Customer communication (ISO 9000:2000 – 7.2.3)

NAFAAD shall ensure that customers are kept up-to-date with the progress of their deliverable and that all of their comments and complaints are dealt with in a speedy and effective manner.

1. Policy and objectives

NAFAAD shall determine and implement arrangements for customer communication and shall define communication requirements relating to:

*   product information;
*   enquiries and order handling (including amendments);
*   customer feedback and complaints – particularly those concerning a non-conforming product;
*   customer responses relating to product performance.

2. Responsibilities

The Managing Director (in consultation with the Quality Manager, Company Secretary and Section Managers) has overall responsibility for establishing, implementing and maintaining this activity.

3. Implementation

SP/3 – Customer Satisfaction
QP/12 – Customer Feedback

Document Ref: **N-51–044RLR13**
Version: 03.01
Date: 1 October 2013
Quality Management System
Part One – Quality Manual
Version 01.00

7.3 Design and development (ISO 9000:2000 – 7.3)

NAFAAD shall plan, control and establish documented procedures for the design and development of a deliverable throughout all processes. Interfaces between different groups involved in the design and development shall be managed to ensure effective communication and clarity of responsibilities.

7.3.1 Design and development planning (ISO 9001:2008 – 7.3.1)

1. Policy and objectives

NAFAAD shall plan and control the design and development of a product, which shall include:

- stage reviews;
- verification and validation activities;
- identification of responsibilities and authorities;
- management of the interfaces between different groups that may be involved;
- provision of effective communication;
- clarity of responsibilities;
- deliverable and planning review procedures.

Planning output **shall** be updated, as appropriate, as the design and development progresses.

Author's Hint

Design and development review, verification and validation have distinct purposes. They can be conducted and recorded separately or in any combination, according to (and most suitable for) the product and the organisation.

2. Responsibilities

Section Managers have overall responsibility for establishing, implementing and maintaining this activity.

	Document Ref: **N-51–044RLR13** Version: 03.01 Date: 1 October 2013 Quality Management System Part One – Quality Manual Version 01.00

3. Implementation

CP/1 – Core Business Process
SP/1 – Compliance and Approval
QP/3 – Internal Audits
QP/8 – Design Control
QP/14 – Change Control
QP/15 – Meetings and Reports

7.3.2 Design and development inputs (ISO 9001:2008 – 7.3.2)

NAFAAD shall review (for adequacy and approval) all design and development inputs.

1. Policy and objectives

NAFAAD shall:

- identify and detail all the relevant standards, specifications and the deliverable's specific requirements that are going to be used during the design stage;
- establish and maintain procedures to ensure that the functions of the design development and planning activities are in agreement with the customer's specified requirements.

Procedures shall be defined and documented, and shall include:

- functional and performance requirements from customer or market;
- applicable statutory, regulatory and legal requirements;
- applicable environmental requirements;
- information derived from previous similar designs;
- any other requirements essential for design and development.

These inputs shall be reviewed for adequacy and incomplete, ambiguous or conflicting requirements shall be resolved.

 Author's Hint

Whilst still expecting organisations to plan and perform product design and development review, verification and validation activities, ISO 9001:2008 now clarifies that these three activities **can** be carried out and recorded separately, if required.

Document Ref: **N-51–044RLR13**
Version: 03.01
Date: 1 October 2013
Quality Management System
Part One – Quality Manual
Version 01.00

2. Responsibilities

Section Managers have overall responsibility for establishing, implementing and maintaining this activity.

3. Implementation

CP/1 – Core Business Process
SP/1 – Compliance and Approval
QP/3 – Internal Audits
QP/8 – Design Control
QP/14 – Change Control
QP/15 – Meetings and Reports

7.3.3 Design and development outputs (ISO 9001:2008 – 7.3.3)

NAFAAD shall ensure that the outputs of design and development are provided in a form that enables verification against the design and development input and shall be approved prior to release.

1. Policy and objectives

NAFAAD shall ensure that all documentation associated with the design output (e.g. drawings, schematics, schedules, system specifications, system descriptions etc.) has been:

- produced in accordance with agreed customer requirements;
- reviewed (by another designer who has not been associated with the initial design) to ensure that it meets the design input;
- identified all characteristics which are critical to the effective operation of the designed system;
- reviewed and approved by the customer prior to acceptance.

 Records of design and development outputs shall be maintained.

Design and development output shall:

- meet the design and development input requirements;
- contain (or make reference to) product and/or service acceptance criteria;
- be approved before being released;

	Document Ref: **N-51–044RLR13**
	Version: 03.01
	Date: 1 October 2013
	Quality Management System
	Part One – Quality Manual
	Version 01.00

and where necessary:

- define the characteristics of the deliverable that are essential to its safe and proper use;
- specify the characteristics of the deliverable that are essential for its safe and proper use.

Author's Hint

Design and development outputs should also include information that explains how products can be preserved during production and service provision.

2. Responsibilities

Section Managers have overall responsibility for establishing, implementing and maintaining this activity.

3. Implementation

CP/1 – Core Business Process
SP/1 – Compliance and Approval
QP/3 – Internal Audits
QP/8 – Design Control
QP/14 – Change Control
QP/15 – Meetings and Reports

7.3.4 Design and development review (ISO 9001:2008 – 7.3.4)

Throughout the design and development stage, NAFAAD shall carry out systematic reviews to confirm its ability to meet requirements.

1. Policy and objectives

At suitable stages, systematic reviews of design and development shall be carried out so as to:

- evaluate the ability of the results of design and development to meet requirements;
- evaluate the ability of a deliverable to fulfil requirements for quality;

Document Ref: **N-51–044RLR13**
Version: 03.01
Date: 1 October 2013
Quality Management System
Part One – Quality Manual
Version 01.00

- identify problems;
- propose follow-up actions;
- ensure adherence to contractual and statutory requirements has been fully met;
- ensure all alternative design concepts and items have been considered;
- ensure all potential design problems have been identified and evaluated;
- ensure all calculations have been correctly performed and re-checked;
- ensure that the deliverable continues to meet customer and/or other statutory requirements.

 Participants of these reviews shall include a representative from the design stage being reviewed.

 Results of the reviews and subsequent follow-up actions **shall** be recorded.

2. Responsibilities

Section Managers have overall responsibility for establishing, implementing and maintaining this activity.

3. Implementation

CP/1 – Core Business Process
SP/1 – Compliance and Approval
QP/3 – Internal Audits
QP/7 – Production of a Quality Document
QP/8 – Design Control
QP/15 – Meetings and Reports

7.3.5 Design and development verification
(ISO 9001:2008 – 7.3.5)

NAFAAD shall ensure that verification processes are planned and implemented to ensure that the design and development output meets the design and development input.

1. Policy and objectives

NAFAAD shall ensure that procedures are available to complete periodic evaluations of the design output against the design input using one (or all) of the following methods:

	Document Ref: **N-51-044RLR13**
	Version: 03.01
	Date: 1 October 2013
	Quality Management System
	Part One – Quality Manual
	Version 01.00

- **comparison** – with other similar designs;
- **alternative calculations** – to verify the precision of the original calculations and their analysis;
- **third-party evaluation** – to verify that the original calculations and other design activities have been correctly carried out;
- **feedback** – from previous designs and experience;
- **customer feedback** – i.e. asking customer representatives.

 The results of the verification and subsequent follow-up actions **shall** be recorded.

2. Responsibilities

Section Managers have overall responsibility for establishing, implementing and maintaining this activity.

3. Implementation

CP/1 – Core Business Process
SP/1 – Compliance and Approval
QP/3 – Internal Audits
QP/8 – Design Control
QP/14 – Change Control
QP/15 – Meetings and Reports

7.3.6 Design and development validation (ISO 9001:2008 – 7.3.6)

Prior to the delivery or implementation of the deliverable's design and development, validation shall be performed to confirm that the resultant deliverable is capable of meeting customer requirements.

1. Policy and objectives

NAFAAD shall:

- ensure that records of all evaluations are maintained;
- ensure that design and development validation is completed in accordance with planned arrangements to ensure that the resulting deliverable is capable of meeting the customer's requirements for its specified application or intended use;

Document Ref: **N-51–044RLR13**
Version: 03.01
Date: 1 October 2013
Quality Management System
Part One – Quality Manual
Version 01.00

- ensure that records of the results of validation and subsequent follow-up actions are maintained and recorded.

Note: Wherever applicable, this validation shall be defined, planned and completed prior to the delivery or implementation of the deliverable. Where it is impossible or impracticable to complete a full validation prior to delivery or implementation, partial validation of the design or development outputs shall be undertaken to the maximum extent practical.

2. Responsibilities

Section Managers have overall responsibility for establishing, implementing and maintaining this activity.

3. Implementation

CP/1 – Core Business Process
SP/1 – Compliance and Approval
QP/2 – Control of Records
QP/3 – Internal Audits
QP/8 – Design Control
QP/14 – Change Control
QP/15 – Meetings and Reports

7.3.7 Control of design and development changes
(ISO 9001:2008 – 7.3.7)

All changes to the design criteria (input and output) shall be subject to strict documentation control and shall be reviewed and verified by the designer and the customer, prior to incorporation within the design.

1. Policy and objectives

NAFAAD shall ensure procedures are available to:

- identify the interaction between the elements of the design and development;
- identify the interaction between the component parts of the resulting deliverable;
- evaluate the effect of these changes on existing products and/or services and/or post-delivery product operations;
- identify need for carrying out re-verification or re-validation for all, or part of, the design and development outputs.

	Document Ref: **N-51–044RLR13** Version: 03.01 Date: 1 October 2013 Quality Management System Part One – Quality Manual Version 01.00

 The results of the review of changes and subsequent follow-up actions **shall** be recorded.

2. Responsibilities

Section Managers have overall responsibility for establishing, implementing and maintaining this activity.

3. Implementation

CP/1 – Core Business Process
SP/1 – Compliance and Approval
QP/3 – Internal Audits
QP/8 – Design Control
QP/14 – Change Control

7.4 Purchasing (ISO 9001:2008 – 7.4)

NAFAAD shall establish documented procedures to ensure that all purchased products conform to the specified purchase requirements. Wherever possible items shall only be purchased from an accredited source.

1. Implementation

SP/2 – Compliance and Approval
QP/1 – Document Control
QP/11 – Purchasing

7.4.1 Purchasing process (ISO 9001:2008 – 7.4.1)

Although the majority of NAFAAD purchases only concern stationery and the maintenance/improvement of IT facilities, NAFAAD, nevertheless, needs to control its purchasing processes to ensure that the purchased product conforms to NAFAAD's requirements. The type and extent of methods to control these processes shall be dependent on the effect of the purchased product upon the final product.

Document Ref: **N-51–044RLR13**
Version: 03.01
Date: 1 October 2013
Quality Management System
Part One – Quality Manual
Version 01.00

Author's Hint

Obviously this sort of statement is only applicable to an organisation such as NAFAAD.

If you are, for example, a manufacturer, then you will need to cover the process of purchasing (and the selection of your subcontracted suppliers) thoroughly.

If, on the other hand you are a supplier then you will need to ensure that you have the relevant controls for ensuring that the item(s) you are supplying meet the purchaser's requirements and that you also have a system for storing and inspecting etc. the item(s).

If you are an installer or maintainer, then this section will also be applicable to you.

If you are in the IT world, then it will be a bit of all the above.

1. Policy and objectives

NAFAAD shall evaluate and select suppliers based on their ability to supply products in accordance with NAFAAD's requirements. Evaluation, re-evaluation and selection criteria for suppliers shall be established, and management shall have procedures for the:

- assessment of suppliers and subcontractors;
- evaluation and selection of suppliers;
- specification of requirements for purchased documents and the verification of goods and services received;
- completion of periodic re-evaluation of suppliers and the purchasing processes.

The results of evaluations and subsequent follow-up actions **shall** be recorded.

The NAFAAD system for the control of purchased goods or subcontracted services shall ensure those products and/or services purchased and received, conform to specified requirements and include provision for the assessment of suppliers and subcontractors. It shall also establish rules for the specification of requirements for purchased documents and the verification of goods and services received.

	Document Ref: **N-51–044RLR13** Version: 03.01 Date: 1 October 2013 Quality Management System Part One – Quality Manual Version 01.00

2. Responsibilities

The Company Secretary (assisted by Section Managers and the Quality Manager), has overall responsibility for establishing, implementing and maintaining this activity.

3. Implementation

SP/2 – Subcontractors and Suppliers
QP/1 – Document Control
QP/11 – Purchasing
Individual (i.e. sectional) subcontract assessment procedures according to product and/or contract.

7.4.2 Purchasing information (ISO 9001:2008 – 7.4.2)

NAFAAD shall ensure the adequacy of specified purchase requirements prior to them being given to the supplier.

1. Policy and objectives

NAFAAD shall ensure procedures are implemented to ensure that all purchasing documents contain information clearly describing the product and/or service ordered and shall include:

*   the requirements for approval and/or qualification of product, procedures, processes and equipment;
*   the requirements for qualification of personnel;
*   requirements for approval or qualification of product and/or service, procedures, processes, equipment and personnel;
*   any other QMS requirements.

 NAFAAD shall ensure the adequacy of specified purchase requirements prior to release.

 Author's Hint

To ensure traceability, it is normal to find that copies of all relevant purchasing documents (including records) are retained for a period of not less than two years or as stipulated in customer or national regulations.

Document Ref: **N-51–044RLR13**
Version: 03.01
Date: 1 October 2013
Quality Management System
Part One – Quality Manual
Version 01.00

2. Responsibilities

The Company Secretary (assisted by Section Managers and the Quality Manager), has overall responsibility for establishing, implementing and maintaining this activity.

3. Implementation

SP/2 – Subcontractors and Suppliers
QP/1 – Document Control
QP/2 – Control of Records
QP/11 – Purchasing
Individual (i.e. sectional) subcontract assessment procedures according to product and/or contract.

7.4.3 Verification of purchased product (ISO 9001:2008 – 7.4.3)

NAFAAD shall establish and implement the procedures necessary for ensuring that the purchased goods and services meet NAFAAD's specified purchase requirements.

1. Policy and objectives

NAFAAD shall ensure that there is a procedure to ensure that all goods and services received are checked to confirm that:

- they are those that were ordered;
- the delivery is on time;
- they are of good quality.

 Note: The amount of inspection will depend on how critical the supplied goods and/or service is to the end product and the amount of inspection should be compatible with the risk or inconvenience if the item is later found to be faulty.

Where NAFAAD (or its customer) needs to carry out verification activities at the supplier's premises, then NAFAAD shall specify the required verification arrangements and the method of product release in the purchasing information.

Document Ref: **N-51–044RLR13**
Version: 03.01
Date: 1 October 2013
Quality Management System
Part One – Quality Manual
Version 01.00

2. Responsibilities

The Company Secretary (assisted by Section Managers and the Quality Manager), has overall responsibility for establishing, implementing and maintaining this activity.

3. Implementation

SP/2 – Subcontractors and Suppliers
QP/1 – Document Control
QP/2 – Control of Records
QP/11 – Purchasing
QP/14 – Change Control
Individual (i.e. sectional) subcontract assessment procedures according to product and/or contract.

7.5 Production and service provision (ISO 9001:2008 – 7.5)

In order to achieve the output targets (and at the same time, to prevent defects) NAFAAD shall plan and carry out production and service provision under controlled conditions.

1. Implementation

QP/1 – Document Control

7.5.1 Control of production and service provision (ISO 9001:2008 – 7.5.1)

1. Policy and objectives

Top Management shall identify the requirements for deliverable realisation and ensure that it has:

- the ability to comply with contractual requirements;
- the ability to train and have available competent people;
- a viable system for communication;
- a process for problem prevention.

Document Ref: **N-51–044RLR13**
Version: 03.01
Date: 1 October 2013
Quality Management System
Part One – Quality Manual
Version 01.00

Top Management shall ensure that the following is available:

- information concerning the deliverable's characteristics;
- appropriate work instructions, documented procedures and reference measurement procedures;
- relevant reference materials;
- suitable office equipment;
- processes to cover the release, delivery and post-delivery activities;
- the resources for the implementation of pre-defined labelling and packaging operations to prevent labelling errors.

Top Management **shall** establish and maintain a record for each deliverable. This batch record shall be verified and approved and shall provide traceability, quantity produced and quantity approved for distribution.

 Author's Hint

Depending on what sort of business you are in, you might also need to consider:

- the use and maintenance of suitable production, installation and maintenance equipment;
- the availability of monitoring and measuring equipment;
- the implementation of suitable monitoring and measuring activities;
- suitable methods for release and delivery and/or installation of a product and/or service.

2. Responsibilities

Top Management (assisted by Section Managers) has overall responsibility for establishing, implementing and maintaining this activity.

3. Implementation

NAFAAD QMS Part 3 – Quality Procedures
NAFAAD QMS Part 4 – Work Instructions
QP/1 – Document Control
QP/14 – Change Control

	Document Ref: **N-51–044RLR13** Version: 03.01 Date: 1 October 2013 Quality Management System Part One – Quality Manual Version 01.00

7.5.2 Validation of processes for production and service provision (ISO 9001:2008 – 7.5.2)

1. Policy and objectives

As NAFAAD's product is exclusively management system documents and reports that are controlled by a Quality Procedure (i.e. QP/1 – Document Control) **this section is not applicable to NAFAAD's business AND IS, THEREFORE, A PERMISSIBLE EXCLUSION.**

Author's Hint

Depending on the sort of business you are in, then it may be necessary for you to validate any processes relevant to production and service provision where the resulting output cannot be verified by subsequent monitoring or measurement and, as a consequence, deficiencies only become apparent after the product is in use or the service has been delivered. Validation should be aimed at demonstrating the ability of these processes to achieve planned results.

If this is relevant to your business, therefore, you will need to consider having a procedure for:

- the review and approval of the processes;
- approval of equipment;
- approval and qualification of personnel;
- use of specific methods and procedures;
- the requirements for maintaining records; and
- the necessity for revalidation.

In some businesses it may be necessary for the organisation to identify, monitor and measure the product **throughout product realisation**. Then (assuming traceability is a requirement) the organisation will also need to control the unique identification of the product and maintain adequate records.

Computer software
If computer software is relevant to your product and/or service then you will need to establish documented procedures for the validation of computer software as well as changes to such software and/or its application.

Document Ref: **N-51–044RLR13**
Version: 03.01
Date: 1 October 2013
Quality Management System
Part One – Quality Manual
Version 01.00

7.5.3 Identification and traceability (ISO 9001:2008 – 7.5.3)

Where traceability is a requirement, NAFAAD shall have procedures for identifying the status of a deliverable.

1. Policy and objectives

Where traceability is a necessity, NAFAAD shall be capable of controlling and recording:

- the identification of a deliverable;
- the identification of the status of a deliverable;
- the traceability of a deliverable.

Note: The identification of deliverable status shall be maintained throughout production and storage to ensure that only deliverables that have passed the required inspections and tests (or released under an authorised concession) are despatched.

2. Responsibilities

Top Management (assisted by Section Managers) has overall responsibility for establishing, implementing and maintaining this activity.

3. Implementation

QP/1 – Document Control
QP/2 – Control of Records
QP/3 – Internal Audits
QP/4 – Non-Conforming Product
QP/5 – Corrective Action
QP/6 – Preventative Action
QP/8 – Design Control
QP/14 – Change Control

7.5.4 Customer property (ISO 9001:2008 – 7.5.4)

NAFAAD shall ensure that all customer property while it is under NAFAAD's supervision (or being used by NAFAAD) is identified, verified, stored and maintained. Any customer property that is lost, damaged or otherwise found to be unsuitable for use shall be recorded and reported to the customer.

	Document Ref: **N-51–044RLR13** Version: 03.01 Date: 1 October 2013 Quality Management System Part One – Quality Manual Version 01.00

 Author's Hint

The term 'Customer property' can also include intellectual property and personal data – particularly information that has been provided in confidence. These need to be controlled with reference to appropriate national data protection acts.

1. Policy and objectives

NAFAAD shall:

- retain records of all customer-provided material;
- protect and maintain all customer-provided property.

Note: All goods received from customers shall be visually inspected at the receipt stage and any undeclared non-conformance immediately reported to the customer.

2. Responsibilities

Top Management (assisted by Section Managers) has overall responsibility for establishing, implementing and maintaining this activity.

3. Implementation

SP/2 – Control of Records
SP/3 – Customer Satisfaction
QP/2 – Control of Records
QP/13 – Customer Awareness and Training

7.5.5 Preservation of product (ISO 9001:2008 – 7.5.5)

NAFAAD shall ensure that during internal processing and final delivery of the product to its intended destination the identification, packaging, storage, preservation and handling do not affect conformity with product requirements.

 Author's Hint

This also applies to parts or components of a product as well as elements of a service.

Document Ref: **N-51–044RLR13**
Version: 03.01
Date: 1 October 2013
Quality Management System
Part One – Quality Manual
Version 01.00

Product release/delivery shall not proceed until all the specified activities have been satisfactorily completed and the related documentation is available and authorised.

1. Policy and objectives

All materials and goods that are received, whether they are the property of NAFAAD or others, shall, as far as practicable, be protected and their quality preserved until such time as they are transferred to a customer, disposed of to a third party or utilised. The overall objective should be to prevent deterioration and damage whilst in storage, or in the process of transportation, installation, commissioning and maintenance.

NAFAAD shall establish procedures for:

- preserving the conformity of the product during internal processing and delivery to the intended destination;
- identifying, handling, packaging, storing and protecting products during internal processing and delivery to their intended destination;
- the control of product with a limited shelf life or requiring special storage conditions.

 Such special storage conditions **shall** be controlled and recorded.

NAFAAD shall ensure that during internal processing and final presentation of a delivery to its intended destination that the identification, packaging, storage, preservation and handling do not affect conformity with the deliverable's requirements.

The release and distribution of a deliverable shall not proceed until all specified activities have been satisfactorily completed and the related documentation is available and authorised.

2. Responsibilities

The Company Secretary (assisted by Section Managers) has overall responsibility for establishing, implementing and maintaining this activity.

3. Implementation

NAFAAD QMS Part 3 – Quality Procedures
NAFAAD QMS Part 4 – Work Instructions

	Document Ref: **N-51–044RLR13** Version: 03.01 Date: 1 October 2013 Quality Management System Part One – Quality Manual Version 01.00

QP/1 – Document Control
QP/2 – Control of Records
QP/4 – Non-Conforming Product
QP/13 – Customer Awareness and Training

7.6 Control of monitoring and measuring equipment (ISO 9001:2008 – 7.6)

1. Policy and objectives

As NAFAAD's product is exclusively management system documents and reports this section is **not** applicable to NAFAAD's business.

 Author's Hint

If your organisation makes use of monitoring and measuring equipment, then the measuring equipment shall:

- be calibrated or verified (or both) prior to use and at specified intervals against workshop-standard equipment that is traceable to international or national measurement standards;
- be adjusted and re-adjusted as necessary;
- have an identification tag to show its calibration status;
- be protected from third parties being able to make adjustments that would invalidate the measurement result;
- be protected from damage and deterioration during handling, maintenance and storage.

 Records of the results of calibration and verification **shall** be maintained.

Note: When computer software is used in the monitoring and measurement process then, **prior** to initial use, the ability of computer software to satisfy the intended application needs to be confirmed and reconfirmed as deemed necessary.

Document Ref: **N-51–044RLR13**
Version: 03.01
Date: 1 October 2013
Quality Management System
Part One – Quality Manual
Version 01.00

8 MEASUREMENT, ANALYSIS AND IMPROVEMENT (ISO 9001:2008 – 8)

8.1 General (ISO 9001:2008 – 8.1)

NAFAAD shall define, plan and implement measurement, monitoring, analysis and improvement of all QMS processes in order to:

- demonstrate conformity to product requirements;
- ensure conformity of the QMS; and
- be capable of continually improving the effectiveness of the NAFAAD QMS.

 Author's Hint

It is also normal for an organisation to identify and make use of statistical tools and the results of data analysis and improvement activities as an input to the management review process.

1. Policy and objectives

NAFAAD shall plan and implement all monitoring, measurement, analysis and improvement processes that are required to demonstrate the conformity of the deliverable so as to maintain the effectiveness of the NAFAAD QMS.

NAFAAD shall define the activities required to measure and monitor:

- deliverable conformity;
- deliverable improvement;
- Quality Plan conformity.

NAFAAD shall ensure that:

- the type, location, timing and frequency of measurements and the requirements for records are defined;
- the effectiveness of implemented measures are periodically evaluated.

2. Responsibilities

Top Management (assisted by Section Managers) has overall responsibility for establishing, implementing and maintaining this activity.

	Document Ref: **N-51–044RLR13** Version: 03.01 Date: 1 October 2013 Quality Management System Part One – Quality Manual Version 01.00

3. Implementation

CP/1 – Core Business Process
QP/1 – Document Control
QP/2 – Control of Records
QP/10 – Quality Management System Review
QP/15 – Meetings and Reports

8.2 Monitoring and measurement (ISO 9001:2008 – 8.2)

8.2.1 Customer satisfaction (ISO 9001:2008 – 8.2.1)

As one of the measurements of the performance of the Quality Plan, NAFAAD shall conduct customer satisfaction surveys to monitor and gauge whether NAFAAD has met customer requirements and to understand the level of customer satisfaction achieved.

1. Policy and objectives

NAFAAD shall monitor information concerning customer satisfaction and/or dissatisfaction as one of the measurements of performance of the QMS. The methods and measures for obtaining and utilising such information and data shall be defined.

 Author's Hint

Monitoring customer perception can include obtaining input from sources such as customer satisfaction surveys, customer data on delivered product quality, user opinion surveys, lost business analysis, compliments, warranty claims and dealer reports etc.

2. Responsibilities

Top Management (assisted by Section Managers) has overall responsibility for establishing, implementing and maintaining this activity.

	Document Ref: **N-51–044RLR13**
	Version: 03.01 Date: 1 October 2013 Quality Management System Part One – Quality Manual Version 01.00

3. Implementation

SP/3 – Customer Satisfaction
QP/12 – Customer Feedback
QP/13 – Customer Awareness and Training
QP/15 – Meetings and Reports

8.2.2 Internal audit (ISO 9001:2008 – 8.2.2)

 Author's Hint

It is a **mandatory** requirement of ISO 9001:2008 for all organisations to have a documented procedure for Internal Audits.

NAFAAD shall establish an internal audit procedure process to assess the strengths and weaknesses of its QMS, to identify potential danger spots, eliminate wastage and verify that corrective action has been successfully achieved. The internal audit process shall also be used to review the efficiency and effectiveness of other organisational activities and support processes.

1. Policy and objectives

NAFAAD shall establish a documented procedure for Internal Auditing and shall complete internal audits at planned intervals to determine whether the QMS:

- has been effectively implemented and maintained;
- conforms to the requirements of ISO 9001:2008.

This audit process, including the schedule, shall be based on the status and importance of the activities and/or areas to be audited, the results of previous audits and shall include:

- the responsibilities and requirements for conducting audits;
- the scope, frequency and methodologies used;
- the method for recording results and reporting to management.

In addition, NAFAAD may carry out audits to identify potential opportunities for improvement.

	Document Ref: **N-51–044RLR13** Version: 03.01 Date: 1 October 2013 Quality Management System Part One – Quality Manual Version 01.00

 Author's Hint

In accordance with ISO 9001:2008, a documented procedure for Internal Auditing needs to be established and this needs to clearly define the responsibilities and requirements for conducting audits, establishing records and reporting and maintaining output results.

To ensure the impartiality of the audit process, auditors should not be permitted to audit their own work.

The management responsible for the area being audited need to ensure that (when necessary) corrective actions are taken quickly so as to eliminate detected non-conformities and their causes.

Also see ISO 19011 for further guidance on auditing.

2. Responsibilities

Top Management has overall responsibility for establishing, implementing and maintaining this activity.

3. Implementation

QP/1 – Document Control
QP/2 – Control of Records
QP/3 – Internal Audits
QP/4 – Non-Conforming Product
QP/5 – Corrective Action
QP/6 – Preventative Action
QP/10 – Quality Management System Review
QP/12 – Customer Feedback
QP/15 – Meetings and Reports

8.2.3 Monitoring and measurement of processes
(ISO 9001:2008 – 8.2.3)

NAFAAD shall identify measurement methodologies, perform measurements to evaluate their process performance and use the results obtained to improve the deliverable(s) realisation process.

Document Ref: **N-51–044RLR13**
Version: 03.01
Date: 1 October 2013
Quality Management System
Part One – Quality Manual
Version 01.00

1. Policy and objectives

NAFAAD shall measure and monitor processes to ensure that:

- they meet customer requirements;
- they satisfy their intended purpose;
- process performance is evaluated;
- results are achieved which can be used to improve the deliverable(s) realisation process; and
- they continue to satisfy their intended purpose.

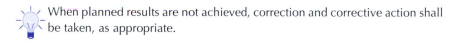 When planned results are not achieved, correction and corrective action shall be taken, as appropriate.

2. Responsibilities

Top Management (assisted by Section Managers) has overall responsibility for establishing, implementing and maintaining this activity.

3. Implementation

SP/1 – Compliance and Approval
SP/3 – Customer Satisfaction
QP/2 – Control of Records
QP/3 – Internal Audits
QP/10 – Quality Management System Review
QP/12 – Customer Feedback
QP/15 – Meetings and Reports

8.2.4 Monitoring and measurement of product
(ISO 9001:2008 – 8.2.4)

NAFAAD shall establish, specify and plan its measurement requirements (including acceptance criteria) for its contracted deliverables.

1. Policy and objectives

NAFAAD shall monitor and measure the characteristics of the product to verify that requirements for the product and/or service are met.

	Document Ref: **N-51–044RLR13**
	Version: 03.01
	Date: 1 October 2013
	Quality Management System
	Part One – Quality Manual
	Version 01.00

When a product is released for delivery to a customer, records must indicate who actually released the product.

NAFAAD shall:

- measure and monitor the characteristics of a deliverable;
- document and maintain evidence of conformity with the acceptance criteria;
- indicate the authority responsible for release of a deliverable;
- record the identity of personnel performing any inspection, verification and validation;
- not proceed with the release of the deliverable until the planned arrangements have been satisfactorily completed.

Evidence conformance **shall** be documented and recorded and these records **shall** indicate the authority responsible for releasing the deliverable.

2. Responsibilities

Top Management (assisted by Section Managers) has overall responsibility for establishing, implementing and maintaining this activity.

3. Implementation

SP/1 – Compliance and Approval
QP/2 – Control of Records
QP/3 – Internal Audits
QP/10 – Quality Management System Review
QP/15 – Meetings and Reports

8.3 Control of non-conforming product (ISO 9001:2008 – 8.3)

Author's Hint

It is a **mandatory** requirement of ISO 9001:2008 for all organisations to have a documented procedure that defines the controls and related responsibilities and authorities for dealing with a non-conforming product and/or service.

Document Ref: **N-51–044RLR13**
Version: 03.01
Date: 1 October 2013
Quality Management System
Part One – Quality Manual
Version 01.00

NAFAAD shall establish a documented procedure for non-conforming product and shall ensure that products that do not conform to requirements are identified and controlled to prevent unintended use or delivery. These non-conformities shall be:

- corrected or adjusted to conform to requirements and re-validated; or
- accepted under concession, with or without correction or adjustment; or
- re-assigned for alternative valid application; or
- rejected as unsuitable.

1. Policy and objectives

NAFAAD shall establish a documented procedure for non-conforming products and ensure that:

- deliverables which do not conform to requirements are prevented from unintended use or delivery;
- non-conforming deliverables that have been corrected are re-verified to demonstrate conformity;
- non-conforming deliverables found after delivery or use are either corrected or removed from service;
- all non-conforming deliverables are only accepted by concession **if** all regulatory requirements are met and the identity of the person(s) authorising the concession has been recorded;
- if a deliverable needs to be reworked (one or more times), the rework shall be subject to the same authorisation and approval procedure as the original work was subject to;
- prior to authorisation and approval, a determination of any adverse effect of the rework upon a deliverable shall be made and documented.

2. Responsibilities

The Quality Manager (assisted by the Section Managers) has overall responsibility for establishing, implementing and maintaining this activity.

3. Implementation

SP/1 – Compliance and Approval
QP/1 – Document Control
QP/2 – Control of Records
QP/3 – Internal Audits

	Document Ref: **N-51–044RLR13** Version: 03.01 Date: 1 October 2013 Quality Management System Part One – Quality Manual Version 01.00

QP/4 – Non-Conforming Product
QP/5 – Corrective Action
QP/6 – Preventative Action

8.4 Analysis of data (ISO 9001:2008 – 8.4)

NAFAAD shall establish documented procedures to determine, collect, collate and analyse appropriate data to demonstrate and confirm to the customer and, when required, to regulatory authorities, that NAFAAD is capable of continuing to produce a quality deliverable. The preferred method of achieving this is via statistical analysis.

1. Policy and objectives

Top Management shall establish documented procedures to collect data for the analysis of:

- customer feedback;
- customer satisfaction (and/or dissatisfaction);
- conformance to customer deliverable requirements;
- processes and procedures used to produce the deliverable;
- characteristics of trends and opportunities for preventive action;
- work originating from third-party suppliers and subcontractors (if applicable);
- the suitability, adequacy and continued effectiveness of the QMS.

2. Responsibilities

Top Management (assisted by Section Managers) has overall responsibility for establishing, implementing and maintaining this activity.

3. Implementation

SP/1 – Compliance and Approval
SP/3 – Customer Satisfaction
QP/2 – Control of Records
QP/3 – Internal Audits
QP/8 – Design Control
QP/10 – Quality Management System Review
QP/12 – Customer Feedback

	Document Ref: **N-51–044RLR13**
	Version: 03.01
	Date: 1 October 2013
	Quality Management System
	Part One – Quality Manual
	Version 01.00

8.5 Improvement (ISO 9001:2008 – 8.5)

NAFAAD shall endeavour to maintain a programme for continual improvement of and to contract deliverables and the NAFAAD QMS.

1. Implementation

QP/5 – Corrective Action
QP/6 – Preventative Action

8.5.1 Continual improvement (ISO 9001:2008 – 8.5.1)

1. Policy and objectives

NAFAAD shall:

- identify and implement any changes necessary to ensure and maintain the continued suitability and effectiveness of the NAFAAD QMS (i.e. through the use of the quality policy, quality objectives, audit results, analysis of data, corrective and preventive actions and management reviews);
- have available documented procedures to identify, manage and ensure the continual improvement of the NAFAAD QMS;
- maintain records of all investigations into customer complaints;
- record any reasons why a customer complaint was not followed by corrective and/or preventive action.

Note: If international, national or local regulations require, NAFAAD shall establish documented procedures to notify the regulatory authorities of those adverse events which meet the reporting criteria.

2. Responsibilities

Top Management has overall responsibility for establishing, implementing and maintaining this activity.

3. Implementation

SP/3 – Customer Satisfaction
QP/2 – Control of Records
QP/3 – Internal Audits
QP/10 – Quality Management System Review
QP/12 – Customer Feedback
QP/15 – Meetings and Reports

	Document Ref: **N-51–044RLR13** Version: 03.01 Date: 1 October 2013 Quality Management System Part One – Quality Manual Version 01.00

8.5.2 Corrective action (ISO 9001:2008 – 8.5.2)

Author's Hint

It is a **mandatory** requirement of ISO 9001:2008 for all organisations to have a documented procedure for Corrective Action.

NAFAAD shall plan and establish a process for corrective action, the results of which shall be included in the management review process.

1. Policy and objectives

NAFAAD shall establish a documented procedure for corrective action and shall define the requirements for:

* identifying non-conformities (including customer complaints);
* determining the causes of non-conformity;
* evaluating the need for actions to ensure that non-conformities do not recur;
* implementing corrective action;
* recording the results of actions taken;
* reviewing that corrective action taken is effective and recorded.

2. Responsibilities

Top Management (assisted by Section Managers) has overall responsibility for establishing, implementing and maintaining this activity.

3. Implementation

SP/3 – Customer Satisfaction
QP/2 – Control of Records
QP/3 – Internal Audits
QP/4 – Non-Conforming Product
QP/5 – Corrective Action
QP/6 – Preventative Action
QP/15 – Meetings and Reports

Document Ref: **N-51–044RLR13**
Version: 03.01
Date: 1 October 2013
Quality Management System
Part One – Quality Manual
Version 01.00

8.5.3 Preventive action (ISO 9001:2008 – 8.5.3)

 Author's Hint

It is a **mandatory** requirement of ISO 9001:2008 for all organisations to have a documented procedure for Preventative Action.

NAFAAD shall use preventive methodologies such as risk analysis, trend analysis, statistical process control, fault tree analysis, failure modes and effects and criticality analysis to identify the causes of potential non-conformances.

1. Policy and objectives

NAFAAD shall establish a documented procedure for preventative action and shall define the requirements for:

- the identification of potential non-conformities;
- determining the causes of the identified potential non-conformities;
- determining the type and amount of preventive action required to eliminate causes of potential non-conformities;
- the implementation of preventive action;
- recording the results of action taken;
- reviewing that the preventive action taken is effective.

2. Responsibilities

Top Management (assisted by Section Managers) has overall responsibility for establishing, implementing and maintaining this activity.

3. Implementation

QP/2 – Control of Records
QP/3 – Internal Audits
QP/4 – Non-Conforming Product
QP/6 – Preventative Action
QP/15 – Meetings and Reports

	Document Ref: **N-51–044RLR13**
	Version: 03.01
	Date: 1 October 2013
	Quality Management System
	Part One – Quality Manual
	Version 01.00

Annex A – NAFAAD Consultancy Ltd's organisation and responsibilities

 Author's Hint

The following roles and responsibilities, although primarily aimed at this particular example organisation, nevertheless represent the primary tasks that all of these managers etc. in any type of business would be responsible for.

When customising these roles and responsibilities for your own organisation, therefore, you will need to include your own organisation-specific tasks as well. This is **not** meant as a 'one-size-fits-all' type of job description!

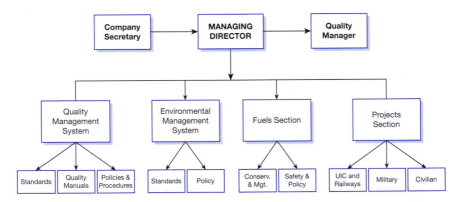

FIGURE 6.1.15 NAFAAD's organisational chart

1. MANAGING DIRECTOR

The Managing Director is responsible for the overall management of NAFAAD. He is responsible for the complete and final success of all contracts undertaken, for providing guidance on all major issues and for ensuring that all NAFAAD's products and services are produced and delivered to the highest possible level.

Document Ref: **N-51–044RLR13**
Version: 03.01
Date: 1 October 2013
Quality Management System
Part One – Quality Manual
Version 01.00

The Managing Director is responsible for:

- supervising the day-to-day running of NAFAAD;
- the overall progress of the work with which he has been entrusted and the budget placed at his disposal;
- controlling budget, time schedules, quality plans, resources and quality within the company;
- approving changes to agreed time schedules, resources and budgets;
- ensuring that the organisation will, at all times, meet the business requirements and objectives (as stipulated in NAFAAD's Memorandum of Articles and Association) as well as keeping to the agreed time schedule;
- maintaining overall responsibility for all sections;
- preparing contracts for section members, in consultation with Section Managers.

2. QUALITY MANAGER

The Quality Manager shall report **directly** to the Managing Director and is responsible for ensuring that NAFAAD's QMS is defined, implemented, audited and monitored in order to ensure that NAFAAD's documents comply with the customers' quality standards as well as the ISO 9000 series of documents concerning the implementation of a '*Quality Management System*'.

His tasks shall include:

- maintenance and effectiveness of NAFAAD's QMS;
- ensuring compliance of NAFAAD's QMS with ISO 9001:2008;
- ensuring the consistency of NAFAAD's QMS;
- ensuring that the quality message is transmitted to and understood by everyone;
- liaising with clients and outside bodies in all aspects of quality management that affect NAFAAD's organisation and type of business.

3. COMPANY SECRETARY

The NAFAAD Administration, Finance and Secretarial Office is headed by the Company Secretary who is responsible for overseeing all of the general administrative activities such as filing and distribution of NAFAAD documents as well

	Document Ref: **N-51–044RLR13** Version: 03.01 Date: 1 October 2013 Quality Management System Part One – Quality Manual Version 01.00

as all aspects of financial and contractual administration. The Company Secretary shall report **directly** to the Managing Director.

His tasks shall include:

- the daily running of the NAFAAD Office;
- issuing financial reports;
- producing monthly financial statements to the Managing Director;
- the organisation of special meetings, workshops, seminars etc. when requested to do so by the Managing Director;
- arranging (and planning) publication of documents when required.

4. SECTION MANAGERS

Section Managers are appointed by the Managing Director and are responsible for the general progress of their section, the budget placed at their disposal, for organising the work of their section and distributing this work between the sectional members according to the directives, procedures and instructions making up NAFAAD's QMS whilst duly observing the requirements of NAFAAD's Memorandum of Articles and Association.

Section Managers shall report **directly** to the Managing Director and their tasks shall include:

- controlling the time schedules, work packages, resources and quality of the tasks allocated to their section;
- ensuring that the section will, at all times, meet the business needs and objectives of NAFAAD;
- directing the studies of the section with the constant aim of achieving an accelerated and sustained tempo of the studies within the scope of their own particular quality plan and individual work packages;
- the progress and time management of all sub task(s).

5. SECTION MEMBERS

Section members shall carry out the accepted tasks assigned by their Section Manager, within the deadlines set.

Document Ref: **N-51–044RLR13**
Version: 03.01
Date: 1 October 2013
Quality Management System
Part One – Quality Manual
Version 01.00

6. SUBCONTRACTORS AND CONSULTANTS

When the work/study of a section falls outside the scope of section members, the Managing Director may authorise the temporary co-operation of subcontractors and consultants.

A contract/agreement for the subcontractor's or consultant's participation will be concluded with his company or with his parent company by the Company Secretary.

The subcontractor or consultant shall be expected to make use of his personal knowledge and experience acquired both in and outside his company without, however, in any way committing the latter. The company that provides sub-contractors or consultants shall, in return, grant them the greatest possible freedom of action and initiative and shall afford them the time and facilities required to carry out whatever work/studies they might be charged with in their capacity as a member of a NAFAAD section concerned.

	Document Ref: **N-51–044RLR13**
	Version: 03.01
	Date: 1 October 2013
	Quality Management System
	Part One – Quality Manual
	Version 01.00

Annex B – ISO 9001:2008 Cross-check

Note: Other than the permissible exclusions shown in the relevant parts of the text, NAFAAD's Quality Manual conforms to **all** of the requirements of ISO 9001:2008.

SECTION 4 – QUALITY MANAGEMENT SYSTEM

Clause No.	ISO 9001:2008 title	Quality Manual	Quality Process	Quality Procedure
4.1	General requirements	Sections 1–2		
4.2	Documentation requirements			
4.2.1	General			CP/1
			SP/1	
			SP/2	
			SP/3	
4.2.2	Quality Manual			CP/1
			SP/1	
			SP/2	
			SP/3	QP/7
				QP/9
				QP/10
4.2.3	Control of documents			QP/1
				QP/7
				QP/9
				QP/10
				QP/14
4.2.4	Control of quality records			QP/2
				QP/10

Document Ref: **N-51–044RLR13**
Version: 03.01
Date: 1 October 2013
Quality Management System
Part One – Quality Manual
Version 01.00

SECTION 5 – MANAGEMENT RESPONSIBILITY

Clause No.	ISO 9001:2008 title	Quality Manual	Quality Process	Quality Procedure
5.1	Management commitment	Sections 5–8		
5.2	Customer focus		SP/1	
			SP/2	
			SP/3	QP/12
				QP/13
5.3	Quality policy	Section 1.4		QP/7
				QP/10
5.4	Planning			
5.4.1	Quality objectives	Section 1.4		QP/7
				QP/10
5.4.2	Quality Management System planning	Sections 1.4, 2.1 and 2.2	SP/1	QP/7
				QP/8
5.5	Responsibility, authority and communication			
5.5.1	Responsibility and authority	Annex A		
5.5.2	Management representative	Annex A		
5.5.3	Internal communication			QP/13
5.6	Management review			
5.6.1	General			QP/2
				QP/10
5.6.2	Review input			QP/2
				QP/10
5.6.3	Review output			QP/2
				QP/10

	Document Ref: **N-51–044RLR13** Version: 03.01 Date: 1 October 2013 Quality Management System Part One – Quality Manual Version 01.00

SECTION 6 – RESOURCE MANAGMENT

Clause No.	ISO 9001:2008 title	Quality Manual	Quality Process	Quality Procedure
6.1	Provision of resources			QP/10
				QP/11
				QP/13
6.2	Human resources			
6.2.1	General	Annex A	SP/1	
			SP/2	QP/11
				QP/13
6.2.2	Competence, training and awareness			QP/13
6.3	Infrastructure			QP/3
				QP/8
				QP/10
				QP/11
				QP/15
6.4	Work environment	HSE Relevant Documents		

Document Ref: **N-51–044RLR13**
Version: 03.01
Date: 1 October 2013
Quality Management System
Part One – Quality Manual
Version 01.00

SECTION 7 – PRODUCTION REALISATION

Clause No.	ISO 9001:2008 title	Quality Manual	Quality Process	Quality Procedure
7.1	Planning of realisation processes		CP/1	
			SP/1	
			SP/2	
			SP/3	QP/8
7.2	Customer-related processes		SP/3	
7.2.1	Determination of requirements related to the product		CP/1	
			SP/1	
			SP/2	
			SP/3	QP/1
				QP/8
7.2.2	Review of requirements related to the product		CP/1	
			SP/1	QP/1
				QP/8
				QP/14
7.2.3	Customer communications		SP/3	QP/12
7.3	Design and development			
7.3.1	Design and development planning		CP/1	
			SP/1	QP/3
				QP/8
				QP/14
				QP/15
7.3.2	Design and development inputs			CP/1
			SP/1	QP/3
				QP/8
				QP/14
				QP/15

Document Ref: **N-51–044RLR13**
Version: 03.01
Date: 1 October 2013
Quality Management System
Part One – Quality Manual
Version 01.00

Clause No.	ISO 9001:2008 title	Quality Manual	Quality Process	Quality Procedure
7.3.3	Design and development outputs		SP/1	CP/1
				QP/3
				QP/8
				QP/14
				QP/15
7.3.4	Design and development review		CP/1	QP/3
			SP/1	QP/7
				QP/8
				QP/15
7.3.5	Design and development verification		CP/1	QP/3
			SP/1	QP/8
				QP/14
				QP/15
7.3.6	Design and development		SP/1	CP/1
				QP/2
				QP/3
				QP/8
				QP/14
				QP/15
7.3.7	Control of design and development changes		CP/1	QP/3
			SP/1	QP/8
				QP/14
7.4	Purchasing		SP/2	QP/1
				QP/11
7.4.1	Purchasing process		SP/2	QP/1
				QP/11
7.4.2	Purchasing information		SP/2	QP/1
				QP/2
				QP/11

Document Ref: **N-51–044RLR13**
Version: 03.01
Date: 1 October 2013
Quality Management System
Part One – Quality Manual
Version 01.00

Clause No.	ISO 9001:2008 title	Quality Manual	Quality Process	Quality Procedure
7.4.3	Verification of purchased product		SP/2	QP/1
				QP/2
				QP/11
				QP/14
7.5	Production and service provision			QP/1
7.5.1	Control of production and service provision	NAFAAD QMS Part 3		QP/1
		NAFAAD QMS Part 4		QP/14
7.5.2	Validation of processes for production and service provision	**PERMISSIBLE EXCLUSION**		
7.5.3	Identification and traceability			QP/1
				QP/2
				QP/3
				QP/4
				QP/5
				QP/6
				QP/8
				QP/14
7.5.4	Customer property		SP/2	QP/2
			SP/3	QP/13
7.5.5	Preservation of product	NAFAAD QMS Part 3		QP/1
		NAFAAD QMS Part 4		QP/2
				QP/4
				QP/13
7.6	Control of measuring and monitoring equipment	**PERMISSIBLE EXCLUSION**		

	Document Ref: **N-51–044RLR13**
	Version: 03.01
	Date: 1 October 2013
	Quality Management System
	Part One – Quality Manual
	Version 01.00

SECTION 8 – IMPROVEMENT

Clause No.	ISO 9001:2008 title	Quality Manual	Quality Process	Quality Procedure
8.1	General		CP/1	QP/1
				QP/2
				QP/11
				QP/15
8.2	Monitoring and measurement			
8.2.1	Customer satisfaction		SP/3	QP/12
				QP/13
				QP/15
8.2.2	Internal audit			QP/1
				QP/2
				QP/3
				QP/4
				QP/5
				QP/6
				QP/10
				QP/12
				QP/15
8.2.3	Monitoring and measurement of processes		SP/1	QP/2
			SP/3	QP/3
				QP/10
				QP/12
				QP/15
8.2.4	Monitoring and measurement of product		SP/1	QP/2
				QP/3
				QP/10
				QP/15

	Document Ref: **N–51–044RLR13** Version: 03.01 Date: 1 October 2013 Quality Management System Part One – Quality Manual Version 01.00

Clause No.	ISO 9001:2008 title	Quality Manual	Quality Process	Quality Procedure
8.3	Control of non-conforming product		SP/1	QP/1
				QP/2
				QP/3
				QP/4
				QP/5
				QP/6
8.4	Analysis of data		SP/1	QP/2
			SP/4	QP/3
				QP/8
				QP/10
				QP/12
8.5	Improvement			QP/5
				QP/6
8.5.1	Continual improvement		SP/3	QP/2
				QP/3
				QP/10
				QP/12
				QP/15
8.5.2	Corrective action		SP/3	QP/2
				QP/3
				QP/4
				QP/5
				QP/6
				QP/15
8.5.3	Preventative action			QP/2
				QP/3
				QP/4
				QP/6
				QP/15

	Document Ref: **N-51–044RLR13** Version: 03.01 Date: 1 October 2013 Quality Management System Part One – Quality Manual Version 01.00

Annex C – List of Quality Procedures

Procedure no.	*Procedure title*
QP/1	**Document Control***
QP/2	**Control of Records***
QP/3	**Internal Audits***
QP/4	**Non-Conforming Product***
QP/5	**Corrective Action***
QP/6	**Preventative Action***
QP/7	Production of a Quality Document
QP/8	Design Control
QP/9	Approval Procedure
QP/10	Quality Management System Review
QP/11	Purchasing
QP/12	Customer Feedback
QP/13	Customer Awareness and Training
QP/14	Change Control
QP/15	Meetings and Reports

* ISO mandatory procedures

Document Ref: **N–51–044RLR13**
Version: 03.01
Date: 1 October 2013
Quality Management System
Part One – Quality Manual
Version 01.00

Annex D – Abbreviations and acronyms

Abbreviation	Definition
BSI	British Standards Institution
CAD	Computer Aided Design
CP	Core Business Process
DCS	Document Control Sheet
EU	European Union
HSE	Health and Safety Executive (UK)
ISO	International Standards Organisation
IT	Information Technology
LMO	Large Multinational Organisation
MD	Managing Director
MTBF	Mean Time Between Failures
NAFAAD	NAFAAD Consultancy Ltd
PDCA	Plan, Do, Check, Act
QA	Quality Assurance
QC	Quality Control
QES	Quality Environmental and Safety
QM	Quality Manual
QMS	Quality Management System
QP	Quality Procedure
RAMS	Reliability, Availability, Maintainability and Safety
SME	Small and Medium sized Enterprise
SP	Supporting Process
SQP	Project-Specific Quality Plan
TQM	Total Quality Management
UK	United Kingdom
UKAS	United Kingdom Accreditation Service
WI	Work Instruction

	Document Ref: **N-51–044RLR13**
	Version: 03.01
	Date: 1 October 2013
	Quality Management System
	Part One – Quality Manual
	Version 01.00

Annex E – References

Ref	Abbreviation	Title	Issue date
1	ISO 9001	Quality Management Systems – Requirements	2008
2	ISO 9004:2009	Managing for the sustained success of an organization – A quality management approach	2009
3	ISO 19011:2011	Guidelines for auditing quality systems	2011
4	3042940	NAFAAD Consultancy Ltd's Memorandum and Articles of Association	1994
5	EN 50126–1	Railway applications. The specification and demonstration of reliability, availability, maintainability and safety (RAMS). Basic requirements and generic process	1999
6	BS EN ISO 14001	Environmental management systems. Requirements with guidance for use	2004
7	BS OHSAS 18001	Occupational health and safety management systems. Requirements	2007

NAFAAD Consultancy Ltd

Quality Management System

Part 2 – Quality Processes

This Quality Manual has been issued on the authority of the Managing Director of NAFAAD Consultancy Ltd for the use of all staff, subcontractors, clients and/or regulatory bodies to whom NAFAAD Consultancy Ltd may be required to provide such information to.

Approved

Date: 1 October 2013

Ray Rekcirt
Managing Director
NAFAAD Consultancy Ltd

© 2013 by NAFAAD Consultancy Ltd, all rights reserved.

Copyright subsists in all NAFAAD Consultancy Ltd deliverables including magnetic, optical and/or any other soft copy of these deliverables. This document may not be reproduced, in full or in part, without written permission.

| Document Ref: **N-52–044RLR13** |
| Version: 03.01 |
| Date: 1 October 2013 |
| Quality Management System |
| Part Two – Quality Processes |
| Version 01.00 |

DOCUMENT CONTROL SHEET

Title	This version	Date
NAFAAD Consultancy Ltd		
Part 2	File Number	No of Pages
Quality Processes	**N-52–045RLR13**	**12**

ABSTRACT

The NAFAAD Associates Ltd Quality Management System is divided into four parts.

This document is Part 2 and describes the Quality Processes that have been developed to implement NAFAAD Associates Ltd's Quality Management System.

The Quality Procedures and Work Instructions designed to meet these processes are contained in Parts 3 and 4.

Name	Function	Level
	Quality Manager	Prepare
	Managing Director	Agree
	Managing Director	Approve

ATTACHMENTS

Attachments	Description

Document Ref: **N-52–044RLR13**
Version: 03.01
Date: 1 October 2013
Quality Management System
Part Two – Quality Processes
Version 01.00

QMS REVISION HISTORY

No.	Chapter	Amendment details	Date
01.00	All	First published version in accordance with ISO 9001:1994	28.06.93
01.01	3	Inclusion of new chapter for customer satisfaction	05.04.94
01.02	4.2.3	Procedure for the control of documents changed	23.12.95
01.03	All	Minor editorial revisions of all sections and annexes	30.07.96
02.00	All	Second published version to conform to ISO 9001:2000	31.12.00
02.01	5	Management responsibility procedure updated to cover new (i.e. Fuels) Division	01.01.02
02.02	All	Minor editorial changes following three years' experience of ISO 9001:2000	01.01.05
03.00	All	Major revision following publication of ISO 9001:2008	01.11.09
03.01	All	Minor editorial changes following five years' experience of ISO 9001:2008	01.10.13

	Document Ref: **N-52–044RLR13**
	Version: 03.01
	Date: 1 October 2013
	Quality Management System
	Part Two – Quality Processes
	Version 01.00

CONTENTS

Abstract 2
Attachments 2
QMS revision history. 3

List of illustrations 4
List of tables 4

1   Documentation. 5

2   Processes 5

3   Core Business Process 6

4   Supporting Processes. 8
     4.1   SP/1 Compliance and approval 9
     4.2   SP/2 – Subcontractors and suppliers 10
     4.3   SP/3 – Customer satisfaction. 10

LIST OF ILLUSTRATIONS

Figure 6.2.1:   Core Business Process 7
Figure 6.2.2:   Supporting Processes 8
Figure 6.2.3:   Compliance and approval 9
Figure 6.2.4:   Subcontractors and suppliers 11
Figure 6.2.5:   The benefits of increasing customer satisfaction 12

LIST OF TABLES

Table 6.2.1:   NAFAAD Associates Ltd's Quality System –
                documentation 5
Table 6.2.2:   Quality Processes 6

Document Ref: **N-52–044RLR13**
Version: 03.01
Date: 1 October 2013
Quality Management System
Part Two – Quality Processes
Version 01.00

1 DOCUMENTATION

NAFAAD Associates Ltd (NAFAAD) has four levels of documentation within its Quality Management System (QMS) which is structured as shown in the table below.

This document is Part 2 and describes the Quality Processes that have been developed to implement NAFAAD's QMS.

TABLE 6.2.1 NAFAAD Associates Ltd's Quality System – documentation

Part 1	Quality Manual	The main policy document that establishes NAFAAD's QMS and how it meets the requirements of ISO 9001:2008.
Part 2	**Quality Processes**	**The Core Business Process plus the primary and secondary Supporting Processes that describe the activities required to implement the QMS and to meet the policy requirements made in the Quality Manual.**
Part 3	Quality Procedures	A description of the method by which quality system activities are managed.
Part 4	Work Instructions	A description of how a specific task is carried out.

2 PROCESSES

NAFAAD is a customer-focused organisation that is committed to understanding, anticipating and responding to all customers' requirements with product and service excellence. This commitment is achieved by relating resources and activities to managed processes and by establishing unity of purpose and direction.

The organisational processes making up the NAFAAD QMS comprise a Core Business Process (CP) (describing the end-to-end activities involved in NAFAAD project management and the production of contract deliverables) supplemented by a number of Supporting Processes (SPs) which describe the infrastructure required to complete NAFAAD projects on time and within budget.

 To ensure achievement of process objectives, a process owner with **full** responsibility and authority for managing the process and achieving process objectives shall be nominated.

	Document Ref: **N-52–044RLR13** Version: 03.01 Date: 1 October 2013 Quality Management System Part Two – Quality Processes Version 01.00

The current list of NAFAAD Processes are:

TABLE 6.2.2 Quality Processes

Process no.	Instruction title
CP/1	NAFAAD's Core Business Process
SP/1	Compliance and Approval
SP/2	Subcontractors and Suppliers
SP/3	Customer Satisfaction
SP/4	TBA
SP/5	TBA
SP/6	TBA

3 CORE BUSINESS PROCESS

As described by ISO, 'A Core business process or business method is a collection of related, structured activities or tasks that produce a specific service or product (serve a particular goal) for a particular customer or customers.'

Within NAFAAD our Core Business Process (see Figure 6.2.1) involves eight steps:

1. Identify a market need for a product or service;
2. Create a market opportunity;
3. Obtain a Contract;
4. Appoint a Project Team;
5. Produce the Deliverable (in our case this is normally a service but can sometimes be a product as well);
6. Deliver the service (or product) to the customer;
7. Receive payment;
8. Investigate further market opportunities and possible ongoing improvements to NAFAAD's QMS.

From the initial identification of the task through to final customer satisfaction, all steps in NAFAAD's Core Business Process are supported by Supporting Processes, which in turn are supported by Quality Procedures that ensure that

Document Ref: **N-52–044RLR13**
Version: 03.01
Date: 1 October 2013
Quality Management System
Part Two – Quality Processes
Version 01.00

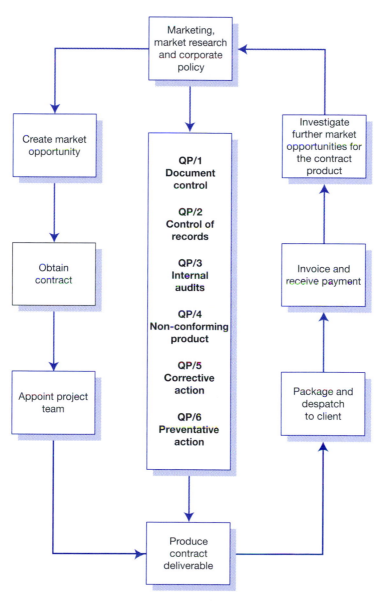

FIGURE 6.2.1 Core Business Process

	Document Ref: **N-52–044RLR13**
	Version: 03.01
	Date: 1 October 2013
	Quality Management System
	Part Two – Quality Processes
	Version 01.00

its activities are fully understood, controlled and documented and that everyone knows exactly what they are supposed to be doing and how they should be doing it.

The Managing Director is responsible for managing the Core Business Process.

4 SUPPORTING PROCESSES

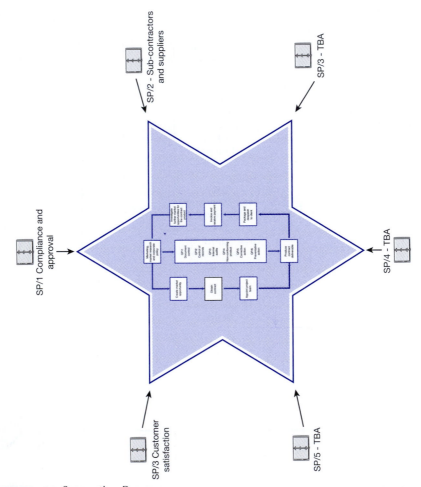

FIGURE 6.2.2 Supporting Processes

Document Ref: **N-52–044RLR13**
Version: 03.01
Date: 1 October 2013
Quality Management System
Part Two – Quality Processes
Version 01.00

In any organisation there always exists a common set of five Supporting Processes (SP) which (particularly in the case of a Small Business) will consist of:

1.   Sales & Marketing;
2.   Accounting & Technology;
3.   Quality & Product/Service Delivery;
4.   Management, HR & Finance;
5.   Product Development.

Within NAFAAD we use three SPs (namely '*Compliance and Approval*', '*Subcontractors and Suppliers*' and '*Customer Satisfaction*') to sustain our Core Business Process and these fully cover the five elements listed above. The SPs, in turn, are then supported by our current set of Quality Procedures.

4.1 SP/1 Compliance and Approval

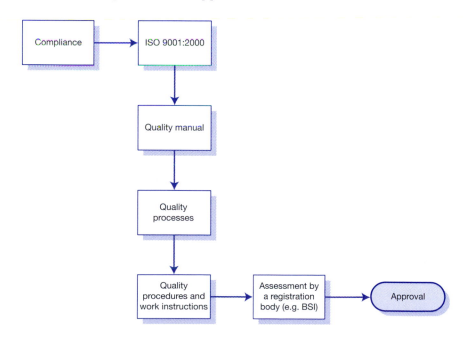

FIGURE 6.2.3 Compliance and Approval

	Document Ref: **N-52–044RLR13**
	Version: 03.01 Date: 1 October 2013 Quality Management System Part Two – Quality Processes Version 01.00

Before NAFAAD can tender for a deliverable, it must comply with all of the applicable regulations and standards. In order to achieve approval, NAFAAD will put into practice the various steps shown in the Compliance and Approval chart above.

The Quality Manager is responsible for managing this Supplementary Process.

4.2 SP/2 – Subcontractors and Suppliers

From the initial Selection process through to Delivery and Storage, all contract requirements will be monitored and assessed for compliance.

The Managing Director is responsible for managing this Supplementary Process.

4.3 SP/3 – Customer Satisfaction

Managing customer expectations and providing great customer service are very important nowadays and this can only be achieved by building customer satisfaction into our NAFAAD business processes. Many organisations tend to only measure customer satisfaction once per year – a long time after the product and/or service has been provided – whilst others measure customer satisfaction after service, project or product has been delivered and then take corrective actions. The main problem with these kinds of approach is that they are reactive, not proactive ways to respond to customer satisfaction.

If customer satisfaction is built into business processes (see QP/12 'Customer Feedback' and QP/13 'Customer Awareness and Training') then you do not have to contend with negative feedback after it is too late to do anything about it. Here are some ideas for how to build customer satisfaction into your business processes:

- 'Keep your systems simple.'

Note: More often than not this is referred to as the KISS approach, i.e. 'Keep It Simple Stupid'!

- 'If it is important to your customer, it belongs in your tracking system.'
- 'The information you gather needs to be available in real-time.'
- 'Because customer preferences change, assumptions are dangerous.'
- 'Customers' moods change, so you need to track them.'

Document Ref: **N-52–044RLR13**
Version: 03.01
Date: 1 October 2013
Quality Management System
Part Two – Quality Processes
Version 01.00

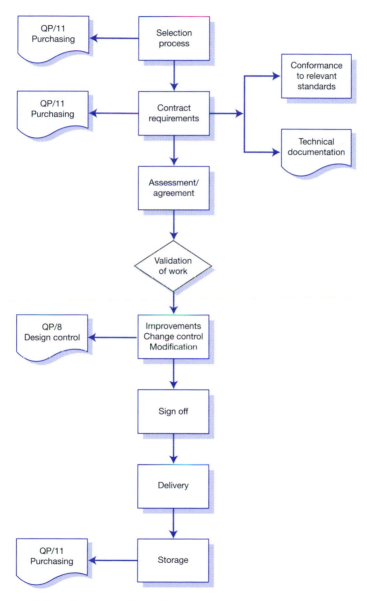

FIGURE 6.2.4 Subcontractors and suppliers

	Document Ref: **N-52–044RLR13**
	Version: 03.01
	Date: 1 October 2013
	Quality Management System
	Part Two – Quality Processes
	Version 01.00

- 'Do not dampen the customer experience with an impersonal delivery.'
- 'Use technology to ask for customers' information sparingly.'

If customer satisfaction is built into business processes, then you do not have to contend with negative feedback after it is too late to do anything about it.

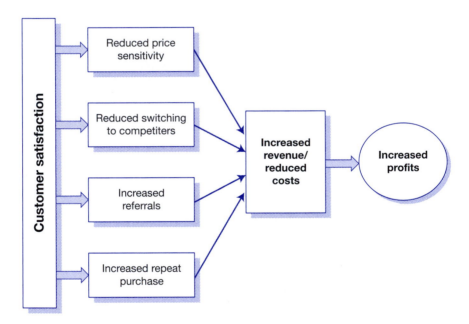

FIGURE 6.2.5 The benefits of increasing customer satisfaction

NAFAAD Consultancy Ltd

Quality Management System

Part 3 – Quality Procedures

This Quality Manual has been issued on the authority of the Managing Director of NAFAAD Consultancy Ltd for the use of all staff, subcontractors, clients and/or regulatory bodies to whom NAFAAD Consultancy Ltd may be required to provide such information to.

Approved	
	Date: 1 October 2013
Ray Rekcirt Managing Director NAFAAD Consultancy Ltd	

© 2013 by NAFAAD Consultancy Ltd, all rights reserved.

Copyright subsists in all NAFAAD Consultancy Ltd deliverables including magnetic, optical and/or any other soft copy of these deliverables. This document may not be reproduced, in full or in part, without written permission.

| Document Ref: **N-53–044RLR13** |
| Version: 03.01 |
| Date: 1 October 2013 |
| Quality Management System |
| Part Three – Quality Procedures |
| Version 01.00 |

DOCUMENT CONTROL SHEET

Title	This version	Date
NAFAAD Consultancy Ltd		
Part 3	File Number	No of Pages
Quality Procedures	**N-53–046RLR13**	**131**

ABSTRACT

The NAFAAD Associates Ltd Quality Management System is divided into four parts.

This document is Part 3 and describes the Quality Procedures that have been developed to implement NAFAAD Associates Ltd's Quality Management System.

The Work Instructions designed to meet these processes are contained in Part 4.

Name	Function	Level
	Quality Manager	Prepare
	Managing Director	Agree
	Managing Director	Approve

ATTACHMENTS

Attachments	Description

Document Ref: **N-53–044RLR13**
Version: 03.01
Date: 1 October 2013
Quality Management System
Part Three – Quality Procedures
Version 01.00

QMS REVISION HISTORY

No.	Chapter	Amendment details	Date
01.00	All	First published version in accordance with ISO 9001:1994	28.06.93
01.01	3	Inclusion of new chapter for customer satisfaction	05.04.94
01.02	4.2.3	Procedure for the control of documents changed	23.12.95
01.03	All	Minor editorial revisions of all sections and annexes	30.07.96
02.00	All	Second published version to conform to ISO 9001:2000	31.12.00
02.01	5	Management responsibility procedure updated to cover new (i.e. Fuels) Division	01.01.02
02.02	All	Minor editorial changes following three years' experience of ISO 9001:2000	01.01.05
03.00	All	Major revision following publication of ISO 9001:2008	01.11.09
03.01	All	Minor editorial changes following five years' experience of ISO 9001:2008	01.10.13

	Document Ref: **N-53–044RLR13**
	Version: 03.01
	Date: 1 October 2013
	Quality Management System
	Part Three – Quality Procedures
	Version 01.00

CONTENTS

Abstract 2

Attachments 2

QMS revision history. 3

1 Documentation 5

2 Quality Procedures 5

LIST OF TABLES

Table 6.3.1:   NAFAAD Associates Ltd's Quality System –
documentation 5

Table 6.3.2:   Quality Procedures 7

Document Ref: **N-53–044RLR13**
Version: 03.01
Date: 1 October 2013
Quality Management System
Part Three – Quality Procedures
Version 01.00

1 DOCUMENTATION

NAFAAD Associates Ltd (NAFAAD) has four levels of documentation within its Quality Management System (QMS) which is structured as shown in the table below.

This document is Part 3 and describes the Quality Procedures that have been developed to implement NAFAAD's QMS.

TABLE 6.3.1 NAFAAD Associates Ltd's Quality System – documentation

Part 1	Quality Manual	The main policy document that establishes NAFAAD's QMS and how it meets the requirements of ISO 9001:2008.
Part 2	Quality Processes	The Core Business Process plus the primary and secondary Supporting Processes that describe the activities required to implement the QMS and to meet the policy requirements made in the Quality Manual.
Part 3	**Quality Procedures**	**A description of the method by which quality system activities are managed.**
Part 4	Work Instructions	A description of how a specific task is carried out.

2 QUALITY PROCEDURES

Quality Procedures (QPs) form the bulk of NAFAAD's QMS and describe how the policy objectives of the Quality Manual (QM) can be met in practice and how their processes are controlled.

QPs contain the basic documentation used for planning and controlling all of NAFAAD activities that impact on quality. By design, the QPs conform to the specific requirements contained in ISO 9001:2008 although (in reality) they often cover more and as such are an efficient method of controlling every aspect of NAFAAD business. Each QP is unique and contains details of procedures directly applicable to NAFAAD.

These documented procedures can be made available and used in either hard copy or electronic format and may be used as separate documents outside the QM in places of work.

	Document Ref: **N-53–044RLR13**
	Version: 03.01
	Date: 1 October 2013
	Quality Management System
	Part Three – Quality Procedures
	Version 01.00

 Note: Some procedures (e.g. '*Investments*') may contain data or information, the knowledge of which must remain restricted to NAFAAD. These procedures are not included in the QM, beyond their title and reference number.

There is absolutely **no** restriction as to how many QPs an organisation can produce, however, **ISO 9001:2008 contains a total of six mandatory ISO 9001 Procedures that MUST be included in every organisation's QMS regardless of its size.** These are listed below.

1.1.1 Control of Documents (QP/1)

A written procedure used to control the approval and re-approval of procedures prior to issue. Used to ensure that the current revision status is displayed, documents are legible and that **only** current versions are available at point of use. To also ensure that obsolete documents are controlled and documents from external parties (such as customers) are maintained correctly.

1.1.2 Control of Records (QP/2)

A procedure to control the identification, storage, protection, retrieval, retention and disposal of all records.

1.2.3 Internal Audits (QP/3)

A procedure to define a planned programme of audits to ensure that all processes and procedures meet both ISO 9001 requirements and an organisation's requirements. Also used for the reporting, follow up and recording of these audits.

1.2.4 Control of Non-conforming Product (QP/4)

A procedure to ensure that a non-conforming product is **not** used and action is taken to prevent any future possible use of it.

1.2.5 Corrective Action (QP/5)

A written procedure to ensure that root causes of problems are identified and actions taken to correct them.

 Note: actions must be verified to ensure effectiveness.

Document Ref: **N-53–044RLR13**
Version: 03.01
Date: 1 October 2013
Quality Management System
Part Three – Quality Procedures
Version 01.00

1.2.6 Preventive Action (QP/6)

A written procedure (similar to that for corrective action) for the identification of potential problems – and to eliminate them before a problem occurs.

Current NAFAAD QPs are shown in Table 6.3.2.

TABLE 6.3.2 Quality Procedures

Procedure no.	Procedure title
QP/1	Document Control
QP/2	Control of Records
QP/3	Internal Audits
QP/4	Non-conforming Product
QP/5	Corrective Action
QP/6	Preventative Action
QP/7	Production of a Quality Document
QP/8	Design Control
QP/9	Approval Procedure
QP/10	Quality Management System Review
QP/11	Purchasing
QP/12	Customer Feedback
QP/13	Customer Awareness and Training
QP/14	Change Control
QP/15	Meetings and Reports

| | Document Ref: **N-53–047RLR13**
Version: 03.01
Date: 1 October 2013
Quality Management System
Part Three – Quality Procedures
QP/1 Document Control – Version 01.00 |

QP/1 – Document Control

Author's Hint

For a **very** small business, the following procedures might be far more than you require. The most important thing – even if you are not intending to go for formal ISO 9001:2008 Certification – is to have some form of reference for each document and for there to be some form of control over its distribution, use and eventual removal.

CONTENTS

1.1   Scope 2
1.2   Responsibility.. 2
       1.2.1   Quality Manager...................................... 2
1.3   Definition 3
1.4   Document administration number............................... 3
1.5   File numbering system 3
1.6   Documents produced by NAFAAD................................. 3
       1.6.1   File reference....................................... 3
       1.6.2   Version numbering 4
1.7   Letters produced by NAFAAD 5
1.8   Faxes produced by NAFAAD 5
1.9   E-mails produced by NAFAAD 5
1.10   Contracts and minutes produced by NAFAAD 6
1.11   Documents received by NAFAAD 6
1.12   E-mails received by NAFAAD personnel 7
1.13   Storing files on the server................................. 7
1.14   Filing of documents (hard copies) 7
1.15   Old and obsolete documents.................................. 8
1.16   Controlled documents 8
1.17   Headed paper.. 8
1.18   Document distribution....................................... 9
1.19   Draft documents 9
1.20   Approved documents 10
1.21   Internal distribution 10

Document Ref: **N-53–047RLR13**
Version: 03.01
Date: 1 October 2013
Quality Management System
Part Three – Quality Procedures
QP/1 Document Control – Version 01.00

1.22   External distribution 10
1.23   Press notices etc. 10
1.24   Software 10
    1.24.1   Word processing 10
    1.24.2   Spreadsheets and graphics 11
1.25   Copyright 11
1.26   Software programs for document control 11
Annex A – Examples of mail in and mail out sheets 13
Annex B – Example of file reference codes 14
Annex C – Identification of changes in a document 16

1.1 SCOPE

Under Section 4.2.3 of ISO 9001:2008, there is a mandatory requirement for NAFAAD to produce a document procedure for the control of documents. QP/1 satisfies this requirement.

Document control is essential for the overall efficiency and quality of NAFAAD and its documents and the following document control procedures shall apply to all documents that are produced by (and for) the organisation, irrespective of where they originate.

QP/1 details the allocation of document codes and the procedures for distributing these documents. It describes the procedures for translating (if required) and for filing (electronically and/or manually) these documents, how document changes are managed and the type of word-processing software and other types of software that are to be used.

1.2 RESPONSIBILITY

1.2.1 Quality Manager

The Quality Manager (in consultation with the Company Secretary) is responsible for the overall planning of document control procedures throughout NAFAAD.

 A centralised filing system shall be retained in the main office.

Document Ref: **N-53–047RLR13**
Version: 03.01
Date: 1 October 2013
Quality Management System
Part Three – Quality Procedures
QP/1 Document Control – Version 01.00

1.3 DEFINITION

The term '*document*' includes all NAFAAD documents, deliverables, letters, faxes, copies of e-mails, reports, minutes and contracts etc.

1.4 DOCUMENT ADMINISTRATION NUMBER

All documents which are received, despatched and/or processed by the main office shall receive a document administration number. A list of all document administration numbers used by individual NAFAAD consultants shall be maintained by them. Personnel, however, based at the Head Office shall share one book, which shall be maintained by the Company Administrator. This document administration number is also the number by which the document is stored on the company computer. The number reverts to '001' at the beginning of each year.

 Author's Hint

Dependent on the size of your business and the amount of correspondence you administer, this number could be increased to, say 0001 or even 00001.

All documents despatched by the Office shall be entered in the 'MAIL OUT' letterbook, while all documents received shall be entered in the 'MAIL IN' letterbook (for examples see Annex A).

1.5 FILE NUMBERING SYSTEM

All NAFAAD personnel shall make use of the company filing and numbering system when originating NAFAAD documents, particularly where documents are to be distributed externally.

1.6 DOCUMENTS PRODUCED BY NAFAAD

1.6.1 File reference

For all documents produced by NAFAAD, the file reference (also known as the document reference number) shall be inserted in the header, to the right, of every

Document Ref: **N-53–047RLR13**
Version: 03.01
Date: 1 October 2013
Quality Management System
Part Three – Quality Procedures
QP/1 Document Control – Version 01.00

page (see top of this page as a typical example of this rule), regardless of whether the page is single or double sided. The format of this reference number shall be as follows:

N-XX-NNNAAAYY, where:

N	Indicates that the document is related to NAFAAD.
XX	Is the file reference code (see Annex B).
NNN	Is the document administration number, which provides a unique reference for a particular document.
AAA	Is the author's (or originator's) initials.
YY	Is the last two digits of the year in which the document was written.

Example: **N-53–029RLR13**, where:

N	Means this is a NAFAAD document
53	Means this is a Quality Procedure (see Annex B)
029	Is the Document administration number (i.e. 29)
RLR	Is the Author's initials (i.e. Ray Rekcirt)
13	Is the year in which the document was written

1.6.2 Version numbering

To indicate the status of the document, a version number shall be included in the header underneath the Document Ref number (see top of this page as a typical example of this rule). The format of this number shall be as follows:

VV Indicates the version number of the document.

Note: For preliminary or draft documents this number will always be '*00*'.

RR Indicates the revision number of the document.

Example: **Version 02.02**, where:

02.02	Means this is version 2 of document 29
02.**02**	Means this is revision 2 of Version 2 of document 29

Document Ref: **N-53–047RLR13**
Version: 03.01
Date: 1 October 2013
Quality Management System
Part Three – Quality Procedures
QP/1 Document Control – Version 01.00

Changes to consecutive revisions (of versions already having a revision number), should be identified by shaded and/or strikethrough type fonts (see Annex C).

Issued documents which have changed significantly from the previous version shall receive a new version number and the revision number will revert to '00'.

1.7 LETTERS PRODUCED BY NAFAAD

All letters produced by NAFAAD shall be produced using the letter template available from the server. The reference number shall be in the relevant space on the first page and this number shall be repeated in the footer of every page, to the right, regardless of whether the page is single or double-sided. The format of this reference number is the same as the example in 1.6.1 (i.e. N-53–029-RLR13).

All letters shall also have a reference indicating the person/persons who dealt with the letter. This reference will consist of the initials of the involved persons separated by a slash (.../...) and shall be placed underneath the document reference number (on the front page only).

The first initials in the reference will be the person who initiated the letter. The last initials are optional and are intended to indicate the person who actually wrote (or in some circumstances translated) the letter.

Example: **MD/QM**, where:

MD   Means that the Managing Director originated the letter;
QM   Means that the Quality Manager wrote the letter.

1.8 FAXES PRODUCED BY NAFAAD

All faxes produced by NAFAAD shall use the fax template available from the server. The reference number need only be included on the first page of the fax.

The format of this reference number is the same as the example in 1.6.1.

1.9 E-MAILS PRODUCED BY NAFAAD

All e-mails produced by NAFAAD shall be produced using the e-mail template available from the server. The reference number need only be included in the subject (i.e. title) of the e-mail.

	Document Ref: **N-53–047RLR13** Version: 03.01 Date: 1 October 2013 Quality Management System Part Three – Quality Procedures QP/1 Document Control – Version 01.00

1.10 CONTRACTS AND MINUTES PRODUCED BY NAFAAD

All contracts and minutes produced by NAFAAD shall be produced using the template available from the server. The reference number shall be included in the header of every page, to the right, in small characters, regardless of whether the page is single or double-sided. The format of this reference number is the same as the example in 1.6.1.

1.11 DOCUMENTS RECEIVED BY NAFAAD

All documents received by NAFAAD shall have the file reference number clearly marked on the left hand side of the document, by hand, as follows:

N-XX-NNN-DDMMYY, where:

N-XX-NNN	Is as shown in 1.6.1 above.
DD	Is the day number of the date when the document was received;
MM	Is the month number of the date when the document was received;
YY	Are the last two digits of the year number of the date when the document was received.

Example: **N-16–1147–260113**, where:

16	Is the place where the document will eventually be stored – e.g. the Financial (Insurance) folder (see Annex B);
1147	Is the document administration number 1147 given by the Secretary, or person receiving the document.
260113	Means that the document was received on 26 January 2013

 Author's Hint

Some organisations do not include the receipt date in the file reference number as they consider it unnecessary because the actual reference is logged against a specific date in the file registry (which is usually a spreadsheet of some description).

	Document Ref: **N-53–047RLR13**
	Version: 03.01
	Date: 1 October 2013
	Quality Management System
	Part Three – Quality Procedures
	QP/1 Document Control – Version 01.00

1.12 E-MAILS RECEIVED BY NAFAAD PERSONNEL

If the e-mail contains important information which needs to be stored for future reference (for example an e-mail concerning a Contract condition or alteration) then a copy of the e-mail shall be filed in accordance with para 1.11 above. This equally applies to any file attachment the e-mail may contain. The decision as to whether the e-mail should be registered lies with the recipient of that e-mail.

1.13 STORING FILES ON THE SERVER

In order to be able to retrieve stored files from the NAFAAD server, each document shall be filed within a specific directory for that particular Contract/section. Each Contract/section shall have a folder, with sub-folders for the various categories within each contract/section such as minutes, correspondence, reports, annexes etc. The document numbering system shall be used for this purpose and it is essential that the file reference number corresponds with the relevant part of the document number – as shown below

XX-NNNAAYY, where:

XX	Is the file reference code (see Annex B) for the folder;
NNN	Is the document administration number (which provides a unique reference for that particular document);
AA	Is the author's (or originator's) initials;
YY	Is the last two digits of the year in which the document was written.

Example: **16–1147RLR13**, where:

16	Is the Financial (Insurance) folder
1147	Is the document administration number (i.e. 1147)
RLR	Is the author's initials (Ray Rekcirt)
13	Is the year in which the document was written.

1.14 FILING OF DOCUMENTS (HARD COPIES)

NAFAAD file cabinets shall be located in the main office and are the responsibility of the Company Secretary; the document reference number, as described above, will indicate where the document is to be filed.

	Document Ref: **N-53–047RLR13**
	Version: 03.01
	Date: 1 October 2013
	Quality Management System
	Part Three – Quality Procedures
	QP/1 Document Control – Version 01.00

 Note: Where possible, different files concerning one particular contract or section shall be grouped together.

If a received document concerns more than one Contract or section, the document reference numbers of **both** documents shall be shown on that document.

1.15 OLD AND OBSOLETE DOCUMENTS

All documents and data relating to NAFAAD shall be reviewed for adequacy prior to issue with appropriate copies being made available, on an as required basis. All obsolete documents shall be promptly removed from all points of issue and/or use.

Old and obsolete documents shall be removed from the file cabinet under the supervision of the Company Administrator. A decision shall be taken (i.e. between the Company Secretary and the originator of the document) concerning how long a particular removed document shall be stored. Documents requiring storage shall be placed in file boxes (adopting the same method used for filing documents) and shall be clearly marked as '*CANCELLED*', and the file box shall show how long the document is to be stored for. File boxes shall be retained in the attic storeroom.

1.16 CONTROLLED DOCUMENTS

A controlled copy of each published document will be held on the server and applicable personnel notified of its publication by e-mail. The names of these personnel shall be recorded by the Quality Manager.

When a controlled document is amended or becomes obsolete, personnel will be informed of the change (by the Quality Manager) and instructed to dispose of any copies (printed or soft copies) that they hold of the document.

The Quality Manager is responsible for ensuring that at least one soft copy of any obsolete controlled document **shall** be retained at least for the lifetime of the product or service – as defined by the client.

1.17 HEADED PAPER

All official NAFAAD correspondence shall be printed on NAFAAD paper using the appropriate NAFAAD logo.

	Document Ref: **N-53–047RLR13**
	Version: 03.01
	Date: 1 October 2013
	Quality Management System
	Part Three – Quality Procedures
	QP/1 Document Control – Version 01.00

1.18 DOCUMENT DISTRIBUTION

Approved documents, working papers, reports and documents may be freely distributed to all NAFAAD personnel as well as any personnel working for and on behalf of NAFAAD. These papers shall all be clearly marked with the file reference number, status, originator, date and a distribution statement (e.g. '**not to be distributed outside NAFAAD**').

Author's Hint

Alternatively you might prefer to use a watermark on the document itself to make it perfectly clear that this particular document is only intended for internal use.

When a document is being sent to someone outside NAFAAD, the document or deliverable shall be approved by the Managing Director before despatch and the cover letter shall include the Managing Director's signature. In exceptional cases the Managing Director may delegate approval of a specific document or documents to another officer (e.g. the Company Secretary).

The actual signing (i.e. per pro) of the cover letter may also be delegated to a third party (e.g. the Company Secretary).

1.19 DRAFT DOCUMENTS

All draft versions of documents shall carry the following text on the front cover of the document:

'This is a draft version and may only be used for information purposes'.

Author's Hint

Again, you could use a watermark if you prefer.

Draft documents that do not pass approval shall be removed from circulation. If such documents have to be retained, they shall be kept in files clearly marked '*NOT APPROVED*'.

Document Ref: **N-53–047RLR13**
Version: 03.01
Date: 1 October 2013
Quality Management System
Part Three – Quality Procedures
QP/1 Document Control – Version 01.00

1.20 APPROVED DOCUMENTS

All approved documents shall be uniquely numbered (see Section 1.6) and the main office will keep a register of all issued documents.

When a new version of an approved document is issued, copies of all previous versions shall be destroyed. This shall be covered by a statement in the covering letter to the effect that:

'On receipt of a new issue number all previous versions are to be destroyed'.

1.21 INTERNAL DISTRIBUTION

The Company Secretary is responsible for the distribution of all approved company documents, working papers, reports and documents within NAFAAD.

1.22 EXTERNAL DISTRIBUTION

The Managing Director is responsible for (and shall decide on) the distribution of all approved documents, working papers, reports and documents outside NAFAAD.

1.23 PRESS NOTICES ETC.

The Managing Director shall decide whether NAFAAD approved documents, working papers, reports and documents shall be made available to the public. The Managing Director shall fix the right-of-use fee for these documents, with the Company Secretary deciding the copy price.

1.24 SOFTWARE

1.24.1 Word processing

All NAFAAD documents, working papers, and reports shall be made and stored using Microsoft® Word version 2007 format.

Document Ref: **N-53–047RLR13**
Version: 03.01
Date: 1 October 2013
Quality Management System
Part Three – Quality Procedures
QP/1 Document Control – Version 01.00

1.24.2 Spreadsheets and graphics

Spreadsheets and graphics for NAFAAD documents, working papers, reports and documents shall be made using Microsoft® Office Professional 2007 and Visio Professional® (2007 version).

1.25 COPYRIGHT

The following shall be included on the front page of each deliverable:

© **2013 NAFAAD. All rights reserved.**

Copyright subsists in all NAFAAD deliverables including magnetic, optical and/or any other soft copy of these deliverables. This document may not be reproduced, in full or in part, without written permission. Enquiries about copyright of NAFAAD deliverables should be made to NAFAAD, Riddiford House, Winkleigh, Devon, EX19 8DW.

If, by permission of the copyright owner, any part of this document is quoted, then a statement specifying the original document shall be added to the quotation. Any such quotation shall be according to the original (text, figure or table) and may **not** be shortened or modified.

1.26 SOFTWARE PROGRAMS FOR DOCUMENT CONTROL

With the acceptance of ISO 9001:2008 as the principal standard for integrated management has come the requirement to see the business in process terms.

One method of achieving this is to use a process mapping software tool which not only describes the organisation's business processes (through a series of multi-layer maps) but also provides immediate access to existing documentation sitting below the process maps. This enables a record to be easily accessed rather than having to cope with searching through a forest of printed papers, with staff having immediate access (i.e. through an intranet desktop PC) to the relevant document(s).

The benefits of using software to manage your documentation and processes are numerous, which is the reason why more organisations are now turning to an IT solution. The advantages include:

Document Ref: **N-53–047RLR13**
Version: 03.01
Date: 1 October 2013
Quality Management System
Part Three -- Quality Procedures
QP/1 Document Control – Version 01.00

- ease of use
- error reductions
- cost savings on print, paper and distribution
- improved functionality
- space and environmental savings
- time no longer wasted on searching for hard copies.

 There are many companies supplying process mapping software tools (as you will see from a quick search on Google) and I am sure that you will be able to quickly locate one to suit your particular requirements (author's fingers crossed however!).

Document Ref: **N-53–047RLR13**
Version: 03.01
Date: 1 October 2013
Quality Management System
Part Three – Quality Procedures
QP/1 Document Control – Version 01.00

QP/1 Annex A –
Examples of mail in and mail out sheets

Mail In sheet

Date	Code	From	Subject	Document admin no.	Action (by whom)	Completed (date)

Code: a letter to describe the document, i.e. F = Fax, M = Minutes, L = Letter, etc.

Mail Out sheet

Date	Code	To	From	Subject	Document admin no.

Code: a letter to describe the document, i.e. F = Fax, M = Minutes, L = Letter, etc.

Document Ref: **N-53–047RLR13**
Version: 03.01
Date: 1 October 2013
Quality Management System
Part Three – Quality Procedures
QP/1 Document Control – Version 01.00

QP/1 Annex B –
Examples of file reference codes

00–09	**Administration**
01	Accommodation – reservations, etc.
02	Internal quality audits
03	Meetings and reports
04	Office equipment
05	Stationery
06	Travel
07	Subcontractors
10–19	**Finance**
10	Audits
11	Annual accounts
12	Budgets
13	Contracts
14	Expenditure
15	Financial management
16	Insurance
17	Time and expense sheets
30–39	**Public Relations**
30	Articles
31	Brochures
32	General
33	Publications and presentations
40–49	**Personnel Matters**
40	Management
41	Social and welfare
42	Training

	Document Ref: **N-53–047RLR13**
	Version: 03.01
	Date: 1 October 2013
	Quality Management System
	Part Three – Quality Procedures
	QP/1 Document Control – Version 01.00

43	Health and safety
50–59	**Quality Management System**
50	Quality – General
51	Quality Manual
52	Quality Processes
53	Quality Procedures
54	Work Instructions
55	Quality Plans
56	Quality Audits
57	ISO 9001:2008 and other standards
60–69	**Environmental**
60	Policy
61	Standards
62	ISO 14001
70–79	**Fuels**
70	Conservation
71	Management
72	Safety
73	Policy
80–89	**Projects**
80	UIC and railways
81	Military
82	Civilian
90–99	**Technical**
90	Manuals
91	Reference documents
92	National standards
93	International standards
94	Information Technology

Document Ref: **N-53–047RLR13**
Version: 03.01
Date: 1 October 2013
Quality Management System
Part Three – Quality Procedures
QP/1 Document Control – Version 01.00

QP/1 Annex C –
Identification of changes in a document

EXAMPLE

In addition to being ideal for ~~handling~~ controlling the quality of manufactured goods, Quality Plans are ~~also very much~~ equally suited to the delivery of processes and/or services. The main requirement of a Quality Plan, however, is to ~~give~~ provide the customer (and the workforce) with clear, concise instructions. These instructions must be clearly and adequately recorded and be made available for examination by the customer. They must leave no room for error but equally they should be flexible and written in such a way that it is possible to modify its/their content to reflect changing circumstances.

Document Ref: **N-53–048RLR13**
Version: 03.01
Date: 1 October 2013
Quality Management System
Part Three – Quality Procedures
QP/2 Control of Records– Version 01.00

QP/2 – Control of Records

Author's Hint

Even if you are an extremely small business (and even if you are not intending to go for formal ISO 9001:2008 Certification) the necessity for looking after your current user documentation and records cannot be over-emphasised.

CONTENTS

2.1	Scope	2
2.2	Responsibilities	2
	2.2.1 Quality Manager	2
	2.2.2 Company Secretary	3
	2.2.3 NAFAAD Staff	3
2.3	Definitions	3
2.4	Purpose	4
2.5	Filing and records management	4
2.6	What records are required?	4
	2.6.1 Approved documents	4
	2.6.2 New Records	5
	2.6.3 Master List of Quality Records	5
	2.6.4 Third-Party documentation	6
2.7	Collection, Indexing and Access of Quality records	6
2.8	Storage of Records	7
2.9	Maintenance of Records	7
2.10	Maintenance of Quality Records	7
2.11	Backup copies of Records	8
2.12	Backup copies of Quality Records	8
2.13	Retention of Records	9
2.14	Archiving Quality Records	9
2.15	Disposal of Records	10
2.16	Disposal of Quality Records	10
2.17	Disposal of Health Records	11

Document Ref: **N-53–048RLR13**
Version: 03.01
Date: 1 October 2013
Quality Management System
Part Three – Quality Procedures
QP/2 Control of Records– Version 01.00

2.1 SCOPE

Under Section 4.2.4 of ISO 9001:2008, there is a mandatory requirement for NAFAAD to produce a formal procedure to control the identification, storage, protection, retrieval, retention and disposal of records. QP/2 satisfies this requirement.

QP/2 also covers the need to make backup copies of records, how to correct records and other associated topics concerning the requirement to ensure that all quality records are maintained, referenced and that associated responsibilities are defined. This procedure applies to all quality-relayed records held by NAFAAD.

Quality records are generated internally within NAFAAD and externally from customers, suppliers and subcontractors.

2.2 RESPONSIBILITIES

2.2.1 Quality Manager

It is the responsibility of the Quality Assurance Manager to ensure that all aspects of this procedure are adhered to.

The Quality Manager (in consultation with the Company Secretary) is responsible for the overall planning of document control procedures throughout NAFAAD. He shall:

- ensure that NAFAAD's quality records are maintained in a systematic and presentable form;
- have the authority to inspect the status of quality records kept by departments and – as the MD's nominated representative – take suitable action against any department that does not maintain its quality records as described in this Procedure and other sections of the NAFAAD QMS;
- be responsible for maintaining an index of all quality records, which shall provide information regarding each type of record, as follows:
  o a unique reference number to facilitate identification;
  o the record title (or suitable description);
  o the location of the record;
  o the retention period for that particular record;
  o the person responsible for retaining the quality record.

Document Ref: **N-53–048RLR13**
Version: 03.01
Date: 1 October 2013
Quality Management System
Part Three – Quality Procedures
QP/2 Control of Records– Version 01.00

2.2.2 Company Secretary

The Company Secretary is responsible for:

* making and maintaining a master list of all quality records;
* ensuring that adequate facilities exist for the safe keeping of quality records; and
* ensuring that a centralised filing system shall be retained in the main office.

2.2.3 NAFAAD Staff

All staff are responsible for ensuring that they provide the necessary records (on an as required basis) from their involvement in implementing NAFAAD's quality systems:

Author's Hint

If you are a manufacturer then you should also include a statement to the effect that:

'The Quality Manager (in consultation with the Technical Manager, Production Manager and Company Secretary) shall ensure that the company is capable of continuing to supply logistic support for the lifetime of the product. This logistic support may include the provision of spares, updating of documentation, details of product improvement etc., depending upon the Purchaser's requirements.'

2.3 DEFINITIONS

Quality records: applies to all quality management system documentation (as described in NAFAAD's QMS), all data produced on any of the company databases and associated software that is quality related and any document that describes the results of an activity such as audits, inspections, meeting minutes, reviews, tests, measurements and training records etc.

Document Ref: **N-53–048RLR13**
Version: 03.01
Date: 1 October 2013
Quality Management System
Part Three – Quality Procedures
QP/2 Control of Records– Version 01.00

2.4 PURPOSE

The purpose of this procedure is to ensure that comprehensive records relating to all projects undertaken and all services supplied are collated and systematically maintained so that both the achievement of quality in the results of work undertaken, conformity to requirements and the effective operation of the NAFAAD QMS, as a whole, can be demonstrated.

2.5 FILING AND RECORDS MANAGEMENT

Filing and records management is a vital – although at times very uninspiring! – part of any business. Information is, however, a major element in many companies' competitive advantage, but it can only be utilised if it is available when needed.

At the same time, every business can benefit from cutting out the wasted effort associated with looking for misfiled information and misplaced files. The same principles apply to both computer and paper records.

2.6 WHAT RECORDS ARE REQUIRED?

Various records are needed to provide evidence of conformity to regulatory and customer requirements (and of the effective operation of the QMS) and it is essential that these records remain legible, readily identifiable and retrievable.

 This particularly applies to Approved Documents.

2.6.1 Approved documents

NAFAAD's Document Control procedure (QP/1) includes the requirement to maintain a list of approved documents and describes the arrangements for approval, issues and changes/modifications to documents.

QP/1 also requires that:

- all approved documents are uniquely numbered;
- a register of all issued documents is maintained;
- when a new version of an approved document is issued, copies of all previous versions are destroyed. (This shall be covered by a statement in the covering letter to the effect that, *'On receipt of a new issue number all previous versions are to be destroyed'.*)

	Document Ref: **N-53–048RLR13** Version: 03.01 Date: 1 October 2013 Quality Management System Part Three – Quality Procedures QP/2 Control of Records– Version 01.00

 Note: Approved Documents become quality records following completion of the quality related information for which each document has been designed. These records are then maintained for reference purposes to demonstrate achievement of the required quality and also the effective operation of the quality system.

2.6.2 New Records

The requirement for a new type of record could arise from a day-to-day operational need or even a customer demand.

Note: The head of department of the concerned functional area representing a specific business task generally carries out this identification.

Once a particular functional area identifies the requirement for a new type of record or the disposal of an existing record, it shall be elevated to Top Management using the procedures described in QP/14 'Change Control'.

2.6.3 Master List of Quality Records

A Master List of all quality records shall be maintained by the Company Secretary and this list shall be updated from time to time to add newly identified quality records and to remove obsolete quality records as they occur.

This Master List will contain details of:

*   the standard and contract requirements that have to be adhered to;
*   the records that need to be documented for each standard;
*   the filing location of the records;
*   the staff members who are responsible for each record;
*   the retention date for the records; and
*   the method of deletion for each record.

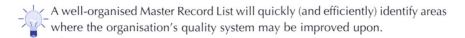 A well-organised Master Record List will quickly (and efficiently) identify areas where the organisation's quality system may be improved upon.

Document Ref: **N-53–048RLR13**
Version: 03.01
Date: 1 October 2013
Quality Management System
Part Three – Quality Procedures
QP/2 Control of Records– Version 01.00

The Document Master List will identify – and list – for each quality record:

- the document code and title;
- the current revision and issue date;
- a description of revision changes;
- the index for sorting or filing the records;
- the location of active records and the person (or position) responsible for maintaining them;
- the active retention time for the records as well as the total retention time for archived records;
- the means for retrieving records;
- the methods for disposing of the records, when their total retention time is up and they are no longer useful.

2.6.4 Third-Party documentation

The system shall include the need to safely retain any relevant information not included in the quality system. For example, pertinent subcontractor quality records, hazard warnings, statutory or national directives, manufacturers' handbooks and records of management review meetings etc.

2.7 COLLECTION, INDEXING AND ACCESS OF QUALITY RECORDS

Records shall be generated in the formats specified and approved in various Quality System procedures. The indexing method and authority for access shall be as specified in the Master List of Quality Records.

All personnel involved with filling out forms and storing company related records are to ensure that these records are:

- filled out properly, accurately and completely;
- documented either on the computer (or other electronic media) or on paper, with a note made of the proper retention period;
- (when appropriate) signed and dated;
- stored so that they are available to the customer or regulatory authority upon request or when required by contract.

Document Ref: **N-53–048RLR13**
Version: 03.01
Date: 1 October 2013
Quality Management System
Part Three – Quality Procedures
QP/2 Control of Records– Version 01.00

In certain circumstances (e.g. when completing field work) the records may be stored on paper (hard copy), in which case they shall be:

- legible and identifiable when hand written;
- printed through all copies of multiple carbons;
- stored in a clean, dry area in such a manner as to prevent damage or deterioration to prevent loss.

2.8 STORAGE OF RECORDS

All records shall be centrally stored at NAFAAD's main office and it is the Company Secretary's responsibility to ensure that:

- a centralised filing system shall be retained in the main office;
- all records are easily retrievable; and
- adequate facilities exist for the safe keeping and retention of **all** quality records.

2.9 MAINTENANCE OF RECORDS

Hard copy records shall be maintained in a suitable form – such as in registers and document files – and these files shall be neatly stored in safe locations.

When using electronic media for the storage of files, it is the originator's responsibility to ensure their adequacy and continued availability.

When a customer or third party (such as an ISO Auditor) demands a record, care shall be taken to only provide them with a copy of the relevant file as a hard copy or on a separate CD or flash drive if the record has to be taken out of the premises.

2.10 MAINTENANCE OF QUALITY RECORDS

The table below identifies the type of quality records that shall be originated by the Quality Manager and how each shall be maintained.

	Document Ref: **N-53–048RLR13**
	Version: 03.01
	Date: 1 October 2013
	Quality Management System
	Part Three – Quality Procedures
	QP/2 Control of Records– Version 01.00

QP2.1 Quality Records and their maintenance

Type of quality record	How it is maintained
Paper	• Protect the record from becoming dirty or soiled. • Keep records away from sources of contamination. • Use a plastic sleeve if appropriate.
Electronic Media (Computers, flash drives, separate hard drives and/or CDs etc.)	• Use virus protection practices. • Backup data on a regular basis. • Maintain backups off site if appropriate.

2.11 BACKUP COPIES OF RECORDS

Generally speaking, records in the form of electronic media shall be kept on the hard disk of their respective computers. A monthly backup of these records shall be taken on another hard disk (or flash drive, hard drive or CD) in order to minimise the risk of data loss due to computer failures.

Similarly, all administrative and non-quality related data shall be backed up by the Company Secretary at least monthly.

 Individuals keeping online data would be well advised to also use an additional form of backup system in case you lose access to your server!

2.12 BACKUP COPIES OF QUALITY RECORDS

To ensure that all quality records are securely maintained and finally discarded, all staff are responsible for ensuring that records that are held on individual computers are backed up **daily** to the company's server.

In addition to user backup copies, the Company Secretary shall make a **weekly** backup copy of **all** these individual backup files and make arrangements for them to be retained off-site so as to ensure that in the event of theft/fire, the worst case scenario would be less than five working days of lost data.

	Document Ref: **N-53–048RLR13**
	Version: 03.01
	Date: 1 October 2013
	Quality Management System
	Part Three – Quality Procedures
	QP/2 Control of Records– Version 01.00

2.13 RETENTION OF RECORDS

All records associated with the administration of the company shall be maintained for a minimum period of five years.

This period may be altered for specified retention requirements established in accordance with the:

- duration of the contract;
- life of the product;
- requirements of applicable standards;
- government, customer, legislative, statutory, regulatory and/or contract requirements.

subject to agreement with the Managing Director.

 Customers with special requirements for record retention shall be noted in the Customer Master List.

2.14 ARCHIVING QUALITY RECORDS

The Company Secretary shall ensure that all quality records are properly archived, as shown below.

TABLE QP2.2 Archiving Quality Records

Step	Task	Action
1	Labelling the box	Indicate the names of the records being archived.
2		Indicate the period covered by the records being archived as follows: • From (the date of the first record). • To (date of the last record). • Disposal (the date that the whole box may be destroyed in accordance with current rules).
3	Storing the box	Place the records in a designated archive storage area that will: • protect the record from becoming dirty or soiled; • keep records away from sources of contamination.

	Document Ref: **N-53–048RLR13** Version: 03.01 Date: 1 October 2013 Quality Management System Part Three – Quality Procedures QP/2 Control of Records– Version 01.00

External storage services shall **not** be used to archive quality records.

2.15 DISPOSAL OF RECORDS

Records may **only** be disposed of after the expiry of a stipulated retention period.

If required, old records may be retained for the purpose of future reference and/or for legal purposes.

2.16 DISPOSAL OF QUALITY RECORDS

The Quality Manager shall ensure that all quality documents are regularly reviewed for their continued retention and use within the organisation as follows:

TABLE QP2.3 Disposal of Quality Records

Step	Action
1	*Ask:* 'Has the useful life of the records ended?' 'Have all the relevant government, customer, legislative, statutory, regulatory requirements been met?' If 'No', do not dispose of the records. If 'Yes', go to Step 2.
2	*Ask:* 'Have the contractual requirements of the records been satisfied?' If 'No', do not dispose of the records. If 'Yes', go to Step 3.
3	Dispose of quality records.

The Quality Manager shall determine the most suitable disposal method for disposal for quality records based on the type of quality record, data contained in the record and/or security requirements.

Document Ref: **N-53–048RLR13**
Version: 03.01
Date: 1 October 2013
Quality Management System
Part Three – Quality Procedures
QP/2 Control of Records– Version 01.00

Records shall be shredded when appropriate and unwanted quality records contained on electronic media shall be all cleared and the media reformatted for future use. All CDs shall either be shredded (where possible) or cut into bits.

2.17 DISPOSAL OF HEALTH RECORDS

Personal health records shall **only** be destroyed in a secure and confidential manner.

	Document Ref: **N-53–0449LR13**
	Version: 03.01
	Date: 1 October 2013
	Quality Management System
	Part Three – Quality Procedures
	QP/3 Internal Audits – Version 01.00

QP/3 – Internal Audits

Author's Hint

If you are a Micro Business (i.e. less than 10 employees) then you probably will not have a full-time Quality Manager and so it would normally be the Owner or Managing Director who performs the audits and checks. If this is the case then the following example needs to be carefully reworded

CONTENTS

3.1   Scope 2
3.2   Responsibilities 2
      3.2.1   Quality Manager 2
      3.2.2   Section Managers 3
      3.2.3   Internal Auditors 3
3.3   Definitions 4
3.4   Purpose 4
3.5   Sectional quality audits 4
      3.5.1   Frequency of audits 4
      3.5.2   Audit preparation and organisation 5
3.6   Internal quality audits 5
      3.6.1   Frequency of audit and audit schedule 5
      3.6.2   Internal Quality Audit Team 5
      3.6.3   Agenda 6
      3.6.4   Audit preparation and organisation 6
      3.6.5   Audit execution 7
      3.6.6   Audit report 8
      3.6.7   Meeting records 8
      3.6.8   Corrective action 8
      3.6.9   Corrective actions 8
      3.6.10 Follow-up 9

Document Ref: **N-53–0449LR13**
Version: 03.01
Date: 1 October 2013
Quality Management System
Part Three – Quality Procedures
QP/3 Internal Audits – Version 01.00

3.1 SCOPE

One of the mandatory requirements of ISO 9001:2008 (i.e. Section 8.2.2) is that:

'The organisation shall conduct internal audits at planned intervals to determine whether the quality management system:

- **conforms to the requirements of the ISO 9001:2008 standard and to the quality management system requirements established by the organisation and,**
- **is effectively implemented and maintained.'**

QP/3 complies with the mandatory need for this quality procedure and details the requirements for internal quality audits within NAFAAD. This procedure also describes the differences between a sectional quality audit and other internal quality audits.

3.2 RESPONSIBILITIES

3.2.1 Quality Manager

The Quality Manager (as the MD's nominated representative) is responsible for implementing and maintaining NAFAAD's QMS. He has the responsibility and the authority to ensure that adequate processes, procedures, plans and instructions are drawn up so as to provide a common approach to quality assurance throughout NAFAAD and to ensure that the quality system is continuously monitored and improved by means of internal audits and management reviews.

The Quality Manager has the overall responsibility for ensuring that all NAFAAD Audits (i.e. quality, health and safety, environmental (i.e. personal), administrative, financial, risk, command control and signalling, power, infrastructure, operations and/or system specific) are conducted according to agreed schedules and to agreed plans.

He is responsible for:

- ensuring the continuing acceptability, validity and effectiveness of the NAFAAD Management System;
- ensuring that the NAFAAD Quality Manual, Quality Procedures, Work Instructions and system-specific Quality Plans are regularly audited, reviewed and remedial action taken whenever appropriate;

Document Ref: **N-53–0449LR13**
Version: 03.01
Date: 1 October 2013
Quality Management System
Part Three – Quality Procedures
QP/3 Internal Audits – Version 01.00

- confirming that all NAFAAD activities are defined and controlled by a Quality Process, Procedure and/or Work Instruction;
- completing regular reviews of the NAFAAD Quality Manual (and its supporting documentation) together with auditing its effective implementation to ensure that the most suitable methods and procedures are still prescribed and used;
- drawing up audit schedules, plans, checklists and programmes for auditing NAFAAD's quality audits;
- conducting planned and 'on the spot' internal audits to ensure that all aspects of this procedure are adhered to;
- identifying and training nominated NAFAAD resources as internal and external third-party (e.g. subcontractor) auditors;
- scheduling (in consultation with the Section Managers) and conducting the quality audits;
- reporting audit results to the Top Management;
- ensuring corrective and preventive actions are taken.

3.2.2 Section Managers

Section Managers are responsible for:

- providing adequate facilities to carry out scheduled quality audits within their areas of responsibility;
- assigning responsible persons within that department to represent the department during audits;
- ensuring that corrective and preventive actions agreed during audits are completed during the stipulated time.

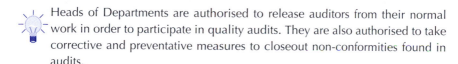

Heads of Departments are authorised to release auditors from their normal work in order to participate in quality audits. They are also authorised to take corrective and preventative measures to closeout non-conformities found in audits.

3.2.3 Internal Auditors

As a result of their broad scope of involvement, many internal auditors may have a variety of higher educational and professional backgrounds.

Document Ref: **N-53-0449LR13**
Version: 03.01
Date: 1 October 2013
Quality Management System
Part Three – Quality Procedures
QP/3 Internal Audits – Version 01.00

Internal auditors, however, are **not** responsible for the execution of company activities, but, drawing on their expertise, training and work experience, are expected to advise management regarding how to better execute their responsibilities.

3.3 DEFINITIONS

Nil.

3.4 PURPOSE

The primary purpose of an audit is to:

- enable an organisation to evaluate its process management systems;
- determine deficiencies, and generate cost effective and efficient solutions;
- check practice against procedure, and to thoroughly document any differences;
- measure an organisation's ability '*to do what it says it is going to do*';
- provide management with an independent, objective assurance that all of NAFAAD's quality activities meet the requirements of the organisation's management system; and
- make recommendations for improvement in key management processes.

This assurance and consulting activity is designed to add value and improve the organisation's operations. It helps NAFAAD accomplish its objectives by bringing a systematic, disciplined approach to evaluate and improve the effectiveness of risk management, quality control and management processes.

3.5 SECTIONAL QUALITY AUDITS

3.5.1 Frequency of audits

During each financial year, **all** sections shall be subject to at least three **complete** quality audits covering all of NAFAAD's relevant procedures. These audits shall be initiated by the Quality Manager and shall be scheduled at key points in relation to the status and importance of the various activities of a section.

It is the Quality Manager's responsibility to prepare (in consultation with the Section Managers) an audit schedule for the Managing Director's approval to cover the next 12 months.

Document Ref: **N-53–0449LR13**
Version: 03.01
Date: 1 October 2013
Quality Management System
Part Three – Quality Procedures
QP/3 Internal Audits – Version 01.00

3.5.2 Audit preparation and organisation

All Sectional Quality audits shall be carried out by an audit team consisting of the Managing Director, Company Secretary and Quality Manager (who will normally perform the function of lead auditor – but this need not always be the case).

The Quality Manager shall decide on the minimum number of attendees for convening that meeting and whether it is necessary to invite additional members and if so, who shall be involved. The exact number of attendees may vary according to circumstances applicable at that time.

In addition to agenda items, the audit team shall review, for adequacy, the Section's Quality Plan together with its associated procedures. They shall resolve all concerns where the Section Quality Plan or the section's organisation is inadequate or inappropriate to meet NAFAAD objectives as stated in the Quality Manual.

3.6 INTERNAL QUALITY AUDITS

Internal quality audits are initiated by the Quality Manager and shall be scheduled in relation to the status and importance of the various activities and contract deliverables.

When deemed necessary, an internal quality audit may be completed by invited personnel (independent of the activity being audited), such as invited specialists from other ISO 9001:2008 certified companies.

The audits and all agreed corrective actions shall be recorded and these records shall be maintained in the company quality file by the Quality Manager.

3.6.1 Frequency of audit and audit schedule

Internal quality audits are either scheduled by the Quality Manager or completed at the request of a company officer (e.g. Managing Director, Company Secretary, Section Manager etc.).

3.6.2 Internal Quality Audit Team

Quality audits shall be carried out by personnel **independent** of the activity being audited. For example, the Marketing Department **shall not** be audited by an auditor belonging to the Marketing Department. Instead it can be audited by an auditor belonging to, say, the Accounts Department.

Document Ref: **N-53–0449LR13**
Version: 03.01
Date: 1 October 2013
Quality Management System
Part Three – Quality Procedures
QP/3 Internal Audits – Version 01.00

As well as being independent in terms of organisational status and personal objectivity of the section being audited, auditors should:

- seek to foster constructive working relationship and mutual understanding with the section concerned;
- exercise due care in fulfilling his responsibilities;
- adequately plan, control and record his work.

 Note: A master list of qualified (as well as potential) internal quality auditors shall be maintained by the Quality Manager.

3.6.3 Agenda

The Quality Manager shall organise an agenda for each audit which shall include:

- scope and objectives of the audit;
- review of all actions raised at previous meetings and progress at subsequent meetings;
- details of the persons having direct responsibilities for the procedure(s) that is to be audited;
- reference documents;
- name of lead auditor and name(s) of assigned auditor(s);
- date when audit is to be concluded;
- audit report distribution.

3.6.4 Audit preparation and organisation

Depending on the complexity and the size of the audit, the Quality Manager may perform the audit himself, or he can assign a lead auditor and a team of auditors.

 Note: This may be required when sections are too large, or when activities from other sections are integrated or are co-operating.

The lead auditor and the assigned auditor(s):

- shall examine all earlier audit reports on the same subject;
- shall prepare an audit check list (containing all of the topics/items to be covered and an audit programme).

The lead auditor shall report directly to the Quality Manager.

Document Ref: **N-53–0449LR13**
Version: 03.01
Date: 1 October 2013
Quality Management System
Part Three – Quality Procedures
QP/3 Internal Audits – Version 01.00

3.6.5 Audit execution

All audits shall be completed in accordance with the recommendations of ISO 10011.

An initial meeting between the auditor(s), the auditee(s) and the Quality Manager shall be held. During this meeting:

- a brief summary of the methods and procedures being used to conduct the audit shall be provided;
- the method of communication between auditor(s) and auditee(s) shall be agreed;
- the audit programme shall be confirmed.

The auditor(s) shall collect evidence via interviews, examination of documents and observation of activities. If possible information provided at interviews shall be checked for accuracy by acquiring the same information through independent sources.

If necessary (and required) changes to the audit programme may be made in order to achieve optimum audit objectives.

Auditors shall record all observations on the Audit Observation Sheet (available as a template on the server).

Auditors shall review the observations and determine which (if any) are to be reported as non-conformities.

Auditors shall discuss all observations with the Quality Manager and all observations of non-conformity shall be acknowledged by the manager (e.g. Section Manager) responsible for the activity being audited.

A closing meeting of auditor(s), auditee(s) and the Quality Manager shall be held during which:

- audit observations are clarified;
- the critical significance of observations are presented;
- conclusions drawn about compliance are presented;
- system effectiveness in achieving the quality objectives are presented;
- corrective actions are agreed;
- the date for completion of the audit report is agreed.

Minutes of **all** relevant meetings, decisions and agreements shall be attached to the audit report.

	Document Ref: **N-53–0449LR13** Version: 03.01 Date: 1 October 2013 Quality Management System Part Three – Quality Procedures QP/3 Internal Audits – Version 01.00

3.6.6 Audit report

The lead auditor shall prepare an audit report using the Audit Report Form (available as a template on the server). The report must be signed by all members of the audit team, plus the Quality Manager, and copies sent to auditee(s) and company management as required.

Audit reports shall be retained in NAFAAD quality files.

3.6.7 Meeting records

The Quality Manager is responsible for ensuring that minutes of the meeting are prepared and distributed promptly.

The minutes shall clearly state the:

- actions agreed on;
- person responsible for implementing these actions (i.e. the Action List);
- agreed completion date (i.e. the Time Plan).

The minutes of the meeting shall be kept in the NAFAAD quality file, by the Quality Manager, with a copy being circulated to all members of the audit team and (in particular!) to the section concerned.

3.6.8 Corrective action

After the closing meeting the lead auditor shall prepare a Corrective Action Request for each **agreed** corrective action. Corrective Action Requests (available as a template on the server) shall state who is responsible for carrying out the corrective action and the timescale for its completion.

3.6.9 Corrective actions

If the results of the audit are such that corrective action or actions are necessary, the audit team shall:

- consider solutions and agree on the corrective action(s);
- agree on responsibility for the implementation;
- agree on a timescale for the implementation and review of corrective action(s) to be taken.

Document Ref: **N-53–0449LR13**
Version: 03.01
Date: 1 October 2013
Quality Management System
Part Three – Quality Procedures
QP/3 Internal Audits – Version 01.00

The review and the agreed corrective actions shall be recorded in the company quality file and a copy shall be retained by the section concerned.

3.6.10 Follow-up

The lead auditor is responsible for ensuring that corrective action has been carried out and for notifying the Quality Manager of the status and/or completion of the corrective actions.

When a non-conformance detected during audits is not removed within the audit period, follow-up audits shall be conducted.

Document Ref: **N-53–050RLR13**
Version: 03.01
Date: 1 October 2013
Quality Management System
Part Three – Quality Procedures
QP/4 Non-conforming Product – Version 01.00

QP/4 – Non-conforming Product

Author's Note regarding manufacturers

If you are a manufacturer then you will probably have to lay more emphasis on the 'deliverable' being a manufactured item and your particular organisation will have to establish processes that provide for a review of the non-conformity by the appropriate individuals. Such processes may have different levels of approval depending on the nature of the action to be taken for the non-conformity. A decision to 'use as is', for example, may require engineering approval because such a decision is effectively a change in design with liability implications. On the other hand, manufacturing management may be permitted to approve a rework or scrap disposition.

CONTENTS

4.1   Scope 2
4.2   Responsibilities 2
    4.2.1   Quality Manager. 2
    4.2.2   Stores Section Chief 2
4.3   Definitions 3
4.4   Purpose 3
4.5   Process. 4
    4.5.1   What is the basic process?. 4
    4.5.2   How to identify a non-conforming product 4
    4.5.3   How are non-conforming products dealt with? 5
    4.5.4   Taking action to eliminate the detected non-conformity 5
    4.5.5   What happens if a non-conformity is detected after
            delivery or use. 7
    4.5.6   Having corrected the non-conformity what then? 7
4.6   Records 8
    4.6.1   The need for initial documentation to be recorded 8
    4.6.2   Documentation regarding status of the product. 9
Annex A – Guidance on non-conforming products 10

Document Ref: **N-53–050RLR13**
Version: 03.01
Date: 1 October 2013
Quality Management System
Part Three – Quality Procedures
QP/4 Non-conforming Product – Version 01.00

4.1 SCOPE

One of the **mandatory requirements** of ISO 9001:2008 (i.e. Section 8.3) is that:

> **'The organization shall ensure that product which does not conform to product requirements is identified and controlled to prevent its unintended use or delivery. A documented procedure shall be established to define the controls and related responsibilities for dealing with a non-conforming producer.'**

To meet this mandatory requirement NAFAAD shall produce a formal, documented procedure to cover the eventuality of a non-conforming product and shall ensure that products that do not conform to specified, regulatory or contractual requirements are identified and controlled to prevent unintended use or delivery. These non-conformities shall be:

- corrected or adjusted to conform to requirements and re-validated; or
- accepted under concession, with or without correction or adjustment; or
- re-assigned for alternative valid application; or
- rejected as unsuitable.

4.2 RESPONSIBILITIES

4.2.1 Quality Manager

The Quality Manager (assisted by the Section Managers) has overall responsibility for establishing, implementing and maintaining this activity.

4.2.2 Stores Section Chief

The Stores Section Chief shall:

- be responsible for ensuring that this procedure is implemented effectively if materials have been purchased from a third party;
- be authorised to take decision on acceptance (after concession) of any non-conforming items arising out of purchased products.

	Document Ref: **N-53–050RLR13**
	Version: 03.01
	Date: 1 October 2013
	Quality Management System
	Part Three – Quality Procedures
	QP/4 Non-conforming Product – Version 01.00

4.3 DEFINITIONS

Non-conforming product – is a deliverable (i.e. product or service) that does not conform to its specified, regulatory or customer requirements and its intended use.

Quarantine – a special area (or just special shelves for non-conforming products) that is set apart from conforming products. This segregation shall be physical as well as logical (e.g. if the non-conforming part is a software element, then it should be separated from the development area and/or test area).

4.4 PURPOSE

The primary purpose of QP/4 is to prevent unintended use or delivery of a product that does not conform to specified requirements and thereby for the organisation to unwittingly provide customers with a product that doesn't come up to expectation. The primary intention of this procedure, therefore, is to **control** non-conforming products by ensuring that:

- deliverables which do not conform to requirements are prevented from unintended use or delivery;
- non-conforming deliverables that have been corrected are re-verified to demonstrate conformity;
- non-conforming deliverables found after delivery or use are either corrected or removed from service;
- all non-conforming deliverables are only accepted by concession **if** all regulatory requirements are met and the identity of the person(s) authorising the concession has been recorded;
- if a deliverable needs to be reworked (one or more times), the rework shall be subject to the same authorisation and approval procedure as the original work was subject to;
- prior to authorisation and approval, a determination of any adverse effect of the rework upon a deliverable shall be made and documented.

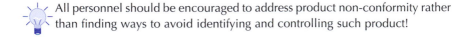 All personnel should be encouraged to address product non-conformity rather than finding ways to avoid identifying and controlling such product!

Document Ref: **N-53–050RLR13**
Version: 03.01
Date: 1 October 2013
Quality Management System
Part Three – Quality Procedures
QP/4 Non-conforming Product – Version 01.00

4.5 PROCESS

4.5.1 What is the basic process?

- As soon as a non-conformity is detected, it must be recorded in order to prevent further use of this product or delivery to the customer before the non-conformity has been evaluated.
- The non-conforming product must be separated physically as well as logically from the other products.
- The procedure shall determine the authorities and responsible parties to handle non-conforming products.
- The procedure will describe a method for eliminating non-conformities that were detected.
- Evaluate the non-conformance in order to determine its type and its severity.
- Releasing a non-conforming product must be approved by a prior authorised function. The release would be under concession with the concession being made by an authorised person or by the customer. The concession shall be recorded.
- When a non-conforming product has been re-processed, it must be revalidated to ensure that it meets the requirements (customer's or regulatory) after rework.
- When a non-conformity is detected after delivering the product, actions must be taken relevant to the nature of the non-conformities.

 All actions and results **must** be recorded.

4.5.2 How to identify a non-conforming product

Non-conforming (defective) items found during quality inspections shall be segregated and stored in designated locations with suitable inspection marks applied according to the relevant Quality System Procedure.

Products may be identified by anyone in NAFAAD during any stage in the process, including:

- receiving inspection and testing (if the deliverable is from a third party);
- in-process inspection and testing;
- final inspection and testing;
- customer returns.

	Document Ref: **N-53–050RLR13**
	Version: 03.01
	Date: 1 October 2013
	Quality Management System
	Part Three – Quality Procedures
	QP/4 Non-conforming Product – Version 01.00

Having identified a non-conforming product, the Quality Manager and the Section Manager concerned shall conduct an initial review of the suspect product to determine if the product definitely **is** non-conforming.

If the answer is:

- '**Yes**' – then the non-conforming product shall be segregated from other products and given either a:
  - **Hold tag** – for a suspect, damaged and non-conforming product and for products returned from customers and awaiting NAFAAD's investigation; or a
  - **Rejected tag** – for a damaged or a non-conforming product.

 When non-conformity is detected **after** delivering the product, actions must be taken relevant to the nature of the non-conformities and the product concerned.

If the answer is:

- '**No**' – then the product is established as being acceptable, all tags shall be removed and the product released for use.

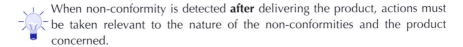 **Note:** Customer supplied products (if any) that are found to be defective during incoming inspection/storage/usage shall be disposed of as per prior agreement between the company and the customers.

4.5.3 How are non-conforming products dealt with?

The organisation shall deal with non-conforming product by either:

- taking action to eliminate the detected non-conformity;
- authorising its use, release or acceptance under concession (either by the customer or appropriate authority); or
- by taking action to prevent its original intended use or application.

4.5.4 Taking action to eliminate the detected non-conformity

As soon as a non-conforming product has been detected, it must be segregated from all other products in a quarantine area and the customer (and where necessary

Document Ref: **N-53–050RLR13**
Version: 03.01
Date: 1 October 2013
Quality Management System
Part Three – Quality Procedures
QP/4 Non-conforming Product – Version 01.00

other relevant parties – organisational, internal, external, or governmental) duly notified.

4.5.4.1 Quarantine area

If a product has been rejected, it shall be quarantined with the reject notice being retained by the Quality Manager (as a quality record), which will become one of the inputs for a future management review and (if applicable) supplier performance information. The non-conforming product shall be suitably marked in accordance with respective Quality System Procedures.

 If the non-conformance has been caused by, or is due from a supplier's non-conformance, a copy of the material reject notice will also be sent to the Purchasing Section to be used for supplier performance information.

 Releasing a non-conforming product **must** be approved by a prior authorised function and this release can only be made on receipt of either a waiver or a concession which can be made either by an authorised person or by the customer. Everything, however, concerning the concession must be thoroughly documented.

4.5.4.2 Evaluation of the non-conformance

Not just for quality control and but also from a business perspective, **all** non-conformities must be evaluated to determine the type of the non-conformance, level of severity and its extent. For example:

- is it a non-conforming product? (i.e. a tangible product that NAFAAD provides to its customers and which does not meet the prior planned requirements); or
- is it a non-conforming process? (e.g. a service that was not executed or performed according to specific instructions, documented or not).

The type of evaluation performed must include a reference to whether the non-conformance requires further investigation of the root cause (and notification to the responsible parties) and whether any other component part of the product or service could be affected from the occurred non-conformance.

	Document Ref: **N-53–050RLR13** Version: 03.01 Date: 1 October 2013 Quality Management System Part Three – Quality Procedures QP/4 Non-conforming Product – Version 01.00

4.5.4.3 Products requiring rework

Products requiring rework shall be reworked and re-inspected in accordance with current NAFAAD procedures.

All reworked products shall be inspected by the Quality Manager, assisted by the Section Manager concerned, prior to releasing the product back to the customer.

4.5.4.4 Products accepted on waiver

Products accepted on waiver must be identified and accepted in writing by the customer and records of this acceptance on waiver will be maintained by the Quality Manager.

4.5.5 What happens if a non-conformity is detected after delivery or use?

 If a non-conforming product is detected after delivery or if use of that product has already commenced, NAFAAD shall:

- quarantine the remainder of the product;
- notify its customers of the non-conformance;
- investigate the causes of the non-conformance;
- take action to eliminate the non-conformity;
- re-inspect the product to demonstrate conformity to its original and agreed requirements;
- authorise its use, release or acceptance (either by the customer or appropriate authority); or
- take action to prevent its original intended use or application.

4.5.6 Having corrected the non-conformity what then?

When a non-conforming product has been corrected it must be re-inspected to demonstrate conformity to the requirements of that particular product.

You may determine the method according to the nature of your product or processes but you **must** thoroughly document it so that everybody who is related to or has a part in the realisation of the product knows exactly what they are required to do if a further non-conformity is detected.

Document Ref: **N-53–050RLR13**
Version: 03.01
Date: 1 October 2013
Quality Management System
Part Three – Quality Procedures
QP/4 Non-conforming Product – Version 01.00

4.6 RECORDS

Records of all non-conformities shall be maintained in accordance with NAFAAD's records control procedure (see QP/2).

These records shall include details of:

- the type (or nature) of the non-conformity;
- any subsequent action(s) that have been taken (including concessions gained or given).

4.6.1 The need for initial documentation to be recorded

The first time a non-conformity occurs it can be reported on any media, be it a form, software, e-mail or just word of mouth (don't forget that customer complaints are also considered as non-conformities!) but whatever happens it is essential that it is thoroughly documented as this is the first step for a later corrective action process.

This record needs to include evidence of the results caused by the non-conforming product (why and how it fails to meet the requirements) as well as identifying whether the non-conforming product has affected other component parts.

It also needs to be as thorough as possible so as to enable the investigator to be able to better understand the non-conformity, its cause and, far more important, be able to come up with an effective corrective action. To enable this to happen, the following details need to be recorded:

- **The non-conformity details** – document any identifying details regarding the non-conformity: customer's name, product's name (and if applicable), the catalogue number, the name of the employee who first detected the non-conformity – indeed, any information that would help the investigation later on.
- **Description of the non-conformity** – include a literal description and attach any other document(s) that might assist in the evaluation of the non-conformity.
- **Categorisation of the non-conformity** – include any initial thoughts as to the cause of the non-conformity and how important it is to the end product or service, as this will assist later with a statistical analysis.

	Document Ref: **N-53–050RLR13** Version: 03.01 Date: 1 October 2013 Quality Management System Part Three – Quality Procedures QP/4 Non-conforming Product – Version 01.00

- **Investigation details** – all reported non-conformities must be thoroughly investigated so as to identify the root cause for the non-conformity as this will assist in determining what type of corrective action should be taken.

4.6.2 Documentation regarding status of the product

Documentation regarding status of the product is also required and shall include details of:

- any repair or rework;
- acceptance or rejection notices;
- any corrective action that is/was required.

Document Ref: **N-53–050RLR13**
Version: 03.01
Date: 1 October 2013
Quality Management System
Part Three - Quality Procedures
QP/4 Non-conforming Product – Version 01.00

Annex A –
Guidance on non-conforming products

By definition, a non-conforming product is a product that does not conform to the agreed product requirements when subjected to a planned (or unplanned) verification and which fails to meet:

- specified customer's requirements;
- intended usage requirements;
- stated or implied needs;
- customer expectations;
- the organisation's own requirements.

 Note: A product that becomes damaged or fails at any other stage is normally considered unserviceable.

A.1 IDENTIFYING NON-CONFORMITIES

Identifying and controlling non-conforming products is a fundamental quality control discipline whose purpose is to prevent unacceptable items or services from reaching customers in the first place.

This discipline is covered by ISO 9001:2008 clause 8.3 which states that '*The organisation shall ensure that a product which does not conform to product requirements is identified and controlled to prevent its unintended use or delivery*'. In simple terms this means that an organisation must identify products that don't conform to requirements. Probably the most common method of carrying this out is just to stick a label to the product warning people of this fact, but there are other ways such as placement in specially marked areas (e.g. quarantine areas).

 Note: Whilst products are often capable of operating even though they do contain certain non-conformities, a service is usually withdrawn once the non-conformity has been detected (no matter how trivial the fault) and this is usually achieved by using notices such as '*Out of Order*' or by announcements such as '*Normal service will be resumed as soon as possible*'.

	Document Ref: **N-53–050RLR13** Version: 03.01 Date: 1 October 2013 Quality Management System Part Three – Quality Procedures QP/4 Non-conforming Product – Version 01.00

A.2 CONTROLLING NON-CONFORMING PRODUCTS

The prime aim for any organisation, of course, is that it should prevent any non-conforming products from reaching the customer in the first place and should remove the root cause of non-conformance. Whilst the most obvious way of achieving this aim is to actually scrap or destroy the product, it might also be possible to eliminate the non-conformity by amending an existing procedure or to repair (or rework) the offending item. This process would, of course, have to be covered by a specific documented procedure which would include requirements for:

- defining responsibilities for the control and maintenance of these documented procedures;
- training employees on the use of these procedures;
- segregating non-conforming products from conforming products;
- securing non-conforming products in locked or protected areas.

A.3 DOCUMENTED PROCEDURES

In addition to section A.2 above, a documented procedure written for the control of a non-conforming product should specify:

- the responsibilities for authorising a product (or service) as a non-conformity, where this is to be recorded and what information should be provided;

 Note: This should also include:

- who can identify non-conforming products?
- who can authorise remedial action to deal with non-conforming products?
- who is responsible for completing this action?
- who can move or handle non-conforming products?
- how should the product be scrapped or recycled? (together with the forms to be used and the authorisations to be obtained);
- what repair procedures should be used (and how should they be produced, selected and implemented)?;
- how should modifications be defined, identified and implemented?;
- how should production permits (deviations) and concessions (waivers) be requested, evaluated, approved or rejected?;

Document Ref: **N-53–050RLR13**
Version: 03.01
Date: 1 October 2013
Quality Management System
Part Three – Quality Procedures
QP/4 Non-conforming Product – Version 01.00

- how should products be returned to their supplier? (the forms to be completed and any identification requirements etc.);
- how is regrading a product to be carried out? (product markings, prior authorisation and acceptance criteria etc.);
- what records must be maintained?

A.4 DEALING WITH NON-CONFORMING PRODUCTS

When a product is found to be non-conforming there are three decisions that should be made based on the following questions:

- can the product be made to conform?
- if the product cannot be made to conform, is it fit for use?
- if the product is not fit for use, can it be made fit for use?

In clause 8.3, ISO 9001:2008 suggests that one of the following methods should be used to control non-conforming products:

By taking action to eliminate the detected non-conformity.	Such as repairing, networking or reprocessing.
By authorising its use, release or acceptance under concession by a relevant authority and, where applicable, by the customer.	If a product non-conforms to the organisation's internal specifications but conforms to the customer's specifications, then a concession (i.e. an agreement to use, release or accept a product) can be issued by the organisation. If the product non-conforms to the customer's specifications then the concession must come from the customer.
By taking action to preclude its original intended use or application.	Such as scrapping, recycling, reprocessing or regrading.

If you need to recall a product that is suspected of being defective you will need to devise a Recall Plan, specify responsibilities and time-scales and put the plan into effect.

	Document Ref: **N-53–050RLR13** Version: 03.01 Date: 1 October 2013 Quality Management System Part Three – Quality Procedures QP/4 Non-conforming Product – Version 01.00

Note: Product recall is a remedial action not a corrective action because it does not prevent a recurrence of the initial problem.

A.5 RECORDS

ISO 9001:2008 requires '*that records of the nature of non-conformities and any subsequent action taken, including concessions obtained, shall be maintained*'.

These records should contain:

- a description of the non-conformity;
- action taken (usually referred to as 'disposition');
- action taken to re-verify the non-conforming product after it has been corrected;
- details of any concessions made or given.

A.6 RE-VERIFYING NON-CONFORMING PRODUCTS

When non-conforming products are corrected, they must be re-verified before being delivered to the customer. This re-verification should be completed using the original (or a modified version of the original) and the records must include:

- evidence of conformity (i.e. actual measurements or observations);
- identification of the person authorising the release (i.e. the person performing the verification or responsible for seeing that the task is carried out).

A.7 NON-CONFORMITIES DETECTED AT A LATER DATE

Occasionally non-conformities will be detected after delivery or after the customer has used the product and in these cases ISO 9001:2008 requires that the organisation '*shall take action appropriate to the effects or potential effects of the non-conformity*'.

Normally this is achieved by the organisation having a procedure to cover a returned goods process. This procedure will include:

- identifying the non-conforming product (see section 1.5.2 above);
- initiating corrective action to determine and eliminate the root cause of the non-conformity (see section 1.5.4 above).

Document Ref: **N-53–050RLR13**
Version: 03.01
Date: 1 October 2013
Quality Management System
Part Three – Quality Procedures
QP/4 Non-conforming Product – Version 01.00

A.8 CORRECTIVE ACTION

ISO 9001:2008 states that '*The organisation shall take action to eliminate the causes of non-conformities in order to prevent recurrence*', which basically means that all non-conformities will be submitted for corrective action and that this corrective action should be appropriate to the type of non-conformity found.

Action to remove the detected non-conformity is a remedial action and can include the completion of operations, rework, repair or modification.

Document Ref: **N-53–051RLR13**
Version: 03.01
Date: 1 October 2013
Quality Management System
Part Three – Quality Procedures
QP/5 Corrective Action – Version 01.00

QP/5 – Corrective Action

CONTENTS

5.1   Scope 1
5.2   Responsibilities 1
      5.2.1   The Quality Manager...................................... 1
5.3   Definitions 2
5.4   Purpose 2
5.5   Procedure 2
      5.5.1   Why are concessions to an approved NAFAAD
              product required?....................................... 3
      5.5.2   Concession scheme 3

5.1 SCOPE

Under Section 8.5.2 of ISO 9001:2008, there is a mandatory requirement for NAFAAD to produce a formal procedure to control requirements for:

- Reviewing non-conformities (including customer complaints);
- determining the causes of non-conformity;
- evaluating the need for actions to ensure that non-conformities do not recur;
- implementing corrective action;
- records of the results of actions taken;
- reviewing that corrective action taken is effective and recorded.

QP/5 satisfies this requirement.

5.2 RESPONSIBILITIES

5.2.1 The Quality Manager

The Quality Manager (assisted by Section Managers) has overall responsibility for:

- establishing, implementing and ensuring adherence to this procedure;
- maintaining a system for reporting and record keeping;
- determining the causes of non-conformances.

Document Ref: **N-53–051RLR13**
Version: 03.01
Date: 1 October 2013
Quality Management System
Part Three – Quality Procedures
QP/5 Corrective Action – Version 01.00

5.3 DEFINITIONS

Corrective action – Corrective actions are steps that are taken to eliminate the causes of existing non-conformities in order to prevent recurrence. The corrective action process tries to make sure that existing non-conformities and potentially undesirable situations do not happen again.

Note: *'Corrective actions'* are steps that are taken to remove the causes of existing non-conformities, while *'**Preventive actions'*** are steps that are taken to remove the causes of potential non-conformities. Corrective actions address actual problems, ones that have already occurred, while preventive actions address potential problems, ones that haven't yet occurred. In general, the corrective action process is a problem solving process, while the preventive action process is a risk analysis process.

5.4 PURPOSE

The purpose of this procedure is to establish and define the process for identifying, documenting, analysing and implementing corrective actions in order to eliminate further non-conformances occurring.

5.5 PROCEDURE

QP5 is a planned and established NAFAAD procedure for corrective actions that may arise from non-conforming products – the results of which **shall** be included in the management review process. This process includes the necessity for corrective action being evaluated in terms of the potential impact on operating costs, costs of non-conformance, performance, dependability, safety and customer satisfaction – but overall, it is designed to:

- define the causes of non-conformances and defects;
- eliminate the causes of these non-conformances and defects;
- take appropriate actions to avoid recurrence of problems (i.e. preventative action – see QP/6);
- make a record of the corrective action that has been taken; and
- review that the agreed corrective action taken is effective and consider the need for actions to ensure that this type of non-conformity does not happen again.

Document Ref: **N-53–051RLR13**
Version: 03.01
Date: 1 October 2013
Quality Management System
Part Three – Quality Procedures
QP/5 Corrective Action – Version 01.00

5.5.1 Why are concessions to an approved NAFAAD product required?

Although NAFAAD are proud to operate and maintain an exceedingly 'state of the art' quality management system and to take every precaution in ensuring that the customer's deliverable is totally in accordance with the agreed specification and requirements of the contract, there are occasions outside our control which may give rise to a non-conforming product.

From a business perspective this is a very serious matter and must be thoroughly investigated, and the route causes identified and remedied.

 Client satisfaction (and continual improvement) are of paramount importance to NAFAAD.

5.5.2 Concession scheme

Having confirmed that a non-conformity has been identified NAFAAD makes use of a *'concession scheme'*, which consists of a form that has to be completed by NAFAAD, the subcontractor (in the case of a supplier and/or manufacturer) **and** the customer.

For this concessionary scheme to operate correctly, NAFAAD has to list details of every document, defect or mistake that has been identified and to record this as well as the action that has been, will be or was taken to rectify, scrap, modify or accept the problem and (of importance to NAFAAD's quality assurance and quality control) identify if the problem is the result of a faulty design or specification.

The concession system is a very important part of NAFAAD's relationship with the customer. It also helps to promote better discipline within the organisation, shows up recurring problem areas and ensures that NAFAAD's standards of workmanship are maintained.

 Although the corrective actions may involve changes to NAFAAD's procedures and systems, they are necessary in order to achieve quality deliverable improvement.

Document Ref: **N-53–052RLR13**
Version: 03.01
Date: 1 October 2013
Quality Management System
Part Three – Quality Procedures
QP/6 – Preventative Action – Version 01.00

QP/6 – Preventative Action

CONTENTS

6.1   Scope 1
6.2   Responsibilities 1
    6.2.1   Quality Manager. 1
    6.2.2   Company Secretary 2
    6.2.3   Section Chiefs 2
6.3   Definitions 2
6.4   Purpose 2
6.5   Procedure 2

6.1 SCOPE

Under Section 8.5.3 of ISO 9001:2008, there is a mandatory requirement for NAFAAD to produce a formal procedure to determine action to eliminate the causes of potential non-conformities in order to prevent their occurrence and that all preventive actions shall be appropriate to the effects of the potential problems.

QP/6 (as required by ISO 9001:2008), therefore, provides a documented procedure to:

- determine potential non-conformities and their root causes;
- evaluate the need for actions to prevent occurrence;
- determine and implement the required action to prevent occurrence;
- maintain records of the results of the action taken;
- review the effectiveness of preventive action taken.

6.2 RESPONSIBILITIES

6.2.1 Quality Manager

It is the responsibility of the Quality Manager to ensure that all aspects of this procedure are adhered to.

	Document Ref: **N-53–052RLR13**
	Version: 03.01
	Date: 1 October 2013
	Quality Management System
	Part Three – Quality Procedures
	QP/6 – Preventative Action – Version 01.00

6.2.2 Company Secretary

The Company Secretary is responsible for ensuring that adequate facilities exist for the safe keeping of Quality Records.

6.2.3 Section Chiefs

All Section Chiefs are responsible for ensuring that all potential problem areas that could give rise to a non-conforming product are immediately reported and acted upon.

6.3 DEFINITIONS

Preventive action – a change implemented to address a weakness in a management system that is not **yet** responsible for causing a non-conforming product or service. An endeavour taken to eliminate the cause of a potential non-conformity or other potentially undesirable situation and to prevent its occurrence.

Note: 'Corrective' actions are steps that are taken to remove the causes of existing non-conformities, while 'Preventive' actions are steps that are taken to remove the causes of potential non-conformities.

Corrective actions address actual problems, ones that have already occurred, while Preventive actions address potential problems, ones that haven't yet occurred.

In general, the Corrective action process is a problem solving process, while the Preventive action process is a risk analysis process.

6.4 PURPOSE

Using preventive methodologies such as risk analysis, trend analysis, statistical process control, fault tree analysis, failure modes and effects and criticality analysis to identify the causes of potential non-conformances, NAFAAD seeks to reduce the chance of non-conforming products being produced.

6.5 PROCEDURE

Preventive action is a procedure used to address a potential weakness in a management system that is not yet responsible for causing a non-conforming

Document Ref: **N-53–052RLR13**
Version: 03.01
Date: 1 October 2013
Quality Management System
Part Three – Quality Procedures
QP/6 – Preventative Action – Version 01.00

product or service. It is part of a proactive process for organisational improvement as opposed to a reaction to problems or complaints.

But first, NAFAAD needs to be aware of a potential problem area and the possibility of a non-conforming product being produced and/or delivered to an unsuspecting customer. Using sources such as those listed below, NAFAAD is able to produce a viable route map for product improvement. Much of this information comes from:

- customer needs and expectations;
- customer complaints
- market analysis;
- outputs from data analysis;
- satisfaction measurements;
- systems that consolidate many sources of customer information.

Preventive action also includes the use of **internal** sources of information obtained from:

- outputs from management reviews;
- process measurements and work operations which affect quality;
- relevant QMS records;
- results from internal audits;
- results of self-assessment;
- processes that provide early warning of approaching out-of-control operating conditions.

All NAFAAD personnel are responsible for ensuring that **immediately** they discover a potential problem, it is elevated to their respective Section Chief for investigation.

The Section Chief (in consultation with the Quality Manager) shall then:

- review the potential problem;
- decide the potential cause of the problem;
- decide the best course of action to eliminate the problem from occurring;
- put the plan into action; and then
- ensure or verify that the action solved the problem or is effective over time.

	Document Ref: **N-53–052RLR13**
	Version: 03.01
	Date: 1 October 2013
	Quality Management System
	Part Three – Quality Procedures
	QP/6 – Preventative Action – Version 01.00

The Quality Manager is ultimately responsible for maintaining quality records of all the actions, and results of those actions are thoroughly documented and retained in NAFAAD's quality records.

The focus for preventive actions is to avoid creating non-conformances, but also commonly includes improvements in efficiency.

Document Ref: **N-53–053RLR13**
Version: 03.01
Date: 1 October 2013
Quality Management System
Part Three – Quality Procedures
QP/7 – Production of a Quality Document – Version 01.00

QP/7 – Production of a Quality Document

CONTENTS

7.1 Scope 1
7.2 Responsibilities 2
    7.2.1 Quality Manager.. 2
7.3 Definitions 2
7.4 Procedure 2
    7.4.1 Initiation of a quality document 2
    7.4.2 Drafting 4
    7.4.3 Headings 4
    7.4.4 Text 4
    7.4.5 Flowchart 5
    7.4.6 Quality Procedures 5
    7.4.7 Work Instructions 5
    7.4.8 Review 6
    7.4.9 Issue authority 7
    7.4.10 Amendments to a draft document 7
    7.4.11 Amendments to approved documents 7
    7.4.12 Cancellation 7
    7.4.13 Quality records 7
    7.4.14 Personnel involved in the identification and production
           of a quality document 8

7.1 SCOPE

To ensure conformity of all documentation it is necessary to establish a process for the production, amendment and cancellation of all NAFAAD Quality Procedures and Work Instructions (collectively known as 'quality documents') covering:

- initiation;
- review;
- authorisation;

Document Ref: **N-53–053RLR13**
Version: 03.01
Date: 1 October 2013
Quality Management System
Part Three – Quality Procedures
QP/7 – Production of a Quality Document – Version 01.00

- issue;
- amendment;
- cancellation.

QP/7 describes the process involved in the production of a Quality Document, from initial identification of the need for a new or amended Quality Document, through to the approval processes and the eventual publication of the final Quality Document.

7.2 RESPONSIBILITIES

7.2.1 Quality Manager

The Quality Manager is responsible for identifying the requirements for a new quality document (or reviewing a recommendation for a new quality document from a member of NAFAAD's staff) and making a decision as to whether a new document should be published.

Author's Hint

If you are a manufacturer then you should possibly also include a statement to the effect that the Technical Manager, Production Manager, Stock Control Manager etc. are also included in this process.

7.3 DEFINITIONS

Nil.

7.4 PROCEDURE

7.4.1 Initiation of a quality document

A written QP or WI shall be required for any NAFAAD activity where consistency of quality output is likely to be impaired by its absence.

Document Ref: **N-53–053RLR13**
Version: 03.01
Date: 1 October 2013
Quality Management System
Part Three – Quality Procedures
QP/7 – Production of a Quality Document – Version 01.00

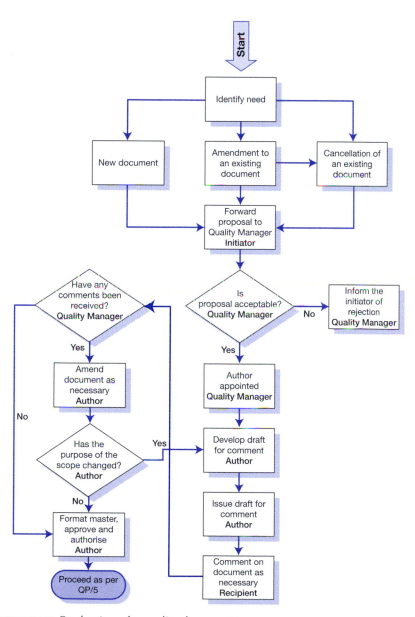

FIGURE QP7.1 Production of a quality document

	Document Ref: **N-53–053RLR13** Version: 03.01 Date: 1 October 2013 Quality Management System Part Three – Quality Procedures QP/7 – Production of a Quality Document – Version 01.00

The need for a written quality document and its scope may be identified by:

- an individual;
- the results from an internal quality audit – see QP/3;
- the results from a company bi-annual QMS review – see QP/10.

Development of a quality document shall be agreed and co-ordinated by the Quality Manager.

A quality document may be drafted by the Quality Manager or by an author nominated by the Quality Manager.

7.4.2 Drafting

Drafts shall be prepared in accordance with QP/1 – Document Control.

7.4.3 Headings

The following headings are the preferred contents:

- Title Page;
- Contents – if required, together with a list of all annexes and attachments;
- Scope – a concise explanation of the specific objectives of the document together with a definition of the context and boundaries to which the document applies. Any exclusions shall also be identified;
- Responsibilities;
- Definitions – if required;
- Detail;
- Annex(es) – if required.

7.4.4 Text

The document should comprise a logical sequence of text which must be easy to:

- read;
- understand;
- use;
- remember.

Document Ref: **N-53–053RLR13**
Version: 03.01
Date: 1 October 2013
Quality Management System
Part Three – Quality Procedures
QP/7 – Production of a Quality Document – Version 01.00

7.4.5 Flowchart

A flowchart is optional. If used, it shall:

- describe the main tasks;
- include decision points and related tasks;
- include details of associated QPs and WIs.

7.4.6 Quality Procedures

Quality Procedures shall be prepared using the report template available from the server.

FIGURE QP7.2 Route to templates

7.4.7 Work Instructions

WIs will normally be in the form of a flowchart. They should be prepared using Microsoft Visio and may be supported (if required and to ease understanding) by a small amount of text.

The flowchart should follow the sequence of events needed to enable the user of the Work Instruction to fulfil the task. Details should include:

- step-by-step instructions for carrying out the task;
- how to deal with problems that may arise, particularly those that may affect quality;
- measurable criteria for workmanship to ensure the required level of quality is being adhered to;
- who can carry out the procedure;
- Annex(es) – if required.

	Document Ref: **N-53–053RLR13**
	Version: 03.01
	Date: 1 October 2013
	Quality Management System
	Part Three – Quality Procedures
	QP/7 – Production of a Quality Document – Version 01.00

7.4.8 Review

In accordance with QP/1 – Document Control, each title page of a draft for review shall be endorsed with the issue number and/or current draft number (e.g. 00.01 – meaning the first draft).

For control purposes, when a draft quality document has been checked into the server it will be issued for comment, the date entry on each page shall be the date of its production.

The author shall circulate (via e-mail) the draft quality document to the Quality Manager and any other relevant members of staff for review.

When an e-mail is received by the member of staff it will show that there is a document awaiting their comment and/or approval. They should then:

- check out the document and review it;
- enter into discussions via e-mail with other staff members;
- send an e-mail to the author giving their views and/or approval.

 Note: If it assists the reviewer, the draft document may be *'marked up'* using the MS Word Tracker facility and reference to this made in the replying e-mail.

Upon return of the reviewed document, the Quality Manager and/or author shall:

- evaluate and assimilate the reviewers' remarks;
- resolve conflictions, by convening meetings if necessary.

 Note: Final arbitration shall always rest with the Quality Manager and shall:

- be documented accordingly;
- incorporate the comments into the revised document, dating affected page(s);
- repeat the review process if it has been necessary to make major changes to the document.

The Quality Manager shall then (with the assistance of the author – if appointed) complete the review and publish the final document.

Document Ref: **N-53–053RLR13**
Version: 03.01
Date: 1 October 2013
Quality Management System
Part Three – Quality Procedures
QP/7 – Production of a Quality Document – Version 01.00

7.4.9 Issue authority

A quality document shall not be issued formally until the review procedure described above has been satisfactorily completed.

Each quality document shall be issued in accordance with QP/1 – Document Control.

7.4.10 Amendments to a draft document

Amendments to a draft quality document shall be controlled in accordance with paragraph 7.3.8 above.

7.4.11 Amendments to approved documents

Amendments to an approved quality document may arise from:

- an individual applying formally to the Quality Manager (with sufficient information to support the case);
- the results from an internal quality audit;
- the results from a company bi-annual QMS review.

Each proposed amendment shall be considered in accordance with 7.3.8 above.

7.4.12 Cancellation

Cancellation of a quality document may be proposed by applying formally (with sufficient background to support the case) to the Quality Manager.

Each proposal for cancellation shall be processed in accordance with QP/1 – Document Control.

Cancellation of a quality document shall be approved and authorised in accordance with QP/1 – Document Control.

7.4.13 Quality records

To ensure traceability and quality control, the Quality Manager shall retain records of all quality documents (new, revised, amended or destroyed) in separate Quality Files.

	Document Ref: **N-53–053RLR13**
	Version: 03.01
	Date: 1 October 2013
	Quality Management System
	Part Three – Quality Procedures
	QP/7 – Production of a Quality Document – Version 01.00

7.4.14 PERSONNEL INVOLVED IN THE IDENTIFICATION AND PRODUCTION OF A QUALITY DOCUMENT

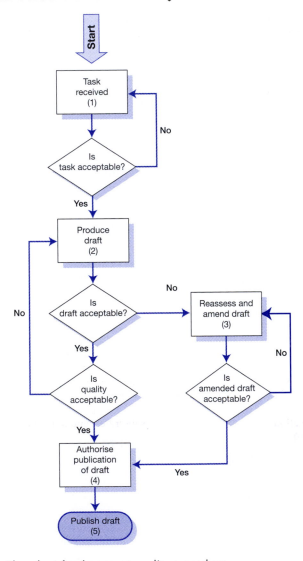

FIGURE QP7.3 Flowchart for document quality procedure

	Document Ref: **N-53-053RLR13**
	Version: 03.01
	Date: 1 October 2013
	Quality Management System
	Part Three – Quality Procedures
	QP/7 – Production of a Quality Document – Version 01.00

TABLE QP7.1 Production and finalisation of NAFAAD Quality Documents

Task	Description	Responsibility	Remarks
1	Potential for a new QP or WI identified	NAFAAD individual	Draft sent to the Quality Manager and other affected personnel for consideration and coordination.
2	Task received, and allocated for completion	Quality Manager	All comments from affected individuals received. Details of requirements, content, format and time frame received and approved by Quality Director.
	Task accepted by Quality Manager	Quality Manager	Task allocated to a Working Group or individual. Work package, time plan etc. agreed.
3	Draft document produced	Working Group or individual	Initial draft produced and checked into the server, relevant staff subscribed to document and notified.
	Re-assess and amend draft	Working Group or individual	Comments received from subscribers and comments assessed and if necessary acted upon.
	Amend draft	Working Group or individual	Draft amended and reissued for comment.
4	Final Draft sent to Quality Manager	Working Group or individual	Final Draft reviewed from a quality perspective and inter-relationship with other NAFAAD QMS documents.
5	Authorise publication of draft	Quality Manager	Draft accepted and authorised by subscribers and Managing Director.
6	Publish document	Quality Manager	Document published and all NAFAAD staff notified of its publication and orders for any previous version to be taken out of use immediately.

	Document Ref: **N-53–053RLR13**
	Version: 03.01
	Date: 1 October 2013
	Quality Management System
	Part Three – Quality Procedures
	QP/7 – Production of a Quality Document – Version 01.00

As the production of a document will normally require considerable time and effort, it is important that the documents themselves are of the required quality and are a reflection of this.

Whilst confirming that the technical and operational content of a document is most important, it is also important to ensure that these documents are correctly formatted and that their content and quality are acceptable. This can only be achieved by monitoring and confirming each stage of the document's production process, from acceptance of a task to the actual distribution of the document.

Figure QP7.3 and Table QP7.1 show the various points during the production of a document that require formal approval. Formal approval is indicated by e-sign off.

In producing and finalising NAFAAD documents, the procedures contained in QP/1 – Document Control shall be observed, especially those concerning the layout of documents.

Document Ref: **N-53–054RLR13**
Version: 03.01
Date: 1 October 2013
Quality Management System
Part Three – Quality Procedures
QP/8 – Design Control – Version 01.00

QP/8 – Design Control

CONTENTS

8.1   Scope 1
8.2   Responsibilities 2
    8.2.1   Quality Manager.....................................2
    8.2.2   Section Managers 2
    8.2.3   Company Secretary 2
8.3   Definitions 2
8.4   Process...2
    8.4.1   Input...3
    8.4.2   Output 3
    8.4.3   Verification 3
    8.4.4   Changes 3

8.1 SCOPE

The primary function of NAFAAD is to:

- provide advice and guidance on all quality matters;
- produce either complete Quality Management Systems, Quality Manuals, Quality Processes, Quality Procedures or Work Instructions (to suit individual customer requirements);
- provide qualified advice on technical, environmental and safety requirements (particularly for the electronics industry), fuel conservation and expert advice in business management, human resources and marketing.

Although this is not a design activity in the true manufacturing sense, the principles described in ISO 9001:2008 for design are, in general, also valid for NAFAAD and QP/8 (i.e. this current document) details the requirements for design control within NAFAAD.

	Document Ref: **N-53–054RLR13**
	Version: 03.01
	Date: 1 October 2013
	Quality Management System
	Part Three – Quality Procedures
	QP/8 – Design Control – Version 01.00

8.2 RESPONSIBILITIES

8.2.1 Quality Manager

The Quality Manager is responsible for ensuring that the planning of all interfaces between the different activities is appropriate and that verification points are allocated and taken into account.

8.2.2 Section Managers

The Managing Director shall assign system specification development responsibilities to Section Managers. Section Managers, in their turn, are responsible for ensuring completion of these tasks, for assigning the work to suitably trained and experienced specialists and for overseeing and supervising their output.

8.2.3 Company Secretary

The Company Secretary is responsible for maintaining a time plan throughout each individual contract's life and for all main NAFAAD activities.

8.3 DEFINITIONS

Nil.

8.4 PROCESS

The Quality Manager shall approve the planning after each change and, where necessary, liaise with the Managing Director to ensure that more detailed plans are made in order that interfaces between the development activities are properly handled. The main objective is to see to it that the appropriate information concerning the requirements and specifications already developed and agreed on, is available to all parties – at any stage.

To facilitate this process, the Quality Manager shall use advance design planning and decision techniques (such as 'Teamwork') to control this requirement wherever appropriate.

To ensure overall task effectiveness, a time plan shall be maintained by the Company Secretary, throughout each individual contract's life and for all main NAFAAD activities.

Document Ref: **N-53–054RLR13**
Version: 03.01
Date: 1 October 2013
Quality Management System
Part Three – Quality Procedures
QP/8 – Design Control – Version 01.00

8.4.1 Input

The input data for each stage of a contract shall (in consultation with the Quality Manager) be identified by the Section Manager concerned, documented by the Company Secretary and agreed with the Managing Director.

For each contract the same structure shall apply and the Quality Manager is responsible for ensuring that this actually happens.

8.4.2 Output

All documents shall be presented in the form as described in QP/1 – Document Control.

8.4.3 Verification

Verification of all NAFAAD documents shall be in accordance with (when available) the relevant project or Contract-specific Quality Plan and shall be documented.

 Note: The Quality Manager will advise the Managing Director concerning this topic on an as-required basis.

Verification that documents are of the required format, content and quality shall be achieved via the procedures described in QP/1 – Document Control and approval shall be in accordance with QP/9 – Approval Procedures.

8.4.4 Changes

All changes that could fundamentally influence the company scope, targets, organisation, budget, overall work breakdown structure, work packages and time plans shall be subject to the formal change control procedures described in QP/14 – Change Control.

Document Ref: **N-53–055RLR13**
Version: 03.01
Date: 1 October 2013
Quality Management System
Part Three – Quality Procedures
QP/9 – Approval Procedures – Version 01.00

QP/9 – Approval Procedures

CONTENTS

9.1   Scope 1
9.2   Responsibilities 1
9.3   Definitions 1
9.4   Process... 1
      9.4.1   The approvals list 1

9.1 SCOPE

To achieve conformity and inter co-operation, all NAFAAD documents (whether these are managerial, quality related, financial or technical) require some form of approval procedure. In addition, all NAFAAD documents shall be presented in the form of an 'official' NAFAAD document, which will require the approval of the Managing Director.

The following Approval Procedure details the requirements for all management and contract-related documents within NAFAAD.

9.2 RESPONSIBILITIES

All Managerial Staff involved in the final approval that a quality related policy, process, procedure or Work Instruction may be published for general NAFAAD usage.

9.3 DEFINITIONS

Nil.

9.4 PROCESS

9.4.1 The approvals list

The list of person(s) required to approve a document before it achieves 'published' status is a function of the area of the server in which the document is to be stored.

	Document Ref: **N-53–055RLR13** Version: 03.01 Date: 1 October 2013 Quality Management System Part Three – Quality Procedures QP/9 – Approval Procedures – Version 01.00

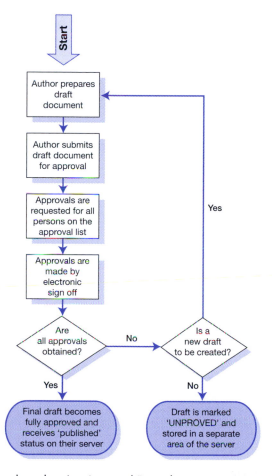

FIGURE QP9.1 Flowchart showing Approval Procedure

For example, the approval list for documents stored in the folder 'Business Plans' may contain the Managing Director, the Marketing Manager and the Financial Manager. That for documents stored in the folder 'Expense Forms' may only contain the Financial Manager.

Document Ref: **N-53–056RLR13**
Version: 03.01
Date: 1 October 2013
Quality Management System
Part Three – Quality Procedures
QP/10 – Quality Management System Review – Version 01.00

QP/10 – Quality Management System Review

CONTENTS

10.1 Scope 1
10.2 Responsibilities 2
     10.2.1 Quality Manager.. 2
     10.2.2 Company Secretary...................................... 2
10.3 Definitions 2
10.4 Process... 2
     10.4.1 Meetings of the Review Board 2
     10.4.2 Frequency of meetings.................................. 4
     10.4.3 Review Board members.................................. 4
     10.4.4 Agenda.. 4
     10.4.5 Meeting contents 5
     10.4.6 Actions.. 5
     10.4.7 Meeting records 6

10.1 SCOPE

In accordance with the principles of ISO 9001:2008, bi-annual NAFAAD QMS reviews are required in order to ensure that:

- NAFAAD is effective in attaining its objectives as described in the Quality Manual;
- the Quality Manual remains effective and suitable for the requirements of NAFAAD (in other words that it 'really works' in practice);
- the requirements and rules as described in the Quality Manual remain workable and are in accordance (as far as possible) with the way NAFAAD personnel prefer to work – without losing the assurance that NAFAAD delivers quality;
- NAFAAD requirements are met and that the relevant rules are agreed on and are adhered to.

QP/10 details the requirements for Quality Management System Reviews within NAFAAD.

Document Ref: **N-53–056RLR13**
Version: 03.01
Date: 1 October 2013
Quality Management System
Part Three – Quality Procedures
QP/10 – Quality Management System Review – Version 01.00

10.2 RESPONSIBILITIES

10.2.1 Quality Manager

The Quality Manager is responsible for overseeing the operation of the QMS; for ensuring that the Quality Manual is fully and effectively implemented and for co-ordinating the writing as well as the availability of the necessary processes, procedures and instructions.

10.2.2 Company Secretary

The Company Secretary is responsible for ensuring that minutes of the meeting are prepared and distributed promptly.

10.3 DEFINITIONS

Nil.

10.4 PROCESS

10.4.1 Meetings of the Review Board

The initiative for meetings of the Review Board shall be taken by the Quality Manager. He shall prepare an agenda and provide all relevant documents (e.g. reports of internal audits, results of product reviews etc.). If necessary the Quality Manager shall draw attention to areas where NAFAAD requirements are not being met or where rules are not followed. Whenever possible he will provide recommendations for improvements.

If the results of the review are such that corrective action is necessary, the Review Board shall agree on the corrective actions and suggest appropriate methods for their implementation. The Managing Director shall be responsible for ensuring the implementation of the agreed corrective actions.

The details of the review and the agreed corrective actions shall be recorded and the records shall be maintained in the company quality files.

The review shall cover all activities related to company and company quality management as described in the Quality Manual, attached Quality Processes, QPs, WIs and Quality Plans.

| | Document Ref: **N-53–056RLR13**
Version: 03.01
Date: 1 October 2013
Quality Management System
Part Three – Quality Procedures
QP/10 – Quality Management System Review – Version 01.00 |

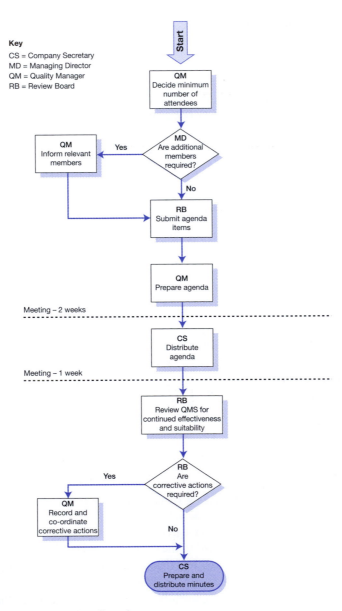

Key

CS = Company Secretary
MD = Managing Director
QM = Quality Manager
RB = Review Board

FIGURE QP10.1 QMS review flowchart

Document Ref: **N-53–056RLR13**
Version: 03.01
Date: 1 October 2013
Quality Management System
Part Three – Quality Procedures
QP/10 – Quality Management System Review – Version 01.00

10.4.2 Frequency of meetings

The Review Board shall meet every six months.

10.4.3 Review Board members

Permanent members of the Review Board are:

- the Managing Director (who acts as Chairman);
- the Company Secretary;
- the Quality Manager (who also acts as Deputy Chairman).

The exact number of attendees may vary according to the circumstances applicable at that time.

The Quality Manager shall decide on the minimum number of attendees for convening that meeting.

The Managing Director (in consultation with the Quality Manager) shall decide whether or not it is necessary to invite additional members and if so, who shall be involved.

10.4.4 Agenda

All members of the Review Board may contribute items for the agenda, but they must be submitted no later than two weeks prior to the actual date of the meeting. Such contributions shall be sent to the Quality Manager.

The Quality Manager shall prepare the agenda in consultation with the Managing Director and ensure that the relevant information documents are attached to it.

The Company Secretary shall distribute the agenda and attached information documents so that these are in the possession of all members of the Review Board at least one week prior to the meeting.

The agenda for a Review Board shall consist of:

- a review of all actions raised at the previous meetings and progressed at subsequent meetings;
- a review of minutes and actions arising from the minutes of the previous meeting;
- implementation and continued effectiveness of the QM, Quality Processes, QPs, WIs and Quality Plans;

Document Ref: **N-53–056RLR13**
Version: 03.01
Date: 1 October 2013
Quality Management System
Part Three – Quality Procedures
QP/10 – Quality Management System Review – Version 01.00

- results of internal NAFAAD audits and details of the corrective actions taken;
- previous NAFAAD audit results;
- previous reports on all major deviations from NAFAAD objectives related to time, costs and quality;
- previous consequences of changes (objectives, organisation, schedules etc.);
- previous results of verifications on major NAFAAD documents;
- previous results of actions agreed at previous meetings;
- customer complaints.

10.4.5 Meeting contents

The nature of the Review Board is such that all major issues affecting NAFAAD shall be considered as appropriate.

In all cases the target shall be:

- to review whether the QMS is still the most effective and suitable way to reach and achieve objectives and to ensure that NAFAAD documents comply with the relevant quality and safety standards; and
- to seek ways of improving NAFAAD's QMS.

10.4.6 Actions

If the results of the review are such that corrective action is necessary, the Review Board shall:

- consider solutions and agree on the corrective action(s);
- agree on responsibility for the implementation of the corrective action chosen;
- agree on a timescale for the implementation and review of corrective action(s) taken.

The review and the agreed corrective actions shall be recorded in the company quality file by the Quality Manager.

The Quality Manager shall also be responsible for co-ordinating the completion of all corrective actions agreed by the Review Board.

All actions raised at previous meetings shall be reviewed and progressed at subsequent meetings.

Document Ref: **N-53–056RLR13**
Version: 03.01
Date: 1 October 2013
Quality Management System
Part Three – Quality Procedures
QP/10 – Quality Management System Review – Version 01.00

10.4.7 Meeting records

The Company Secretary is responsible for ensuring that minutes of the meeting are prepared and distributed promptly.

The minutes shall clearly state:

- actions agreed upon;
- the person responsible for implementing these actions (i.e. the Action List);
- the agreed completion date (i.e. the Time Plan).

The minutes of the meeting shall be kept in the company quality file.

Document Ref: **N-53–057RLR13**
Version: 03.01
Date: 1 October 2013
Quality Management System
Part Three – Quality Procedures
QP/11 – Purchasing – Version 01.00

QP/11 – Purchasing

CONTENTS

11.1 Scope 1
11.2 Responsibilities 1
    11.2.1 Company Secretary 1
11.3 Definitions 2
11.4 Company Procedure 2
11.5 Financial management 3
    11.5.1 Delegation of financial authority 3
    11.5.2 NAFAAD budget forecast 3
    11.5.3 Comparison of committed costs with approved budget 4
    11.5.4 Administrating income and expenditure 4
    11.5.5 Company financial audit 5
11.6 Resource management 5
    11.6.1 Contracts with subcontractors and consultants 5
    11.6.2 Other contracts and purchases 5
11.7 Invoices 6
    11.7.1 Subcontractors' invoices 6
    11.7.2 Filing of invoices 6
Annex A – Delegation of financial and contractual authority 7

11.1 SCOPE

For all NAFAAD contracts, the two main resources required are finance and manpower. QP/11 describes how both of these resources shall be managed within NAFAAD.

11.2 RESPONSIBILITIES

11.2.1 Company Secretary

Total cost management shall be computerised and controlled by the Company Secretary.

Document Ref: **N-53–057RLR13**
Version: 03.01
Date: 1 October 2013
Quality Management System
Part Three – Quality Procedures
QP/11 – Purchasing – Version 01.00

11.3 DEFINITIONS

Nil.

11.4 COMPANY PROCEDURE

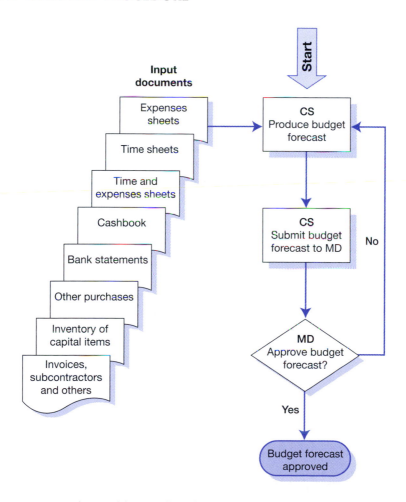

FIGURE QP11.1 Budget and finance flowchart

	Document Ref: **N-53–057RLR13**
	Version: 03.01
	Date: 1 October 2013
	Quality Management System
	Part Three – Quality Procedures
	QP/11 – Purchasing – Version 01.00

11.5 FINANCIAL MANAGEMENT

11.5.1 Delegation of financial authority

The Managing Director each year approves the NAFAAD budget and delegates part of his authority to the Company Secretary.

The table in Annex A shows the delegation of authority for signing contracts and initiating orders, accepting deliveries (i.e. approving invoices), authorising payments and signing bank transfers. The amount each person is authorised to sign for is also indicated in this table.

Contracts, material orders or services may only be signed, or ordered, by the persons for whom an amount is listed in the columns 'Initiate orders and accept deliveries' or 'Sign contracts'. In cases where the Managing Director has to sign, the Section Manager is required to co-sign first.

Deliveries and invoices may only be accepted and approved by the persons for whom an amount is listed in the column 'Initiate orders and accept deliveries'. In cases where the Managing Director has to sign, the Section Manager is required to co-sign first.

In some circumstances a staff member's signature might be required prior to the Section Manager's signature.

Authorising payment and signing the bank transfers for invoices shall be limited to the persons for whom an amount is listed in the column 'Sign bank transfers and approve invoices'. This action can only be completed after the delivery has been accepted.

11.5.2 NAFAAD budget forecast

The NAFAAD budget forecast shall consist of detailed financial budget planning for each contract and activity. The budget forecast shall include the following information:

- description;
- account;
- approved budget for each individual year and grand total;
- committed cost for each individual year and grand total;
- paid cost up to and including the cut-off date;
- result (i.e. difference between committed total and approved budget total);
- forecasted cost for succeeding years.

Document Ref: **N-53–057RLR13**
Version: 03.01
Date: 1 October 2013
Quality Management System
Part Three – Quality Procedures
QP/11 – Purchasing – Version 01.00

The budget forecast shall provide full details of **all** expenditures related to each contract and activity.

From the NAFAAD budget forecast it shall be possible to extract the financial information for any particular year. The Company Secretary is responsible for this activity and shall provide details to the Managing Director.

11.5.3 Comparison of committed costs with approved budget

The Company Secretary shall carry out a continuous check on committed costs and the actual expenditures against the approved budget.

The Company Secretary shall inform the Manager concerned if the total committed costs are higher than the approved budget for their particular activity or section.

The Company Secretary shall inform the Managing Director when it becomes likely that the total committed costs will exceed the total approved budget.

11.5.4 Administrating income and expenditure

All income to and expenditure from the NAFAAD bank account shall be recorded by the Company Secretary in the NAFAAD cashbook, which shall be kept in the main office.

The Company Secretary shall be responsible for the proper administration of the NAFAAD bank account.

Copies of all transfer orders, bank statements and documents related to the NAFAAD bank transfers shall be kept in one binder in the main office.

At the end of each month the Company Secretary shall present the cashbook to the Managing Director for pre-audit.

Author's Hint

According to the size of your organisation this could be a simple hard copy cashbook or (for example) an Excel spreadsheet containing many interwoven Work Sheets and/or macro links to other files etc.

	Document Ref: **N-53–057RLR13**
	Version: 03.01
	Date: 1 October 2013
	Quality Management System
	Part Three – Quality Procedures
	QP/11 – Purchasing – Version 01.00

11.5.5 Company financial audit

The Company Secretary shall, when requested, present all the required financial documents to the Company Auditor for verification.

11.6 RESOURCE MANAGEMENT

All manpower resources (e.g. permanent and part-time staff, subcontractors and consultants) require a separate agreement/contract. These shall be initiated by the Company Secretary and signed by the Managing Director.

11.6.1 Contracts with subcontractors and consultants

All subcontractors and/or consultants working for (or on behalf of) NAFAAD shall be required to agree to a contract which shall include the following elements:

- detailed task description (including documents);
- duration of the contract;
- fees;
- travel expenses and allowances;
- payment conditions;
- other terms and conditions.

The contract may be extended by mutual arrangement. Normally either party can terminate a contract by giving three months' notice.

11.6.2 Other contracts and purchases

Requests for the purchase of all other products or services (including major assets such as furniture and computers etc.) shall be submitted in writing (by the person requiring that product or service) to the Company Secretary. The Company Secretary shall, prior to requisition, obtain the Managing Director's approval.

The Company Secretary shall maintain an inventory of all capital items purchased for NAFAAD.

Document Ref: **N-53–057RLR13**
Version: 03.01
Date: 1 October 2013
Quality Management System
Part Three – Quality Procedures
QP/11 – Purchasing – Version 01.00

11.7 INVOICES

The Company Secretary shall stamp, date and sign all invoices received by NAFAAD using the company stamp.

11.7.1 Subcontractors' invoices

Subcontractors and consultancies shall submit invoices for the manpower resourcing carried out and travel expenses incurred by their staff, directly to the Company Secretary for processing.

The Company Secretary shall check these invoices against the agreement/contract previously signed. If inconsistencies are discovered, the Company Secretary shall contact the subcontractor/consultant concerned for further clarification.

Following verification by the Company Secretary, invoices shall then be sent to the Managing Director for endorsement.

Payment for invoices shall (following authorisation) be made from the NAFAAD bank account by the Company Secretary.

11.7.2 Filing of invoices

After payment, all original invoices shall be filed, together with the following documents:

- a copy of the order form or letter (in case of a telephone order, a handwritten note from the initiating person will suffice);
- the original delivery note and a signed receipt by the initiator or the person authorised to sign on his behalf;
- a copy of the bank transfer note or cheque.

	Document Ref: **N-53–057RLR13**
	Version: 03.01
	Date: 1 October 2013
	Quality Management System
	Part Three – Quality Procedures
	QP/11 – Purchasing – Version 01.00

Annex A –
Delegation of financial and contractual authority

TABLE QP11.1 Delegation of Financial and Contractual Authority

Name	Maximum amounts			
	Initiate orders and accept deliveries	*Sign bank transfers and approve invoices*	*Sign contracts*	*Example of signature*
	Delivery as ordered	*Payment authorised*		
Managing Director	unlimited	unlimited	unlimited	
Section Managers	£6,000	£6,000	£6,000	
Company Secretary	£2,000	*	*	

* No authorisation

Document Ref: **N-53–058RLR13**
Version: 03.01
Date: 1 October 2013
Quality Management System
Part Three – Quality Procedures
QP/12 – Customer Feedback – Version 01.00

QP/12 – Customer Feedback

CONTENTS

12.1   Scope 1
12.2   Responsibilities 1
     12.2.1   Quality Manager.................................... 1
12.3   Definitions 2
12.4   Process.. 2
     12.4.1   Initiation and assessment 2
     12.4.2   Initial review 2
     12.4.3   Local action 2
     12.4.4   Action taken by the Quality Manager................ 4
     12.4.5   Analysing non-conformances 4
     12.4.6   Customer interface................................. 4
     12.4.7   Quality records 5
     12.4.8   Customer Feedback Form............................. 5
Annex A – Customer satisfaction 6

12.1 SCOPE

The successful completion of any deliverable relies on the customer commenting on the technical and operational contents of this deliverable.

QP/12 has been designed to ensure that any customer feedback and complaints raised against NAFAAD reports, documents and/or specifications are adequately reviewed, appropriate action is taken, and trends analysed.

12.2 RESPONSIBILITIES

12.2.1 Quality Manager

The Quality Manager (in consultation with the Company Secretary) is responsible for maintaining quality records demonstrating conformance to the requirements and the effective operation of the QMS.

	Document Ref: **N-53–058RLR13**
	Version: 03.01
	Date: 1 October 2013
	Quality Management System
	Part Three – Quality Procedures
	QP/12 – Customer Feedback – Version 01.00

12.3 DEFINITIONS

Nil.

12.4 PROCESS

12.4.1 Initiation and assessment

All customer feedback including complaints received by the company office, shall (following registration) be directed to the appropriate Section Manager for assessment.

Unless the issue raised by the customer is of a minor nature (e.g. a grammatical or typographic error) or a request for information that can be dealt with directly, the Section Manager shall initiate a Customer Feedback Form (see Annex A).

The Section Manager initiating a Customer Feedback Form shall ensure that:

- there is sufficient detail in Part A for the problem to be self-explanatory;
- all customer details are included;
- any related documents are attached.

The form shall then be signed, dated and forwarded for review.

12.4.2 Initial review

The initial review shall be made either by the originating Section Manager or referred to another Internal Section Manager, or be discussed at the next QMS review meeting. The review procedure shall ascertain if the problem can be resolved locally and if so, agree to the appropriate action required.

12.4.3 Local action

If it is agreed that action shall be taken locally, then the originating Section Manager is responsible for ensuring that it is carried out and the results are detailed in Part B of the Customer Feedback Form. In taking action, full consideration shall be given to the root cause of the problem and how this may be resolved.

This form shall then be signed and dated, with copies being forwarded to the Quality Manager.

Document Ref: **N-53–058RLR13**
Version: 03.01
Date: 1 October 2013
Quality Management System
Part Three – Quality Procedures
QP/12 – Customer Feedback – Version 01.00

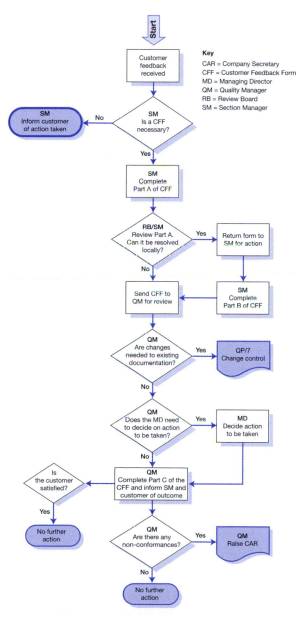

FIGURE QP12.1 Customer feedback flowchart

Document Ref: **N-53–058RLR13**
Version: 03.01
Date: 1 October 2013
Quality Management System
Part Three – Quality Procedures
QP/12 – Customer Feedback – Version 01.00

'If' it is agreed that action shall **not** be taken locally, then the original of the form shall be forwarded to the Quality Manager.

 Local recommendations may be made in Part B by the originating Section Manager if considered necessary and relevant.

12.4.4 ACTION TAKEN BY THE QUALITY MANAGER

The Quality Manager shall review all forms received. Where action has been taken locally, the Quality Manager shall check that the action taken:

*   is adequate;
*   has no implications for other sections;
*   has no implications for the NAFAAD QMS.

Where action has not been taken locally, the Quality Manager shall review the problem and decide if it necessitates action through a change control procedure (as described in QP/14 – Change Control) for consideration by the Managing Director.

The Quality Manager shall ensure that at all times the review considers the root cause of the problem and how this may be resolved.

Upon completion of the appropriate action, the Quality Manager shall ensure that Part B and Part C of the form are completed and a copy of the original is returned to the Section Manager who initiated the form.

12.4.5 Analysing non-conformances

The Quality Manager shall regularly review all Customer Feedback Forms to detect any trends that may have a detrimental effect on a contract deliverable. When such a trend is found, the Quality Manager shall raise a Corrective Action Report (available from the Company Secretary) for review by the Managing Director.

12.4.6 Customer interface

The Quality Manager and/or Section Manager concerned shall ensure that the customer, having made an enquiry, is kept fully informed of its progress. They shall also seek comments from the customer on any action implemented.

Document Ref: **N-53–058RLR13**
Version: 03.01
Date: 1 October 2013
Quality Management System
Part Three – Quality Procedures
QP/12 – Customer Feedback – Version 01.00

12.4.7 Quality records

To ensure traceability and quality control, all records appertaining to customer feedback (and/or complaints) shall be retained by the Quality Manager in a separate quality file.

12.4.8 Customer Feedback Form

CUSTOMER FEEDBACK FORM

Ref No: _____ No of attached sheets ___

Customer: _____

Related documents: _____

PART A

Nature of feedback/ _____
complaint _____

Input: Face-to-face / letter / fax / phone / e-mail
(delete as appropriate)

Signed: Name _____ Date _____

PART B

Action to be taken _____
(Section Manager/Review Board)

Date action completed _____

Signed: Name _____ Date _____

PART C

Review by Quality Manager: _____

Refer to Managing Director? Yes / No   Raise to CAR? Yes / No
                             (delete as   (delete as
                             appropriate)   appropriate)

                                              Car No. _____

Signed: Name _____ Date _____

	Document Ref: **N-53–058RLR13**
	Version: 03.01
	Date: 1 October 2013
	Quality Management System
	Part Three – Quality Procedures
	QP/12 – Customer Feedback – Version 01.00

Annex A –
Customer satisfaction

Customer satisfaction is not just a perception; it is also a question of degree which can vary from high satisfaction to low satisfaction. If customers believe that you have met their requirements, then they experience high satisfaction. If they believe that you have not met their requirements, then they experience low satisfaction.

A.1 THE REQUIREMENT

Section 8.2.1, ISO 9001:2008 requires an organisation to '*monitor information relating to customer perception as to whether the organisation has met customer requirements*' and requires '*the methods of obtaining and using this information to be determined*'.

As you can see, the emphasis here is on monitoring customer perception (systematic checks on a periodic or continuous basis) rather than measuring customer satisfaction during a one-off event. Whilst customers may accept a product, they may not necessarily be entirely satisfied with either that particular product or the service they have received and, quite legitimately, believe that you have not met their expectations. To overcome this possibility, you should always strive to provide a service or product that exceeds the customer's stated requirements – provided that it can be kept within budget.

Satisfied customers are always good for business for not only will they return but they will also recommend your organisation to other people. Getting your customers to tell you what's good about your products or services and where there is room for improvement, helps you to ensure that your business meets or exceeds their expectations. You obviously want your customers to be happy with the products and services that you provide and if they feel they have received good value for their money, then your business will prosper.

Market research can help you to track and monitor customer satisfaction. But first you must consider which form of market research you want to employ.

A.2 BRIEF OVERVIEW OF MARKET RESEARCH

Within market research there are two main methodologies – Quantitative and Qualitative.

Document Ref: **N-53–058RLR13**
Version: 03.01
Date: 1 October 2013
Quality Management System
Part Three – Quality Procedures
QP/12 – Customer Feedback – Version 01.00

Quantitative Research – is the gathering of information from a large sample group to create statistically viable data. It is the basis for monitoring customer satisfaction but needs to be completed systematically and regularly in order to monitor and track changes effectively.

Qualitative Research – is an in-depth investigation of topics using a small sample group. Although this will provide an indication of how the target market is feeling and how they will react to a given topic, it cannot be relied upon as statistically viable data.

Often both methodologies will be used in the monitoring and evaluation of customer satisfaction. Each has its place, each will deliver important and useful information but, in order to make best use of these research tools, you must have a clear idea of what you want to achieve in the first place and then use the most effective tool to deliver the results you want.

It must be remembered that customer satisfaction surveys will only give you a status quo and an indication of what customers would like to see changed. Unless you react and respond to these customer needs, things will never change. Research can give you a quick way to see whether your changes are impacting on them, positively or negatively.

A.3 QUALITATIVE RESEARCH

In general, qualitative research is used by researchers at the beginning of a survey to give a snapshot of the general trends that may come up when they complete the main survey and which will help them to ensure that they ask the correct questions in the main survey. Qualitative research may also help to establish some possible solutions to customer issues which can then be tested in the main survey and the results evaluated before radical changes are made to the way a business is run, product produced or service undertaken.

Qualitative research can also be used in the middle stage of a research programme to re-investigate general trends, explore whether things have changed in the consumer's mind and evaluate whether different questions should now be asked. Finally it will often be used at the end of the programme to gain a clear understanding of how customers are feeling and if anything has changed for them.

Qualitative research can be divided up into a number of different methodologies, but the main methodologies that you will probably encounter are:

- focus groups; and
- depth interviews.

Document Ref: **N-53–058RLR13**
Version: 03.01
Date: 1 October 2013
Quality Management System
Part Three – Quality Procedures
QP/12 – Customer Feedback – Version 01.00

A.3.1 Focus groups

Focus groups are effectively a brainstorming session. They are usually small groups comprising 10 or fewer people who are tasked to examine a particular product, service, policy or idea by '*focussing*' on a comparatively short list of issues and then thoroughly exploring every aspect of it.

Focus groups are especially good at generating ideas early in the product development cycle, when it's too expensive or too complex to develop multiple prototypes. Whilst the conclusions of a focus group can sometimes be very revealing, it should nevertheless be remembered that a focus group only represents a small sample of the population and should, therefore, not be relied upon to be statistically robust.

Choice of membership of a focus group is unlimited. It can include all types of professional, managerial, as well as a working level of expertise to encourage interactive thinking and enable all aspects of an issue or problem to be investigated.

Generally speaking, however, certain people should **not** be asked to participate in the same focus group. These include managers and subordinates, direct competitors, family members, experts and novices, and those who hold drastically different opinions from the other participants. Members won't fully engage with the rest of the group if they're intimidated or unduly influenced by some of its members. To ensure that the participants are able to interact constructively, it is often better to choose people with somewhat similar backgrounds and/or demographics.

For most types of research it is also advisable to recruit people who do not previously know each other. This will avoid the possibility of divisions within the group and friends ganging up on others! Sounds crazy, but it happens!

Note: Sometimes strongly opposing views can be very useful in raising and discussing challenging topics. However, caution should be taken if considering a '*conflict*' focus group as the moderator of the group will have to be very experienced and capable of controlling and managing the situation, which could easily get out of hand.

In order to control and manage the focus group a moderator (often referred to as the '*facilitator*') is used to preside over the session. His or her main task is to ensure a free-flowing discussion that continues to move in the right direction and to ensure that all pertinent details are recorded.

Document Ref: **N-53–058RLR13**
Version: 03.01
Date: 1 October 2013
Quality Management System
Part Three – Quality Procedures
QP/12 – Customer Feedback – Version 01.00

Moderation of focus groups is a tricky business and should be left to those with experience – it certainly isn't the same as chairing a meeting with colleagues or clients! It is, therefore, advisable to use the services of a professional moderator, either through a research agency or by employing a freelance moderator to work directly for you.

To avoid anybody coming to the session with preconceived ideas or a closed opinion on a topic, generally speaking participants will not be informed of the topics to be discussed prior to the start of the focus group because if they have already considered a topic, they could be quite fixed in their views. It has been statistically proven that advance research can often influence a participant's thoughts and opinions during the group discussion which will inevitably result in flawed information for the researchers. You want responses and thoughts to be spontaneous and honest.

Typical topics and lines of questioning could include:

* *What do you like about this product/policy/idea?*
* *What do you dislike?*
* *How does it compare to other products/policies/ideas?*
* *What would you change about it?*

Focus groups are generally held in a relaxed setting, with a circle of seats, coffee table in the middle, with refreshments available. All this will help to relax the participants. Participants will become comfortable with the topic and with each other and this will enable them to focus on the details.

 It is important not to let a focus group last more than two hours as participating in a lively discussion can consume a considerable amount of energy.

In order to ensure that all the topics and areas that need to be covered are covered, the moderator will need to have some form of agenda to work to. This is commonly known as a topic guide and it is just that – a guide. The topic guide should **not** be seen as a strict guide to be followed, however! The discussions may veer off and circle around but as long as all the topics are covered eventually, then that is fine.

 If the moderator was to stop the participants mid-flow and pull them back to the agenda this could embarrass them and maybe stop them from speaking out again.

	Document Ref: **N-53–058RLR13** Version: 03.01 Date: 1 October 2013 Quality Management System Part Three – Quality Procedures QP/12 – Customer Feedback – Version 01.00

In normal circumstances moderators will not make any notes themselves as this will only act to stop the free flow of the discussions, and can remind the participants that the moderator is noting down everything they are saying. Nevertheless, some form of record should be kept of the meeting and this can be either a manual record or some form of electronic means. Nowadays focus group's discussions are almost always recorded using audio recorders and/or video cameras, as they are particularly useful for recording the emotions, opinions, interactions and 'hot topics' that the group uncovers.

In order to ensure that you achieve a good mix of your customer sample, a number of different focus groups may be required and your customer base will need to be split accordingly. This could include doing focus groups separately for men and women, old and young, regionally or nationally to ensure that no biases exist, and if they do, you will discover them.

A.3.2 Depth interviews

Depth interviews follow the same pattern as focus groups (i.e. they are in a relaxed setting, they use a topic guide, they are recorded etc.), but they are carried out with smaller numbers of people. Generally a depth interview will be a one-to-one discussion between a moderator and a selected individual and can be used in cases where you either have a small number of very important customers to interview, or where the topic is of a confidential or sensitive nature and participants would not open up in a general conversation. In all other ways depth interviews follow the same pattern as focus groups.

A.4 TYPES OF QUANTITATIVE SURVEY

Quantitative (often known as '*Quant*') surveys are probably the best way of gathering vital information on customer satisfaction. There are many different Quant methodologies that can be employed, but of these, the main ones are:

- postal/e-mail;
- telephone;
- on street;
- house to house; and
- mystery shopping.

Document Ref: **N-53–058RLR13**
Version: 03.01
Date: 1 October 2013
Quality Management System
Part Three – Quality Procedures
QP/12 – Customer Feedback – Version 01.00

Some of these will be more appropriate to your market and customer base than others; all have their advantages and disadvantages and below are the key pros and cons to each methodology.

A.4.1 Postal and telephone surveys

Sometimes these two methodologies are referred to as '*impersonal surveys*', because by their nature they have less of the human touch to them. Postal surveys are, however, recognised as being the most impersonal of them all, as you are asking your customer to go through a questionnaire completely alone. With a telephone you do at least have a member of your staff (or an agency working on your behalf) interacting with the customer. The main benefits to both of these methodologies are the relatively low cost per response.

Postal (and e-mail) surveys are cheap to produce, with only printing costs, postage and reply postage to consider before you get to the point of analysis. In addition a postal or e-mail survey can be an ideal way of communicating with your customer base if you have a wide spread of customers across the UK (or Europe or the world) and where face-to-face work would not be cost effective.

In general terms, apart from the set up and form of delivery, most of the pros and cons of a postal survey will hold true for an e-mail study too. An added benefit, however, is that as you are conducting an electronic survey, you can thank everyone who responded by only having to send **one** multi-addressed e-mail!

 Currently there are a wide number of specialist software packages and specialist research companies who can assist in the setting up of an e-mail survey.

The main things to remember when compiling a postal/e-mail survey is that the questionnaire itself must be very user-friendly and self-explanatory and mustn't be too long or you will not get your customers to even consider answering the questions. In addition, as with all postal marketing activity, the response rate to a postal survey could be very low indeed and in general you should only anticipate a 5–10% response rate to this type of survey. Some types of business may well get a better response than this, especially where businesses have a very good and close relationship with their customers, or where their product or service is of vital importance to them. In these cases, customers will **want** to contribute, but if your product has low importance to a consumer, or is a commodity or service that is seen as the norm, then you will probably get a very apathetic response.

	Document Ref: **N-53–058RLR13**
	Version: 03.01
	Date: 1 October 2013
	Quality Management System
	Part Three – Quality Procedures
	QP/12 – Customer Feedback – Version 01.00

Postal surveys can and will take time to complete as they have to be posted out (anticipating potential delays in delivery!), then you have to allow customers time to complete and send back their survey forms (again allowing time for the post) before any analysis can commence. E-mail surveys, on the other hand, are increasingly being used as they have two distinct advantages over the old traditional postal surveys – response time (i.e. e-mail surveys can be turned around in days if not hours) and ease of completion. E-mail surveys are much easier to complete and less confusing than paper questionnaires which often include advice (i.e. routing) such as '*if answered YES go to Question xx*' and '*if answered NO go to Question yy*' etc. An electronic survey, on the other hand, will automatically route the respondent in the correct way, ensuring that they answer fully and correctly. More information on routing and single and multiple response questions etc. are explored in Section A.5 *Writing a questionnaire*.

Another consideration with this type of survey is that they are, of course, self-selecting in nature. You have no control over who responds, thus you cannot ensure that you achieve a good and representative sample of your customer demographics. This sort of problem does not occur with telephone surveys.

A.4.2 Telephone surveys

Telephone surveys are not dissimilar to the postal or e-mail route discussed above. The main difference of course is that they are conducted over the phone by a member of your staff or a person employed by you to complete the survey.

The three main advantages to this type of survey over postal are the speed of response, accuracy of response and control of the sample profile.

By using a telephone methodology you can ensure that you get to the right people at the appropriate time, but it is important that you target them in the right place and at the right time. For most general customer surveys, this means that calls should be made in the evening, in their home, when they are available and where they will be in a (hopefully!) relaxed atmosphere and more responsive.

The opposite of course applies if you are contacting them about a business-related product or service, then you can get them at their office during working hours and avoid possibly annoying someone relaxing at home 'after a hard day's work'.

Secondly, accuracy of response can be assured. By using trained staff to fill in the survey with the customer you can ensure that all the right questions are

Document Ref: **N-53–058RLR13**
Version: 03.01
Date: 1 October 2013
Quality Management System
Part Three – Quality Procedures
QP/12 – Customer Feedback – Version 01.00

answered and explanations given are relevant (as far as possible that is, because you will always get some people who will start a questionnaire and then get bored and just hang up half way through!). This is especially true if you are employing a research company, which will no doubt use a computerised system of recording the information called CATI (Computer Assisted Telephone Interviewing) which like e-mail ensures that all the correct questions are asked and answered. Again the data is automatically captured and analysis can begin immediately, in fact some analysis can be done '*on the fly*' during the research to give you an emerging picture. Thirdly (and this is very important to ensure your data is statistically viable), by controlling those who answer your survey you will ensure that you get the correct cross sample of customers answering the questions. This will ensure that the results you get give you the correct indicators and directions for your business. This is explored further in Section A.6 Sample profile.

A.4.3 On-street or house-to-house surveys

On-street or house-to-house surveys (often referred to as '*face-to-face*' surveys) are to all intents and purposes one and the same thing. It is just the location that changes! The most appropriate methodology will depend on the type of product or service you offer, who your customer is, and how easy it is to find these people on the street or in a specific location, town, road, estate etc. In addition, this kind of survey will be necessary if you need to show your customers something.

Whereas postal, e-mail and telephone surveys will be ideal if you have a customer base that is widely dispersed, on-street and house-to-house are more relevant if you know your customers are easy to find and/or you can be in one spot and get them as they pass you by. You will need to consider if this is the case before you go for the on-street or house-to-house option, because if you get it wrong and find yourself chasing for days to get one or two people to answer your questions, then costs will soon mount up.

One of the main advantages of on-street and house-to-house surveys is that you can generally have a longer survey. This is more true of house-to-house, when you can sit down and chat to the customer over (possibly!) a cup of tea!

As previously described, quantitative studies are a way of discovering what customers may want in the future. If you discover that they would like an additional service, revised packaging etc., then a pictorial representation of this (called a *show card*) will help customers to understand what you are suggesting and therefore help them to make a more informed decision on the possible benefits of this (a picture is worth a thousand words!).

	Document Ref: **N-53–058RLR13** Version: 03.01 Date: 1 October 2013 Quality Management System Part Three – Quality Procedures QP/12 – Customer Feedback – Version 01.00

Being face-to-face with the customer may or may not be an advantage, depending on your product or service and the relationship customers might have with it. Customers may want to tell you face-to-face, however some may be embarrassed to. Even if you employ a third-party company to complete the research for you, customers will often consider that that person represents your company. Again you should know your customer and be able to judge whether this will be an advantage or a disadvantage.

The main disadvantage about on-street and house-to-house surveys is the time and expense of carrying it out. Fieldworkers (i.e. the staff to carry out the interviewing) need to be organised and their locations agreed.

 If you are carrying out on-street interviews in shopping centres, high streets etc., permission may need to be sought from the council or centre management.

Surveys need to be sent out to fieldworkers along with all their instructions, show cards and so on. Fieldworkers then need to be given time to familiarise themselves with the survey before they go out. The fieldwork (i.e. the survey itself) is then carried out, usually over the space of a few days to ensure that a correct sample is obtained. After this, the surveys need to be posted back to the research company before analysis can begin. Again some of the larger research companies will have automated systems for collecting data which is then downloaded, but these do come with a price tag attached – and let's not forget the fieldworkers' travel and subsistence expenses!

The following flow chart and accompanying table describe a typical procedure for this process (see Figures QP12A and B).

Finally: Review the process to see where improvements can be made for future surveys.

 Note: A customer satisfaction index or ACSI (American Customer Satisfaction Index) uses data obtained from customer interviews to produce an independent measure of performance that is useful to economists, investors and potential customers. It is frequently used in North America, Sweden and Germany.

	Document Ref: **N-53–058RLR13** Version: 03.01 Date: 1 October 2013 Quality Management System Part Three – Quality Procedures QP/12 – Customer Feedback – Version 01.00

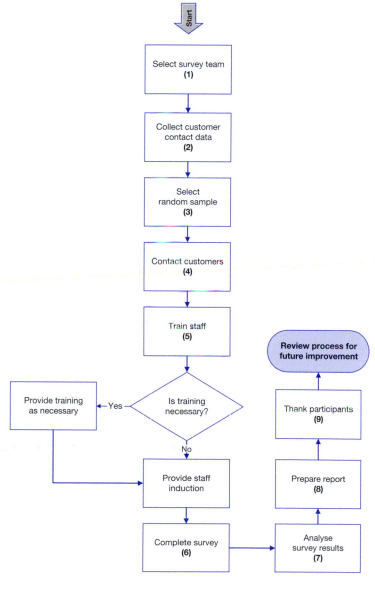

FIGURE QP12A Survey process

Document Ref: **N-53–058RLR13**
Version: 03.01
Date: 1 October 2013
Quality Management System
Part Three – Quality Procedures
QP/12 – Customer Feedback – Version 01.00

1	Select and assemble the survey team (use people who have a good telephone manner, are knowledgeable about the organisation and its business and who are capable of remaining neutral at all times) either from your own organisation or by employing a specialist research company.
2	Collect customer contact data (i.e. name, address, telephone number).
3	Select a random sample of customers for the survey (geographical as well as according to the size of the customer's business) using quotas – see Section B6 Sample Profile.
4	Contact the customers (via e-mail is probably the cheapest method) telling them about the forthcoming survey, the reasons for the survey, why they have been selected and ask for their support. This is a nice thing to do, but may not be appropriate for all types of businesses and could in some instances have a detrimental effect on the outcome of the main survey, because you could put people off from doing the survey in the first place.
5	Provide interviewer training for staff and volunteers. (Prior to beginning the telephone interviews, team members should review the role of the interviewer, explore interview scenarios, review fall back statements and role-play an interview to obtain a 'feel' for how the interview will work and review the record keeping procedures for the survey.)
6	Contact the customers and complete a Customer Satisfaction Survey for each person. (The interviewer should be as natural as possible. Do not apologise for the call; it's better to make the person feel they are contributing to something important rather than suggesting it is unimportant with an apology.)
7	Send the completed survey and call sheets to an evaluator for analysis.
8	Summarise survey results and prepare a report.
9	Consider communicating the key findings of the survey in an executive overview to your customers. This may not always be necessary or indeed appropriate.

FIGURE QP12B Survey process

Document Ref: **N-53–058RLR13**
Version: 03.01
Date: 1 October 2013
Quality Management System
Part Three – Quality Procedures
QP/12 – Customer Feedback – Version 01.00

A.4.4 Mystery shopping

Although not strictly a tool to measure customer satisfaction, mystery shopping is a revealing way to experience the reality first hand. Mystery shopping is where someone impersonates a customer on behalf of the organisation, paying close attention to product or service quality. The undercover customer's findings are often very beneficial and frequently reveal patterns about the effectiveness of the organisation's processes.

The mystery shopper can be an employee of the organisation or someone hired specifically for this purpose and should focus on the organisation's system, processes and procedures. The sort of areas that could be investigated include:

- courtesy of personnel;
- degree of knowledge;
- accuracy of information received;
- adherence to organisational policies;
- timeliness of service;
- efficiency of processes;
- conformity of the final product;
- past results.

There is no set rule to the type of questioning that can be used by a mystery shopper. Generally there will be a questionnaire of sorts, but this will be completed after the mystery shop is over as obviously writing up notes whilst in the shop would give the game away somewhat! Generally mystery shoppers will be given a 'scenario' (or story) of why they are there and this scenario will allow them to ask all the relevant questions required.

Whilst the mystery shop is normally unscripted, the data is generally captured on predefined questionnaires with some elements of free text to allow them to include any exceptional information. This is again relayed back to the research company for analysis.

Mystery shopping is an expensive but valuable tool in the quest to fully gauge the reality of the service you are offering. Expensive because a statistically robust sample must be achieved in the same way as with any other Quant study, and seasonal and regional variations also need to be considered.

> This technique is widely used in the retail industry (e.g. restaurants, hotels, mail order businesses and car dealerships) and can produce some very interesting results!

Document Ref: **N-53–058RLR13**
Version: 03.01
Date: 1 October 2013
Quality Management System
Part Three – Quality Procedures
QP/12 – Customer Feedback – Version 01.00

A.5 WRITING A QUESTIONNAIRE

There are a number of considerations that must be made when setting out to write a questionnaire.

Firstly you must be very clear what your objectives are. What do you want to find out, and what are you going to do with the information once you have it? How will you judge whether you are succeeding or failing? It sounds simple, but until you know what you want to find out, there is no point moving on.

Next create yourself a logical question plan. Start with the general and get more specific as you move through the questionnaire. It may be that you do not want your customer to know it is you asking the questions and, therefore, you will need to start with general questions about your marketplace before getting down to the specifics of your product and service later. It can help to remain anonymous and leave it to the customers to work it out. In this way they can have no preconceived ideas of how they 'should' answer the question and will respond more honestly, and not answer how they think you will want them to answer.

Types of question are vital. For the most part, you should keep to closed questions and avoid open questions. With closed questions you will ensure that all customers answer exactly the same question, but if you give 100 people an open question you will probably get 100 different answers and how will you be able to analyse that?! By all means let your customers have their say, but in a controlled way (i.e. by including an '*any other comments*' after each section of questioning).

Example of open and closed questioning:

Closed question – '*Do you agree or disagree with the following statement*' . . .

Open question – '*How do you feel about the following statement*' . . .

The length of the questionnaire is also important. There is no such thing as a survey that is too short but there is such a thing as a survey that is too long! However, is there any point in only asking one or two questions? You have, after all, a captive audience so why not ask them at least 10–12 questions?!

A survey that is too long is a waste of time from a postal point of view because many people will look at it and not even bother to start, or they may start but then give up half way through.

Whether customers are expected to answer the questionnaire on their own or with the help of a researcher, the questions should be easy to understand and logical. Avoid unnecessary use of jargon (you may understand it, but will they?).

Document Ref: **N-53–058RLR13**
Version: 03.01
Date: 1 October 2013
Quality Management System
Part Three – Quality Procedures
QP/12 – Customer Feedback – Version 01.00

A.5.1 Routing

Routing is a vital part of any quantitative survey. This allows you to have all eventualities covered. If customers say 'yes' to a question, then ask them more, if they say 'no' to a question, move them on to the next section (we've all seen it on tax returns!). Routing is very usual but it is essential to get it right. You don't want to confuse your customers and you want all the relevant people to answer all the relevant questions, not miss swathes out of important parts of the questionnaire by a previous routing error. This is why planning of the questionnaire is vital, and why starting with the general and honing into the specific is key.

A.5.2 Rating scales

For many closed questions (and in order to gauge levels of agreement to statements) rating scales are important. There will be very few questions which you will want just a yes/no answer as opposed to a lot of maybe/sometimes answers! Rating scales will allow you to capture this information. There are a number of schools of thought on the rating scales, how many levels should you allow, whether you should have an odd or an even number of scales. In general terms it will fall to you to decide what is best for your particular company, but it is most normal to see an even number of levels in a rating scale usually of 4 or more. Again this will depend on what information you expect to find out and what you will do with that incremental information. Odd numbers are generally avoided as this would allow people to choose the middle number to sit on the fence. Below is an example of a rating scale question and how you could use the information.

> Question – *On a scale of 1–10 (where 10 = agree completely and 1 = disagree completely) would you agree that the service that company X offers is better than the competition?*

Say you asked 10 people this question, you may get the following data:

> *1 person said '1' – disagree completely;*
>
> *3 people said '4';*
>
> *1 person said '7';*
>
> *4 people said '8';*
>
> *1 person said '10'.*

Document Ref: **N-53–058RLR13**
Version: 03.01
Date: 1 October 2013
Quality Management System
Part Three – Quality Procedures
QP/12 – Customer Feedback – Version 01.00

That would mean that 60% of people agreed to some degree with the question, of that number, 50% agreed to some degree (e.g. they rated it 7–9), and 10% of people categorically agreed, whilst 40% disagreed to some degree and 10% categorically disagreed.

This information is giving you degrees of agreement. If you did not have the scale how would those who answered '4' have answered, if they could only choose to agree or disagree? This could have skewed your data all of a sudden and you would have had 40% disagreeing with your statement, instead of only 10% strongly opposed, with 30% wavering.

A.6 SAMPLE PROFILE

Sample profiles are a complex issue and are only described here in the briefest and most broad brushstroke of ways. Sampling, at its most complex, is a highly sophisticated process of statistics and demographic profiling. However there are some basics that we should look at.

Essentially the sample profile is a definition of your customer base. The sample should be a direct representation of the breakdown of your customer base, in all aspects (for example to reflect the split of male to female, old to young, home-owners to those who rent properties etc.). When national polls are undertaken they don't ask every member of the population, but a representative sample of that population.

Although sample profiles should cover all elements of your customer base don't try to get too sophisticated with it – stick to exploring the views of the majority rather than the minority. When establishing the profile you will want to set broad 'quotas' for each of your main profile groups – for example you may need to achieve 70% male and 30% female respondents to reflect your customer base.

> **Note:** Some quantitative methodologies (such as postal surveys) will not allow you to control the quota and you should consider whether this will pose a problem for you. If the majority of your customer base is broadly the same, then this will not be an issue at all. If, on the other hand, you have a wide diversity in your customer base then you need to be able to control the sample.

Whilst undertaking your research, the sample breakdown should be monitored to ensure you are covering all of the vital groups and so that a plan of action can be put in place if you find you are missing a vital group at this stage – it is difficult to do this later on.

	Document Ref: **N-53–058RLR13** Version: 03.01 Date: 1 October 2013 Quality Management System Part Three – Quality Procedures QP/12 – Customer Feedback – Version 01.00

A.7 AREAS SUITABLE FOR ANALYSIS

The possibilities for analysing customer satisfaction can vary from one organisation to another but probably the three most important areas are:

Type of analysis	Reason	Type of data
Conformance to customer requirements	Targets should be established for product conformity as a measure of achievement. Data needs to be collected and analysed for all products in order to determine whether these objectives are being achieved.	Data generated whilst monitoring and measuring the characteristics of a product as well as data generated during design, purchasing, production, installation and operation, and data collected from customer feedback.
Product and process characteristics	Opportunities for preventive action may arise when the trend in a series of measured values indicates deterioration in performance and if the deterioration were allowed to continue, non-conformity would result.	Variation in product such as characteristics dimensions, voltage, power output and strength.
Supplier data	Information relating to suppliers concerning their performance regarding product and service quality, delivery and cost.	Suppliers are a key contributor to the performance of an organisation and therefore information on the performance of suppliers is necessary to determine the adequacy, suitability and effectiveness of the management system.

A.8 ANALYSIS OF CUSTOMER SATISFACTION DATA

Customer satisfaction is not something one can monitor directly by simply installing a sensor. One has first to collect the data and then analyse it in order to draw conclusions, to identify the key areas where action is necessary and where major opportunities for improvement are indicated. This data can be collected from a number of sources (see table below) and the results can then be used as the basis

	Document Ref: **N-53–058RLR13**
	Version: 03.01
	Date: 1 October 2013
	Quality Management System
	Part Three – Quality Procedures
	QP/12 – Customer Feedback – Version 01.00

for business and process development plans for current and future products and services.

Type	How collected	Result
Repeat orders	From the order process.	Whilst the number of repeat orders is not necessarily a measure of whether a customer is completely satisfied, it does show loyalty and provides useful data when analysing customer satisfaction.
Competition	This data is more subjective and results from market research.	Monitoring the workload of competitors is an indicator of your success or failure.
Referrals	From sales personnel during the transaction or later on follow-up calls.	When you obtain a new customer you should try to find out why they chose your organisation in preference to others. It could be that one of your existing customers referred them to you, which is a sign of that customer's satisfaction.
Demand	From sales trends.	Monitoring the actual demand for your products and services relative to the predicted demand is also an indicator of success or failure to satisfy customers.
Effects of product transition	From sales trends following new product launch.	When you market a new product or service, it is important to gauge whether you still retain your existing customers – or do they go elsewhere?
Surveys	From survey reports.	A customer satisfaction survey is one way of gathering this vital information and there are two main types of surveys that can be used, the impersonal form and the personal form.
Focus meetings	From the meeting.	A focus meeting is another form of personal reports survey where a meeting is arranged between people from within the customer's organisation and people internal to your own organisation (e.g. Marketing, Purchasing, Quality Assurance, Manufacturing departments, etc.).

	Document Ref: **N-53–058RLR13**
	Version: 03.01
	Date: 1 October 2013
	Quality Management System
	Part Three – Quality Procedures
	QP/12 – Customer Feedback – Version 01.00

Type	How collected	Result
Complaints	From complaints recorded by customers or by staff on speaking with customers.	Complaints relating to fitness for purpose, delivery deadlines, product information, conditions of sale, use of personal data, after-sales service and guarantees are an important method for capturing customer feedback (see note below).
Compliments	From written compliments sent in by customers or by staff speaking with customers.	Compliments can vary from a casual remark during a conversation to something included in correspondence. These are usually unsolicited on remarks and a sure sign of customer satisfaction.

When analysing your customer satisfaction data you can compare your data with industry norms to evaluate whether your company is performing above or below the norm for your sector. This is achieved through a customer satisfaction index or ACSI (American Customer Satisfaction Index) which uses data obtained from customer interviews to produce an independent measure of performance that is useful to economists, investors and potential customers.

Note: ISO 10002 (Quality Management, Customer Satisfaction – Guidelines for complaints handling) is part of a forthcoming trio of international best practice codes of conduct (the others being ISO 10001 for complaints handling and ISO 10003 for an external customer disputes resolution system). This standard provides guidelines for handling complaints in a way that will not only benefit the organisation but also the unhappy customer. In addition to meeting the requirements of ISO 9001:2008, ISO 10002 is also capable of being used as a stand-alone process in support of other quality management and customer satisfaction tools such as Customer Relation Management, Six Sigma and the EFQM Models.

A.9 OTHER CONSIDERATIONS

- Make it easy for your customers to complain – customers who are dissatisfied tell 10 times as many people about it as those who are happy with your service.
- Respond to complaints quickly and courteously – a speedy response can add 25% to customer loyalty.
- Resolve complaints on the first contact – reduce the cost of unnecessary additional contacts.

Document Ref: **N-53–058RLR13**
Version: 03.01
Date: 1 October 2013
Quality Management System
Part Three – Quality Procedures
QP/12 – Customer Feedback – Version 01.00

- Use your computers to develop a database of complaints – an electronically compiled customer complaint system enables an organisation to better align its services and products to meet customer expectations.
- Recruit and hire well motivated, front-line employees to deal with customer complaints – it is important that all personnel who come into contact with customers should have a non-intrusive method for conveying to the customer that the complaint is appreciated and will be passed on to the staff involved.
- Be sure to keep your customers informed about any change in procedure that you have introduced because of the survey.
- Document and follow up on all the comments you receive. If you have to change a procedure, then you need to ensure that everyone involved in that procedure is aware of the changes.
- Advertise the fact that you are doing things differently and in a more qualitative manner.
- Above all the survey process needs to be free from bias, prejudice and political influence.

Document Ref: **N-53–059RLR13**
Version: 03.01
Date: 1 October 2013
Quality Management System
Part Three – Quality Procedures
QP/13 – Customer Awareness and Training – Version 01.00

QP/13 – Customer Awareness and Training

CONTENTS

13.1 Scope 1
13.2 Responsibilities 2
    13.2.1 Managing Director. 2
    13.2.2 Section Managers 2
    13.2.3 Quality Manager. 3
13.3 Definitions 3
13.4 Process. 3
    13.4.1 Identification of training needs 3
    13.4.2 Training review. 4
    13.4.3 Planning of training requirements 4
    13.4.4 Implementation of training requirements 4
13.5 Training of new personnel. 4
13.6 Training of subcontractors and consultants 5
13.7 Quality training 5
13.8 Training courses and records 5

13.1 SCOPE

In compliance with ISO 9001:2008, one of the requirements of our QMS is to ensure that all NAFAAD personnel are provided with training that will assist them in acquiring the skills and knowledge to perform their duties effectively, to comply with NAFAAD Quality (Environmental and Safety) Management Systems and to ensure that their part in satisfying customer requests and requirements are fully and professionally met.

Document Ref: **N-53–059RLR13**
Version: 03.01
Date: 1 October 2013
Quality Management System
Part Three – Quality Procedures
QP/13 – Customer Awareness and Training – Version 01.00

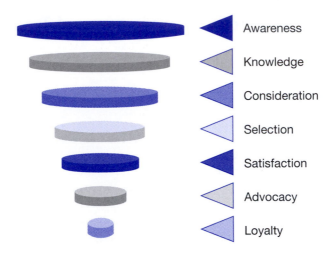

FIGURE QP13.1 Requirements for customer awareness and training within NAFAAD

13.2 RESPONSIBILITIES

13.2.1 Managing Director

The Managing Director identifies the need for staff training to handle the expected workload where specialist techniques or items (e.g. software, customers supplied equipment, test equipment etc.) are involved.

The Managing Director is responsible for ensuring that appropriate training is carried out so as to ensure that all staff involved are aware of the requirements, rules and procedures to which they are to conform and against which they will be audited.

13.2.2 Section Managers

Section Managers are responsible for ensuring that project tasks and activities are **only** assigned to staff qualified for that particular task or activity. This is on the basis of appropriate education, training and experience, in relation to staffing levels and NAFAAD's current recruitment policy.

	Document Ref: **N-53–059RLR13**
	Version: 03.01
	Date: 1 October 2013
	Quality Management System
	Part Three – Quality Procedures
	QP/13 – Customer Awareness and Training – Version 01.00

13.2.3 Quality Manager

The Quality Manager is responsible for providing NAFAAD QMS induction and refresher training courses.

13.3 DEFINITIONS

Nil.

13.4 PROCESS

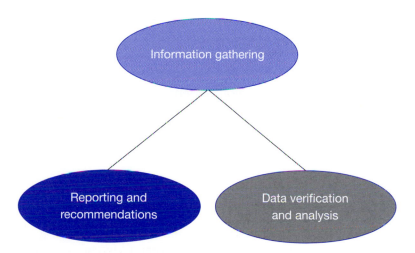

FIGURE QP13.2 Process

13.4.1 Identification of training needs

A training review may be carried out at any time, as necessitated by any of the following:

- appointment of new personnel;
- new equipment or working practices;
- change of duties or responsibilities;
- as a result of an audit or management review.

Document Ref: **N-53–059RLR13**
Version: 03.01
Date: 1 October 2013
Quality Management System
Part Three – Quality Procedures
QP/13 – Customer Awareness and Training – Version 01.00

13.4.2 Training review

The Section Manager or other Manager undertaking the review shall, with the post-holder:

- review training completed since the previous review;
- review and reschedule, where necessary, uncompleted training since the previous review;
- review the training needs of individual positions;
- review and identify current training requirements and ensure that the quality and safety requirements are fully covered;
- review and identify career development (where appropriate);
- ensure that the results of the review are recorded on the appropriate forms and forwarded to the Quality Manager.

13.4.3 Planning of training requirements

The Managing Director (with the assistance of the Company Secretary and the Quality Manager) shall budget and plan the training programme for all personnel under his responsibility. This shall also include any on-the-job training requirements.

13.4.4 Implementation of training requirements

The Manager (e.g. Section Manager) responsible for planning training requirements may either arrange training locally or subcontract formal external courses via the Company Secretary.

13.5 TRAINING OF NEW PERSONNEL

The Company Secretary shall ensure that all new personnel receive a local introduction briefing as detailed in the appropriate administration procedure (currently being prepared).

The Quality Manager is responsible for the initial training of all new personnel in the requirements of the NAFAAD QMS – particularly with regard to Environmental and Health & Safety aspects of working within and for NAFAAD.

Document Ref: **N-53–059RLR13**
Version: 03.01
Date: 1 October 2013
Quality Management System
Part Three – Quality Procedures
QP/13 – Customer Awareness and Training – Version 01.00

13.6 TRAINING OF SUBCONTRACTORS AND CONSULTANTS

The Manager (e.g. Section Manager) employing subcontractors or consultants is responsible for either ensuring that they are already fully competent or that they can be trained to meet the contracted specification. The Manager is also responsible for ensuring that all contracted personnel are made aware and fully understand the local arrangements for both quality and safety.

13.7 QUALITY TRAINING

The Quality Manager, as well as being responsible for providing NAFAAD QMS induction courses, shall also run a series of refresher training courses for all personnel – including Top Management.

13.8 TRAINING COURSES AND RECORDS

If external training is required then it shall only be obtained from established and recognised sources from which documented course content is available.

The appropriate Section Manager shall retain records of all training. This shall include details of attendance, achievements, course content, scope, personnel who provided the training and those who received it.

Document Ref: **N-53–060RLR13**
Version: 03.01
Date: 1 October 2013
Quality Management System
Part Three – Quality Procedures
QP/14 – Change Control – Version 01.00

QP/14 – Change Control

CONTENTS

14.1 Scope 1

14.2 Responsibilities 1

     14.2.1 Managing Director...................................... 1

14.3 Definitions 1

14.4 Procedure 2

14.5 Impact assessment... 3

Annex A – Change Proposal Form...................................... 5

Annex B – Impact Assessment Form 6

14.1 SCOPE

When a contract document reaches the stage where the information that it contains is being used (or relied on) by other sections, it is imperative that any proposed changes to the original document are not completed without the knowledge of all concerned.

In order to prevent this sort of situation occurring, a decision will be made (by the Managing Director, endorsed by the Section Managers) that at a particular stage **no** further changes, alterations, modifications, insertions or deletions will be made without the Change Control procedure described below being adopted.

QP/14 details the requirements for Change Control within NAFAAD and is a company requirement.

14.2 RESPONSIBILITIES

14.2.1 Managing Director

The Managing Director has overall responsibility for this procedure.

14.3 DEFINITIONS

Nil.

Document Ref: **N-53–060RLR13**
Version: 03.01
Date: 1 October 2013
Quality Management System
Part Three – Quality Procedures
QP/14 – Change Control – Version 01.00

14.4 PROCEDURE

All changes to NAFAAD documents, procedures and specifications are, in principle, subject to a formal Change Control procedure.

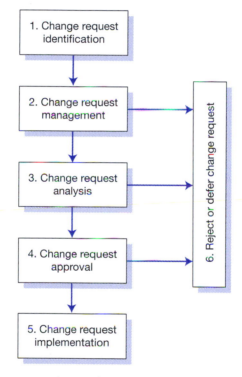

FIGURE QP14.1 Change control procedure

Author's Hint

Manufacturers will need to carefully customise parts of this particular procedure so as to cover their design, manufacturing and installation etc. practices.

Document Ref: **N-53–060RLR13**
Version: 03.01
Date: 1 October 2013
Quality Management System
Part Three – Quality Procedures
QP/14 – Change Control – Version 01.00

Changes that could fundamentally influence the scope, targets, organisation, budget, overall work breakdown structure and time schedules (in addition to changes to approved NAFAAD quality documents and other official documents), will have to be agreed by the Section Managers and approved by the Managing Director.

Proposals for changes shall be submitted to the Managing Director, in writing, using the Change Proposal Form shown at Annex A (the template for this form is available from the server).

The Managing Director will ask the Company Secretary to distribute the proposals for changes to all Section Managers for discussion. The proposal for change will have to be distributed and received by all Section Managers at least four weeks prior to the next Section Managers' meeting.

Depending on the importance and impact of the proposed change(s) the Managing Director can decide to discuss the proposal in a scheduled Section Managers' meeting or call a special meeting.

A description of the types of impact and relevant approvals are listed in Table QP14.1.

1.5 IMPACT ASSESSMENT

Depending on the classification of the proposed change, an 'impact assessment' may be required. The change classification (and, therefore, the need for an impact assessment) will ultimately have to be sanctioned by the Managing Director. If the time, resources and budget required for an impact assessment are expected to be significant, formal approval by the Managing Director for carrying out this assessment is required. An example of an Impact Assessment Form is included at Annex B (the template for this form is available from the server).

When the Section Managers have agreed to the proposed change it will be submitted to the Managing Director for final approval.

The Managing Director shall be responsible for implementing approved changes and shall make sure that all aspects which are affected by these changes are taken into consideration.

The Company Secretary shall be responsible for:

- incorporating the approved changes into existing technical documents;
- distributing these documents to the appropriate people;
- incorporating the approved changes into existing non-technical documents.

Document Ref: **N-53–060RLR13**
Version: 03.01
Date: 1 October 2013
Quality Management System
Part Three – Quality Procedures
QP/14 – Change Control – Version 01.00

TABLE QP14.1 Types of impact and relevant approvals

Change classification	Impact assessment	Final approval by
(A) Minor impact: No other section or area affected No change in man days, time schedule and costs	No	Managing Director on advice from the Section Managers
(B) Medium impact: At least one other section or area affected No (or little) change in man days, time schedule and costs	To be decided by the Managing Director	Section Managers' meeting
(C) Major impact: More than one other section or area affected Significant change in man days, time schedule and costs	Yes	Management Review Board Meeting

	Document Ref: **N-53–060RLR13** Version: 03.01 Date: 1 October 2013 Quality Management System Part Three – Quality Procedures QP/14 – Change Control – Version 01.00

Annex A –
Change Proposal Form

Originator:		Section:	
File ref.:		Date:		Serial No.:	

Reason for and description of change:	
Area(s) affected:	
Product(s) affected:	
Classification:	A/B/C	Impact assessment required?	Yes/No
Impact assessment summary: (including man days, schedules, costs and risks)	
	Full impact assessment attached:		Yes/No

Authorisation/ Approval	Function	Name	Date	Signature
Change preparation				
Classification approval	Managing Director			
Recommendation (submit/reject)	Section Manager			
Approval	Managing Director			

Other points:	

Document Ref: **N-53–060RLR13**
Version: 03.01
Date: 1 October 2013
Quality Management System
Part Three – Quality Procedures
QP/14 – Change Control – Version 01.00

Annex B –
Impact Assessment Form

Originator:		Change Proposal Serial No.:	

Description of proposed change:	
Impact (upon time, resources, cost, quality, etc.)	
Estimated cost of Implementation of change:	
Benefits:	
Recommendation:	Accept/Reject/Change Proposal
Comments:	

Signed:		Name:		Date:	

Document Ref: **N-53–061RLR13**
Version: 03.01
Date: 1 October 2013
Quality Management System
Part Three – Quality Procedures
QP/15 – Meetings and Reports – Version 01.00

QP/15 – Meetings and Reports

CONTENTS

15.1 Scope 1
15.2 Responsibilities 1
    15.2.1 Managing Director 1
    15.2.2 Quality Manager 2
15.3 Definitions 2
15.4 Procedure 2
    15.4.1 Management Review Board meetings 2
    15.4.2 Section Managers' meetings 2
15.5 Discussion documents 2
15.6 Agenda of meetings 3
15.7 Guidelines for meetings 3
15.8 Minutes 3
15.9 Reporting 4
    15.9.1 Company Status Report 4
    15.9.2 Financial reporting 4

15.1 SCOPE

QP/15 describes how Management Review Board and Section Manager meetings are convened, the proposed agenda and how minutes should be produced.

QP/15 also lays down the guidelines for the reporting procedure adopted by NAFAAD.

15.2 RESPONSIBILITIES

15.2.1 Managing Director

The Managing Director shall hold regular Section Manager meetings to discuss the methods and programme to be adopted for the results, reports or other documents that have to be published.

Document Ref: **N-53–061RLR13**
Version: 03.01
Date: 1 October 2013
Quality Management System
Part Three – Quality Procedures
QP/15 – Meetings and Reports – Version 01.00

15.2.2 Quality Manager

Every six months the Quality Manager is responsible for compiling and writing a Company Status Report.

15.3 DEFINITIONS

Nil.

15.4 PROCEDURE

15.4.1 Management Review Board meetings

Management Review Board meetings shall normally take place twice a year in order to discuss important issues and to approve final documents. The Managing Director may convene additional meetings if required.

15.4.2 Section Managers' meetings

The Managing Director shall hold regular Section Managers' meetings to discuss the methods and programme to be adopted for the results, reports or other documents that have to be published. The preparation and detailed editing of reports and technical documents shall be carried out by section working groups or by small editing groups set up for that purpose.

Normally subcontractors and/or consultants will only be invited to attend these meetings when their presence is deemed necessary by the Managing Director.

15.5 DISCUSSION DOCUMENTS

The dates set for these meetings should allow sufficient time for the documents being discussed to be distributed far enough in advance of the meeting so as to enable members to consider them beforehand. In practice this means **not** later than two weeks prior to the meeting.

	Document Ref: **N-53–061RLR13**
	Version: 03.01
	Date: 1 October 2013
	Quality Management System
	Part Three – Quality Procedures
	QP/15 – Meetings and Reports – Version 01.00

15.6 AGENDA OF MEETINGS

In addition to those items covering technical aspects/problems, the agenda shall be established by the Company Secretary and the Section Managers (in agreement with the Managing Director) and shall contain the following points:

- approval of the minutes of the previous meeting;
- matters arising from the minutes of the last meeting;
- status report(s) (verbal or written);
- budget and costs;
- date by which the work is to be completed;
- decision list and action list;
- place and date of the next meeting.

15.7 GUIDELINES FOR MEETINGS

It is to be expected that a frank and objective atmosphere should prevail at all NAFAAD Management Review Board and Section Managers' meetings, as well as with a mutual willingness to overcome problems so as to arrive, whenever possible, at a valid agreed solution.

The Chair of the meeting shall direct the discussions towards a rapid solution of the problem raised without, however, sacrificing the liberty to exchange views, experience and ideas amongst the participants.

15.8 MINUTES

The minutes of the Management Review Board and Section Managers' meetings shall be concise and only contain the essential points, the conclusions of the discussions and distribution of tasks between the members (i.e. the Action List).

The minutes shall, special cases excepted, normally only be sent to the Managing Director, the participants of the meeting and the Quality Manager. The minutes shall always be distributed within one week following the actual meeting.

Document Ref: **N-53–061RLR13**
Version: 03.01
Date: 1 October 2013
Quality Management System
Part Three – Quality Procedures
QP/15 – Meetings and Reports – Version 01.00

15.9 REPORTING

15.9.1 Company Status Report

Every six months a Company Status Report shall be compiled and written by the Quality Manager. This report will then be presented at the next Management Review Board meeting.

Following approval by the Managing Director, the Company Status Report will then be distributed to the members of the Management Review Board. These reports will contain an update of:

- overall progress;
- technical status;
- contractual status;
- financial status;
- liaison with the railways;
- liaison with industry;
- outstanding actions.

15.9.2 FINANCIAL REPORTING

See QP/11 Purchasing.

NAFAAD Consultancy Ltd

Quality Management System

Part 4 – Work Instructions

This Quality Manual has been issued on the authority of the Managing Director of NAFAAD Consultancy Ltd for the use of all staff, subcontractors, clients and/or regulatory bodies to whom NAFAAD Consultancy Ltd may be required to provide such information to.

Approved	
	Date: 1 October 2013
Ray Rekcirt Managing Director NAFAAD Consultancy Ltd	

© 2013 by NAFAAD Consultancy Ltd, all rights reserved.

Copyright subsists in all NAFAAD Consultancy Ltd deliverables including magnetic, optical and/or any other soft copy of these deliverables. This document may not be reproduced, in full or in part, without written permission.

	Document Ref: **N-54–062RLR13**
	Version: 03.01
	Date: 1 October 2013
	Quality Management System
	Part Four – Work Instructions
	Version 01.00

DOCUMENT CONTROL SHEET

Title	This version	Date
NAFAAD Consultancy Ltd		
Part 4	File Number	No of Pages
Work Instructions	**N-54–062RLR13**	**22**

ABSTRACT

The NAFAAD Associates Ltd Quality Management System is divided into four parts.

This document is Part 4 and describes the Work Instructions that have been developed to implement NAFAAD Associates Ltd's Quality Management System.

The Work Instructions designed to meet these processes are contained in Part 4.

Name	Function	Level
	Quality Manager	Prepare
	Managing Director	Agree
	Managing Director	Approve

ATTACHMENTS

Attachments	Description

Document Ref: **N-54–062RLR13**
Version: 03.01
Date: 1 October 2013
Quality Management System
Part Four – Work Instructions
Version 01.00

QMS REVISION HISTORY

No.	Chapter	Amendment details	Date
01.00	All	First published version in accordance with ISO 9001:1994	28.06.93
01.01	3	Inclusion of new chapter for customer satisfaction	05.04.94
01.02	4.2.3	Procedure for the control of documents changed	23.12.95
01.03	All	Minor editorial revisions of all sections and annexes	30.07.96
02.00	All	Second published version to conform to ISO 9001:2000	31.12.00
02.01	5	Management responsibility procedure updated to cover new (i.e. Fuels) Division	01.01.02
02.02	All	Minor editorial changes following three years' experience of ISO 9001:2000	01.01.05
03.00	All	Major revision following publication of ISO 9001:2008	01.11.09
03.01	All	Minor editorial changes following five years' experience of ISO 9001:2008 plus the addition of a new WI for the control of e-mails	01.10.13

ISO 9001:2008 for Small Businesses

CONTENTS

Documentation 451
Procedure 452
1   WI/1 – Travel and hotel arrangements 454
     1.1   Scope 454
     1.2   Procedure 454
Annex A – Travel form. 455

2   WI/2 – Time sheets and Expense sheets 456
     2.1   Scope and objectives 456
     2.2   Time and expense sheets. 456
     2.3   Time sheets 456
     2.4   Expense sheets 457
     2.5   Time and Expense Reports. 457

Annex A – Time Sheet 458
Annex B – Expense Sheet. 459
Annex C – Time and Expense Report 460

3   WI/3 – Subcontractors' Invoices 461
     3.1   Scope 461
     3.2   Approval of invoices 461
     3.3   Payment of invoices. 461
     3.4   Invoice records. 461

4   WI/4 – CD-ROM Distribution 462
     4.1   Scope 462
     4.2   Procedure 462
     4.2.1   Distribution list 462
     4.2.2   Updating previous distributions 462
     4.2.3   Price guidelines. 463
     4.2.4   CD type 463
     4.2.5   CD Labelling. 463
     4.2.6   Plastic case – front. 464
     4.2.7   Plastic case – back 464
     4.2.8   Plastic case – spine. 464
     4.2.9   Internal matter 464
     4.2.10 Draft deliverables. 464
     4.2.11 Approved deliverables. 465

Document Ref: **N-54–062RLR13**
Version: 03.01
Date: 1 October 2013
Quality Management System
Part Four – Work Instructions
Version 01.00

5   WI/5 – Procedure for the control of NAFAAD e-mails 466
         5.1   Scope 466
         5.2   Field of application 466
         5.3   Procedure 467
         5.3.1   The Author 467
         5.3.2   The Receiver 467
         5.4   Archiving Process 468
         5.4.1   Selection of e-mails 468
         5.4.2   Archive mail box 468
         5.5   Duties of the Company Secretary 468

DOCUMENTATION

NAFAAD Associates Ltd (NAFAAD) has four levels of documentation within our Quality Management System (QMS) which is structured as shown in the table below.

This document is Part 4 and describes the Work Instructions that have been developed to implement NAFAAD's QMS.

WIs describe how to perform specific operations and are produced for all of the relevant activities of NAFAAD so as to ensure that the whole company can work to the same format.

TABLE 6.4.1 NAFAAD Associates Ltd's Quality System – documentation

Part 1	Quality Manual	The main policy document that establishes NAFAAD's QMS and how it meets the requirements of ISO 9001:2008.
Part 2	Quality Processes	The Core Business Process plus the primary and secondary Supporting Processes that describe the activities required to implement the QMS and to meet the policy requirements made in the Quality Manual.
Part 3	Quality Procedures	A description of the method by which quality system activities are managed.
Part 4	**Work Instructions**	**A description of how a specific task is carried out.**

WIs describe how individual tasks and activities are to be carried out. They describe, in detail, what is to be done, who should do it and when it has to be completed. They can, for example, cover simple issues such as making travel and hotel arrangements to more complex issues such as the structure of NAFAAD reports.

	Document Ref: **N-54–062RLR13**
	Version: 03.01
	Date: 1 October 2013
	Quality Management System
	Part Four – Work Instructions
	Version 01.00

They are produced for all of NAFAAD's relevant activities so as to ensure that the whole company can work to the same format.

> **Author's Hint**
>
> As previously explained, Work Instructions (WIs) are used to explain how a procedure is implemented.
>
> There is no restriction on the number of WIs an organisation writes and it is probably best to go by the maxim that if you have to constantly explain a certain procedure – then it is time you wrote a WI!
>
> I have provided a few examples in this section to give you an idea of what is required.

TABLE 6.4.2 Work Instructions

WI No.	Work Instruction Title
WI/1	Travel and Hotel Arrangements
WI/2	Timesheets and Expense Sheets
WI/3	Subcontractors' Invoices
WI/4	CD-ROM Distribution
WI/5	Procedure for the control of NAFAAD e-mails

PROCEDURE

The approval procedure for all WIs is as follows:

1. The Quality Manager evaluates the requirement for a new WI, researches all available information (e.g. existing work procedures, work practices, standards etc.) and produces an '*Initial Background Draft*'. This is then issued, for comment, to selected NAFAAD staff who are directly involved in the WI.
2. The Quality Manager evaluates comments received; co-ordinates all the necessary alterations, amendments, proposed modifications etc.; and produces a Draft to the Managing Director for comment.
3. Upon approval (or after modification) by the Managing Director, the WI is then issued as official NAFAAD policy.

Document Ref: **N-54-062RLR13**
Version: 03.01
Date: 1 October 2013
Quality Management System
Part Four – Work Instructions
Version 01.00

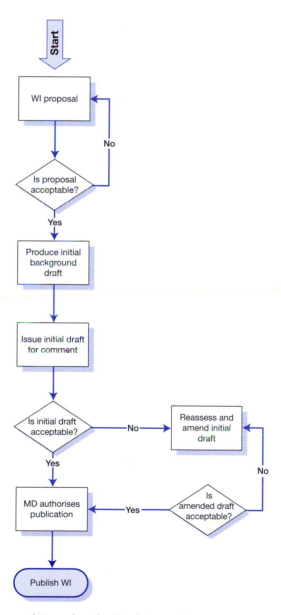

FIGURE 6.4.1 Approval Procedure for Work Instructions

	Document Ref: **N-54–063RLR13** Version: 03.01 Date: 1 October 2013 Quality Management System Part Four – Work Instructions WI/1 – Travel and Hotel Arrangements Version 01.00

WI/1 – Travel and hotel arrangements

1.1 SCOPE

This procedure defines the actions to be taken for ensuring the timely and efficient handling of all travel requests.

1.2 PROCEDURE

When NAFAAD staff are required to travel away from their normal place of work for meetings etc. they shall complete a Travel Form (see W1/1 Annex A), specifying the:

- name of the traveller;
- reason for the meeting(s);
- budget(s) to which the costs must be charged;
- start and end dates of the meeting(s);
- where the meeting is taking place;
- predicted departure and arrival times;
- hotel reservation and travel tickets, if required.

The Travel Form (template available from the server) will be signed by the initiator and an information copy sent to the Company Secretary.

If hotel reservations and travel tickets are required, an information copy shall also be sent to the Company Secretary, who will make the appropriate arrangements.

After the staff member has returned from the journey he/she will add the actual data to the Travel Form, sign it and then submit it to the Company Secretary for reimbursement of expenses.

An allowance for travel expenses will be given on the basis of a lump sum per absence of (or fractions of) 24 hours, as determined by the departure and in conformance with the current, published, NAFAAD rates.

Document Ref: **N-54–063RLR13**
Version: 03.01
Date: 1 October 2013
Quality Management System
Part Four – Work Instructions
WI/1 – Travel and Hotel Arrangements
Version 01.00

WI/1 Annex A – Travel form

Name:	
Reason for travel:	
Reservations to be made by NAFAAD?	Yes/No

Meeting information

Start date	End date	Where	Client to be billed

Travel Information

		Predicted		Actual	
		Date	Time	Date	Time
From					
To					
From					
To					

Signed: (Initiator)		**Name:**		**Date:**	
Signed: (Company Secretary)		**Name:**		**Date:**	

Document Ref: **N-54–064RLR13**
Version: 03.01
Date: 1 October 2013
Quality Management System
Part Four – Work Instructions
WI/2 – Time Sheets and Expense Sheets
Version 01.00

WI/2 – Time Sheets and Expense Sheets

2.1 SCOPE AND OBJECTIVES

To enable Section Managers to properly account for the hours spent by NAFAAD staff (including Management), it is necessary for this information to be freely available to them.

WI/2 describes the procedure for keeping track of all man-hours spent and shall be used by all NAFAAD staff.

2.2 TIME AND EXPENSE SHEETS

The purpose of the time and expense sheets (see WI/2 Annexes A and B) is to indicate the actual time spent on company and contract work as well as recording the actual travel cost (i.e. transport charges, meals, hotel and other authorised expenditure), incurred in connection with company and contract work.

During the agreement/contract period subcontractors and consultants shall (having first obtained the signature of the Section Manager concerned) send their time and expense sheets to the Company Secretary on the last day of each month.

The Company Secretary shall check the consistency of these reports **before** submitting them to the Managing Director for approval.

 Note: This WI should be read in conjunction with QP/11 – Purchasing.

2.3 TIME SHEETS

The time sheet shall contain the following information:

- actual office hours (hours or days, depending on what is stated in the agreement or contract);
- travel time (for official NAFAAD business);
- productive travel time (normally 50% of travel time).

The Company Secretary shall compare the time sheets with the budget and adjust the forecast when required.

Document Ref: **N-54–064RLR13**
Version: 03.01
Date: 1 October 2013
Quality Management System
Part Four – Work Instructions
WI/2 – Time Sheets and Expense Sheets
Version 01.00

2.4 EXPENSE SHEETS

Travel costs (i.e. transport charges, meals, hotel, telephone charges and other authorised expenditure) may be charged to the company in accordance with the agreement/contract.

All costs shall be in the same currency as per the agreement/contract unless otherwise stipulated and/or agreed.

The Company Secretary shall compare the expense sheets with the budget and adjust the forecast when required.

The Company Secretary shall check and sign the expense sheets if he agrees with the contents. The expense sheets will then require approval by the Managing Director.

Personal expenditure incurred by a subcontractor/consultant is considered to be the responsibility of the subcontractor's/consultant's parent organisation. They are, therefore, responsible for reimbursing the subcontractor/consultant directly.

2.5 TIME AND EXPENSE REPORTS

On a monthly basis, NAFAAD staff shall consolidate the details contained in the Time and Expense sheets into a monthly Time and Expense Report (see WI/2 Annex C).

	Document Ref: **N-54–064RLR13**
	Version: 03.01
	Date: 1 October 2013
	Quality Management System
	Part Four – Work Instructions
	WI/2 – Time Sheets and Expense Sheets
	Version 01.00

WI/2 Annex A – Time Sheet

TIME SHEET

Name:		
Month:		Year:

Day	Actual office hours	Travel time	Productive travel time	Total productive hours
1				
2				
3				
4				
5				
6				
7				
8				
9				
10				
11				
12				
13				
14				
15				
16				
17				
18				
19				
20				
21				
22				
23				
24				
25				
26				
27				
28				
29				
30				
31				

Form NAFAAD-WI/2–1-01.00

	Document Ref: **N-54–064RLR13**
	Version: 03.01
	Date: 1 October 2013
	Quality Management System
	Part Four – Work Instructions
	WI/2 – Time Sheets and Expense Sheets
	Version 01.00

WI/2 Annex B – Expense Sheet

Name:	
Month:	Year:

Week No	(1)						TOTALS
Week ending	(2)						
Air fares	(3)						(10)
Tube & train fares	(3)						(10)
Coach fares	(3)						(10)
Taxi fares	(3)						(10)
Hotel	(4)						(10)
Meals	(5)						(10)
Entertainment	(6)						(10)
Telephone	(7)						(10)
Other expenses	(8)						(10)
TOTALS	(9)						(11)

Signed:		Name:		Date:	
Approved:		Name:		Date:	

Document Ref: **N-54–064RLR13**
Version: 03.01
Date: 1 October 2013
Quality Management System
Part Four – Work Instructions
WI/2 – Time Sheets and Expense Sheets
Version 01.00

WI/2 Annex C – Time and Expense Report

Name	Month:	Year:																
		Time Card	Week ending	Subject	Days spent	Location	Expenses	Travel Expenses Train/Air Fares	Hotel	Taxi	Meals	Other expenses	Totals					End total:
							Allowance:											
			Totals:				Totals:											

Form NAFAAD-WI/2–1-03.00

Document Ref: **N-54–065RLR13**
Version: 03.01
Date: 1 October 2013
Quality Management System
Part Four – Work Instructions
WI/3 – Subcontractors' Invoices
Version 01.00

WI/3 – Subcontractors' Invoices

3.1 SCOPE

WI/3 covers the approval procedure and payment for invoices from subcontractors.

3.2 APPROVAL OF INVOICES

Invoices from subcontractors shall be sent directly to the Company Secretary who shall:

- stamp the invoice and fill in the date and data as appropriate;
- keep a copy of the invoice;
- send the stamped original to the Section Manager for agreement against the planned work achievement/payment schedule as indicated in the contract.

3.3 PAYMENT OF INVOICES

All invoices submitted for approval must be accompanied by a copy of the approved Subcontract Approval Form.

Invoices shall be paid within one month of receipt of the invoice or of the work being completed, whichever is the latest.

3.4 INVOICE RECORDS

The Company Secretary shall keep records of the invoices received and their subsequent payment.

Document Ref: **N-54–066RLR13**
Version: 03.01
Date: 1 October 2013
Quality Management System
Part Four – Work Instructions
WI/4 – CD-ROM Distribution
Version 01.00

WI/4 – CD-ROM Distribution

4.1 SCOPE

NAFAAD is frequently requested to provide copies of contract deliverables to clients, section team members and third parties. The simplest and most cost effective way of distributing this information is via e-mail or (occasionally) via CD-ROM. WI/4 describes this process for CD-ROM distribution.

4.2 PROCEDURE

Section Managers and specified individuals are responsible for (and shall decide on) the external distribution of all approved deliverables, working papers, reports and documents outside NAFAAD. (Also see QP/1 – Document Control.)

Section Managers (and specified individuals) shall determine:

- the requirement (need) to distribute copies (or parts of) NAFAAD deliverables;
- the manner in which NAFAAD deliverables may be distributed to clients, section team members and third parties;
- their availability and distribution.

4.2.1 Distribution list

The distribution of all NAFAAD CDs shall be completed by the Company Secretary who shall maintain a distribution list, which will be updated every time a new delivery is made. The list shall include details of the person to whom the CD was distributed, its contents, the date of distribution and the selling price.

4.2.2 Updating previous distributions

Section Managers shall advise the Company Secretary every time a new version of a CD is issued and the Company Secretary shall inform all persons having received a previous version of that CD that a new version is available and (on request) provide replacement (i.e. updated) copies of that CD.

| Document Ref: **N-54–066RLR13** |
| Version: 03.01 |
| Date: 1 October 2013 |
| Quality Management System |
| Part Four – Work Instructions |
| WI/4 – CD-ROM Distribution |
| Version 01.00 |

4.2.3 Price guidelines

The price charged by NAFAAD for a CD (new or an updated version) shall depend on:

- the type of contract;
- the method of transmitting (i.e. sending) this information to the company;
- the type and amount of information contained on the CD;
- the time spent preparing the CD.

4.2.4 CD type

All NAFAAD deliverables shall be distributed using electronic files formatted onto a CD-ROM which is readable by any standard CD-ROM reader.

4.2.5 CD Labelling

All CD-ROMs provided by NAFAAD shall be labelled. These shall be a circular label (see example below) containing the NAFAAD logo and details of the contract deliverable.

FIGURE 6.4.2 Example of a CD-ROM label

	Document Ref: **N-54–066RLR13**
	Version: 03.01
	Date: 1 October 2013
	Quality Management System
	Part Four – Work Instructions
	WI/4 – CD-ROM Distribution
	Version 01.00

4.2.6 Plastic case – front

The front of the CD-ROM's plastic case shall be similar to the CD-ROM label and shall contain the NAFAAD logo together with details of the contract deliverable and a copyright statement as follows:

> **NAFAAD MANAGEMENT SYSTEMS**
>
> **All rights reserved.**
>
> **This document may not be reproduced – even in part – without the written authorisation of NAFAAD.**

4.2.7 Plastic case – back

The back of the CD-ROM's plastic case shall contain the following text:

4.2.8 Plastic case – spine

The spine of the CD-ROM's plastic case shall contain details of the contract deliverable.

4.2.9 Internal matter

An optional sheet (the same size as the CD case) may be included at the discretion of the Section Manager so as to include details of the deliverable, its potential use, any limitations etc.

4.2.10 Draft deliverables

All draft versions of NAFAAD deliverables shall carry text inside the front cover of the CD case, for example:

> **'This is a preliminary version distributed for information purposes only. It should not, therefore, be used to extract definitive information from. Neither Stingray nor its participating members are liable for any damage (including, but not limited to, claims from third parties) caused by information extracted from this preliminary version.'**

Document Ref: **N-54–066RLR13**
Version: 03.01
Date: 1 October 2013
Quality Management System
Part Four – Work Instructions
WI/4 – CD-ROM Distribution
Version 01.00

4.2.11 Approved deliverables

When a new version of an approved deliverable is issued, copies of all previous versions shall be destroyed. This shall be covered by a statement in the covering letter to the effect that:

'On receipt of this CD, all previous versions are to be destroyed.'

Document Ref: **N-54–067RLR13**
Version: 03.01
Date: 1 October 2013
Quality Management System
Part Four – Work Instructions
WI/5 – Procedure for the control of NAFAAD E-mails
Version 01.00

WI/5 – Procedure for the Control of NAFAAD E-mails

5.1 SCOPE

The aim of this Work Instruction is to:

- set up a series of rules and requirements that will more efficiently manage NAFAAD's electronic e-mail process;
- reduce and limit the number of e-mails that are being sent and received;
- provide a method for archiving incoming or outgoing e-mails that might be relevant to the concerned person and other interested persons, in the NAFAAD database.

E-mails that do not meet the requirements of this procedure shall be considered 'unofficial e-mails' and as a consequence do not require the person who received the e-mail (i.e. the Receiver) to respond and/or initiate any action demanded by the originator (i.e. the Author) of that e-mail.

5.2 FIELD OF APPLICATION

This procedure shall be considered as a NAFAAD-wide methodology for minimising unnecessary e-mails. It shall be applied to all types of incoming and/or outgoing e-mails, issued internally or externally to and/or from the client's personnel, subcontractors, suppliers, supporting elements as well as other third parties, stakeholders, regulatory officials etc.

Within NAFAAD this procedure is particularly relevant to all Section Managers and personnel having an e-mail address and using it for electronic communication internally or externally with the client, suppliers and/or subcontractors.

Although this instruction may be applied to any type of incoming or outgoing e-mail that is issued internally or externally, it is most applicable to documents and/or messages sent or received as attachments to e-mails and which may:

- contain important information for concerned people prior to sender (or recipients) taking any action;

Document Ref: **N-54–067RLR13**
Version: 03.01
Date: 1 October 2013
Quality Management System
Part Four – Work Instructions
WI/5 – Procedure for the control of NAFAAD E-mails
Version 01.00

- contain draft proposals (e.g. Minor Versions of Quality Documents) for information and review;
- identify a consequential risk (design, quality, environmental, health & safety, financial etc.) which may require subsequent action being taken.

5.3 PROCEDURE

The principle behind this procedure is that e-mails should ideally **only** be sent by the originator (i.e. the Author) to one person (i.e. the Receiver) for action with an information copy being sent to that person's direct hierarchy.

Note: In exceptional cases (e.g. an invitation to a meeting or an attached document requiring review by a number of people) there may be more than one Actionee and additional copies being sent to a restricted number of other persons for information purposes.

5.3.1 The Author

The Author of an e-mail is responsible for determining:

- its content and attachments;
- the Actionee;
- the circulation of information copies.

5.3.2 The Receiver

- receives the e-mail, notes its content, due date for response and priority;

Note: Normally, the Receiver will have two working days to respond to an e-mail. If the Receiver is on holiday or mission, then his direct hierarchy or designated competent person shall respond in accordance with the due date.

- determines whether other people need to be informed or involved in the response;
- if necessary, sends out copies of the e-mail to other concerned people together with a due date for response;
- if appropriate circulates the information contained in, or attached to, the e-mail to other concerned people for action or information as required;

| | Document Ref: **N-54–067RLR13**
Version: 03.01
Date: 1 October 2013
Quality Management System
Part Four – Work Instructions
WI/5 – Procedure for the control of NAFAAD E-mails
Version 01.00 |

- prepares an appropriate response to the received e-mail;
- sends the response to the original Author of the e-mail with an internal copy to his direct hierarchy for information purposes.

Note: If considered appropriate, information copies may also be sent to other concerned and/or possibly involved people but this should **only** be on a need to know basis.

5.4 ARCHIVING PROCESS

All relevant e-mails shall be archived for future use and reference by the receiver or sender of those e-mails as well as other NAFAAD Contractor personnel.

5.4.1 Selection of e-mails

The selection of relevant e-mails is the prerogative of the Receiver and/or Sender of those mails and that person is the **only** person who shall decide whether or not the e-mail he received, or sent, should concern other persons.

5.4.2 Archive mail box

When an e-mail is considered relevant, the Receiver will forward this particular e-mail to the Company Secretary via a specific Archive e-mail address specifically created for that purpose.

When authorised (see below) the Company Secretary shall upload these e-mails to the '*Archive e-mail box*' where it will remain available for subsequent referral by NAFAAD staff.

5.5 DUTIES OF THE COMPANY SECRETARY

- The Archive e-mail file is the sole responsibility of the Company Secretary. He shall open and check this mail-box at least once a day.
- The Company Secretary shall supply the Managing Director and the Quality Manager with a list of all e-mails received during the past seven days.
- The Quality Manager shall review the list of e-mails and prepare a short list of e-mails which shall be archived.
- The Company Secretary shall then upload the relevant e-mails and their attachments to the Archive mail box.

Self-assessment

Author's Note

Assuming that you now have your own organisation-specific Quality Management System up and running, how do you monitor its effectiveness? How can you be sure that you will be capable of continuing to meet ISO 9001:2008 requirements?

And, more importantly, if you intend going on to seek ISO 9001:2008 Certification, how can you be sure that you will be able to meet the exacting requirements of the UKAS appointed Accredited Certification Body?!

Chapter 7 covers the often-overlooked topic of self-assessment. Methods for completing management reviews and quality internal audits (internal and/or third-party assessments) are discussed. Also included are Annexes explaining:

- the QMS documentation that an organisation will require;
- the ISO 9001:2008 requirements of management;
- typical auditors' questions to assess ISO 9001:2008 compliance;
- example internal stage audit checks.

Note: Once more this chapter assumes that your organisation is of a similar size to the NAFAAD example used in Chapter 6 (i.e. an organisation of about 45–50 people, which has a full-time Quality Manager plus a small part-time Quality Team).

If your organisation does not have a Quality Team, then you should leave out the irrelevant passages.

If you are a Micro Business (i.e. less than 10 employees) then you probably will not have a full-time Quality Manager and in that case it would normally be the Owner or Managing Director who performs the audits and checks.

For a more comprehensive explanation about the concepts of auditing perhaps I should recommend that you have a look at my associated publication 'ISO 9001:2000 Audit Procedures', which, although it was written around the previous version of the standard (i.e. ISO 9001:2000) is still

> very relevant because there have been no actual changes to the quality management structure requirements made by the new ISO 9001:2008 version – and so the actual 'rules' for auditing ISO 9001 remain virtually the same.
>
> '*ISO 9001:2000 Audit Procedures*' follows on from where '*ISO 9001:2008 for Small Businesses*' leaves off and is a guide to assist auditors in completing internal, external and third-party audits of all existing and newly implemented ISO 9001: 2008 Quality Management Systems, as well as organisational (non-registered) QMSs. It also includes background notes for auditors as well as lots of checklists and example audit forms etc.

7.1 HOW ISO 9000 CAN BE USED TO CHECK SMALL BUSINESSES' QUALITY MANAGEMENT SYSTEMS

Having set up your own Quality Management System (QMS), it may be necessary for you to prove to a potential customer that it fully meets the recommendations, requirements and specifications of ISO 9001:2008. On the other hand, you may need to know how to check a subcontractor's or a supplier's QMS is up to your required standard. Or, you are considering seeking ISO 9001:2008 Certification, from a UKAS appointed Accredited Certification Body!

If your organisation has complied with the requirements for setting up a compliant QMS as described so far, then you will be well on your way to running a quality organisation. The requirements of QMS do not rest there, however. Your organisation must **continually** review its QMS to confirm its continued suitability and success, reveal defects, danger spots or irregularities, suggest possible improvements, eliminate wastage or loss, check the effectiveness of management at all levels and to be sure that managerial objectives and methods are effective and achieving the desired result. Above all your organisation must be prepared to face up to an audit of its quality procedures **from** potential customers!

 Note: Also see Annex B for 'ISO 9001:2008 requirements of management'.

7.2 INTERNAL AUDIT

The purpose of an internal quality audit is to identify potential danger spots, eliminate wastage and verify that corrective action has been successfully achieved. The procedures with which to carry out these audits should always be documented and available.

An audit plan determines whether the QMS is effectively achieving its stated quality objectives and should be established as soon as possible. Indeed, it is a requirement of ISO 9001:2008 that an assessment is regularly completed by the organisation of all the elements, aspects and components belonging to its QMS.

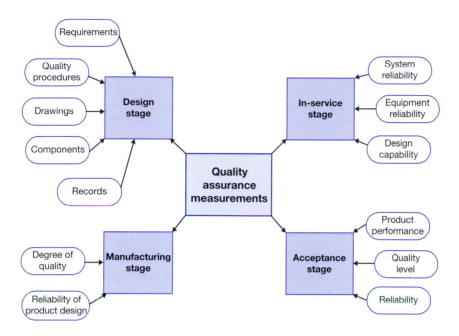

FIGURE 7.1 Quality assurance measurements

The type and content of an internal audit, obviously, varies with the size of the organisation. In some circumstances it can, however, mean going as far as having to resort to statistical control analysis to indicate and/or predict the need to carry out corrective action.

Another very important reason for carrying out an internal audit is clearly that it provides a comparison between what the QMS or Quality Plan stipulates **should** be done – and what is actually **being** done.

The main aim, however, of an internal audit is to confirm that everything is OK.

This verification activity will, depending on the size and activities of the organisation, include testing and monitoring the design, production, delivery, installation and possibly after sales processes, design reviews and the method of auditing the QMS.

The audit should be capable of identifying such things as non-compliance with previously issued instructions and deficiencies within the QMS. In addition the audit should recommend any corrective actions that can be achieved to improve the system.

It is essential that management ensure that timely corrective action is taken on all deficiencies found during the audit. Follow-up actions should include the verification and implementation of corrective action, and reporting of results.

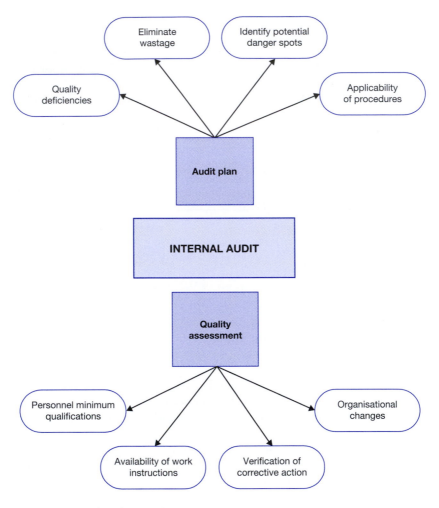

FIGURE 7.2 Internal audit

7.2.1 Audit plan

To be effective, an '*internal audit*' must be completed by trained personnel and where possible by members of the quality control staff – provided, that is, that they are **not** responsible for the quality of that particular product.

This does not, of course, stop the management from using an outside agency (i.e. third-party certification) if they wish to, and in so doing gain a completely unbiased view of the general success of their organisation's QMS.

The selection of the department or section to be audited should always be conducted on a random basis and normally these internal audits will be completed every three months or so. In an ideal world the audit should be pre-planned so that it covers all aspects of quality control within one calendar year.

The audit plan should:

- cover all the specific areas and activities that are to be audited;
- cover the reasons why an internal audit is being completed (e.g. organisational changes, reported deficiencies, survey or routine check);
- stipulate the minimum qualifications of the personnel who are to carry out the audit;
- describe how the audit report should be finalised and submitted.

7.2.2 Internal audit programme

As shown in Figure 7.3, an internal audit programme normally consists of eight separate (but inter-related) steps:

FIGURE 7.3 Internal audit programme

Step 1 – Audit schedule

Internal quality audits are usually planned and initiated by the Quality Manager in relation to the status and importance of the various activities of a section and/or deliverable. For large organisations, it would be quite normal for all departments and sections to be subject to at least three **complete** quality audits every year as shown in Example 1 below:

FUNCTION/ DEPARTMENT	JAN	FEB	MAR	APR	MAY	JUN	JULY	AUG	SEPT	OCT	NOV	DEC
Administration and finance	x				x				x			
Drawing office		x				x				x		
Workshops			x				x				x	
Stores				x				x				x

EXAMPLE 1 Annual quality audit schedule

 Note: For smaller organisations (e.g. those employing just a handful of people) an audit every four months or so of selected areas would probably be sufficient.

Step 2 – Audit preparation and organisation

Depending on the complexity and the size of the audit, the Quality Manager may perform the audit him- or herself, or (when sections are too large, or when activities from other sections are involved) he or she can assign a lead auditor and a team of auditors to complete the task.

The Quality Manager (or lead auditor) is then responsible for organising an agenda which (see Example 2) will include the:

- scope and objectives of the audit;
- persons having direct responsibilities for the procedure(s) to be audited;
- reference documents;
- name of lead auditor and name(s) of assigned auditor(s);
- date when audit is to be concluded.

Following a review of earlier audit reports on the same section or the same subject, the lead auditor and the assigned auditor(s) will prepare an audit check list containing all of the topics/items to be covered together with an audit programme (see Examples 3 and 4).

Audit Reference No:	File No: ....
Purpose of audit:	
Scope of audit:	
Lead Auditor assigned:	
Location(s) of audit:	
Unit or area to be audited:	
Reference documents:	
Team members:	
Date of audit:	Anticipated duration of audit: ....
Time of opening meeting:	Anticipated time of closing meeting: .....
Facilities requested:	

EXAMPLE 2 Internal audit plan

AUDIT CHECKLIST	FUNCTION/PROCESS AUDITED: .... DOCUMENT REFERENCES:			AUDIT NO:....... AUDIT DATE:.......
ITEM NO	AUDIT QUESTIONS	REFERENCE	RESULT	NOTES/ OBSERVATIONS
	PREPARED BY:	PAGE ... OF ...		DATE PREPARED: ....

EXAMPLE 3 Audit checklist

TIMETABLE	TEAM A	TEAM B	AUDITEE PARTICIPATION
0900–0930	Opening meeting		Senior Management & Department Heads
0930–1030	Managing Director Quality Policy Management Review	Laboratory 1	Technical Director
1030–1100	Review of: Document Control Non-conformity	Laboratory 2	Department Heads
1100–1200	Purchasing	Laboratory 2	Department Heads
1200	Lunch		
1330–1500	Purchasing	Laboratory 2 (cont)	Department Heads
1500–1600	Personnel Training	Electrical Test House	Department Heads
1600–1700	Commercial/ Sales	Calibration Service	Department Heads

EXAMPLE 4 Audit programme

Step 3 – Audit execution

Assuming that the organisation is large enough to warrant having an audit team then an initial meeting between the auditor(s), the auditee(s) and the Quality Manager is held during which:

*   a brief summary of the methods and procedures that will be used to conduct the audit is given;
*   the method of communication between auditor(s) and auditee(s) is agreed; and
*   the audit programme is confirmed.

In accordance with ISO 9001:2008 (Section 8.2.2) all organisations are required to have a documented procedure for conducting internal quality audits and normally this procedure will distinguish between two kinds of internal quality audits, namely a *'standards audit'* and a *'procedures audit'*.

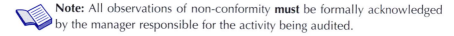

Note: The standards audit evaluates how well the ISO standard is being applied, while the procedures audit evaluates how effective the organisation's quality procedures, policies, plans and instructions are.

Using the standards audit the auditor will begin collecting evidence of compliance by interviewing auditee personnel, reading documents, reviewing manuals, checking records, examining data, observing activities and studying working conditions. As the evidence is collected the auditor will answer each audit question and record his or her observations as either:

Yes	means that this activity is in compliance with the standard;
No	means that this activity is not in compliance;
Not applicable	means that this question is not applicable in this activity's situation.

Once the auditor has completed the audit questionnaire, he or she makes a list of all the non-conformities (i.e. the 'Nos') and summarises his or her evidence.

Similarly, using the procedures audit each applicable quality procedure, policy, plan and Work Instruction will be looked at from the point of view of *Is it documented? Is it being followed? Is it effective?* On the basis of evidence collected, the auditor will record his or her observation as:

Yes	means that this activity is in compliance;
No	means that this activity is not in compliance.

Auditors will record all their observations on the audit observation sheet (see Example 5) and all non-compliances will then be listed on a 'non-compliance worksheet' which will eventually form part of the final audit report.

Step 4 – Summarise audit results

Auditors will then meet to discuss all of their observations (particularly any non-compliance that they may have found) with the Quality Manager.

Note: All observations of non-conformity **must** be formally acknowledged by the manager responsible for the activity being audited.

A closing meeting of auditor(s), auditee(s) and Quality Manager will then be held during which:

- audit observations will be clarified;
- the critical significance of observations will be presented;
- conclusions drawn about compliance will be presented;

Section or project to be audited:	
Reason for audit:	

Audit No:		Date:
Auditor:		Sheet ... of ...

Serial No	Observation/supporting evidence	
	Action required	Yes/No

Circulation:	
Attached Sheets:	

Signed:		Name:		Date:	

EXAMPLE 5 Audit observation sheet

- system effectiveness in achieving the quality objectives will be presented;
- corrective actions will be agreed;
- the date for completion of the audit report will be agreed.

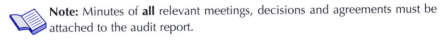 **Note:** Minutes of **all** relevant meetings, decisions and agreements must be attached to the audit report.

Step 5 – Prepare audit report

The lead auditor now needs to prepare an audit report using an audit report form similar to the one shown in Example 6.

The report must be signed by all members of the audit team, plus the Quality Manager, and copies sent to auditee(s) and company management as required.

The audit report will list all non-conformities discovered, observations made and discuss any conclusions drawn. It will also detail (in the summary)

Section or project audited:					
Reason for audit:					
Audit No:		Date:			
Auditor:		Sheet ... of ...			
Audit area(s):					
Reference document(s):					
Summary:					
Audit observation sheet number	Observation number	Comments		Corrective action requirement	
Prepared:		Name:		Date:	
Agreed:		Name:		Date:	
Circulation:		Attached sheets:			

EXAMPLE 6 Audit report form

recommendations that should be implemented in order to correct or prevent non-conformities occurring and to make improvements.

Step 6 – Corrective action

After the closing meeting, the lead auditor will prepare a corrective action request (see Example 7) for each agreed corrective action.

 Note: Corrective action requests should always state who is responsible for carrying out the corrective action and the timescale for its completion.

 Note: One sheet should be used for **each agreed** corrective action.

Section or project audited:	
Reason for audit:	
Audit No:	Audit Date:
Auditor(s):	Auditee(s):
Audit area(s):	
Reference document(s):	

Non-conformance details:			
Signed: (Auditor)	Name:	Date:	

Agreed corrective action:			
Signed: (Auditee)	Name:	Date:	

Agreed time limit:			
Signed: (Actionee)	Name:	Date:	

Progress:	Signed:	Date:

EXAMPLE 7 Corrective action request

Step 7 – Take remedial action

The section/department that has been audited is then responsible for ensuring that the agreed corrective actions are implemented and that any observations, comments and recommendations made by the audit team have been taken into account.

Step 8 – Follow up

Finally, the lead auditor is then responsible for ensuring that corrective action has been carried out and for notifying the Quality Manager of the status and/or completion of corrective actions.

7.3 EXTERNAL AUDIT

Although the supplier may have been able to convince the purchaser that its QMS is effective, it is in the interests of the purchaser to conduct its own evaluation (i.e. audit) of the supplier. This is usually done on an irregular basis.

The supplier must, of course, agree to the principle of purchaser evaluations being carried out and it is usual to find this as a separate clause in the contract.

FIGURE 7.4 External audit

Normally these audits are pretty simple, but – particularly when the material, product or service being purchased is complex – the **purchaser** will need to have a reasonably objective method of evaluating and measuring the efficiency of the quality control of the supplier's promises and be certain that the quality system (i.e. quality control) established by the supplier complies with laid down standards and is, above all, effective. This method is known as the *'supplier evaluation'*.

7.3.1 Supplier evaluation

Part of the initial contract will stipulate that the supplier provides access to the purchaser's inspectors and sometimes even accommodation and facilities to enable the purchaser's representatives to conduct their activities and evaluations. These facilities depend upon the level of surveillance, but could possibly require the supplier to provide:

- suitable office and administrative facilities;
- adequate work space for product verification;
- access to those areas where work is in progress or to those which affect the work;
- help in documenting, inspecting and releasing material and services;
- the use of inspection and test devices and availability of personnel to operate them are necessary.

7.3.1.1 Evaluation team

Again, assuming that the purchaser's organisation is a large one, then two or more inspectors will form the evaluation team. These inspectors must be thoroughly skilled in the requirements of quality assurance and are normally selected by the Quality Manager from the purchaser's own quality control section.

Note: In some cases the Quality Manager may decide to lead the team or conduct the audit by him- or herself – particularly if the supplier is a micro business (i.e. less than 10 employees).

7.3.1.2 Pre-evaluation meeting

Before the evaluation team visits the supplier's premises they must first be given the chance to:

- meet the supplier's staff to discuss the procedures being used;
- identify the supplier's sections/areas that will be tested;
- decide which representatives of the organisation will be required to accompany the evaluation team during their inspection;
- agree dates and outline timetables, etc.

7.3.1.3 Study of the quality manual

The purchaser must then be given a copy of the supplier's Quality Manual. The Quality Manual will be inspected not only for its accuracy and clarity but also its position compared to national and international standards and to see that it conforms to the relevant sections of ISO 9001:2008.

Having thoroughly examined the manual, the purchaser is then in a position to be able to send a team of inspectors to the supplier's premises to fully scrutinise every aspect of the supplier's design office, purchasing, storekeeping, manufacturing activities, assembly, test and storage facilities to see that the work carried out complies with the procedures (promises!) made in its Quality Manual.

7.3.1.4 The evaluation

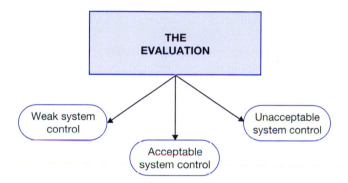

FIGURE 7.5 The evaluation

Having completed the pre-evaluation, the purchaser is now able to visit the supplier's premises for a complete inspection.

During the actual evaluation, the supplier's department heads will first be required to describe to the team exactly how their quality control system works. They will have to provide examples of their quality control documentation and possibly even be required to prove that certain sections have the correct documentation and that it is up to date. The department heads will then have to show how stock is received, accounted for and withdrawn from stores, how the appropriate drawings are issued, updated and eventually disposed of.

 Note: Quite often the evaluation team will want to see the route cards and/or 'travellers' that accompany partially completed work.

The purchaser will, as part of its QMS audit, possibly carry out an evaluation of the sampling procedures used by the supplier – to ascertain whether they conform to those laid down in the Quality Plan for that particular product.

During their evaluation it is also possible for the purchaser's team to ask for a previously inspected batch to be rechecked so that they can see if a similar or comparable result is obtained.

Other aspects of the manufacturer's facilities that the inspectors might well want to look at (particularly if the supplier is an organisation actually manufacturing a product) could include:

- evidence that its test equipment and other instruments have been regularly maintained and calibrated against a known source;
- that rejected or unacceptable components and assemblies are clearly marked and segregated to avoid any chance of their accidental inclusion with other items that have already been accepted.

At the end of this evaluation, a meeting will be arranged between the evaluation team and the factory organisations to discuss their findings and to be sure that there are not any misunderstandings, etc.

The eventual evaluation report will then be formally presented at a meeting with the management. The result of this meeting could be one of the following:

7.3.1.5 Acceptable system control

This means that the evaluation has shown that the supplier has a satisfactory QMS, there are no deficiencies and the supplier has been able to give an assurance of quality. When this happens, there should be no reason why the purchaser should feel it necessary to demand any radical changes to the supplier's system.

Note: But even though the supplier may have proved that it is up to a satisfactory standard, the purchaser will still have the right to (and often does) insist on making further inspections throughout the duration of the contract.

7.3.1.6 Weak system control

This covers the situation where the evaluation team find several significant weaknesses in the supplier's system.

If this happens, the supplier will have to take steps to overcome these failures and improve its QMS. Having done this, the supplier can then ask for another evaluation to be carried out to confirm that its quality now meets the required standards.

7.3.1.7 Unacceptable system control

This is the result of the purchaser's evaluation team finding that the number of deficiencies – or the lack of quality discipline at the supplier's premises – mean that the supplier will have to make radical changes to improve its overall QMS before it is anything like acceptable to the potential purchaser.

When the supplier has completed the necessary changes, it will then require a second evaluation to see that its improvements are satisfactory. Unfortunately this could be as much as a year later, by which time the purchaser may well have found an alternative source or decided that the initial organisation's quality is definitely not up to standard – and virtually blacklisted that particular supplier!

Having been inspected, it is important that the records of this inspection are safely filed away in case they may be required to reinforce some point at a later stage or to provide statistical data for the analysis of a supplier's performance. This is sometimes referred to as 'vendor rating'.

7.4 THE SURVEILLANCE OR QUALITY AUDIT VISIT

Although an organisation might have successfully passed an initial evaluation of its facilities and the purchaser may well be satisfied that the supplier is capable of providing an assurance of quality, it cannot be assumed that the supplier will be able to, or even capable of, retaining this status forever. Many things can happen to change this situation such as staff moving through promotion or natural wastage, changes in the product design that may or have been necessary, or perhaps even a new man-management philosophy.

The purchaser needs, therefore, to be informed of any changes in the organisation and personnel that might affect the overall quality of the product.

It is quite possible that the purchaser might also want to make irregular surveillance visits of the supplier's premises to examine a particular aspect of its QMS. These surveillance or audit visits by the purchaser will be run on exactly the same lines as the supplier evaluation and are aimed at providing the purchaser with a confidence in the supplier and an assurance that it is capable of in fact still providing the purchaser with the quality of goods that it requires. The aim of these audit visits should be that all the important aspects of the quality control system are checked, in rotation.

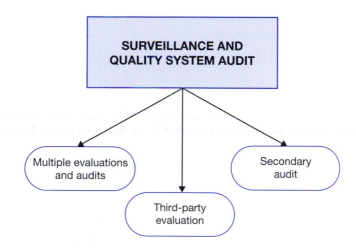

FIGURE 7.6 The surveillance

7.4.1 Multiple evaluations and audits

It is likely that a supplier might well be providing the same product to several different customers and it could just happen that all of these customers ask to have an audit – at the same time! This obviously cannot be allowed to happen as the supplier and/or the manufacturer would forever have people visiting its premises and disturbing, not only the labour force, but also the production line! Thankfully there are quite a number of ways around this problem, such as a secondary audit or third-party evaluation.

7.4.2 Secondary audit

If a purchaser indicates that it wants to carry out an audit, the supplier can offer to provide the details of another customer's audit that has recently been carried out at its premises. If this does not quite cover the problem area sufficiently, then the supplier could offer to check in more detail the appropriate points raised by the purchaser.

7.4.3 Third-party evaluation

As an alternative to the secondary audit, a third-party evaluation team (i.e. one that is not directly involved in either the supply or purchase of the deliverable) could be employed to carry out an audit.

There are several firms that have been specifically set up to do this and these are capable of determining whether a supplier's product, premises and management are capable of meeting (and still meet) the laid down standards.

7.4.4 Conformity assessment

In these days of international markets and cross-border trading, many national regulations require that a product or deliverable is first tested for compliance with an internationally agreed specification for safety, environmental and/or quality conformance before it can be released to the market.

This sort of testing is referred to as '*conformity assessment*' and in its simplest form means that a product, material, service, system (or in some cases, person(s)) has been measured against the specifications of a relevant standard – which, in most cases, will be an internationally agreed standard.

Although some conformity assessment can be completed using internal facilities, when a product has health and/or environmental implications, national legislation will probably stipulate that testing is carried out by an independent Registrar, Notified Body or specialist organisation; in other words, by a third party.

There exist many testing laboratories and certification bodies which offer independent conformity assessment services performed either as a commercial venture, or under mandate to their national government.

7.5 SELF ASSESSMENT CHECKLISTS

Self-assessment can be a very useful tool to identify possible areas for improving an organisation's capability and ISO 9004:2009 ("*Managing for the sustained success of an organization. A quality management approach*") helps organisations by providing an annex containing '*guidelines for self-assessment*'.

As this is an important consideration I have included a number of appendices to this chapter specifically aimed at helping small businesses complete a self-assessment of their QMS and cost-effectively work in conformance with the requirements of ISO 9001:2008. These consist of:

7.5.1 Documentation required by an organisation to meet ISO 9001:2008 requirements

A brief explanation of the specific requirements (i.e. the '*shalls*') of each element of ISO 9001:2008 together with a description of the likely documentation that an organisation would need to have in place to meet the requirements, as well as an outline of this content (Annex A).

7.5.2 ISO 9001:2008 requirements of management

Another list of the sections and sub sections that make up ISO 9001:2008, but this time identifying the areas that management need to address when they document their Quality Management System (Annex B).

> **Note:** Most independent Registrars and Notified Bodies will use a similar 'check sheet' to determine whether an organisation's QMS complies with the requirements of ISO 9001:2008.

7.5.3 Example checklists of typical auditors' questions for ISO 9001:2008 compliance

Annex C contains a list of the most important questions an external Quality Auditor (e.g. BSI, ISOQAR, TÜV, AFNOR, etc.) would be likely to ask when completing an external or conformity audit. If an organisation can honestly answer '*yes*' to all these questions then it would be quite entitled to say that it '*fully complies with the requirements of ISO 9001:2008*'.

> **Note:** Parts of these checklists could, of course, **also** be used when conducting internal quality audits.

7.5.4 Example internal stage audit checklists

Author's Note

These types of checklist, although relevant to most organisations, would probably be of more use to manufacturing companies.

Note: These checklists could also be used for internal audits.

Lists of the most important questions that an external Quality Auditor (e.g. purchaser) is likely to ask when evaluating an organisation for the:

* design stage;
* manufacturing stage;
* acceptance stage;
* in-service stage.

(See Annex D).

7.6 DOCUMENTATION REQUIREMENTS

In addition to providing a simplified set of standards that are equally applicable to small as well as medium and/or large organisations, the main objectives behind the 2008 revision of the ISO 9000 series of standards were that:

* organisations would be allowed more flexibility in the way they chose to document their management systems;
* the amount of detailed documentation that was required by the standard would be limited;
* the amount of documentation required by individual organisations would be significantly reduced – provided that it was still capable of demonstrating the effective planning, operation and control of their processes as well as the implementation (and continual improvement) of their QMS;
* the type and extent of the documentation would depend on the nature of the organisation's products and processes.

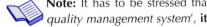

Note: It has to be stressed that whilst ISO 9001 requires a *'Documented quality management system'*, **it does not** require a *'system of documents'*!

To achieve these aims, organisations will need to document – either electronically or on paper – their quality policy, objectives, procedures, planning and operations. They will need to describe how they control quality in these areas and will also need to retain quality records to prove that these procedures have been followed (i.e. inventory control listings, travellers, work orders, signed contracts, etc.).

There are no specific requirements on the actual type or form of documentation. It can differ from one organisation to another depending on size, type of activities, or complexity of processes.

7.6.1 The requirement

ISO 9001:2008 clause 4.1 General requirements requires an organisation to *'establish, document, implement, and maintain a quality management system and continually improve its effectiveness in accordance with the requirements of this International Standard'.*

The standard then goes on to explain that the QMS documentation shall include:

- documented statements of a quality policy and quality objectives;
- a quality manual;
- documented procedures required by this International Standard;
- documents needed by the organisation to ensure the effective planning, operation and control of its processes; and
- records required by this International Standard;

and that these documents may be in any form or type of medium **such as:**

- paper;
- magnetic;
- electronic or optical computer disk;
- photograph;
- master sample.

 Note: For additional advice on documentation see ISO/TR 10013 *Guidelines for quality management systems documentation.*

7.6.1.1 Documented statements regarding quality policy and quality objectives

These will normally be included in the Quality Manual.

7.6.1.2 Quality Manual

Clause 4.2.2 of ISO 9001:2008 specifies the minimum content for a quality manual. The format and structure of the manual, however, will vary between organisations depending on the organisation's size, culture and complexity. For example, a small organisation may find it appropriate to include the description of its entire QMS within a single manual, including all the documented procedures required by the standard. On the other hand, large, multi-national organisations may need several manuals at the global, national and/or regional level together with a more complex hierarchy of documentation. Alternatively, some organisations may choose to use the quality manual for other purposes besides that of simply documenting the QMS.

 Note: The Quality Manual is a document that has to be controlled in accordance with the requirements of clause 4.2.3.

7.6.1.3 Documented procedures required by ISO 9001:2008

 ISO 9001:2008 specifically **requires** the organisation **shall** have '*documented procedures*' for the following six activities:

*   Control of documents (4.2.3);
*   Control of quality records (4.2.4);
*   Internal audits (8.2.2);
*   Control of non-conforming products (8.3);
*   Corrective actions (8.5.2);
*   Preventative actions (8.5.3).

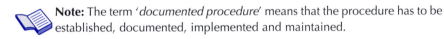 **Note:** The term '*documented procedure*' means that the procedure has to be established, documented, implemented and maintained.

By implication documented procedures should **also** be included for:

*   Customer communications (7.2.3) – which states '*The organisation shall determine and implement effective arrangements for communication with customers*'; and
*   Purchasing process (7.4.1) which states '*Criteria for selection, evaluation and re-evaluation shall be established*'.

Procedures can take any suitable form. They can be a narrative, a flow chart, a process map, or indeed any other suitable structure. As long as the procedure is effective, it really doesn't matter what it looks like.

Whilst some organisations may find it convenient to combine the procedure for several activities into a single documented procedure (for example, Corrective action and Preventive action), others may choose to document a given activity by using more than one documented procedure (for example, Internal Audits). Both are acceptable.

Some organisations (particularly larger organisations, or those making use of more complex processes) may also require additional documented procedures (especially those relating to product realisation processes) in order to implement an effective QMS. This will clearly vary depending on the size of the organisation, the kind of activities in which it is involved and their complexity.

7.6.1.4 Documents required by the organisation to ensure the effective planning, operation and control of its processes

The two main objectives of an organisation's documentation should be to provide communication of information (as a means of disseminating information about the aims, objectives and requirements for quality management) and evidence of conformity (i.e. the availability of evidence that all planned activities are being achieved in an efficient and effective manner).

Although the only documents specifically mentioned in ISO 9001:2008 are for quality management, quality policy, quality objectives and the actual quality manual itself, there are also several requirements in the standard where an organisation can demonstrate conformity by preparing additional documentation such as:

- process maps, process flow charts and/or process descriptions;
- organisation charts;
- specifications;
- work and/or test instructions;
- documents containing internal communications;
- production schedules;
- approved supplier lists;
- test and inspection plans;
- quality plans.

7.6.1.5 Records required by ISO 9001:2008

Records specifically required by ISO 9001:2008 are as shown on the following page.

There is, of course, no restriction on an organisation developing other records that may be needed to demonstrate conformity of its processes, products and/or quality management system.

7.6.2 Control of documents

'*Proper control of documents*' is required by the standard, which means that you need to ensure that all your QMS documents have been correctly identified, reviewed, authorised, issued and distributed. You need to take care that old (i.e. obsolete) documents are not being used and that they are stored in a secure location if they are required for future reference. You also need to make sure that any external documents that you use in your QMS are identified within your system and that the access to these documents is controlled.

7.6.3 Software programs for document control

With the acceptance of ISO 9001:2008 as the principal standard for integrated management has come the requirement to see the business in process terms.

One method of achieving this is to use a process mapping software tool which not only describes the organisation's business processes (through a series of multi-

Self-Assessment

Clause	Type of record required
4.2.1	Records of QMS documentation.
5.6.1	Management reviews.
6.22(e)	Education, training, skills and experience.
7.1 (d)	Evidence that the realisation processes and resulting product fulfil requirements.
7.2.2	Results of the review of requirements related to the product and actions arising from the review.
7.3.2	Design and development inputs relating to product requirements.
7.3.4	Results of design and development reviews and any necessary actions.
7.3.5	Results of design and development verification and any necessary actions.
7.3.6	Results of design and development validation and any necessary actions.
7.3.7	Results of the review of design and development changes and any necessary actions.
7.4.1	Results of supplier evaluations and any necessary actions arising from the evaluations.
7.5.2 (d)	As required by the organisation to demonstrate the validation of processes where the resulting output cannot be verified by subsequent monitoring or measurement.
7.5.3	The unique identification of the product, where traceability is a requirement.
7.5.4	Customer property that is lost, damaged or otherwise found to be unsuitable for use.
7.6 (a)	Basis used for calibration or verification of measuring equipment where no international or national measurement standards exist.
	Validity of the previous measuring results when the measuring equipment is found not to conform to requirements.
	Results of calibration and verification of measuring equipment.
8.2.1	Results of customer satisfaction and opinion polls.
8.2.2	Internal audit results and follow-up actions.
8.2.3	Indication of the person(s) authorising release of product.
	Nature of the product non-conformities and any subsequent actions taken, including concessions obtained.
8.5.2	Results of corrective action.
8.5.3	Results of preventive action.

layer maps) but also provides direct access to existing documentation sitting below the process maps. This enables staff to have immediate access (i.e. through an intranet connected desktop PC or laptop) to the relevant documents, rather than having to cope with searching through a forest of printed documents. It also ensures that only the latest issues of these documents are available to staff.

More organisations are now turning to an IT solution, as the benefits of using software to manage documentation and processes are numerous, including:

- ease of use;
- error reductions;
- cost savings on print, paper and distribution;
- improved functionality;
- space and environmental savings; and
- time no longer wasted on searching for hard copies.

Annex A –
Documentation required by an organisation
to meet ISO 9001:2008 requirements

Section no.	ISO 9001:2008 title	Explanation	Likely documentation
4	QMS		
4.1	General requirements	A definition of the processes necessary to ensure that a product conforms to customer requirements that are capable of being implemented, maintained and improved.	Core Business Processes supplemented by: • Supporting Processes (SPs); • quality procedures (QPs); and • work instructions (WIs).
4.2	Documentation requirements		
4.2.1	General	Documented proof of a QMS.	QM. High-level policy statement on organisational objectives and quality policies. Procedures. Quality records.
4.2.2	QM	A document which describes an organisation's quality policies, procedures and practices that make up the QMS.	A QM containing everything related to quality controls within an organisation.
4.2.3	Control of documents	How an organisation's documents are approved, issued, numbered, etc. How revisions are recorded and implemented and obsolete documents removed.	Document control procedures.
4.2.4	Control of records	What quality records need to be kept to demonstrate conformance with the requirements of an organisation's QMS and how they are identified, stored, protected, etc.	Record keeping procedures.

Section no.	ISO 9001:2008 title	Explanation	Likely documentation
5	Management responsibility	Management responsibility and quality requirements.	QM.
5.1	Management commitment	A written demonstration of an organisation's commitment to: • Sustaining and increasing customer satisfaction; • Establishing quality policies, objectives and planning; • Establishing a QMS; • Performing management reviews; • Ensuring availability of resources; • Determining the legal and mandatory requirements its products and/or services have to meet; and • Continuous improvement.	High-level policy statement on organisational objectives and quality policies. A list of Government regulatory, legal and customer-specific requirements. • Procedures describing: – Resource management; – Contract review procedures; – Management reviews; and – Financial business plan(s).
5.2	Customer focus	How an organisation ensures that customer expectations and needs, requirements are determined, fully understood and met.	Procedures describing: • Resource management; • Contract review procedures; • Management reviews; and • Financial business plan(s).
5.3	Quality policy	How an organisation approaches quality and the requirements for meeting expectations, ensuring that: • They are appropriate for both customer and an organisation; • There is a commitment to continually meet customer requirements; • These commitments are communicated, understood and implemented throughout an organisation; and • There is a commitment for continual improvement.	High-level managerial statement on an organisation's quality policy containing clear responsibilities, training and resources required for each organisational activity.

Section no.	ISO 9001:2008 title	Explanation	Likely documentation
5.4	Planning	The planning of resources, etc. to meet an organisation's overall business objectives.	QM.
5.4.1	Quality objectives	The quality objectives that an organisation expects to achieve within each level of the organisation.	Policy statements defining the objectives of the company and those responsible for achieving the objectives.
5.4.2	QMS planning	The identification and planning of activities and resources required to meet an organisation's quality objectives.	The processes and procedures used by senior management to define and plan the way that the organisation is run.
5.5	Responsibility, authority and communication	How the organisation has documented its QMS.	A QM containing everything related to quality controls within the organisation.
5.5.1	Responsibility and authority	A definition of the roles, responsibilities, lines of authority, reporting and communication relevant to quality.	Job descriptions and responsibilities. Organisation charts showing lines of communication.
5.5.2	Management representative	The identification and appointment of a 'Quality Manager' (who is an existing member of the organisation – as opposed to a part-time outsider) with responsibility for the QMS.	Job description and responsibilities. Organisation charts showing lines of communication.
5.5.3	Internal communication	How the requirements of an organisation's QMS are communicated throughout the company.	Team briefings, organisational meetings, notice boards, in-house journals/magazines, audio-visual and other forms of e-information.
5.6	Management review	How senior management reviews the QMS to ensure its continued suitability, adequacy and effectiveness, in the context of an organisation's strategic planning cycle.	Procedures concerning: • Process, product and/or service audit procedures; • Customer feedback; • Process and product performance;

Section no.	ISO 9001:2008 title	Explanation	Likely documentation
			• Corrective and preventive action; • Supplier performance; and • Record keeping.
5.6.1	General	The requirement for management to establish a process for the periodic review of the QMS.	Management review and QMS audit procedures.
5.6.2	Review input	The documents and information required for management reviews.	Results of audits, customer feedback, analysis of process performance and product conformance, corrective and preventive action reports and supplier performance records.
5.6.3	Review output	Result of the review.	Minutes of the meetings where the overall running of the company is discussed.
6	Resource management	A description of resources with regard to training, induction, responsibilities, working environment, equipment requirements, maintenance, etc.	QPs, Quality Plans and WIs.
6.1	Provision of resources	How resource needs (i.e. human, materials, equipment and infra-structure) are identified.	Quality Plans identifying the resources required to complete a particular project or activity.
6.2	Human resources	Identification and assign-ment of human resources to implement and improve the QMS and comply with contract conditions.	QPs, Quality Plans and WIs.
6.2.1	General	How an organisation assigns personnel on the basis of competency, qualification, training, skills and experience to relevant specific tasks.	Job descriptions and responsibilities. Training records. Staff evaluations. Project plans identifying the human resources required to complete the task.

Section no.	ISO 9001:2008 title	Explanation	Likely documentation
6.2.2	Competence, training and awareness	Documents showing how an organisation selects, trains and assigns personnel to specific tasks.	System level procedures for: • Training; • Staff evaluations; • Review of work assignments; • Staff assessments; and • Records.
6.3	Infrastructure	How an organisation defines, provides and maintains the infrastructure requirements to ensure product conformity (e.g. infrastructure, plant, hardware, software, tools and equipment, communication facilities, information systems, transport and supporting services, etc.).	Policies, procedures and regulatory documents stating the infrastructure requirements of an organisation and/or their customers. Financial documents. Maintenance plans. Project plans identifying the human resources required to complete the task.
6.4	Work environment	How an organisation defines and implements the human and physical factors of the work environment required to ensure product conformity (health and safety, work methods, ethics and ambient working conditions).	Environmental procedures. Project plans. Budgetary and legal processes and procedures.
7	Product realisation	The requirements for process control, purchasing, handling and storage, measuring devices, etc.	QM and associated Processes, QPs, Quality Plans and WIs.
7.1	Planning of product realisation	The availability of documented plans for all product processes required to realise a product, and the sequences in which they occur.	Process models (flow charts) showing the sequence of activities that an organisation goes through to produce a product. Documented QPs and WIs to ensure that staff work in accordance with requirements. Records that prove the results of process control. Quality Plans.

Section no.	ISO 9001:2008 title	Explanation	Likely documentation
7.2	Customer-related processes	The identification, review and interaction with customer requirements and customers.	QM and Quality Plans.
7.2.1	Determination of requirements related to the product	How an organisation determines and implements customer requirements.	Contract review procedures. Regulatory and legal product requirements. Formal contracts. Audit procedures. Corrective action.
7.2.2	Review of requirements related to the product	How an organisation reviews product and customer requirements to check that they can actually do the job.	Contract review procedures. Regulatory and legal product requirements. Project plans showing lines of communication with the customer.
7.2.3	Customer communication	How an organisation communicates (i.e. lines of liaises) with their customers, keeps them informed, handles their enquiries, complaints and feedback.	Project plans showing communication with the customer.
7.3	Design and development	The control of design and development within an organisation.	Processes and procedures for design and development. Design plans.
7.3.1	Design and development planning	How an organisation goes about planning and controlling the design of a product (e.g. design stages, development processes, verification and validation, responsibilities and authorities).	Design and development plans. Procedures detailing the design process and how designs are verified and validated. Risk assessment. Job descriptions and responsibilities.
7.3.2	Design and development inputs	How an organisation identifies the requirements to be met by a product.	Project Plans (detailing policies, standards and specifications, skill requirements). Specifications and tolerances. Regulatory and legal requirements. Information derived from previous (similar) designs or developments. Environmental requirements. Health and safety aspects.

Section no.	ISO 9001:2008 title	Explanation	Likely documentation
7.3.3	Design and development outputs	How an organisation ensures that the design output meets the design input requirements. How it ensures and considers the preservation of the product.	Drawings, schematics, schedules, system specifications, system descriptions, etc.
7.3.4	Design and development review	How an organisation evaluates its ability to fulfil product requirements, identify problems and complete follow-up actions.	Procedures detailing how changes are made to designs and how they are approved, recorded and distributed. Design process review procedures. Management reviews and audit procedures. Records.
7.3.5	Design and development verification	How an organisation ensures that product specifications are fulfilled and that the design and development output meets the original input requirements.	Design process review procedures. Procedures for periodic reviews. Records.
7.3.6	Design and development validation	How an organisation ensures that the design is actually capable of doing its intended job.	Procedures for in-process inspection and testing. Final inspection and test. Records.
7.3.7	Control of design and development changes	How changes to a design are approved, together with consideration of how these changes may influence other aspects of the business.	Procedures detailing how changes are made to designs and how they are approved, recorded and distributed. Design process review procedures. Management reviews and audit procedures. Records.
7.4	Purchasing	How an organisation controls the purchase of materials, products and services from suppliers and third parties.	Documented procedures for purchasing and the evaluation of suppliers.
7.4.1	Purchasing process	The controls that an organisation has in place to ensure that purchased products and services are of an acceptable standard.	Approved list of suppliers. Supplier evaluations. Purchasing procedures. Purchase orders.
7.4.2	Purchasing information	The details provided by an organisation when placing an order with a supplier and the	Approved list of suppliers. Supplier evaluations. Purchasing

Section no.	ISO 9001:2008 title	Explanation	Likely documentation
		approval process for purchasing documentation.	procedures. Purchase orders. Stock control procedures.
7.4.3	Verification of purchased product	The controls that an organisation has in place to ensure that products and services provided by suppliers meet their original requirements.	Approved list of suppliers. Supplier evaluations. Purchasing procedures. Purchase orders. Stock control procedures.
7.5	Production and service provision	The availability of a process to cover all production and service operations.	Documented Processes, QPs and WIs for production and service operations.
7.5.1	Control of production and service provision	The provision of anything required to control production and service operations.	Procedures for the provision of everything necessary for staff to carry out their work. Project plans and resources required to carry out a job.
7.5.2	Validation of processes for production and service provision	How an organisation identifies processes which cannot be verified by subsequent monitoring/testing/inspection (including the validation of these processes to demonstrate their effectiveness).	Procedures for tasks which cannot subsequently be proved to be acceptable.
7.5.3	Identification and traceability	The means by which the status of a product can be identified at all stages of its production/ delivery. How the organisation ensures that inspection and test status has and will be identified 'throughout product realisation'.	Procedures for the provision of everything necessary for staff to carry out their work. Project plans and resources required to carry out a job.
7.5.4	Customer property	How an organisation looks after property before provided and personal data by a customer including identification, verification, storage and maintenance.	Procedure for the control of customer property.
7.5.5	Preservation of product	How an organisation looks after its own products (i.e. identification, handling, packaging, storing and protecting) including authorisation of release to a customer.	Product approval procedures. Procedures which ensure the safety and protection of products.

Section no.	ISO 9001:2008 title	Explanation	Likely documentation
7.6	Control of monitoring and measuring equipment	The controls that an organisation has in place to ensure that equipment (including software) used for proving conformance to specified requirements is properly maintained, calibrated and verified.	Equipment records of maintenance and calibration. WIs.
8	Measurement, analysis and improvement	The measurement, monitoring, analysis and improvement processes an organisation has in place to ensure that the QMS processes and products conform to requirements.	Procedures for inspection and measurement.
8.1	General	The definitions of procedures to ensure product conformity and product improvement.	Procedures for: • Product conformity; • Product improvement; and • Statistical process review.
8.2	Monitoring and measurement	The analysis of customer satisfaction and the control of products and processes.	Procedures for inspection and measurement.
8.2.1	Customer satisfaction	The processes used to establish whether a customer is satisfied with a product.	Documented Procedures for: • Customer feedback; • Change control; • Customer complaints; • Customer satisfaction and opinion surveys; • Necessary corrections and corrective actions; and • Records of audits and audit results.
8.2.2	Internal audit	The in-house checks determine if the QMS is functioning properly, that it continues to comply with the requirements of ISO 9001:2008 and to identify possibilities for improvement.	Audit procedure, made to Audit schedules. Audit plans, check sheets and records.
8.2.3	Measurement and monitoring of processes	The methods used to check if processes continue to meet their intended purpose.	Audit schedules. Audit plans, check sheets and records. Approval

Section no.	ISO 9001:2008 title	Explanation	Likely documentation
			procedures for product acceptance. Processes for failure cost analysis, conformity, non-conformity, life cycle approach, self-assessment. Compliance with environmental and safety policies, laws, regulations and standards. Procedures for testing and monitoring processes. Performance and product measurement procedures.
8.2.4	Monitoring and measurement of product	How an organisation measures and monitors product characteristics to meet the customer's specified requirements.	Audit schedules. Audit plans, check sheets and records. Approval procedures for product acceptance. Processes for failure cost analysis, conformity, non-conformity, life-cycle approach and self-assessment. Compliance with environmental and safety policies, laws, regulations and standards. Procedures for testing and monitoring processes. Performance and product measurement procedures. Supplier approval procedures.
8.3	Control of non-conforming product	The methods used to prevent the use or delivery of non-conforming products and to decide what to do with a non-conforming product.	Documented procedure to identify and control the use and delivery of non-conforming products. Approval procedures. Quarantine procedures. Change control procedure. Corrective and preventive action procedures. Audits.
8.4	Analysis of data	The methods used to review data that will determine the effectiveness of the QMS,	Any data or statistics produced as a result of audits, customer

Section no.	ISO 9001:2008 title	Explanation	Likely documentation
		especially with regard to customer satisfaction, conformance to customer requirements and the performance of processes and products.	satisfaction surveys, complaints, non-conformances, supplier evaluations, etc.
8.5	Improvement	How an organisation controls corrective and preventive actions and plans for ongoing process and product improvement.	Documented procedures for: • Corrective action; • Preventive action; • Product/process improvement; • Customer complaints/ feedback; • Non-conformity reports; • Management reviews; and • staff suggestions scheme.
8.5.1	Continual improvement	How an organisation goes about continually improving its QMS.	Procedures, minutes of meetings where improvement to the organisation's business is discussed. Management reviews.
8.5.2	Corrective action	What an organisation does to identify and put right non-conformities.	Process for eliminating causes of non-conformity. Documented complaints. Complaints procedure. Staff suggestions scheme.
8.5.3	Preventive action	The proactive methods an organisation employs to prevent non-conformities from happening in the first place.	Process for the prevention of non-conformity. Documented complaints. Complaints procedure. Staff suggestions scheme. Review process to ensure the effectiveness of the preventative action taken.

Annex B –
ISO 9001:2008 requirements
of management

Systemic Requirements

Section no.	ISO 9001:2008 title	Requirement	Explanation
4	QMS Requirement	Establish your quality system	So that it meets the requirements of ISO 9001:2008.
4.1	General requirements	Develop your processes *Note:* Outsourced controls shall be defined in the QMS.	• Identify the processes that make up your quality system; • Describe your quality management processes; • Implement your QMS; • Use quality system processes; • Manage process performance; • Improve your QMS; • Monitor process performance; • Improve process performance; • Outsourced controls shall be defined in the QMS
4.2	Documentation requirements	Document your quality system	
4.2.1	General	Develop quality system documents *Note*: A single document may address the requirements for one or more procedures and that a requirement for a documented procedure may be covered by more than one document.	• Develop documents to implement your quality system (QMS documentation **also** includes records); • Develop documents that reflect what your organisation does; and • Ensure that QMS documentation **also** includes records.
4.2.2	QM	Prepare quality system manual	• Document your procedures;

Section no.	ISO 9001:2008 title	Requirement	Explanation
			• Describe how your processes interact; and
			• Define the scope of your quality system.
4.2.3	Control of documents	Control quality system documents	• Approve documents before you distribute them;
		Note: Only external documents that the organisation believes are necessary for the planning and operation of the QMS, need to be identified and for their distribution to be controlled.	• Provide the correct version of documents at points of use;
			• Review and reapprove documents whenever you update them;
			• Specify the current revision status of your documents;
			• Monitor documents that come from external sources;
			• Prevent the accidental use of obsolete documents; and
			• Preserve the usability of your quality documents.
			Note: Only external documents that the organisation believes are necessary for the planning and operation of the QMS, need to be identified and for their distribution to be controlled.
4.2.4	Control of records	Maintain quality system records	• Use your records to prove that requirements have been met;
			• Develop a procedure to control your records; and
			• Ensure that your records are established and maintained to provide evidence of conformity.

Management Requirements

Section no.	ISO 9001:2008 title	Requirement	Explanation
5	Management responsibility		
5.1	Management commitment	Support quality	• Promote the importance of quality; • Promote the need to meet customer requirements; • Promote the need to meet regulatory requirements; • Promote the need to meet statutory requirements; • Develop a QMS; • Support the development of a quality system; • Formulate your organisation's quality policy; • Set your organisation's quality objectives; • Provide quality resources; • Implement your QMS; • Provide resources to implement your quality system; • Encourage personnel to meet quality system requirements; • Improve your QMS; • Perform quality management reviews; and • Provide resources to improve the quality system.
5.2	Customer focus	Satisfy your customers	• Identify customer requirements; • Expect your organisation to identify customer requirements;

Section no.	ISO 9001:2008 title	Requirement	Explanation
			• Meet your customers' requirements; • Expect your organisation to meet customer requirements; • Enhance customer satisfaction; and • Expect your organisation to enhance customer satisfaction.
5.3	Quality policy	Establish a quality policy	• Define your organisation's quality policy; • Ensure that it serves your organisation's purpose; • Ensure that it emphasises the need to meet requirements; • Ensure that it facilitates the development of quality objectives; • Ensure that it makes a commitment to continuous improvement; • Manage your organisation's quality policy; • Communicate your policy to your organisation; and • Review your policy to ensure that it is still suitable.
5.4	Planning	Carry out quality planning	
5.4.1	Quality objectives	Formulate your quality objectives	• Ensure that objectives are set for functional areas; • Ensure that objectives are set at organisational levels; • Ensure that objectives facilitate product realisation; • Ensure that objectives support the quality

Section no.	ISO 9001:2008 title	Requirement	Explanation
			policy; and • Ensure that objectives are measurable.
5.4.2	QMS planning	Plan your QMS	• Plan the development of your QMS; • Plan the implementation of your QMS; • Plan the improvement of your QMS; and • Plan the modification of your QMS.
5.5	Responsibility, authority and communication	Control your quality system	
5.5.1	Responsibility and authority	Define responsibilities and authorities	• Clarify responsibilities and authorities; and • Communicate responsibilities and authorities.
5.5.2	Management representative	Appoint management representative *Note*: The management representative **must** be a member of the organisation's own management and '*outsiders*' may no longer perform this important function.	• Oversee your QMS; • Report on the status of your QMS; and • Support the improvement of your QMS.
5.5.3	Internal communication	Support internal communications	• Ensure that internal communication processes are established; and • Ensure that communication occurs throughout the organisation.
5.6	Management review	Perform management reviews	
5.6.1	General	Review QMS	• Evaluate the performance of your quality system; and • Evaluate whether your quality system should be improved.

Section no.	ISO 9001:2008 title	Requirement	Explanation
5.6.2	Review input	Examine management review inputs	• Examine audit results; • Examine product conformity data; • Examine opportunities to improve; • Examine feedback from customers; • Examine process performance information; • Examine corrective and preventive actions; • Examine changes that might affect your system; and • Examine previous quality management reviews.
5.6.3	Review output	Generate management review outputs	• Generate actions to improve your quality system; • Generate actions to improve your products; and • Generate actions to address resource.

Resource Requirements

Section no.	ISO 9001:2008 title	Requirement	Explanation
6	Resource management		
6.1	Provision of resources	Provide quality resources	• Identify quality resource requirements; • Identify resources needed to support the quality system; • Identify resources needed to improve customer satisfaction; • Provide quality system resources; • Provide resources needed to support the

Section no.	ISO 9001:2008 title	Requirement	Explanation
			quality system; and
			• Provide resources needed to improve customer satisfaction.
6.2	Human resources	Provide quality personnel	
6.2.1	General	Use competent personnel *Note*: Where training needs to be provided, itshould be in order '*to achieve the necessary competence*'.	• As any QMS task could directly or indirectly influence product quality, ensure that all QMS personnel are competent; • Ensure that your personnel have the right experience; • Ensure that your personnel have the right education; • Ensure that your personnel have the right training; and • Ensure that your personnel have the right skills.
6.2.2	Competence, training and awareness	Support competence	• Define acceptable levels of competence; • Identify training and awareness needs; • Deliver training and awareness programs; • Evaluate effectiveness of training and awareness; and • Maintain a record of competence.
6.3	Infrastructure	Provide quality infrastructure *Note*: The new standard expects an organisation to provide the infrastructure (including information systems) that is needed *to ensure that product requirements are being met*.	• Identify infrastructure needs; • Identify building needs; • Identify workspace needs; • Identify hardware needs; • Identify software needs; • Identify utility needs; Identify equipment needs;

Section no.	ISO 9001:2008 title	Requirement	Explanation
			• Identify support service needs; • Provide needed infrastructure; • Provide needed buildings; • Provide needed workspaces; • Provide needed hardware; • Provide needed software; • Provide needed utilities; • Provide needed equipment; • Provide needed support services; • Maintain your infrastructure; • Maintain your buildings; • Maintain your workspaces; • Maintain your hardware; • Maintain your software; • Maintain your utilities; • Maintain your equipment; and • Maintain your support services.
6.4	Work environment *Note*: 'Work environment' includes conditions (i.e. environmental conditions such as noise, temperature; humidity,	Provide quality environment	• Identify needed work environment; • Identify factors needed to ensure products meet requirements; • Manage needed work environment; and • Manage factors needed to ensure that products meet requirements.

Section no.	ISO 9001:2008 title	Requirement	Explanation
	lighting and weather) under which work is performed.		

Realisation Requirements

Section no.	ISO 9001:2008 title	Requirement	Explanation
7	Product realisation		
7.1	Planning and realisation	Control realisation planning	• Plan product realisation processes; • Define product quality objectives and requirements; • Identify product realisation needs and requirements; • Develop product realisation processes; • Develop product realisation documents; • Develop product realisation record keeping systems; • Develop product measurement processes; and • Develop methods to control quality during product realisation.
7.2	Customer-related processes	Control customer processes	
7.2.1	Determination of requirements related to product	Identify customers' product requirements *Note: 'Post delivery activities' also include* things like warranty provisions, contractual obligations (e.g. maintenance), and supplementary services (e.g. recycling and final disposal).	• Identify the requirements that customers want you to meet; • Identify the requirements that are dictated by the product's use; • Identify the requirements that are imposed by external agencies; and

Section no.	ISO 9001:2008 title	Requirement	Explanation
			• Identify the requirements that your organisation wishes to meet.
7.2.2	Review of requirements related to product	Review customers' product requirements	• Review requirements before you accept orders from customers; • Maintain a record of your product requirement reviews; and • Control changes in product requirements.
7.2.3	Customer communication	Communicate with your customers	• Develop a process to control communications with customers; and • Implement your customer communications process.
7.3	Design and development	Control product development	
7.3.1	Design and development planning	Plan design and development *Note*: Whilst organisations are expected to plan and perform product design and development review, verification, and validation activities, these three activities can be carried out and recorded separately.	• Define your product design and development stages; • Clarify design and development responsibilities and authorities; • Manage interactions between design and development groups; • Update your design and development plans as changes occur.
7.3.2	Design and development inputs	Define design and development inputs	• Specify product design and development inputs; • Record product design and development input definitions; and • Review product design and development input definitions.

Section no.	ISO 9001:2008 title	Requirement	Explanation
7.3.3	Design and development outputs *Note*: Design and development outputs should also include information that explains how products can be preserved during production and service provision.	Generate design and development outputs	• Create product design and development outputs • Approve design and development outputs prior to release; and • Use design and development outputs to control product quality.
7.3.4	Design and development review	Carry out design and development reviews	• Perform product design and development reviews; and • Record product design and development reviews.
7.3.5	Design and development verification	Perform design and development verifications	• Carry out product design and development verifications; and • Record product design and development verifications.
7.3.6	Design and development validation	Conduct design and development validations	• Perform product design and development validations; and • Record product design and development validations.
7.3.7	Control of design and development changes	Manage design and development changes	• Identify changes in product design and development; • Record changes in product design and development; • Review changes in product design and development; • Verify changes in product design and

Section no.	ISO 9001:2008 title	Requirement	Explanation
			development; • Validate changes in product design and development; and • Approve changes before they are implemented.
7.4	Purchasing	Control purchasing function	
7.4.1	Purchasing process	Control purchasing process	• Ensure that purchased products meet requirements; and • Ensure that suppliers meet requirements.
7.4.2	Purchasing information	Document product purchases	• Describe the products being purchased; and • Specify the requirements that must be met.
7.4.3	Verification of purchased product	Verify purchased products	• Verify purchased products at your own premises; and • Verify purchased products at suppliers' premises (when required).
7.5	Production and service operations	Control operational activities	
7.5.1	Control of production and service provision	Control production and service provision	• Control production and service processes; • Control production and service information; • Control production and service instructions; • Control production and service equipment; • Control production and service measurements; and • Control production and service activities.
7.5.2	Validation of processes for production and service provision	Validate production and service provision	• Prove that special processes can produce planned outputs; • Prove that process

Section no.	ISO 9001:2008 title	Requirement	Explanation
			personnel can produce planned results; and • Prove that process equipment can produce planned results.
7.5.3	Identification and traceability	Identify and track your products	• Establish the identity of your products (when appropriate); • Maintain the identity of your products (when appropriate); • Identify the status of your products (when appropriate); • Record the identity of your products (when required); and • Identify inspection and test status throughout product realisation.
7.5.4	Customer property	Protect property supplied by customers *Note*: Personal data can also include property and personal data.	• Identify property supplied to you by your customers; • Verify property supplied to you by your customers; and • Safeguard property supplied to you by your customers.
7.5.5	Preservation of product	Preserve your products and components	• Preserve products and components during internal processing; and • Preserve products and components during final delivery.
7.6	Control of measuring and monitoring equipment	Control monitoring devices	• Identify monitoring and measuring needs; • Identify the monitoring and measuring that should be done; • Select monitoring and measuring equipment;

Section no.	ISO 9001:2008 title	Requirement	Explanation
			• Select equipment that meet your monitoring and measuring needs;
			• Calibrate monitoring and measuring equipment;
			• Perform calibrations;
			• Record calibrations;
			• Protect monitoring and measuring equipment;
			• Protect your equipment from unauthorised adjustment;
			• Protect your equipment from damage or deterioration;
			• Validate monitoring and measuring software;
			• Validate monitoring and measuring software before you use it;
			• Revalidate monitoring and measuring software when necessary;
			• Use equipments to ensure that your products meet requirements; and
			• Ensure that verification and configuration management of computer software has not been overlooked.

Remedial Requirements

Section no.	ISO 9001:2008 title	Requirement	Explanation
8	Measurement, analysis and improvement		
8.1	General	Perform remedial processes	• Plan remedial processes;

Section no.	ISO 9001:2008 title	Requirement	Explanation
			• Plan how remedial processes will be used to assure conformity; • Plan how remedial processes will be used to improve the system; • Implement remedial processes; • Use remedial processes to demonstrate conformance; and • Use remedial processes to improve QMS.
8.2	Monitoring and measurement	Monitor and measure quality	
8.2.1	Customer satisfaction	Monitor and measure customer satisfaction *Note*: Customer satisfaction and opinion surveys may be used for this purpose. Auditing has to include '*necessary corrections and corrective actions*' and records of audits **must** include audit results.	• Identify ways to monitor and measure customer satisfaction; • Monitor and measure customer satisfaction; and • Use customer satisfaction information.
8.2.2	Internal audit *Note*: a documented procedure for Internal Auditing **must** define the responsibilities and requirements for conducting audits; establishing records and; reporting and maintaining output results.	Plan and perform regular internal audits	• Set up an internal audit program; • Develop an internal audit procedure; • Plan your internal audit projects; • Perform regular internal audits; • Solve problems discovered during audits; and • Verify that the problems have been solved.
8.2.3	Monitoring and measurement of processes	Monitor and measure quality processes	• Use suitable methods to monitor and measure your processes; and

Section no.	ISO 9001:2008 title	Requirement	Explanation
			• Take action when your processes fail to achieve planned results. *Note*: When products are released for delivery to customers, records must indicate who releases the products for delivery to customers.
8.2.4	Monitoring and measurement of product	Monitor and measure product characteristics	• Verify that product characteristics are being met; and • Keep a record of product monitoring and measuring activities.
8.3	Control of non-conforming product	Control non-conforming products	• Develop a procedure to control non-conforming products; • Define how non-conforming products should be identified; • Define how non-conforming products should be handled; • Identify and control your non-conforming products; • Eliminate or correct product non-conformities; • Prevent the delivery or use of non-conforming products; • Avoid the inappropriate use of non-conforming products; • Reverify non-conforming products that were corrected; • Prove that corrected products now meet requirements;

Section no.	ISO 9001:2008 title	Requirement	Explanation
			• Control non-conforming products after delivery or use; • Control events when you deliver or use non-conforming products; • Maintain records of non-conforming products; • Describe your product non-conformities; and • Describe the actions taken to deal with non-conformities.
8.4	Analysis of data	Analyse quality information	• Define quality management information needs; • Define the information you need to evaluate your quality system; • Define the information you need to improve your quality system; • Collect QMS data; • Monitor and measure the suitability of your quality system; • Monitor and measure the effectiveness of your quality system; • Provide quality management information; • Provide information about your customers; • Provide information about your suppliers; • Provide information about your products; and • Provide information about your processes.
8.5	Improvement	Make quality improvements	
8.5.1	Continual improvement	Improve QMS	• Use your audits to generate improvements;

Section no.	ISO 9001:2008 title	Requirement	Explanation
			• Use your quality data to generate improvements; • Use your quality policy to generate improvements; • Use your quality objectives to generate improvements; • Use your management reviews to generate improvements; • Use your corrective actions to generate improvements; and • Use your preventive actions to generate improvements.
8.5.2	Corrective action	Correct actual non-conformities	• Review your non-conformities; • Figure out what causes your non-conformities; • Evaluate whether you need to take corrective action; • Develop corrective actions to prevent recurrence; • Take corrective actions when they are necessary; • Record the results that your corrective actions achieve; and • Examine the effectiveness of your corrective actions.
8.5.3	Preventive action	Prevent potential non-conformities	• Review the effectiveness of the preventative action taken; • Detect potential non-conformities; • Identify the causes of potential non-conformities;

Section no.	ISO 9001:2008 title	Requirement	Explanation
			• Study the effects of potential non-conformities; • Evaluate whether you need to take preventive action; • Develop preventive actions to eliminate causes; • Take preventive actions when they are necessary; • Record the results that your preventive actions achieve; and • Examine the effectiveness of your preventive actions.

Annex C –
Example checklists of typical
auditors' questions for ISO 9001:2008
compliance

Systematic Requirements

Section no.	ISO 9001:2008 title	Typical auditor's questions
4	Quality System	Management requirement
4.1	General requirements	• Does the company have a copy or access to a copy of ISO 9001:2008? • Has a QMS been established in accordance with the requirements of ISO 9001:2008? • Have all references been amended to reflect an upgrade to ISO 9001:2008? • Is the QMS: – Documented? – Implemented? – Maintained? – Continually improved? • Does the organisation have all the documents necessary to ensure the effective operation and control of its processes? • Has the organisation: – Identified the sequence of processes and subprocesses needed for the QMS? – Determined the sequence and interaction of these processes? – Determined the criteria and methods required to ensure the effective operation and control of these processes? – Ensured that information necessary to support the monitoring and operation of these processes is available? – Confirm that any outsourced process is fully controlled where there is potential for an impact on the product or service provided.

Section no.	ISO 9001:2008 title	Typical auditor's questions
		Note: This should be controlled through clause 7.4. The type and extent of control should also be defined. • Does the organisation measure, monitor and analyse these processes? • Is the necessary action implemented to achieve planned results and continual improvement of the processes? • Does the organisation manage these processes in accordance with the requirements of ISO 9001:2008?
4.2	Documentation requirements	
4.2.1	General	Does the QMS include: • AQM • Statements concerning quality policy and quality objectives? • Documented procedures? • Quality records?

4.2.2	QM	• Is the QM
		  – Controlled?
		  – Maintained?
		• Does it include details concerning:
		  – The scope of the QMS?
		  – Justifications for any exclusion from the ISO 9001:2008 requirements?
		  – Associated documented procedures?
		  – The sequence and interaction of processes?

4.2.3	Control of documents	• Has the organisation established a documented procedure to control all of its QMS documents?
		• Does this procedure include methods for:
		  – Controlling their distribution?
		  – Approving documents prior to issue?
		  – Reviewing, updating and re-approving documents?
		  – Identifying the current revision status of documents?
		  – Ensuring that documents fulfil a useful purpose in the organisation?
		  – Ensuring that relevant versions of all applicable documents are available at points of use?
		  – Ensuring that documents remain legible, readily identifiable and retrievable?

Section no.	ISO 9001:2008 title	Typical auditor's questions
		– Ensuring that information is kept up to date? – Identifying, distributing and controlling of documents received from an external source? – Ensuring that classified information is restricted to those who are authorised to receive it? – The identification and control of obsolete documents that have been retained for any purpose?

4.2.4	Control of records	• Does the organisation have a documented procedure for records covering:
		  – Control, maintenance and identification?
		  – Storage and retrieval?
		  – Protection and retention?
		• Do these records provide evidence of:
		  – The organisation's conformance to the ISO 9001:2008 requirements?
		  – The effective operation of the QMS?

Management Requirements

Section no.	ISO 9001:2008 title	Typical auditor's questions
5	Management responsibility	

5.1	Management commitment	• Does the organisation demonstrate its commitment to developing, establishing and improving the organisation's QMS through:
		  – Management commitment?
		  – An established quality policy?
		  – Determining customer requirements and achieving customer satisfaction?
		  – A quality policy?
		  – Regularly reviewing the QMS documentation?
		• Does the organisation:
		  – Ensure that all personnel are aware of the importance of meeting customer, regulatory and legal requirements?
		  – Establish the quality policy and quality objectives?

Section no.	ISO 9001:2008 title	Typical auditor's questions
		– Conduct internal management reviews? – Ensure the availability of necessary resources to administer the QMS?
5.2	Customer focus	• Does the organisation ensure that customer needs and expectations are recognised and established? • Are these customer needs and expectations converted into requirements? • Does the organisation ensure that customer requirements are fulfilled?
5.3	Quality policy	• Is the organisation's quality policy: – Controlled? – Appropriate? – Regularly reviewed for continued suitability? – Committed to meeting requirements? – Communicated and understood throughout the company? – Capable of continual improvement? – Capable of providing a framework for establishing and reviewing quality objectives?
5.4	Planning	
5.4.1	Quality objectives	• Is the organisation's quality planning documented? • Does it include: – Quality objectives? – Resources? • Has the organisation established quality objectives for each relevant function and level within the company? • Are the organisation's quality objectives measurable and consistent with quality policy? • Do they include: – A commitment for continual improvement? – Product requirements?
5.4.2	QMS planning	• Does the organisation's quality planning cover: – The processes required for a QMS (as mentioned in Section 4)? – The identification and availability of resources and information?

Section no.	ISO 9001:2008 title	Typical auditor's questions
		– Any permissible exclusion (to the requirements of ISO 9001:2008)? – The requirements for continual improvement? – The requirements for change control? • Does the organisation's quality planning ensure that the QMS is maintained during planned changes?
5.5	Responsibility, authority and communication	• Has the organisation defined and implemented a QMS that addresses its quality objectives? • Is the administration of the organisation's QMS documented? • Does it cover: – Responsibilities and authorities? – Management representative's duties? – Internal communication? – The QM? – Control of documents? – Control of quality records?
5.5.1	Responsibility and authority	• Are the functions and interrelationships of all staff defined? • Are staff responsibilities and authorities defined?
5.5.2	Management representative	• Has the organisation appointed a Quality Manager who (regardless of all other duties) has sole responsibility for the implementation and management of the QMS? • Confirm that the Management Representative is a member of the organisation's own management. • Is the administration of the organisation's QMS documented? • Does the organisation's QMS adequately cover: – Responsibilities and authorities? – Management representative's duties?
5.5.3	Internal communication	• Does the organisation ensure that there are lines of communication between all members of staff to ensure the effectiveness of the QMS processes? • Is there a procedure for internal communication?

Section no.	ISO 9001:2008 title	Typical auditor's questions
5.6	Management review	• Does the organisation's Top Management regularly review the QMS at planned intervals?

5.6.1	General	• Does the QMS review cover the continuing suitability, adequacy and effectiveness of the QMS?
		• Does the review evaluate the:
		  – Need for changes?
		  – Quality policy?
		  – Quality objectives?

5.6.2	Review input	• Does the management review include:
		  – Internal audit results?
		  – External and third party audit results?
		  – Customer feedback?
		  – Process performance?
		  – Product conformance?
		  – Implemented preventive and corrective actions?
		  – Outstanding preventive and corrective actions?
		  – Results from previous management reviews?
		  – Changes that could affect the QMS?

5.6.3	Review output	• Do the outputs of management reviews include recommendations for:
		  – The improvement of the QMS and its processes?
		  – The improvement of product related to customer requirements?
		  – Confirming and establishing resource needs?
		  – Are the results of management reviews recorded?
		  – Are the results (e.g. minutes and action sheets) circulated?

6	Resource management	

6.1	Provision of resources	• Does the organisation provide the resources required to:
		  – Implement and improve the QMS processes?
		  – Ensure customer satisfaction?
		  – Meet customer requirements?

6.2	Human resources	• Has the organisation established procedures for:

Section no.	ISO 9001:2008 title	Typical auditor's questions
		– The assignment of personnel? – Training? – Awareness? – Competency?

6.2.1	General	• Has the organisation established procedures for the assignment of personnel on the basis of:
		  – Competency?
		  – Qualification?
		  – Training?
		  – Skill and experience?
		  – Ensure that any person performing work affecting 'conformity of the product/service' is competent.

6.2.2	Competence, awareness and training	• Does the organisation:
		  – Identify training requirements?
		  – Provide appropriate training?
		  – Evaluate the training provided?
		• Does the organisation ensure that all staff appreciates the relevance and importance of their activities and how they contribute towards achieving quality objectives?
		• Does the organisation keep staff records covering education, experience, qualifications, training, etc.?

6.3	Infrastructure	• Does the organisation identify, provide and maintain the necessary:
		  – Workspace and associated facilities?
		  – Equipment, hardware and software?
		  – Supporting services (e.g. information systems)?

6.4	Work environment	• Does the organisation identify and manage the work environment (including human and physical factors) to ensure conformity of product? • Confirm that all applicable work environment conditions have been considered?
7	Product realisation	• Has the organisation established the processes necessary to achieve the product?
7.1	Planning and realisation	• Has the organisation: – Identified the sequence of processes and subprocesses needed for the QMS?

Section no.	ISO 9001:2008 title	Typical auditor's questions
		– Determined the sequence and interaction of these processes? – Determined the criteria and methods required to ensure the effective operation and control of these processes? – Ensured that information necessary to support the monitoring and operation of these processes is available? – Ensured that resources necessary to support the monitoring and operation of these processes are available? • Within this sequence of processes and subprocesses has the following been determined: – The quality objectives for the product, project or contract? – Product-specific processes, documentation, resources and facilities? – Verification and validation activities? – Criteria for acceptability? – Required records? • Does the organisation have a documented procedure for records covering: – Control, maintenance and identification? – Storage and retrieval? – Protection and retention? • Do these records provide evidence of: – The organisation's conformance to the ISO 9001:2008 requirements?
7.2	Customer-related	• Has the organisation established processes procedures for the: – Identification of customer requirements? – Review of product requirements? – Customer communication?
7.2.1	Determination of requirements related to product	• Has the organisation established a process for identifying customer requirements? • Does this process determine: – Customer-specified product requirements (e.g. availability, delivery and support)? – Non-specified customer requirements (e.g. those affecting the product)?

Section no.	ISO 9001:2008 title	Typical auditor's questions
		– Mandatory requirements (such as regulatory and legal obligations)? – Ensure that any post delivery activity is covered (e.g. warranty, recycling, disposal obligation)?
7.2.2	Review of requirements related to product	• Has the organisation established a process for ensuring that product requirements have been fully established? • Does the process ensure that (prior to submission of tender or acceptance of contract): – All customer requirements have been defined and can be met? – Where no written requirements are available, that verbal customer requirements are confirmed? – Any contract or order requirements differing from those previously expressed (e.g. in a tender or quotation) are resolved? – The organisation has the ability to meet the defined requirements?
7.2.3	Customer communication	• Has the organisation an established process for: – Providing customers with product information? – Handling customer enquiries, contracts or orders (including amendments)? – Customer feedback and customer complaints?
7.3	Design and development	• Has the organisation developed a process and adequate procedures for their design and development activities?
7.3.1	Design and development planning	• Does the organisation plan and control design and development of the product? • Do these processes include: – Stage review, verification and validation activities? – Identification of responsibilities and authorities? – Management of the interfaces between different groups that may be involved? – Provision of effective communication and clarity of responsibilities?

Section no.	ISO 9001:2008 title	Typical auditor's questions
		– Product and planning reviews? • Are these processes adequate? • Has the design review, verification and validation been conducted and recorded as suitable for the product and/or the organisation?

7.3.2	Design and development inputs	• Does the organisation have a process for developing Project Plans?
		• Does the organisation define and document product requirement inputs?
		• Do these input requirements include:
		  – Function and performance requirements?
		  – Applicable regulatory and legal requirements?
		  – Applicable standards, specifications and tolerances?
		  – Applicable requirements derived from previous similar designs?
		  – Any other requirements essential for design and development?
		• Are inadequate, incomplete, ambiguous or conflicting input requirements resolved?

7.3.3	Design and development outputs	• Are all products approved prior to release?
		• Does the organisation define and document their product outputs?
		• Do these critical requirements ensure that the product:
		  – Meets the design and development input requirements?
		  – Provides appropriate information for production and service operations?
		  – Contains or makes reference to product acceptance criteria?
		  – Defines the characteristics of the product that are essential to its safe and proper use?
		• The preservation of the product has been considered?

7.3.4	Design and development review	• Are systematic reviews of the design and development carried out at suitable stages? – Evaluate the ability of the product to fulfil the requirements?

Section no.	ISO 9001:2008 title	Typical auditor's questions
		– Include representatives from the functions concerned with the design and development stage being reviewed?
		• Are follow-up actions from the reviews recorded?
7.3.5	Design and development verification	• Does the organisation verify that the design output meets the design and development input? • Are these results of this verification (and any necessary subsequent follow-up actions) recorded?
7.3.6	Design and development validation	• Does the organisation validate that the product is capable of meeting the requirements of intended use? • Are these results and any necessary subsequent follow-up actions recorded? • Wherever applicable, is the validation completed prior to the delivery or implementation of the product? • If full validation is impractical prior to delivery or implementation of the product, is a partial validation performed to the maximum extent applicable?
7.3.7	Control of design and development changes	• Does the organisation have a procedure that identifies the need for a design and development change? • Are these results of implementing this procedure (and any necessary subsequent follow-up actions) recorded? • Are the effects of these changes reviewed, verified and validated before implementation?
7.4	Purchasing	• Does the organisation have processes for: – Purchasing control? – Purchasing information? – Verification of purchased product?
7.4.1	Purchasing process	• Does the organisation have processes for: – Purchasing control? – Purchasing information? – Verification of purchased product?
7.4.2	Purchasing information	• Does the organisation have documentation describing: – The product to be purchased?

Section no.	ISO 9001:2008 title	Typical auditor's questions
		– Requirements for approval or qualification (i.e. product, procedures, processes, equipment and personnel)? – QMS requirements? – Does the organisation ensure the adequacy of the specified requirements contained in the purchasing documents prior to their release?
7.4.3	Verification of purchased product	• Does the organisation identify (and implement) the activities necessary for the verification of a purchased product? • Are these verification arrangements specified by the organisation or its customer (particularly if verification is to be carried out at the supplier's premises)? • Is the method of product release specified in the purchasing documents (particularly if verification is to be carried out at the supplier's premises)?
7.5	Production and service operations?	• Does the organisation have procedures for the control of: – Production and service operations? – Identification and traceability? – Customer property? – Preservation of product? – Validation of processes?
7.5.1	Control of production	• Does the organisation plan and control and service provision production and service operations? • Is this achieved through: – Information concerning the characteristics of the product? – Appropriate WIs? – The use and maintenance of suitable equipment for production and service operations? – The availability and use of measuring and monitoring devices?
7.5.2	Validation of processes for production and service provision	• Where the resulting output cannot be verified by subsequent measurement or monitoring, does the organisation validate production and service processes to demonstrate the ability of the processes to achieve planned results?

Section no.	ISO 9001:2008 title	Typical auditor's questions

		• Does this validation demonstrate the ability of the processes to achieve planned results?
		• Does the validation include:
		  – Qualification of processes?
		  – Qualification of equipment and personnel?
		  – Use of defined methodologies and procedures?
		  – Requirements for records?
		  – Re-validation?
		  – Does this validation include any processes where deficiencies may become apparent only after the product is in use or the service has been delivered?

7.5.3	Identification and traceability	• Does the organisation have procedures available to identify the product throughout production and service operations? • Is the product status identifiable with respect to measurement and monitoring requirements? • When traceability is a requirement, does the organisation control and record the unique identification of a product?
7.5.4	Customer property *Note*: Personal data and intellectual property (e.g. software) may now be considered as customer property and reported if unsuitable.	• Does the organisation exercise care with customer property? • Does the organisation verify, protect and maintain customer property provided for use or incorporated into a product? • Are records maintained of any customer property that is lost, damaged or otherwise found to be unsuitable for use?
7.5.5	Preservation of product	• Does the organisation have set procedures for the identification, handling, packaging, storage and protection of products during internal processing and delivery to the intended destination?

7.6	Control of measuring and monitoring equipment:
	
	Note: In most circumstances, computer software may not be subject to traditional calibration.
		• Where applicable, are measuring and monitoring devices:
		  – Calibrated and adjusted periodically, or prior to use, against devices traceable to international or national standards?
		  – Safeguarded from adjustments that would invalidate the calibration?

Section no.	ISO 9001:2008 title	Typical auditor's questions
	In these cases, '*calibration*' may be focused on verification and configuration management.	– Protected from damage and deterioration during handling, maintenance and storage? – Are the results of the calibration recorded? *Note*: Calibration status identification does not have to be physically on the equipment, **provided** that the identification employed can determine the calibration status. – Is the validity of previous results re-assessed if they are subsequently found to be out of calibration, and corrective action taken? – If software is used for measuring and monitoring, has it been validated prior to use?
8	Measurement, analysis and improvement	• Does the organisation define the activities needed to measure and monitor: – Product conformity? – Product improvement?
8.1	General	• Does the organisation define the activities needed to measure and monitor: – product conformity? – product improvement? • Does the organisation continually strive to improve the effectiveness of its QMS?
8.2	Monitoring and measurement	• Does the organisation have procedures available to: – Ensure customer satisfaction? – Control internal audits? – Ensure effective measurement and monitoring of products and processes?
8.2.1	Customer satisfaction	• Does the organisation monitor information regarding customer satisfaction? • Does the organisation monitor information regarding customer dissatisfaction? • Are the methods and measures for obtaining such information defined? • Is there an agreed change control procedure? • Is there an agreed customer complaints procedure?

Section no.	ISO 9001:2008 title	Typical auditor's questions
		• Are these methods and measures utilised as part of the performance measurements of the QMS?

8.2.2	Internal audit	• Has the organisation a documented QP for conducting internal audits?
		• Does the organisation conduct periodic internal audits?
		• Do these audits determine whether the QMS:
		  – Conforms to the requirements of ISO 9001:2008?
		  – Has been effectively implemented and maintained?
		• Are audits only carried out by personnel who are not associated with the activity or department being audited?
		• Are the audits planned to take into account:
		  – The status and importance of the activities and areas to be audited?
		  – The results of previous audits?
		• Are the audit scope, frequency and methodologies defined?
		• Does the organisation have a documented procedure for audits that includes:
		  – The responsibilities and requirements for conducting audits?
		  – The method for recording results?
		  – The method for reporting to management?
		• Does the management implement correction and corrective action on deficiencies found during an audit?
		• Do these follow-up actions include the verification of the implementation of corrective action and the reporting of verification results?

8.2.3	Monitoring and measurement of processes	• Does the organisation apply suitable methods for the measurement and monitoring of processes:
		  – To meet customer requirements?
		  – To confirm the process's continuing ability to satisfy its intended purpose?
		  – Confirm that appropriate monitoring and measurement processes have

Section no.	ISO 9001:2008 title	Typical auditor's questions
		been implemented, dependent on the impact of the product/service and the effectiveness of the management system?
8.2.4	Monitoring and measurement of product	• Does the organisation apply suitable methods to measure and monitor the characteristics of the product at appropriate stages of the product realisation process? • Is there a documented evidence of conformity with the acceptance criteria? • Are the responsibilities and authorities defined with regard to the release of product? • Does the organisation ensure that the product is not released or the service delivered until all specified activities have been satisfactorily completed (unless otherwise approved by the customer)? • When products are released to the customer, does the organisation maintain records of who is responsible to sign off on the product for delivery?

8.3	Control of non-conforming product
	
	Note: Corrective action taken should be appropriate to the effects or the potential effects of the non-conformity when non-conforming product is detected **after** delivery or use has started.
		• Has the organisation defined a procedure for the control of non-conformities?
		• Does this procedure ensure that:
		  – Products which do not conform to requirements are prevented from unintended use or delivery?
		  – Non-conforming products that have been corrected are subject to reverification to demonstrate conformity?
		  – Non-conforming products detected after delivery or use are either corrected or removed from service?
		• Is there a provision for the notification of the customer, end user, regulatory or other body when required?

8.4	Analysis of data	• Does the organisation collect and analyse data to determine suitability and effectiveness of the QMS? • Does the organisation analyse the data to provide information regarding: – Possible improvement that can be made to the QMS?

Section no.	ISO 9001:2008 title	Typical auditor's questions
		– Customer satisfaction and dissatisfaction? – Conformance to customer requirements? – The characteristics of processes, products and their trends? – Suppliers?
8.5	Improvement	• Does the organisation have procedures available for: – Planning continual improvement? – Corrective action? – Preventive action?
8.5.1	Continual improvement	• Does the organisation plan and manage the processes necessary for the continual improvement of the QMS? • Is the continual improvement of the QMS facilitated by the use of: – The quality policy? – Quality objectives? – Audit results? – Analysis of data? – Corrective and preventive action? – Management reviews? – Concessions and approvals? – Concession scheme? – Defects and defect reports? – Bonded store?
8.5.2	Corrective action	• Has the organisation a documented procedure to enable corrective action to be taken to eliminate the cause of non-conformities and prevent recurrence? • Does this procedure define the requirements for: – Identification of non-conformities (including customer complaints)? – Determining the causes of non-conformities? – Evaluating the need for action to ensure that non-conformities do not recur? – Determining and implementing the corrective action needed? – Ensuring that results of action taken are recorded? – Reviewing the effectiveness of the corrective action taken?

Section no.	ISO 9001:2008 title	Typical auditor's questions

8.5.3	Preventive action	• Has the organisation a documented procedure to enable preventative action to be taken to eliminate the cause of non-conformities and prevent recurrence?
		• Does this procedure define the requirements for:
		  – Identification of non-conformities (including customer complaints)?
		  – Determining the causes of non-conformities?
		  – Evaluating the need for action to ensure that non-conformities do not recur?
		  – Determining and implementing the preventative action needed?
		  – Ensuring that results of action taken are recorded?
		  – Reviewing the effectiveness of the preventative action taken?

Annex D –
Example internal stage audit checklists

Design Stage

Item		Related item		Remark
1	Requirements	1.1	Information	• Has the customer fully described his requirement? • Has the customer any mandatory requirements? • Are the customer's requirements fully understood by all members of the design team? • Is there a need to have further discussions with the customer? • Are other suppliers or subcontractors involved? • If yes, who is the prime contractor?
		1.2	Standards	• What international standards need to be observed? • Are they available? • What national standards need to be observed? • Are they available? • What other information and procedures are required? • Are they available?
		1.3	Procedures	• Are there any customer-supplied drawings, sketches or plans? • Have they been registered?
2	QPs	2.1	Procedures Manual	• Is one available? Does it contain detailed procedures and instructions for the control of all drawings within the drawing office?
		2.2	Planning, Implementation and Production	• Is the project split into a number of Work Packages? • If so: – Are the various Work Packages listed? – Have Work Package Leaders been nominated? – Is their task clear? – Is their task achievable? – Is a time plan available? – Is it up-to-date?

	Item		Related item	Remark
				– Regularly maintained? – Relevant to the task?
3	Drawings	3.1	Identification	• Are all drawings identified by a unique number? Is the numbering system strictly controlled?
		3.2	Cataloguing	• Is a catalogue of drawings maintained? • Is this catalogue regularly reviewed and up-to-date?
		3.3	Amendments and Modifications	• Is there a procedure for authorising the issue of amendments and changes to drawings? Is there a method for withdrawing and disposing of obsolete drawings?
4	Components	4.1	Availability	• Are complete lists of all the relevant components available?
		4.2	Adequacy	• Are the selected components currently available and adequate for the task? • If not, how long will they take to procure? • Is this acceptable?
		4.3	Acceptability	• If alternative components have to be used, are they acceptable to the task?
5	Records	5.1	Failure reports	• Has the Design Office access to all records, failure reports and other relevant data?
		5.2	Reliability data	• Is reliability data correctly stored, maintained and analysed?
		5.3	Graphs, diagrams and plans	• In addition to drawings, is there a system for the control of all graphs, tables, plans, etc.? • Are CAD (Computer Aided Design) facilities available? (If so, go to 6.1)
6	Reviews and Audits	6.1	Computers	• If a processor is being used: – Are all the design office personnel trained in its use? – Are regular backups taken? – Is there an anti-virus system in place?
		6.2	Manufacturing Division	• Is a close relationship being maintained between the design office and the manufacturing division?

Item	Related item	Remark
	6.3	• Is notice being taken of the manufacturing division's exact requirements, their problems and their choices of components, etc.?

Manufacturing Stage

Item		Related item		Remark
1	Degree of quality	1.1	Quality control procedures	• Are they relevant to the task? • Are they understood by all members of the manufacturing team? • Are they regularly reviewed and up-to-date? • Are they subject to control procedures?
		1.2	Quality control checks	• What quality checks are being observed? Are they relevant? • Are there laid down procedures for carrying out these checks? • Are they available? • Are they regularly updated?
2	Reliability of product design	2.1	Statistical data	• Is there a system for predicting the reliability of the product's design? • Is sufficient statistical data available to be able to estimate the actual reliability of the design, before a product is manufactured? • Is the appropriate engineering data available?
		2.2	Components and parts	• Are the reliability ratings of recommended parts and components available? • Are probability methods used to examine the reliability of a proposed design? • If so, have these checks revealed design deficiencies such as: – Assembly errors? – Operator learning, motivational, or fatigue factors? – Latent defects? – Improper part selection?

Note: If necessary, use additional sheets to list actions taken.

Acceptance Stage

	Item		Related item	Remark
1	Product performance			• Does the product perform to the required function? • If not, what has been done about it?
2	Quality level	2.1	Workmanship	• Does the workmanship of the product fully meet the level of quality required or stipulated by the user?
		2.2	Tests	• Is the product subjected to environmental tests? • If so, which ones? • Is the product field tested as a complete system? • If so, what were the results?
3	Reliability	3.1	Probability function	• Are individual components and modules environmentally tested? • If so, how?
		3.2	Failure rate	• Is the product's reliability measured in terms of probability function? • If so, what were the results? • Is the product's reliability measured in terms of failure rate? • If so, what were the results?
		3.3	Mean time between failures	• Is the product's reliability measured in terms of mean time between failures? • If so, what were the results?

In-service Stage

	Item		Related item	Remark
1	System reliability	1.1	Product basic design	• Are statistical methods being used to prove the product's basic design? • If so, are they adequate? • Are the results recorded and available? • What other methods are used to prove the product's basic design? • Are these methods appropriate?
2	Equipment reliability	2.1	Personnel	• Are there sufficient trained personnel to carry out the task? • Are they sufficiently motivated? • If not, what is the problem?
		2.1.1	Operators	• Have individual job descriptions been developed? • Are they readily available?

Item	Related item		Remark
			• Are all operators capable of completing their duties?
	2.1.2	Training	• Do all personnel receive appropriate training? • Is a continuous on-the-job training programme available to all personnel? • If not, why not?
	2.2	Product dependability	• What proof is there that the product is dependable? • How is product dependability proved? • Is this sufficient for the customer?
	2.3	Component reliability	• Has the reliability of individual components been considered? • Does the reliability of individual components exceed the overall system reliability?
	2.4	Faulty operating procedures	• Are operating procedures available? • Are they appropriate to the task? • Are they regularly reviewed?
	2.5	Operational abuses	• Are there any obvious operational abuses? • If so, what are they? • How can they be overcome?
	2.5.1	Extended duty cycle	• Do the staff have to work shifts? • If so, are they allowed regular breaks from their work? • Is there a senior shift worker? • If so, are his duties and responsibilities clearly defined? • Are computers used? • If so, are screen filters available? • Do the operators have keyboard wrist rests?
	2.5.2	Training	• Do the operational staff receive regular on-the-job training? • Is there any need for additional in-house or external training?
3 Design capability	3.1	Faulty operating procedures	• Are there any obvious faulty operating procedures? • Can the existing procedures be improved upon?

What are the costs involved in an organisation obtaining Registration to this standard?

☼ Author's Note

Having customised the NAFAAD QMS example shown in Chapter 6 as a template for producing your own Quality Manual together with your associated Processes, Procedures and Work Instructions, and (following the guidelines contained in Chapter 7) having conducted a full internal audit of not only your own internal management system but also that of your suppliers and sub consultants – you are now in a position to seek Registration for becoming an ISO 9001:2008 Accredited Organisation.

Chapter 8 is intended to give you an indication of how to go about this in the easiest and most cost effective manner. It will tell you how to choose an Accreditation or Notified Body and how they will complete their audit in terms of what they will need from you; potential costs; and, most importantly, how you can help the process go smoothly so as to reach a successful completion.

If you have any problems getting yourself ready for this next important step, please feel free to contact me via ray@herne.org.uk and I will help you as much as I can.

Many of today's contracts (particularly those for the military or government – but also for many large businesses) insist that applicants hold a current up-to-date ISO 9001:2008 certificate before they will even be considered for the job – be it a deliverable, product or service.

Indeed, in many tender documents this is the first question that has to be answered, and to a small business (that has probably never envisaged going outside its own particular market) it can cause a lot of anguish.

If, as briefly mentioned in Chapter 1, the organisation has a well documented, properly audited, management-led Quality Management System in place that is subject to continuous improvement and always seeking customer satisfaction, then the road to gaining ISO 9001:2008 certification need not be too onerous.

The obvious question that a small business is going to ask, though, is 'how much is it going to cost to implement and operate?' And 'Is it going to be worth having the ISO Certificate hanging on the Managing Director's Wall?!!'

Obviously, each business is different and the cost of ISO 9001 Registration will vary depending on the size and complexity of your organisation and on whether you already have some elements of a quality management system in place.

Consequently, no book could possibly answer this question with any accuracy, however the following tables with examples may, I hope, be beneficial to you.

 But the first question that has to be answered is **do** you actually **need** to become an ISO 9001 registered company or would simply *'working in compliance with ISO 9001:2008'* be sufficient? – and only your Top Management will know the answer to that one!

8.1 CAN I JUST WORK 'IN COMPLIANCE' WITH ISO 9001?

If your organisation simply needs to prove that it only has to work in compliance with the requirements of ISO 9001:2008, then all that is required is to fully read and understand Chapter 6 of this book. This chapter contains a generic QMS that can be customised to suit any form of business no matter whether it produces equipment, widgets, software or simply professional advice etc.

As mentioned before, to save you having to copy or retype the Quality Manual, Quality Procedures and/or Work Instructions contained in the 160 something-page Chapter 6, 'unlocked', fully accessible, non .PDF, soft copies of all of the files presented in the book are available – at no additional charge – direct from the author.

To obtain copies of these files, simply send an e-mail to me at ray@herne.org.uk containing details of your name, address and where you purchased the book from, and I will send you the link to download a full copy.

But please remember, this generic example of a complete QMS is **not** meant as a simple 'get quick, pretty meaningless cut and paste exercise!!' **You** will need to carefully go through the whole of the generic QMS contained in Chapter 6, cutting out the bits that do not apply to your sort of organisation, inserting or modifying others so that they replicate exactly how your organisation operates.

8.2 SO WHY SHOULD I BOTHER ABOUT GETTING ISO 9001 CERTIFICATION?

- ISO 9001 certification by an accredited certification body shows commitment to quality, customers and a willingness to work towards improving efficiency.
- It demonstrates the existence of an effective quality management system that satisfies the rigours of an independent, external audit.
- ISO 9001 certification enhances company image in the eyes of customers, employees and shareholders alike.
- It also gives a competitive edge to an organisation's marketing.

An organisation can also decide to seek certification because it:

- is a contractual or regulatory requirement;
- is necessary to meet customer preferences;
- falls within the context of a risk management programme; and
- helps motivate staff by setting a clear goal for the development of its management system.

8.3 BUT WHAT IS THE DIFFERENCE TO BEING A CERTIFIED, ACCREDITED AND/OR A REGISTERED ISO 9001:2008 ORGANISATION?

Certification – is the provision by an independent body of written assurance (a certificate) that the deliverable (product, service or system in question) meets specific requirements.

Registration – Certification is very often referred to as Registration in North America – but it is one and the same thing.

Accreditation – this is the formal recognition by an independent Accreditation Body (e.g. in the UK, UKAS), that a Certification Body has been formally approved as being capable of carrying out the certification of an organisation's QMS. Accreditation is not obligatory but it adds another level of confidence, as 'accredited' means the Certification Body has been independently checked to make sure it operates according to international standards.

8.4 BUT IS IT WORTH THE COST AND TROUBLE TO BECOME ISO 9001:2008 CERTIFIED?

Table 8.4 at the end of this chapter clearly shows how much ISO 9001:2008 has grown over the last decade into a world-wide business requirement so that by the end of 2011, just within Europe, there were nearly half a million companies certified to ISO 9001:2008 – 10% of whom were from the UK! Figure 8.1 unmistakably shows how Europe and Central and South Asia are the main regions in which companies hold Certificates around the world.

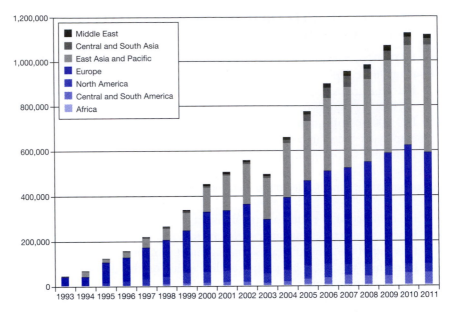

FIGURE 8.1 Worldwide accreditation to ISO 9001:2008 (Courtesy of ISO)

8.5 WHAT ARE THE BENEFITS OF ISO INTERNATIONAL STANDARDS?

The whole aim of companies becoming accredited to the ISO 9001:2008 Standard is to ensure that their products and services are safe, reliable and of good quality. For business, the Standards are strategic tools that reduce costs by reducing waste and errors whilst at the same time increasing productivity. Accreditation helps companies not only to access new markets, but in doing so to become more professional as an organisation and improve their client relationships – as shown by the results of a recent ISO study of 1,000 mixed businesses. As can be seen in Figure 8.2, 44% of organisations surveyed said that they had won more business as a direct result of having achieved ISO 9001 certification.

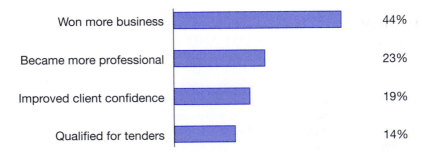

FIGURE 8.2 Benefits from achieving ISO 9001 Accreditation

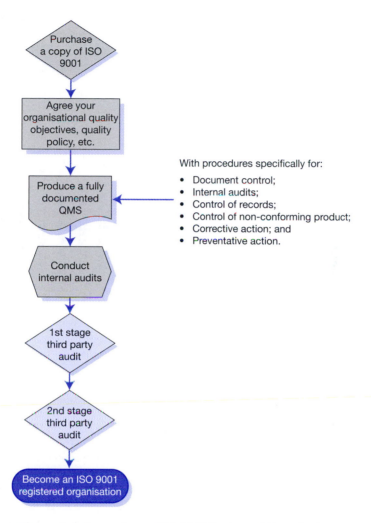

With procedures specifically for:

- Document control;
- Internal audits;
- Control of records;
- Control of non-conforming product;
- Corrective action; and
- Preventative action.

FIGURE 8.3 The route to becoming an ISO 9001 Registered Organisation

8.6 HOW DO I BECOME AN ISO 9001 REGISTERED ORGANISATION?

Assuming that you definitely need to be ISO 9001 certified then you will need to:

- (Normally,) purchase a copy of ISO 9001:2008 (but in your case, this book contains everything that you need!!);
- Identify which requirements of the ISO 9001:2008 standard are applicable to your type of organisation;
- Agree your organisational quality objectives, quality policy and quality plans;

- Produce a fully documented Quality Management System (consisting of a Quality Manual plus its associated Quality Processes, Procedures and Work Instructions) that is fully compliant with the requirements of ISO 9001:2008 – paying particular attention to the **six mandatory quality procedures that your organisation must produce**, i.e.:

  1   Document control;
  2   Internal audits;
  3   Control of records;
  4   Control of non-conforming product;
  5   Corrective action; and
  6   Preventative action.

- Implement these Processes and Procedures throughout your organisation;
- Complete a series of internal audits to ensure that these procedures are suitable and adhered to.

Once all the requirements of ISO 9001 have been met within your organisation and all non-compliances identified by your internal audit have been rectified, it is time for an external audit by a third party certification body.

The Certified Body who is going to be used for this audit is entirely your choice – but preferably (i.e. in order to be officially recognised) it should always be a company which has been fully accredited by an Accreditation Service (such as UKAS in the UK).

 See http://www.ukas.com/about-accreditation/accredited-bodies for a current list of UKAS accredited certification bodies.

The chosen certification body will then thoroughly review your Quality Manual and procedures etc. to see that your organisation's management programme is measurable and achievable.

Note: For a small business this could either consist of a desktop study or a one-day visit to your organisation's premises. For a large organisation, a site visit would probably be required – dependent on your product or service. The certification body may also send you a few simple questionnaires to complete, such as that shown in Table 8.1 for Management Systems.

Assuming that this Stage 1 audit is successful then this is followed at a later date by a full, on-site audit to ensure that working practices observe all of your policies, procedures and stated objectives and that appropriate records are maintained.

If this Stage 2 audit is successful, then the certification body will issue you with a certificate of registration to ISO 9001 and this will then be followed by annual (or in some cases, depending on the size and complexity of your organisation, bi-annual) surveillance visits to ensure that the system continues to work.

TABLE 8.1 Quality Management System: documentation requirements

Number	Question	Yes/No	ISO Clause	Remarks
1	Do you have a documented Quality Manual which includes or makes reference to the scope of your quality management?		4.2.2	
2	Does your Quality Manual include details of any exclusions from your management system?		4.2.2	
3	Do you have mandatory documented procedure for the Control of Documents?		4.2.3	
4	Do you have mandatory documented procedure for the Control of Records?		4.2.4	
5	Do you have mandatory documented procedure for Internal Audits?		8.2.2	
6	Do you have mandatory documented procedure for the Control of Non-conforming Product?		8.3	
7	Do you have mandatory documented procedure for Corrective Action?		8.5.2	
8	Do you have mandatory documented procedure for Preventative Action?		8.5.3	

8.7 WHAT OTHER NATIONAL CERTIFICATION BODIES ARE THERE?

Whilst the UKAS Registration is recognised worldwide under ISO agreements, many countries have their own Certification Bodies and as I have been advised that my 'ISO 9001:2008 for Small Businesses' book is being used elsewhere, for your assistance I have listed some of these other National Certification Bodies that might apply to you in Table 8.2.

> **Note: Please** let me know if there is any alternative Accreditation Service concerning your own particular country (or indeed if I have missed any!) – and I will make sure that these are included in the next edition of this book. Just e-mail me at ray@herne.org.uk with the details that you think should be included.

TABLE 8.2 Some of the worldwide accreditation bodies

Country	Logo	Body	Contact Details
Australia and New Zealand	JAS-ANZ	Joint Accreditation Systems of Australia & New Zealand (JAS-ANZ)	http://www.jas-anz.com.au
Canada		The Standards Council of Canada (SCC)	http://www.scc.ca/en/accreditation/management-systems
France	cofrac	Comité Français d'Accréditation (COFRAC)	http://www.cofrac.fr/en/activites/certification.php
Germany	DAkkS Deutsche Akkreditierungsstelle D-PL-12012-01-01	The Deutsche Akkreditierungsstelle GmbH (DAkkS)	http://www.dakks.de/en
India	NABCB	National Accreditation Board for Certifications (NABCB)	http://qcin.org/nabcb
Ireland	INAB ACCREDITED	Irish National Accreditation Board (INAB)	http://www.inab.ie
People's Republic of China	CNAS	China National Accreditation Service (CNAS)	http://eng.cnas.org.cn
Singapore	ACCREDITED CERTIFICATION BODY SAC	Singapore Accreditation Council (SAC)	http://www.sac-accreditation.gov.sg
United Kingdom	UKAS UNITED KINGDOM ACCREDITATION SERVICE	United Kingdom Accreditation Service (UKAS)	http://www.ukas.com
USA	ANAB ACCREDITED	ANSI-ASQ National Accreditation Board (ANAB)	http://www.anab.org

8.8 WHAT WILL BE THE BUDGETARY COSTS FOR DOING ALL THIS?

The cost for an organisation seeking Registration in the UK would (at the time of publication) be in the region of the figures shown in Table 8.3.

TABLE 8.3 Budgetary costs for obtaining ISO 9001:2008 Certification

Enterprise category	Headcount	First Stage	Second Stage	Yearly assessments
		Third party audit	Third party audit	
Medium sized	< 250	£600	£2400	£1200
Small	< 50	£600	£1200	£600–£1200
Micro	< 10	£300	£600	£600

8.9 HOW LONG WILL IT TAKE TO BECOME CERTIFIED?

With the right preparation and a good understanding of what is required for ISO 9001 certification, most organisations can expect to achieve certification within three to six months depending on their size and complexity – but I cannot over-emphasise the importance of having **the complete backing** of Top Management and it is absolutely vital that you have someone (either internal or perhaps in the case of a micro business, an external consultant) who has experience of implementing Quality Management Systems and who knows what will be required in order to gain ISO 9001:2008 Accreditation.

8.10 HOW IS THE CERTIFICATION COMPLETED?

Once the groundwork has been done and the ISO 9001 Quality Manual and its associated Processes, Procedures and Work Instructions are completed, you will be ready for your first assessment.

The assessor (an independent third party, Accredited Certification Body chosen by you from the local Certification Bodies list) will check that your written Quality Management System completely matches what you are actually doing and make any recommendations for change that may be needed.

 In most cases this initial assessment will be a desk top study.

Once any changes have been carried out you will then be ready for the actual audit that will be carried out against the requirements of ISO 9001:2008 by the chosen Accredited Certification Body.

Provided that you have addressed every single requirement and recommendation made in the current edition of ISO 9001 (for example by having a fully customised version of the generic QMS contained in Chapter 6 of this book) AND everyone in your organisation is working in accordance with the procedures of your QMS, then the audit should be plain sailing – **BUT**, you need to make sure that everything has been fully checked before the assessor arrives!

8.11 WHAT HAPPENS DURING THE ACTUAL ISO 9001 AUDIT?!

From my experience, provided that you are well prepared and **everybody** (including Top Management!!) is doing what they are supposed to be doing and completing their work in accordance with your documented management system, then there should be nothing really to worry about.

Most independent Assessors and Notified Bodies (e.g. BSI, ISOQAR, TÜV, AFNOR etc.) will use a '*check sheet*' that is very similar to the lists contained in Annex 7C of this book to determine whether an organisation's QMS complies with the requirements of ISO 9001:2008.

 And so, if you can honestly answer '*yes*' to all the questions contained in Annex C, then the Assessors should be able to say that you '*fully comply with the requirements of ISO 9001:2008*' – and then it is time to think about which wall to hang the certificate on!!

8.12 WHAT HAPPENS AFTER CERTIFICATION AND BEYOND?

When you have passed the formal assessment you will receive an ISO 9001 certificate, which is valid for three years. Your assessor will stay in touch during this time, paying you regular visits to make sure your system doesn't just remain compliant, but that it continually improves.

8.13 HOW CAN I MAINTAIN MY CERTIFICATION?

Once you've achieved a standard you need to maintain it. How? Through training, self-assessment tools, newsletters and so on.

8.14 WHAT ARE THE ADVANTAGES OF MAINTAINING MY ISO 9001:2008 CERTIFICATION?

As previously mentioned, many of the governmental and national body contracts (particularly if you are tendering for a job in a foreign country), as well as a lot of everyday businesses, are now demanding (yes 'demanding'!) that you are a ISO 9001:2008 Certified company before they will even consider you.

Once you have achieved this standard you will, therefore, become one of the ever-growing fully ISO 9001:2008 Certified organisations shown in Table 8.4.

 Note: Although this particular table concentrates on the European sector, the ISO website – www.iso.org – provides details of other continents and countries.

TABLE 8.4 ISO 9001 – Europe

Year	1993	1994	1995	1996	1997	1998	1999	2000	2001	2002	2003	2004	2005	2006	2007	2008	2009	2010	2011
Country	37779	55400	92611	109961	143674	166255	190247	269332	269648	292878	242455	320748	377172	414208	431479	455303	500286	530039	492248
Albania								1	1	2	2	2	11	28	23	43	155	52	164
Andorra							1	5	5	3	1	1	6	12	26	33	27	27	28
Armenia							4	3	3	12	16	26	55	34	79	68	78	61	35
Austria	200	434	1133	1824	2627	3245	3421	4000	4000	4094	2809	3259	3368	3806	4203	4272	4277	5161	4138
Azerbaijan							1	1	1	1	2	203	213	171	55	153	148	103	122
Belarus					6	14	26	78	78	115	102	447	658	882	1308	1749	2014	151	171
Belgium	464	870	1716	1871	3042	3176	3495	4670	4670	4725	3167	4471	4810	3865	4822	4875	3950	3715	3207
Bosnia and Herzegovina					2	10	34	57	57	62	47	209	350	242	652	811	909	944	1119
Bulgaria			3		14	96	199	469	469	629	842	1685	2220	3097	4663	5323	5322	6248	5001
Croatia		2	2	22	38	121	336	415	415	590	580	966	1273	1676	2073	2302	2567	2102	2117
Cyprus	1	5	5	11	42	62	184	334	334	352	314	573	530	683	440	555	677	645	742
Czech Republic	18	47	180	366	746	1443	1500	5627	5627	8489	2565	10781	12743	12811	10458	10089	14031	16242	12697
Denmark	608	916	1314	1387	1902	2200	1962	2163	2163	1900	935	1050	1219	1840	1794	1574	1683	1856	1505
Estonia			1	1	4	26	77	202	202	281	261	438	489	577	625	691	746	773	835
Finland	324	496	772	951	1445	1450	2105	1870	1870	1872	1861	1784	1914	1986	1804	1975	2243	2147	2265
France	1586	3359	5536	8079	11920	14194	16028	20919	20919	19870	15073	21769	21700	21349	22981	23837	23065	29713	29215
Georgia							2	260	7	8	7	20	24	52	88	107	114	72	77
Germany	1534	3470	10236	12979	20656	24055	30150	41629	41629	35802	23598	26654	39816	46458	45195	48324	47156	50583	49540
Gibraltar (UK)									1	25	28	47	55	49	29	30	32	28	28

TABLE 8.4 ISO 9001 – Europe

Year	1993	1994	1995	1996	1997	1998	1999	2000	2001	2002	2003	2004	2005	2006	2007	2008	2009	2010	2011
Greece	46	90	248	348	682	764	1050	2325	2325	3180	1615	2572	3255	4753	5132	6747	5034	4322	4168
Hungary	23	58	309	423	1341	1660	3282	6362	6362	9254	7750	10207	15464	15008	10473	10187	7122	8083	6825
Iceland	3	4	12	44	59	62	28	30	30	27	25	28	19	13	16	20	22	27	35
Ireland	893	1132	1617	2056	2534	2854	3100	3700	3700	2845	1132	1683	2055	2225	1999	2237	2136	2359	1875
Italy	864	2008	4814	7321	12134	18095	21069	48109	48109	61212	64120	84485	98028	105799	115359	118309	130066	138892	171947
Latvia				1	1	14	39	67	67	93	73	484	561	625	342	500	708	809	787
Liechtenstein		14	19	5	3	85	111	73	73	73	69	71	75	81	99	170	73	78	64
Lithuania			2	3	29	40	91	202	202	280	324	487	591	697	809	815	1111	1207	1168
Luxembourg	10	21	48	46	89	106	113	108	108	148	110	108	147	145	197	246	247	107	156
Macedonia			1	3	8	21	46	69	69	59									
Malta	1	3	12	28	45	49	56	207	207	222	204	230	302	342	349	355	420	476	437
Moldova					6	10	14	7	7	15	16	26	33	41	50	96	167	82	86
Monaco	1	2	5	10	20	20	20	26	26	27	45	22	37	38	54	36	39	25	33
Montenegro														33	136	160	157	85	146
Netherlands	1502	2718	5284	7986	10380	10570	10620	12745	12745	13198	9917	6402	9160	18922	18922	13597	12260	11213	11072
Norway	172	400	890	1109	1273	1503	1509	1703	1703	1344	1171	1368	1410	1467	1703	1666	1871	1882	1756
Poland	1	16	130	260	669	768	1012	2622	2622	3091	3216	5753	9718	8115	9184	10965	12707	12195	10984
Portugal	85	181	389	535	819	944	1131	2474	2474	3061	3417	4733	5820	5851	5283	5128	5051	5588	4638
Romania		6	42	61	214	269	466	1670	1670	2463	2052	5183	6097	9426	9633	10737	15865	16200	19405
Russian Federation*	5	8	22	56	95	132	541	1517	1517	1710	962	3816	4883	6398	11527	16051	53152	62265	12663

TABLE 8.4 ISO 9001 – Europe

Year	1993	1994	1995	1996	1997	1998	1999	2000	2001	2002	2003	2004	2005	2006	2007	2008	2009	2010	2011
San Marino (Republic of)					19	19	25	30	30			18	18	24	35	36	40	30	37
Serbia											103			1551	1987	2091	2733	1790	2863
Serbia and Montenegro												696	1209						
Slovakia	5	11	59	135	404	575	560	827	827	1544	1148	2008	2050	2195	2840	3476	3475	3895	3787
Slovenia	16	43	99	152	467	502	521	1026	1026	973	465	1811	2114	2182	1886	1945	1688	1701	1658
Spain	320	586	1492	2496	4268	6412	8699	17749	17749	28690	31836	40972	47445	57552	65112	68730	59576	59854	53057
Sweden	365	618	1095	1931	2789	3489	3786	4652	4652	4039	3107	4687	4744	4839	5233	5377	5346	5687	4901
Switzerland	569	945	2065	3701	4653	6426	7124	8605	8605	10299	8300	11549	12413	10984	11077	11724	11581	12110	10182
The former Yugoslav Republic of Macedonia											47	133	154	217	255	271	295	333	290
Turkey	65	106	434	606	1284	1607	1672	2949	2949	3941	3248	5009	10929	12350	12802	13217	13705	10680	9446
Yugoslav Republic	1	1	8	8	136	148	255	14	269	893									
Ukraine	1	4	8	14	30	56	82		314	405	308	934	1375	1808	2150	2453	3252	2592	1207
United Kingdom	28096	36825	52595	53099	56696	58963	63700	66760	66760	60960	45465	50884	45612	40909	35517	41150	41193	44849	43564

(Table courtesy of ISO)

Abbreviations and acronyms

AAD	Automatic Activation Device
ACSI	American Customer Satisfaction Index
AFNOR	Association Français de Normalisation
ANAB	ANSI-ASQ National Accreditation Board
ANSI	American National Standards Institute
AQAPs	NATO Allied Quality Assurance Publications
BSI	British Standards Institution
CAD	Computer Aided Design
CCIR	International Radio Consultative Committee
CCITT	International Telegraph and Telephony Consultative Committee
CECC	CENELEC Electronic Components Committee
CEN	Comité Européen de Normalisation
CENELEC	Comité Européen de Normalisation Électrotechnique (i.e. the European Committee for Electrotechnical Standardization)
CMI	Chartered Management Institute
CNAS	China National Accreditation Service
COFRAC	Comité Français d´Accréditation
COS	Corporation of Open Systems
CP	Core Business Process
CQI	Chartered Quality Institute
CSA	Canadian Standards Association
DakkS	The Deutsche Akkreditierungsstelle GmbH
DCS	Document Control Sheet
DEF STANS	Defence Standards
DIN	Deutsch Institut fur Normung e.v.
DOD	American Division of Defense
DTI	Department of Trade and Industry
EU	European Union
FMEA	Failure Mode and Effects Analysis
FR	Failure Rate
FRS	Functional Requirements Specification
FTA	Fault Tree Analysis

HSE	Health and Safety Executive (UK)
IEC	International Electrotechnical Commission
IECQ	Quality Assessment System for Electronic Components
ILU	Integrated Logistic Unit
INAB	Irish National Accreditation Board
IRCA	International Register of Certificated Auditors
ISO	International Organization for Standardization
IT	Information Technology
ITU	International Telecommunications Union
JAS-ANZ	Joint Accreditation Systems of Australia and New Zealand
LAN	Local Area Network
LMO	Large Multinational Organisations
MD	Managing Director
MDD	Medical Devices Directive
Mil-Stds	Military Standards
MOD-UK	United Kingdom Ministry of Defence
MTBF	Mean Time Between Failures
NABCB	National Accreditation Board for Certification Bodies
NAFAAD	North American Field Advanced Audit Division
NATO	North Atlantic Treaty Organisation
NOBO	Notified Body
NSO	National Standards Organisation
OHS	Occupational Health and Safety
OHSAS	Occupational Health and Safety Assessment Series
OJT	On-The-Job-Training
OSI	Open Systems Interconnection
PF	Probability Function
QA	Quality Assurance
QC	Quality Control
QES	Quality Environmental and Safety
QM	Quality Manual
QMS	Quality Management System
QP	Quality Procedure
QuE dzST	Quality Excellence for Suppliers of Telecommunications Leadership
RAMS	Reliability, Availability, Maintainability and Safety
SCC	The Standards Council of Canada
SEVEN	Nickname for HQ USAF programs usually connected with surveys
SME	Small and Medium-sized Enterprises
SP	Supporting Process
SQP	Project-Specific Quality Plan
TENS	Transcutaneous Electrical Nerve Stimulation
TQM	Total Quality Management
UK	United Kingdom

UKAS	United Kingdom Accreditation Service
WAMH	Workplace Applied Medical Health
WAUILF	Workplace Applied Uniform Indicated Low Frequency (application)
WI	Work Instruction
YFR	Yearly Forecast Rationale

Books by the same author

Wiring Regulations in Brief

(Third edition)

"*Wiring Regulations in Brief*"

(Second Edition)

- Tired of trawling through the Wiring Regs?
- Perplexed by Part P?
- Confused by cables, conductors and circuits?

Then look no further! This handy guide provides an on-the-job reference source for Electricians, Designers, Service Engineers, Inspectors, Builders, Students, DIY enthusiasts.

Topic-based chapters link areas of working practice – such as cables, installations, testing and inspection, special locations – with the specifics of the Regulations themselves. This allows quick and easy identification of the official requirements relating to the situation in front of you.

The requirements of the regulations, and of related standards, are presented in an informal, easy-to-read style that strips away confusion. Packed with useful hints and tips, and highlighting the most important or mandatory requirements, this book is a concise reference on all aspects of the seventeenth edition IEE Wiring Regulations.

Publisher:	Routledge
Published:	21 August 2012
Paperback:	978–0–415–52687–6
eBook:	978–0–203–11571–8

Building Regulations in Brief

(Seventh edition)

The most popular and trusted guide to the building regulations, *Building Regulations in Brief* is updated regularly to reflect constant changes. Now in its seventh edition, it has sold over 28,000 copies since its first publication in 2003.

This new edition includes the latest on all the significant amendments to Building Regulations, Planning Permission and the Approved Documents that occurred in October 2010 and includes changes to Parts F and L, as well as Approved Documents A, C, and J. There are also changes reflecting the consolidation of the building regulations included.

The no-nonsense approach has made it a firm favorite with all involved in the building industry including designers, building surveyors and inspectors, students and architects. A ready reference giving practical information, it enables compliance in the simplest and most cost-effective manner possible. *Building Regulations in Brief* cuts through the confusion to explain the meaning of the regulations, their history, current status, requirements, and associated documentation and how local authorities view their importance, as well as emphasising the benefits and requirements of each regulation. It's an essential purchase for anyone needing to comply with the building regulations.

Publisher: Routledge
Published: 9 February 2012
Paperback: 978–0–415–80969–6
eBook: 978–0–203–13485–6

Water Regulations in Brief

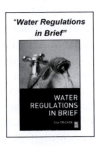

"Water Regulations in Brief"

Water Regulations in Brief is a unique reference book, providing all the information needed to comply with the regulations, in an easy to use, full colour format.

Crucially, unlike other titles on this subject, this book doesn't just cover the Water Regulations; it also clearly shows how they link in with the Building Regulations, Water Bylaws and the Wiring Regulations, providing the only available complete reference to the requirements for water fittings and water systems.

Structured in the same logical, time saving way as the author's other bestselling '. . .in Brief' books, *Water Regulations in Brief* will be a welcome change to anyone tired of wading through complex, jargon heavy publications in search of the information they need to get the job done.

Publisher: Routledge
Published: 30 September 2009
Paperback: 978–1–85617–628–6
eBook: 978–0–08–095094–5

Scottish Building Standards in Brief

"Scottish Building Standards in Brief"

Scottish Building Standards in Brief takes the highly successful formula of Ray Tricker's *Building Regulations in Brief* and applies it to the requirements of the Building (Scotland) Regulations 2004. With the same no-nonsense and simple to follow guidance but written specifically for the Scottish

Building Standards it's the ideal book for builders, architects, designers and DIY enthusiasts working in Scotland.

Ray Tricker and Roz Algar explain the meaning of the regulations, their history, current status, requirements, and associated documentation and how local authorities view their importance, and emphasises the benefits and requirements of each one.

There is no easier or clearer guide to help you to comply with the Scottish Building Standards in the simplest and most cost-effective manner possible.

Publisher:	Routledge
Published:	11 August 2008
Paperback:	978–0–7506–8558–0
eBook:	978–0–08–094251–3

ISO 9001:2000 The Quality Management Process

(Third edition)

With the publication of ISO 9001:2000, there is now a single quality management requirements standard that is applicable to all organisations, products and services. ISO 9001:2000 is the only standard that can be used for the certification of a QMS and its generic requirements can be used by any organisation. ISO 9001:2000 applies to all types of organisations. It is the quality standard which specifies the requirements of quality management systems for use where organisations need to demonstrate their capability to provide products and services which meet both customer needs and relevant regulatory requirements. It will prove invaluable to all quality managers, internal auditors and anyone involved in the management and understanding of ISO 9001:2000. It also acts as a handy reference for professional auditors to the requirements for auditing ISO 9001:2000.

Publisher:	Van Haren Publishing
Published:	1 August 2006
Paperback:	978–0–7506–8558–0
ISBN-13:	978–9077212776

ISO 9001:2008 Quality Manual & Audit Checksheets

(Second edition)

A CD containing a soft copy of the generic Quality Management System featured in *ISO 9001 for Small Businesses* (fourth edition) plus a soft copy of all the check sheets and example audit forms contained in '*ISO 9001 Audit Procedure*' (second edition).

A comprehensive CD containing all the vital documentation, information and guidance to develop a full Quality Management System.

Publisher: Herne European Consultancy Ltd
Published: 2011
ISBN-13:   978–0954864798

Quality Management System for ISO 9001:2008

(Second edition)

Quality Management System for ISO 9001:2008 and accompanying CD is probably the most comprehensive set of ISO 9001:2008 compliant documents available world-wide.

Fully customisable, it can be used as a basic template for any organisation wishing to work in compliance with, or gain registration to, ISO 9001.

"Quality Management system for ISO 9001:2000"

Publisher: Herne European Consultancy Ltd
Published: 2011
ISBN-13:   978–0954864743

ISO 9001:2000 Audit Procedures

(Second edition)

In order to meet the recommendations, requirements and specifications of ISO 9001:2000, organisations must undertake an audit of their own quality procedures and those of their suppliers. Likewise, when supplying ISO 9001:2000 accredited customers, suppliers must be prepared to undergo a similar audit. Revised, updated and expanded, *ISO 9001:2000 Audit Procedures* describes the methods for completing management reviews and quality audits, and outlines the experiences of working with 9001:2000 since its launch in 2000. It also includes essential new material on process models, generic processes, the requirements for mandatory documented procedures, and detailed coverage of auditor's questionnaires.

"ISO 9001:2000 Audit Procedures"
(Second Edition)

Publisher: Routledge
Published: 17 June 2005
Paperback: 978–0–7506–6615–2
eBook: 978–0–08–045862–5

Optoelectronics and Fiber Optic Technology

An introduction to the fascinating technology of fiber optics.

Students, technicians and professional readers could benefit from this publication.

Simply written in an easily accessible style which does not put the reader off and covers all of the basic topics in an appropriate and logical order.

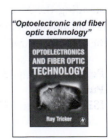

"Optoelectronic and fiber optic technology"

Topical areas such as optoelectronics in LANs and WANs, cable TV systems, and the global fiber-optic highway make this book essential reading for anyone who needs to keep up with the technology of modern data communications.

Publisher: Elsevier (Imprint Newnes)
Published: 1 May 2002
ISBN-13:   978–0750653701

Auditing Quality Management Systems

(Second edition)

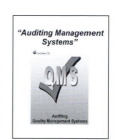

This publication is the result of over a decade's experience of all major international standards for Integrated Quality Management Systems. It is a comprehensive CD containing all of the major audit check sheets and forms that are required to conduct either a simple internal audit or an external assessment of an organisation against the formal requirements of ISO 9001:2008.

Now fully updated to include checklists for:

*   Project Management
*   Health & Safety in the workplace

Also includes '*background notes for auditors*'.

Publisher: Herne European Consultancy Ltd
Published: 2011
ISBN-13:   978–0954864774

MDD Compliance using Quality Management Techniques

The Medical Device Directive (MDD) is difficult to understand and interpret, but this book covers the subject superlatively.

In summary, the book is a good reference for understanding the Medical Device Directive's requirements and would aid companies of all sizes in adding these requirements to an existing QMS.

Publisher: Butterworth Heinemann
Published: 1 May 2000
ISBN-13:   978–0750644419

CE Conformity Marking

CE Marking can be regarded as a product's trade passport for Europe. It is a mandatory European marking for certain product groups to indicate conformity with the essential health and safety requirements set out in the European Directive.

This book contains essential information for any manufacturer or distributor wishing to trade in the European Union.

Practical and easy to understand.

Publisher: Elsevier (Imprint Butterworth Heinemann)
Published: 1 May 2000
ISBN-13:   978–0750648134

ISO 9001:2000 in Brief

(Second edition)

This 'hands on' book provides practical information on how to cost effectively set up an ISO 9001: 2000 compliant Quality Management System.

The new ISO 9000:2000 family is an all-encompassing series of standards that lay down requirements for incorporating the management of quality into the design, manufacture and delivery of products, services and software.

To achieve its main objectives, ISO 9001:2000 requires the manufacturer, or supplier, to possess a fully auditable Quality Management System consisting of Quality Policies, Quality Processes, Quality Procedures and Work Instructions. It is this Quality Management System that will provide the auditable proof that the requirements of ISO 9001:2000 have been and are still being met.

This secoISO 9001:2000 In Brief explains the meaning of ISO 9000, its history, current status, requirements and changes being made to it. It also covers how ISO 9001 will affect businesses, and how they can easily and cost-effectively satisfy their customers' requirements for quality control and quality assurance.

Publisher: Butterworth Heinemann
Published: 1 May 2000
ISBN-13:   978–750648141

Environmental Requirements for Electromechanical and Electronic Equipment

"Environmental Requirements for Electromechanical and Electronic Equipment"

Companion to *Quality and Standards in Electronics*.

Covers essential tests and regulations for equipment designers and manufacturers.

Likely to be of interest to major companies worldwide.

This is the definitive reference containing all of the background guidance, typical ranges, details of recommended test specifications, case studies and regulations covering the environmental requirements on designers and manufacturers of electrical and electromechanical equipment worldwide.

Publisher: Elsevier (Imprint Newnes)
Published: 5 January 1999
ISBN-13: 978–0750639026

Quality and Standards in Electronics

"Quality and Standards in Electronics"

A manufacturer or supplier of electronic equipment or components needs to know the precise requirements for component certification and quality conformance to meet the demands of the customer.

This book ensures that the professional is aware of all the UK, European and International necessities, knows the current status of these regulations and standards, and where to obtain them.

Publisher: Elsevier (Imprint Newnes)
Published: 5 June 1997
ISBN-13: 978–0750625319

And for those who would like to relax with some cooking recipes – based on Cyder and apples why not try . . .

The Cyder Book

THE CYDER BOOK

A unique combination of an historical overview of Cider Making through the ages, the cider making process and a collection of recipes using cider and cider apples.

Publisher: Herne European Consultancy Ltd (Imprint Stingray)
Published: 14 Oct 2007
ISBN-13: 978–0954864767

References

STANDARDS

Number	Date	Title
AS 9100	2009	The Standard for Aerospace
ASTM E1212–12	2012	Standard Practice for Quality Management Systems for Non-destructive Testing Agencies
BS 10012	2009	Data protection. Specification for a personal information management system
BS 4778–2	1991	Quality vocabulary. Quality concepts and related definitions
BS 4778–3.1	1991	Quality vocabulary. Availability, reliability and maintainability terms. Guide to concepts and related definitions
BS 4778–3.2	1991	Quality vocabulary. Availability, reliability and maintainability terms. Glossary of international terms
BS 5701–1	2003	Guide to quality control and performance improvement using qualitative (attribute) data. Uses and value of attribute charts in business, industry, commerce and public service
BS 5701–2	2003	Guide to quality control and performance improvement using qualitative (attribute) data. Fundamentals of standard attribute charting for monitoring, control and improvement
BS 5701–3	2003	Guide to quality control and performance improvement using qualitative (attribute) data. Technical aspects of attribute charting. Special situation handling
BS 5701–4	2003	Guide to quality control and performance improvement using qualitative (attribute) data. Attribute inspection performance control and improvement

Number	Date	Title
BS 6001	2006	Sampling procedures for inspection by attributes
BS 6002	2007	Sampling procedures for inspection by variables
BS 6143–1	1992	Guide to the economics of quality. Process cost model
BS 6143–2	1990	Guide to the economics of quality. Prevention, appraisal and failure model
BS 7850–1	1992	Total quality management. Guide to management principles
BS EN 12798	2007	Transport quality management system. Road, rail and inland navigation transport. Quality management system requirements to supplement EN ISO 9001 for the transport of dangerous goods, with regard to safety
BS EN 15224	2012	Health care services. Quality management systems. Requirements based on EN ISO 9001:2008
BS EN 16224	2012	Healthcare provision by chiropractors
BS EN 9101	2008	Aerospace series. Quality management systems. Assessment based on ISO 9001:2000
BS EN 9104–001	2013	Aerospace series. Quality management systems. Requirements for aviation, space, and defence Quality Management System Certification Programmes
BS EN 9104–003	2010	Aerospace series. Quality management systems. Requirements for aerospace quality management system (AQMS) auditor training and qualification
BS EN 9110	2010	Quality management systems. Requirements for aviation maintenance organisations
BS EN 9115	2013	Quality Management Systems. Requirements for aviation, space and defence organisations. Deliverable software (Supplement to EN 9100)
BS EN 9131	2009	Aerospace series. Quality management systems. Non-conformance documentation
BS EN 9137	2012	Quality management systems. Guidance for the application of AQAP 2110 within an EN 9100 Quality Management System
BS EN ISO 10012	2003	Measurement management systems. Requirements for measurement processes and measuring equipment

Number	Date	Title
BS EN ISO 13485	2012	Medical devices. Quality management systems. Requirements for regulatory purposes
BS EN ISO 14001	2004	Environmental management systems. Requirements with guidance for use
BS EN ISO 14004	2010	Environmental management systems. General guidelines on principles, systems and support techniques
BS EN ISO 15189	2012	Medical laboratories. Requirements for quality and competence
BS EN ISO 15378	2011	Primary packaging materials for medicinal products. Particular requirements for the application of ISO 9001:2008, with reference to Good Manufacturing Practice (GMP)
BS EN ISO 19011	2011	Guidelines for auditing management systems
BS EN ISO 22000	2005	Food safety management systems. Requirements for any organisation in the food chain
BS EN ISO 50001	2011	Energy management systems. Requirements with guidance for use
BS EN ISO 8402	1995	Quality management and quality assurance. Vocabulary
BS EN ISO 9000	2005	Quality management systems. Fundamentals and vocabulary
BS EN ISO 9001	2008	Quality management systems. Requirements
BS EN ISO 9004	2009	Managing for the sustained success of an organisation. A quality management approach
BS EN ISO/IEC 17025	2005	General requirements for the competence of testing and calibration laboratories
BS EN ISO/IEC 80079–34	2011	Explosive atmospheres. Application of quality systems for equipment manufacture
BS ISO 10004	2012	Quality management. Customer satisfaction. Guidelines for monitoring and measuring
BS ISO 10012–2	1997	Quality assurance for measuring equipment. Guidelines for control of measuring processes
BS ISO 10018	2012	Quality management. Guidelines on people involvement and competence
BS ISO 15161	2001	Guidelines on the application of ISO 9001:2000 for the food and drink industry
BS ISO 28000	2007	Specification for security management systems for the supply chain

Number	Date	Title
BS ISO 30000	2009	Ships and marine technology. Ship recycling management systems. Specifications for management systems for safe and environmentally sound ship recycling facilities
BS ISO/IEC 27001	2005	Information technology. Security techniques. Information security management systems. Requirements
BS ISO/IEC 90003	2004	Software engineering. Guidelines for the application of ISO 9001:2000 to computer software
CEN ISO/TS 29001	2011	Petroleum, petrochemical and natural gas industries. Sector-specific quality management systems. Requirements for product and service supply organisations
ISI/IEC 80079–34	2011	Explosive atmospheres. Application of quality systems for equipment manufacture
ISO 10001	2007	Quality management. Customer satisfaction
ISO 10005	2005	Quality management. Guidelines for quality plans
ISO 10011	2002	Guidelines for auditing quality systems
ISO 10012	2003	Measurement management systems. Requirements for measurement processes and measuring equipment
ISO 13444	2012	Technical product documentation (TPD). Dimensioning and indication of knurling
ISO 13485	2112	Medical devices. Quality management systems. Requirements for regulatory purposes
ISO 1538	2011	Primary packaging materials for medicinal products. Particular requirements for the application of ISO 9001:2008, with reference to Good Manufacturing Practice (GMP)
ISO 16106	2006	Packaging. Transport packages for dangerous goods. Dangerous goods packagings, intermediate bulk containers (IBCs) and large packagings. Guidelines for the application of ISO 9001
ISO 16192	2010	Space systems. Experience gained in space projects (Lessons learned). Principles and guidelines
ISO 16949	2009	Quality management systems. Particular requirements for the application of ISO 9001:2008

Number	Date	Title
		for automotive production and relevant service part organisations
ISO 17025	2005	General requirements for the competence of testing and calibration laboratories
ISO 22000	2005	Food safety management systems. Requirements for any organisation in the food chain
ISO 22006	2009	Quality management systems. Guidelines for the application of ISO 9001:2008 to crop production
ISO 27001	2005	Information technology. Security techniques. Information security management systems. Requirements
ISO 28000	2007	Specification for security management systems for the supply chain
ISO 29001	2010	Petroleum, petrochemical and natural gas industries. Sector-specific quality management systems. Requirements for product and service supply organisations
ISO 30000	2009	Ships and marine technology. Ship recycling management systems. Specifications for management systems for safe and environmentally sound ship recycling facilities
ISO 50001	2011	Energy management systems. Requirements with guidance for use
ISO 90003	2009	Software engineering. Guidelines for the application of ISO 9001:2008 to computer software
ISO IWA 1	2005	Quality Management Systems. Guidelines for process improvements in health service organisations
ISO TR 10017	2003	Guidance on statistical techniques for ISO 9001:2000
ISO/IEC 80079–34	2011	Explosive atmospheres – Part 34: Application of quality systems for equipment manufacture
ISO/IEC TR 90005	2008	Systems engineering. Guidelines for the application of ISO 9001 to system life cycle processes
ISO/IECTR 90005	2008	Systems engineering. Guidelines for the application of ISO 9001 to system life cycle processes

Number	Date	Title
ISO/IWA 4	2009	Quality management systems. Guidelines for the application of ISO 9001:2008 in local government
ISO/TR 10013	2001	Guidelines for quality management system documentation
ISO/TR 10017	2003	Guidance on Statistical Techniques for ISO 9001:2000
ISO/TR 16949	2009	Quality management systems. Particular requirements for the application of ISO 9001:2008 for automotive production and relevant service part organisations
ISO/TS 21003–7	2008	Multilayer piping systems for hot and cold water installations inside buildings – Part 7: Guidance for the assessment of conformity
ISO/TS 8000–150	2011	Data quality. Master data. Quality management framework
ISO 19001	2002	In vitro diagnostic medical devices. Information supplied by the manufacturer with in vitro diagnostic reagents for staining in biology
IWA 1	2005	Quality management systems. Guidelines for process improvements in health service organisations
IWA 2	2007	Quality management systems. Guidelines for the application of ISO 9001:2000 in education
IWA 4	2009	Quality management systems. Guidelines for the application of ISO 9001:2008 in local government
OHSAS 18001	2007	Occupational Health and Safety management systems. Requirements
OHSAS 18002	2008	Occupational health and safety management systems. Guidelines for the implementation of OHSAS 18001:2007
SO IWA 2	2007	Quality Management Systems. Guidelines for the application of ISO 9001:2000 in education
TL 9000		Quality management standard for the telecommunication sector

Note: Extracts from British Standards are reproduced with the kind permission of the British Standards Institute. Complete copies of all British Standards can be obtained, by post, from Customer Services, BSI Standards, 389 Chiswick High Road, London W4 4AL

Index

Abbreviations used [in index]: QMS = Quality Management Systems; QP = Quality Procedure; WI = Work Instruction

abbreviations and acronyms [listed] 561–3; worked example 301
acceptance stage: quality during 18
accreditation 73, 549
accreditation services 73, 549, 552, 553, 554
adherence to standards: worked example 221
administration 64
aerospace standards 52
Allied Quality Assurance Publications (AQAPs) xii, 29
American Customer Satisfaction Index (ACSI) 429
American National Standards Institute (ANSI) 27
ANSI 90 series of standards 33
approval procedures: WIs 452–3; worked example 392–3
approval, worked example 311–12
approved documents, worked example 331, 341–2
approved suppliers and subcontractors list 163
archiving: e-mails 468; quality records 346–7
AS/EN/JIS Q 9100:2009 52
asset inventory 404
auditing of QMS 135
audits 68–70; purpose of 69, 352; types 69–70, 136; see also external audit; financial audit; internal audit
authority, management 132–3

automotive industry standard 52
awareness 141; worked example 251

bonded store 192–3
British Standards Institution (BSI) xii, 10, 27
BS 5750 series of standards xii, 32–3, 36
budget forecast: committed costs compared with 403; worked example 401, 402–3

calibration: measuring and monitoring equipment 175–7
CD-ROM distribution example 462–5
certification 71–3; and accreditation 73, 549; advantages and benefits 549, 550; companies that carry out 72; compared with compliance 72–3; costs involved xv, 22–3, 555; European data 557–9; meaning of term 72, 549; post-certification actions 556; reasons to obtain 71, 549; and registration 72, 549; requirements for 72, 552; route to 551–2; time to become 555; see also registration
certification audits 70
change control: in design and development 162–3, 265–6; form 438, 440; impact assessment 438–9, 441; procedure 437–8; worked example 436–41
Chartered Management Institute (CMI) 19
Chartered Quality Institute (CQI) 1–2

communications: customer communications 103, 150, 258; internal 134, 246
company management system: worked example 214–17
company profile example 210–11
Company Secretary [worked example] 289–90; responsibilities 252, 269, 270, 275, 289–90, 328, 340, 344, 345, 376, 390, 395, 438
Company Status Report 445
competence 142; worked example 251
compliance 1, 73, 548; compared with certification 72–3; worked example 311–12
compliance audits 70
components/parts/materials: and design office 155
Computer Aided Design (CAD) 16–17, 156
Computer Assisted Telephone Interviewing (CATI) 419
computer software see software
concessions 191–2, 374
confidentiality 233
configuration management 171
conformity assessment 486
consultants: contracts with 404; invoices 405; training of 435; worked example 291
consumable items: checking of 166
continual improvement 5, 47, 77, 79, 190, 225; worked example 285
contract documents 122, 149; signature 149; worked example 327, 404
contract review 107
controlled documents 329
copyright 332
core business process (CP) 85–6, 98, 101; worked example 228, 229, 307, 308–10
Corporation of Open Systems (COS) 33
corrective action 68, 181, 186–7, 189, 190–3; bonded store 192–3; compared with preventive action 194, 373, 376; concessions and approvals 191–2, 374; defect reports 192; definition 373; documented procedure for 190, 286,

320, 372, 490, 552, 553; and internal audit 181, 356, 479–81; for non-conforming items 189, 371; permanent changes resulting from 187; QMS review 398; Quality Procedure for 372–4; worked example 286, 320, 372–4
cost considerations example 211
crop production standard 53–4
customer awareness and training 431–5; requirements 432; see also training
customer communications 103, 150; documented procedure 103, 197, 490; worked example 258
customer complaints handling 429–30
customer feedback example 407–11; customer interface 410; flowchart 409; form 411; initial review 408; initiation and assessment 408; local action 408–10; non-conformity analysis 410; quality records 411
customer focus 5, 45–6, 63, 123, 126; worked example 225, 241–2
customer property 66, 171–2; worked example 273–4
customer-related processes 65, 145, 147–50; worked example 256–8
customer requirements 155
customer satisfaction, monitoring of 67, 179–80, 278–9, 412–30; areas suitable for analysis 427; data analysis 427–9; qualitative research 413–16; quantitative surveys 413, 416–23; questionnaires 424–6; requirement 412; sample profile 426
customer satisfaction, worked example 278–9, 312, 314, 412–30
customer-supplied product 108, 172, 362

dangerous goods packaging standard 56
data analysis 68, 187–8; customer satisfaction 427–9; records 188; statistical analysis 188; worked example 284
data control 107
data quality management standard 54
decision making: factual approach to 5, 47, 225

defect reports 192; *see also* non-conforming products
Defence Standard (DEF STAN) series xii, 29
delivery of product 174
Deming, William Edwards 79, 222
depth interviews 416
design control 107; changes 391; input 391; output 391; Quality Procedure for 389–91; verification of documents 391
design criteria 152
design and development 150–63; change control 162–3, 265–6; inputs 153–6, 260–1; outputs 156–7, 261–2; planning 65, 151–2, 259–60; review 158–9, 262–3; validation 161–2, 170, 264–5; verification 160, 170, 263–4; worked example 259–66
design office: functions and responsibilities 16, 152, 155, 157
design process control 158
design process review 159
design stage: quality during 15–17
development *see* design and development
document: definition [worked example] 324
document changes 122; worked example 326, 337
document control 62, 120–2; approved documents 331, 341–2; contracts produced 327; controlled documents 329; copyright 332; document administration number 324, 325; document reference number 324–5; documented procedure for 120, 237, 320, 323, 490, 552, 553; documents received 327–8; draft documents 330; e-mails 326, 327; faxes 326; file numbering system 324–6, 327; file storage on server 328; filing 328–9, 341; letters produced 326; minutes produced 327; old and obsolete documents 329; press notices 331; in Quality Plan 107; Quality Procedure for 322–37; self-assessment of 491, 493; software for 332–3, 491, 493; version numbering 325–6; worked example 202, 226–7, 237–8, 322–37

document distribution 121–2, 330, 331
documentation: contract documents 122; of processes 88, 90, 100–1; purchasing 164, 165–6; QMS 62, 72, 98, 225, 307, 319, 451; support documentation 121; value of 121; worked example 225, 307, 319, 451
documentation requirements 118–23, 552, 553; self-assessment 487, 488–93, [checklist]494–504; worked example 235–9
documented procedures 102–3, 120, 173; mandatory 120, 122, 180, 185, 190, 193, 237, 238, 279, 282, 286, 287, 323, 339, 349–50, 359, 372, 373, 375; mandatory [listed] 99, 102, 196, 300, 320–1, 490, 552, 553; meaning of term 102, 118, 121, 196, 233, 490; recommended additional procedures 103, 197, 490; worked example 196, 223, 237, 238, 279, 282, 283, 286, 287, 320–1, 323, 339, 349–50, 359, 372, 373, 375

educational organisations standard 53
e-mail surveys 417, 418
e-mails 326, 328; control procedure example 466–8
EN 29000:1987 33, 36
EN 50126-1 302
energy management systems standard 54
environmental management standards 50–1
Europe: accreditation bodies in 554; ISO 9001 certified companies in 557–9; producers of national standards in 27, 28
European Union (EU) 26, 29
evaluation of QMS 135
expense sheet example 456, 457, 459
explosive atmospheres standard 54
external audit 70, 136, 481–5; self-assessment example, checklists of auditors' questions 487, 524–41, 556; supplier evaluation 482–5

face-to-face surveys 419–22
faxes 326

filing 328–9, 341; file numbering system 324–6, 327; file reference code 325, 335–6; file storage on server 328; of invoices 405

final inspection and testing 161–2; product 184

financial authority: delegation of 402, 406

financial considerations: of quality management 182

financial management: worked example 402–4

first-party audits 70, 136, 181; see also internal audits

flowchart(s): approval procedure 393; budget and finance 401; customer feedback 409; document quality procedure 386; QMS review 396; quality document production 381; Work Instruction 383

FOCUS committee 33

focus groups 414–16

food safety management systems standard 54

free issue products 172

general specification 9

good manufacturing practice standard 55

graphics software 332

headed paper 329

health care standards 55

health records: disposal of 348

health and safety requirements 156

hotel arrangements example 454–5

house-to-house surveys 419–22

human resources 64, 138, 140–2; worked example 250–2

improvement 68, 189–94; continual 5, 47, 77, 190, 285; corrective action 68, 189, 190–3, 286; preventive action 68, 189, 193–4, 287; worked example 285–7

income and expenditure: administration of 403

information security management systems standard 55

infrastructure 64, 138, 143; worked example 252–3

in-inspection 166–7

in-process inspections 161

in-service stage: quality during 18–20

inspection 109; final inspection 161–2, 184; in-process inspection 161; product 162, 184; of purchased products 166–8

inspection equipment 109

inspection status 157

internal audit 67, 68, 70, 136, 180–2; acceptance stage [self-assessment checklist]545; agenda 354; audit categories 69–70; audit execution 354–5, 476–7; audit frequency 353; audit preparation and organisation 354, 474–6; audit report 355, 478–9; audit schedule 353, 474; audit team 354; corrective action(s) 181, 356, 479–81; design stage [self-assessment checklist]542–4; documented procedure for 180, 279, 320, 349, 490, 552, 553; follow-up actions 181, 357, 481; in-service stage [self-assessment checklist]545–6; manufacturing stage [self-assessment checklist]544; meeting minutes 355, 356; purpose of 69, 352, 470; Quality Procedure for 349–57; sectional quality audits 352–3; self-assessment 470–81, [checklist]542–6; worked example 279–80, 349–57

internal auditors 351

internal communication 134; worked example 246

International Electrotechnical Commission (IEC) 30

International Organization for Standardization (ISO) 30, 34–5; membership 34, 35; see also ISO… standards

International Telecommunications Union (ITU) Committees 29

invoices 405; filing of 405; subcontractors' 405, 461

ISO 1538:2011 55

ISO 9000 series 25; background to 35–42; compared with ISO 14000 series 51; future evolution of 74; standards that make up 42–4

ISO 9000:1987 33, 36
ISO 9000:1994 xii–xiii, 36–7
ISO 9000:2005 42–3, 60, 104
ISO 9001:1994 38
ISO 9001:2000 37–9
ISO 9001:2008 39–40, 44; advantages and benefits 197, 549, 550; applicability of clauses 114, 196; auditing 68–71; background to xii–xiii; basic process 58–9; certification/registration 71–3, 549–53; changes in 39; compatibility with other management systems 48–51; future revisions 40; industry standards based on 51–8; quality management principles in 45–8; requirements 68
ISO 9001:2008, structure 60–8, 113–94; cross-check list [worked example] 292–9; introduction 60; management responsibility 63–4, 123–38; measurement, analysis and improvement 67–8, 177–94; normative reference(s) 60, 114; product realisation 65–7, 144–77; quality management system 62–3, 116–23; resource management 64–5, 138–44; scope 60, 113–14; terms and definitions 61, 115
ISO 9001:2015 41–2
ISO 9002:1994 38
ISO 9003:1994 38
ISO 9004:2005 105–6, 117
ISO 9004:2009 38, 43–4, 302, 487
ISO 10001/10002/10003 429
ISO 10005:2005 57
ISO 10012 55
ISO 13444 58
ISO 13485 48, 56
ISO 14000 series of standards 50–1; compared with ISO 9000 series 51
ISO 14001 38, 39, 51, 59, 302
ISO 14004 51
ISO 16106:2006 56
ISO 16192:2010 57
ISO 19011 71, 302
ISO 22000:2005 54
ISO 22006:2009 53–4
ISO 28000:2007 57
ISO 30000:2009 57
ISO 50001:2001 54

ISO/IEC 17025:2005 58
ISO/IEC 27001:2005 55
ISO/IEC 80079–34:2011 54
ISO/IEC 90003:2004 52
ISO/TR 10013 489
ISO/TR 90005:2008 57
ISO/TS 8000–150:2011 54
ISO/TS 15887–7:2009 56
ISO/TS 16949:2009 52
ISO/TS 21003–7:2008 56
ISO/TS 29001 56
IWA 1:2005 55
IWA 2:2007 54
IWA 4:2009 55

leadership 5, 46, 225
letters: document control 326
Local Area Network (LAN) standardisation 33
local government QMS standard 55

mail-in sheet 324, 334
mail-out sheet 324, 334
management audits 69
management commitment 63, 123, 124–5; worked example 241
management representative 64, 73–4, 133–4; worked example 245–6
management requirements: self-assessment checklist for 487, 505–23
management responsibility 63–4, 106–7, 123–38; cross-check list [worked example] 293; customer focus 63, 123, 126, 241–2; external auditors' questions 526–9; management commitment 63, 123, 124–5, 241; management review 64, 124, 134–8, 246–9; planning 63, 123, 129–31, 242–4; quality policy 63, 123, 127–8, 242; responsibility, authority and communication 64, 123, 132–4, 244–6; self-assessment checklists 495–7, 507–10; worked example 240–9
management review 64, 124, 134–8; input 137, 247–8; objectives 135, 247; output 137–8, 248–9; worked example 246–9
Management Review Board meetings 443

Managing Director [worked example]
  288–9; responsibilities 213–14, 250,
  256, 258, 288–9, 310, 312, 432, 436,
  438, 442
mandatory documented procedures 120,
  122, 180, 185, 190, 193; listed 99, 102,
  196, 300, 320–1, 490, 552, 553; worked
  example 196, 237, 238, 279, 282, 286,
  287, 320–1, 323, 339, 349–50, 359, 372,
  373, 375
manufacturing stage: quality during 17
marine technology standard 57
market demand 154–5
market readiness 155
market research 412–23
marketing implications: of design and
  development 154–5
measurement, analysis and improvement
  67–8, 177–94; control of non-
  conforming product 68, 177, 185–7,
  282–4; cross-check list [worked
  example] 298–9; data analysis 68, 177,
  187–8, 284; improvement 68, 177,
  189–94, 285–7; monitoring and
  measurement 67–8, 177, 178–85,
  278–82; planning for 67; self-
  assessment checklists 502–4, 518–23;
  worked example 277–87; see also
  monitoring and measurement
measurement management systems:
  standard for 55
measuring and testing equipment 109
medical devices QMS standard 48, 56
meetings and reports: agenda 444;
  Company Status Report 445; discussion
  documents 443; guidelines 444;
  Management Review Board meetings
  443; minutes 356, 444; Section
  Managers' meetings 443; worked
  example 442–5
Military Specifications (Mil Specs) xii
Military Standards (Mil-Stds) 29
minutes 327, 444; internal audits 355,
  356
mission statement example 209
monitoring and measurement 67–8, 177,
  177–85; of customer satisfaction 67,
  179–80, 278–9; by internal audits 67,
  180–2, 279–80; of processes 68, 182–3,

280–1; of products 68, 183–5, 281–2;
  worked example 278–82
monitoring and measuring equipment:
  calibration of 175–7; control of 66,
  174–7, 276; software 175, 276
multilayer piping systems standard
  56
mystery shopping 423

National Certification Bodies 553–4
national standards organisations 10,
  27–8
NATO Allied Quality Assurance
  Publications (AQAPs) xii, 29
natural gas industry standard 56
non-compliance: purchased products
  168
non-conforming product 109, 171; control
  of 68, 177, 185–7, 282–4, 358–71;
  corrective action 189, 190–3, 286, 371,
  372–4; dealing with 362–4, 369;
  definition 360, 367; documented
  procedure for control of 185, 282, 320,
  359, 368–9, 490, 552, 553; identification
  of 361–2, 367; post-delivery/use
  detection 364, 370; preventive action
  189, 193–4, 287, 375–8; Quality
  Procedure for 358–71; re-inspection
  after correction 364, 370; records
  365–6, 370; rework 364; worked
  example 282–4, 358–71
non-conforming service 109, 367
normative reference(s) 60, 114
North America: producers of national
  standards in 27, 28, 29

Occupational Health & Safety
  Management Systems 49
OHSAS 18000 series 49–50
OHSAS 18001 49–50, 302
OHSAS 18002 50
on-street surveys 419–22
Open Systems Interconnection (OSI)
  33
organisational chart example 212, 288
organisational culture 5
organisational goals: example 215, 217,
  223–4
overall performance specification 10

part numbers/labels 172
people: involvement of 5, 46, 225
petrochemicals industry standard 56
petroleum industry standard 56
Plan–Do–Check–Act (PDCA) cycle 79, 81; worked example 222
planning 63; business processes 83–8; design and development planning 65, 151–2, 259–60; management responsibility 63, 123, 129–31, 242–4; for measurement, analysis and improvement 67; process planning 146; product realisation 65, 144, 145–6, 254–6; QMS planning 123, 129–31, 242–4; SMART approach 129; training requirements 434; worked example 242–4, 254–6
plastics piping systems standard 57
policy statement example 208
postal surveys 417, 418
press notices 331
preventive action 68, 189, 193–4; compared with corrective action 194, 373, 376; definition 376; documented procedure for 193, 287, 321, 375, 490, 552, 553; Quality Procedure for 375–8; worked example 287, 375–8
prime contractor 165; responsibility for quality inspection 167
procedural audits 69
procedure: meaning of term 83
procedures audit 477
procedures manual [design office] 16
process approach [to quality management] 5, 46, 59, 75–83, 225
process audits 69
process control 108
process control and instructions 154
process mapping software 332–3, 491, 493
processes 72, 77, 83, 100–2; business processes, planning of 83–8; core business process (CP) 85–6, 98, 101, 228, 229, 307, 308–10; cross-check list [worked example] 292–9; customer-related processes 65, 145, 147–50; documentation of 88, 90, 100–1; examples in small business 78; flow chart(s) 78; identification of 146; listed

[worked example] 308; mandatory processes 79; monitoring and measurement of 68, 182–3, 280–1; primary supporting processes 87–8, 98, 101; secondary supporting processes 88, 89, 98, 101; supporting processes (SPs) 86–8, 98, 101, 228, 307, 310–14; worked example 228–9, 303–14
product: definition 115; delivery of 174; determinants and measurements of quality 95, 96, 219; identification and traceability 108, 171, 273; monitoring and measurement of 68, 183–5, 281–2; non-conforming product 68, 109, 171, 177, 185–7, 282–4; preservation of 172–4, 274–6; protection of 172; storage of 173–4
product audits 69
product life cycle 14, 15; acceptance stage 18; design stage 15–17; in-service stage 18–20; manufacturing stage 17; quality assurance in 14–20
product realisation 65–7, 144–77; cross-check list [worked example] 295–7; customer-related processes 65, 145, 147–50, 256–8; design and development 65, 145, 150–63, 259–66; external auditors' questions 530–7; monitoring and measurement equipment control 66, 145, 174–7, 276; planning of 65, 144, 145–6, 254–6; production and service provision 66, 145, 168–74, 270–6; purchasing 65, 145, 163–8, 266–70; self-assessment checklists 498–502, 513–18; worked example 254–76
production provision 66, 168–74; control of 169, 270–1; and customer property 66, 171–2; identification and traceability 108, 171, 273; validation of processes 170, 272; worked example 270–6
production stage: quality during 17
purchaser: costs of quality failure 22; responsibilities 12–13
purchaser-supplied product(s) 172
purchasing 65, 108; documentation 164, 165–6, 267, 268; documented procedure 103, 197, 490; financial

management 402–4; information
165–6, 268–9; invoices 405; processes
and procedures 164–5, 266–8; Quality
Procedure for 400–6; verification of
purchased product 166–8, 269–70;
worked example 266–70, 400–6

quality: definitions 2–3, 25, 26;
determinants and measurements of 95,
96; importance of 2–3; integration of
business and quality 80
Quality Assurance (QA) 4, 6–7; benefits
and costs 20–1; costs of quality failure
21–2; definition 6; during product life
cycle 14–20; worked example 209–14
Quality Control (QC) 4, 5–6; definition 5;
purchased products 168
quality document production example
379–88; amendments 385; cancellation
385; document quality procedure 386,
388; drafting 382; flowchart 383;
headings 382; initiation of document
380–2; issue authority 385; personnel
involved 387; Quality Procedures 383;
quality records 385; review 384; text
requirements 382; Work Instructions
383
quality loop 94; worked example 216
quality management principles 5, 45–8;
continual improvement 5, 47, 77, 190,
225; customer focus 5, 45–6, 225;
factual approach to decision making 5,
47, 225; leadership 5, 46, 225; mutually
beneficial supplier relationships 5, 47,
226; people involvement 5, 46, 225;
process approach 5, 46, 59, 75–83, 225;
system approach 5, 47, 225; worked
example 225–6
Quality Management System (QMS) 62–3,
116–23; additional information,
procedures and support 103, 197;
approach 96–7; audits, guidelines on
71; cross-check list [worked example]
292; documentation 62, 72, 98, 225,
307, 319, 451–2; documentation
requirements 72, 97–103, 118–23, 225,
235–9; external auditors' questions
524–6; and financial considerations
182; fundamentals and vocabulary
42–3; general requirements 117, 233–4;
ISO standards 42–4; management
responsibilities 82–3; performance-
improvement guidelines 43–4;
planning 131; principles 93–6;
processes 62, 75–7, 98, 100–3; purpose
[worked example] 217, 221–2; Quality
Manual 62, 98, 99–100, 119–20; Quality
Plan 104–10; Quality Procedures 62,
98, 102–3; quality records 62, 110–11,
122–3; requirements 44, 91–3, 218,
233–4; revision history [worked
example] 203, 305, 317, 449; self-
assessment checklists 494, 505–6;
structure 97–8, 224; Work Instructions
62, 98, 103, 447–68; worked example
201–468
Quality Management System review 128,
223; actions 398; agenda 397–8;
meetings of Review Board 395, 397–8;
minutes 399; Review Board members
397; worked example 394–9
Quality Manager 74, 133–4;
responsibilities 133–4; worked example
213–14, 223, 233, 236, 245–6, 247, 248,
249, 252, 283, 289, 312, 323, 339,
350–1, 359, 372, 375, 380, 390, 395,
407, 433, 443
Quality Manual 62, 72, 79, 98, 99–100,
119–20, 195; administration 233;
component inputs 99, 227;
confidentiality 233; cross-check list
[worked example] 292–9; document
control of 121, 226–7; documentation
requirements 489–90; as overview of
QMS 99–100, 119, 196, 228, 232–9;
versus quality system 97; worked
example 201–302
quality objectives 130
Quality Plan 104–10; contract review 107;
customer-supplied product 108;
definition 104; design control 107;
document and data control 107;
inspection and testing 109;
management responsibility 106–7;
non-conforming service/product 109;
process control 108; product
identification and traceability 108;
project-specific 232; purchasing 108;

standard for 57; worked example 232, 255
quality policy 63, 123, 127–8; worked example 212–13, 218–32, 242
Quality Procedures (QPs) 62, 72, 98, 99, 102–3; cross-check list [worked example] 292–9; documented procedures for 320–1, 323, 339, 349, 359, 372, 375; generation and control of 230, 379–88; listed [worked example] 300, 321; worked example 230–1, 315–446
quality processes: cross-check list [worked example] 292–9; worked example 303–14; see also processes
quality records 62, 110–11; archiving of 346–7; backup copies 345; collection, indexing and access 343–4; control of 122–3, 238–9, 338–48; disposal of 347–8; maintenance of 344–5; master list 342–3; meaning of term 110, 340; see also records
quality system 97; assessments 70; audits 69; responsibility [worked example] 213–14; versus quality manual 97
quality training 435
quarantine area 360, 363
questionnaire writing 424–6; open/closed questions 424; rating scales 425–6; routing 425

record control 122–3, 238–9; documented procedure for 122, 238, 320, 339, 490, 552, 553; Quality Procedure for 338–48
records 62, 110–11, 188, 491, 492; approved documents 341–2; backup copies 345; control of 122–3, 238–9, 338–48; disposal of 347, 348; maintenance of 344; management of 341; new records 342; retention of 111, 346; storage of 111, 188, 344; third-party documentation 343; training 435; versus WIs 103; worked example 232, 238–9, 338–48; see also quality records
registration: and certification 72, 549; costs involved xv, 22–3, 555; meaning of term 549; requirements for 72, 552; route to 551–2, 555–6; see also certification

reliability data 188
reliability measures 18
resource management 64–5, 138–44; cross-check list [worked example] 294; external auditors' questions 529–30; human resources 64, 138, 140–2, 250–2; infrastructure 64, 138, 143, 252–3; provision of resources 64, 138, 139–40, 250; self-assessment checklists 497–8, 510–13; work environment 64, 138, 143–4, 253; worked example 249–53, 404
resources 140
responsibilities: Design Office's 16, 157; Quality Manager's 133–4, 213, 223, 233, 236, 245–6; see also management responsibility
Review Board [QMS Review Board]: actions 398; agenda 397; meetings 395, 397; members 397; records 399
risk assessment 159

scope 60, 113–14
second-party audits 70, 136, 181; see also external audits; vendor audits
secondary audit 486
Section Managers [worked example] 290; meetings 443; responsibilities 251, 253, 258, 259, 261, 262, 263, 264, 265, 266, 290, 351, 359, 376, 390, 432, 435
self-assessment 117, 182, 469–546; documentation requirements 487, 488–93, [checklist]494–504; external audit 481–5, [checklist]524–41; internal audit 470–81, [checklist]542–6; management requirements 487, [checklist]505–23; surveillance audit 485–6; typical auditors' questions 487, 524–41
self-certification 73
service: determinants and measurements of quality 95, 96, 218
service audits 69
service provision 66, 168–74; control of 169, 270–1; identification and traceability 108, 171, 273; validation of processes 170, 272; worked example 270–6
servicing 149

Shewhart, Dr Walter 79
ship recycling standard 57
small businesses 113; advantages xiv;
    certification/registration of 71–3;
    definition xiv; management
    commitment 125; problems faced by xv
small and medium-sized enterprises
    (SMEs): definition xiv
SMART approach [to quality planning]
    129
software: document control 332–3, 491,
    493; measuring and monitoring
    equipment 175; spreadsheet and
    graphics 332; standard for 52; word
    processing 331
space systems standard 57
special processes 185; control system for
    154; inspection and testing procedures
    185
specifications 7–13; purchaser's
    responsibilities 12–13; significance 8;
    supplier's responsibilities 10–12;
    tolerance specifications 155; types
    8–10
spreadsheet software 332
staff: design and development staff 154;
    training of 142, 251–2, 431–4, 435;
    worked example 288–91
standard specification 10
standards: civilian and military 29, 30;
    international 30–1; quality-specific,
    growth of 31–3
standards audit 477
statistical analysis 188
stock rotation 173
storage: of product(s) 173–4; of records
    111, 188
Stores Section Chief [worked example]:
    responsibilities 359
subcontractors: approved subcontractors
    list 163; contracts with 404; invoice
    examples 405, 461; responsibilities 187,
    291; training of 435; worked example
    291, 312
supplier 140, 164–5; approved suppliers
    list 163; costs of quality failure 22;
    mutually beneficial relationships 5, 47,
    226; responsibilities 10–12, 186–7;
    worked example 312, 313

supplier evaluation 482–5; acceptable
    system control 484; evaluation 483–4;
    evaluation team 482; pre-evaluation
    meeting 482; Quality Manual study
    483; unacceptable system control
    484–5; weak system control 484–5
supply chain 61, 115; management
    standard 57
supporting processes (SPs) 86–8, 98, 101;
    worked example 228, 307, 310–14
surveillance/quality audit visit 485–6;
    conformity assessment 486; multiple
    evaluations and audits 486; secondary
    audit 486; third-party evaluation 486
sustainable development: of ISO 9001
    40
system approach to management 5, 47,
    225
system audits 69
systems engineering standard 57

telecommunications industry standard 57
telephone surveys 417, 418–19
terminology 42–3
terms and definitions 61, 115
test status 157
testing 109; final testing 161–2; in-process
    testing 161; product 161, 184; of
    purchased products 167
testing and calibration laboratories:
    standards for 58
testing equipment 109
third-party audits 70, 136, 181
third-party evaluation 486
time and expense report example 457, 460
time sheet example 456, 458
TL 9000 57
tolerance specifications 155
Total Quality Management (TQM) 44, 219
training 142; courses 435; identification of
    training needs 433; new personnel 434;
    plan 142; planning of 434; quality 435;
    records 435; review 434; subcontractors
    and consultants 435; worked example
    251–2, 431–5
travel arrangements example 454–5

United Kingdom Accreditation Service
    (UKAS) 73, 549, 552, 553, 554

validation: design and development 161–2, 170, 264–5; production and service provision processes 170, 272
vendor audit 70
vendor rating 485
verification: design and development 160, 170, 263–4; purchased product 166–8, 269–70

welding materials and fluxes: standard for 58

word processing software 331
work environment 64, 138, 143–4; worked example 253
Work Instructions (WIs) 72, 98, 99; approval procedure for 452–3; flowcharts 383; generation and control of 231, 379–88; travel and hotel arrangements [worked example] 454–5; versus records 103; worked example 231–2, 447–68
workshop standard 175, 176

Taylor & Francis

eBooks

FOR LIBRARIES

ORDER YOUR
FREE 30 DAY
INSTITUTIONAL
TRIAL TODAY!

Over 23,000 eBook titles in the Humanities, Social Sciences, STM and Law from some of the world's leading imprints.

Choose from a range of subject packages or create your own!

Benefits for you

- ▶ Free MARC records
- ▶ COUNTER-compliant usage statistics
- ▶ Flexible purchase and pricing options

Benefits for your user

- ▶ Off-site, anytime access via Athens or referring URL
- ▶ Print or copy pages or chapters
- ▶ Full content search
- ▶ Bookmark, highlight and annotate text
- ▶ Access to thousands of pages of quality research at the click of a button

For more information, pricing enquiries or to order a free trial, contact your local online sales team.

UK and Rest of World: **online.sales@tandf.co.uk**

US, Canada and Latin America:
e-reference@taylorandfrancis.com

www.ebooksubscriptions.com

ALPSP Award for
BEST eBOOK
PUBLISHER
2009 Finalist
sponsored by

Taylor & Francis eBooks
Taylor & Francis Group

A flexible and dynamic resource for teaching, learning and research.